MURDER

A Multidisciplinary Anthology of Readings

Joseph G. Weis and Robert D. Keppel

MURDER

A Multidisciplinary
Anthology of Readings

SECOND EDITION

THOMSON

™

CUSTOM PUBLISHING

Editor: Kathleen Abraham
Production Manager: Staci Powers
Production Coordinator: Spring Greer
Marketing Coordinator: Sara L. Hinckley

Table of Contents

Chapter 3
The Characteristics & Distribution of Murder

Chapter 4
Types of Murder

Chapter 5
Perspectives & Theories of Murder

Chapter 6
The Control of Murder

Introduction

MURDER is a multidisciplinary anthology of readings. It examines the most serious form of violence—lethal violence or criminal homicide, which is the intentional, malicious killing of one human being by another. The public's fear of violence, particularly of murder, is at an all-time high. This reflects, in part, the fact that many high-profile killers and murder victims are turned into celebrities by the media. Notorious killers who have been caught include many familiar names: Ted Bundy, Jeffrey Dahmer, John Wayne Gacy, Richard Speck, Wayne Williams, George Russell, Richard Ramirez, Kenneth Bianchi, the Menendez Brothers, and many others. And even murderers whose identities remain unknown are public figures, including Jack the Ripper, the Zodiac, and the Green River Killer. Victims are equally well-known, whether they were celebrities before they were killed—John F. Kennedy, John Lennon, Tupac Shakur—or, ironically, because of their murder—Nicole Brown, Ronald Goldman, Polly Klaas, JonBenet Ramsey, Ennis Cosby. They may collectively personify the "murder problem," even though they do not truly represent the typical killer or victim. Murder is a rare phenomenon, hovering at less than 10/100,000 population for most of the 20th century, committed for the most part by ordinary people who kill victims they know, including family members, friends, and acquaintances.

Politicians and criminal justice administrators are searching for solutions, to both citizens' concerns and the pervasive physical, emotional, and financial damage caused by the more than 20,000 murders committed every year in the United States. The "clearance rate"—or the percent of murder cases that are solved—has also dropped dramatically during recent years, to a national average of approximately 60%, with some jurisdictions reporting that more than one-half of their cases are unsolved.

Unfortunately, research has had little impact in the quest for answers to the murder problem. Scholarship on murder is at an elementary stage of development and, consequently, the literature is uneven in quality, scattered across a number of disciplines, and is disorganized. Research on murder has not kept stride with studies of other types of crime, including related acts of violence like rape, robbery, and aggravated assault. Theories of the causes of murder borrow heavily from more general theories of crime, ignoring the enormous behavioral, motivational, and situational differences between murder and more ordinary crimes, particularly the vast majority of property offenses.

MURDER synthesizes and organizes some of the best research and thinking on murder, produced by a number of eminent scholars from a variety of disciplines, including criminology, psychiatry, sociology, psychology, law, history, economics, and criminal justice. The six substantive chapters cover a broad range of topics, including: 1) the history and laws of homicide and murder; 2) available data sources and measures; 3) the characteristics and distribution of murder; 4) different types of murder (mass, serial, juvenile, sexual, domestic, and stranger); 5) perspectives and theories of murder (biological, psychiatric, psychological, cultural, social psychological, routine activities, and social structural); and 6) the control of murder (police investigation, profiling, deterrence, gun control, and prevention).

The book is designed for use in courses in criminology, sociology, criminal justice, public affairs, law, psychology, and other disciplines that address violence, crime control, and the administration of justice, as well as in criminal investigation training. MURDER can be used as a primary or supplementary set of readings in a variety of classes on deviant behavior, crime, violence, homicide investigation, crime control policy, abnormal psychology, general forensics, law enforcement, criminal justice, or homicide. Each of the readings included in MURDER has undergone some editing, to make them more accessible to students, particularly those who may not be familiar with the substance of criminology or the methodological and statistical procedures used in some papers.

The editors bring together a unique combination of scholarship, teaching, and homicide investigation experience. Joseph G. Weis is a Professor of Sociology, and the Director of the Center for Law and Justice, at the University of Washington, where he teaches courses on criminology, juvenile delinquency, deviant behavior, and murder. Robert D. Keppel is the Chief Criminal Investigator for the Washington State Attorney General's Office, with experience in over 2,000 homicide investigations. He has a Ph.D. in Criminal Justice from the University of Washington, and has taught classes on homicide investigation at a number of colleges in Washington state, as well as in many training sessions for law enforcement personnel. Drs. Weis and Keppel have collaborated for a number of years on research and writing about murder, and are currently conducting a national study for the U.S. Department of Justice on child abduction murders.

CHAPTER I

[Handwritten note:] Homicide rate was much higher that it is today in other countries & the US.

[Handwritten note:] Humans are among only a minority of species that kill their own kind. but we kill eachother intentionally — Since prehistoric times.

Contrary to what many p [...] most violent time in hist [...] the homicide rate was much higher than it is today, in other countries, as well as in the United States.

In fact, human beings are among a minority of species that, historically, have killed their own kind. What truly sets us apart from other intraspecies killers, though, is that we kill each other intentionally, rather than as an act of self-defense or survival. It [...]

[Handwritten note:] Characteristics of killers and victims from 13th century Britan & today are very similar — economically & socially marginalized young males.

being by another—has exis[...] define in law as criminal hon[...] definition in the *Revised C*[...] much higher than today's.

We have been killing e[...] aforethought, before the forn[...] research of Chesnais and of C[...] rates, some almost ten time[...] century England, before the[...] legislated later as a criminal a[...]

early time, Given reports that the characteristics of the killers and their [...] were similar to those of today—economically and socially marginalized young males. Chesnais concludes that homicide rates have declined over the centuries in a "civilizing of manners," as educational levels rise, life expectancy lengthens, poverty is reduced, and systems of control become more powerful.

Historical evidence from the U.S. during the 20th century, compiled by Zahn, shows major fluctuations in murder, with the highest rates peaking near the second and last quarters of the century, with the fewest murders per capita being committed at mid-century. More recent data indicate that, contrary to the expectations and beliefs of many, the murder rate has actually been dropping for about the past five years. Of course, what is most intriguing about the changing rates is "How much?" and "Why?" To answer those questions, accurate measures and data are necessary, as well as viable theories, both of which will be addressed in subsequent chapters.

The History of Violence:
Homicide and Suicide Through the Ages

JEAN-CLAUDE CHESNAIS

How, in the course of history, have people's attitudes to life changed, as measured by homicide and suicide statistics?

In general, the suicide rate tends to increase along with the stages of social and economic development, whilst the homicide rate tends to change in the opposite direction. In societies with a high standard of education, the frequency of suicide is high and that of homicide is low, whilst in traditional societies in which illiteracy predominates, the situation is the opposite, murder being widespread and suicide rare. International comparisons confirm the results of historical analysis. In highly structured societies in which duties and rules are strictly codified, the suicide/homicide ratio is high, whilst the converse prevails in less advanced societies.

The historical study of violence will be dealt with here under seven headings:

1. Trends in homicide
2. History of the duel
3. Suicide trends
4. A case-study: England from the thirteenth century to the present day
5. History of the death penalty
6. The causes of the reduction in violence with the passage of time
7. The mythology of violence

1 . TRENDS IN HOMICIDE

In modern developed countries, death caused intentionally by another individual has become rare. The only exception to this is the United States, and, to a lesser extent, over the past few years, the Soviet Union.

International comparisons

Setting aside the very special case of the United States which has a homicide rate almost ten times the average of other Western nations, the annual rate of death by homicide in the West is today of the order of one death per 100,000 inhabitants. Over the past two centuries, a convergence has been taking place between the countries of North West Europe, at the apex of industrial modernization, and the agricultural countries in Southern and Eastern Europe. In Italy, for example, a century ago, in 1890, crimes of violence were the cause of 1,500 deaths per year, i.e. five per 100,000 persons. By 1930 this rate had fallen by half, and then further decreased until it reached a low point of one per 100,000 during the 1960s. Only two periods stand out in this great historical decrease, these being the peaks at the end of each of the two World Wars (settling of scores, vengeance, purges etc.). In the majority of European societies the changes have been similar. From one decade to the next, up to the middle of the present century, the homicide rate has tended to decrease. Thus in the period 1860–80, in Sweden and in England, death by homicide was of the order of two per 100,000 inhabitants but in the following decade it fell below one per 100,000.

In many Western countries, however, the trend has reversed since the middle of the 1960s. Factors such as the breakdown of the urban social fabric, the splitting up of family structures and the growth of drug addiction and unemployment, particularly amongst the most disadvantaged minorities (immigrants especially), may be at the root of this reversal. In the United States, the contrast between the last two decades and the preceding ones is even clearer and the effect of the factors mentioned above could be more profound, especially amongst the Blacks, who are more affected by homicide. But even in the United States, crimes against property (theft, burglary, fraud etc.) have increased much more rapidly than crimes against the person (assassination, murder, theft, assault and wounding etc.). Except for certain dangerous neighborhoods, the United States is, in reality, safer and more law-abiding than is generally imagined. International comparisons are useful in this respect.

In El Salvador, for example, the homicide rate is consistently close to 30 per 100,000 inhabitants. In 1970, in Thailand and the Philippines, it was around 20 and in Mexico and Colombia 15. In the regions which produce and sell drugs, the incidence is even greater and murder is the prime cause of death amongst young males adults. This can be seen in several parts of Peru, Ecuador, Bolivia and Colombia.

Whether kept by the judicial authorities (the Courts) or by health authorities (medical bodies), infanticide statistics give similar results. The report infanticide rates are decreasing appreciably and in the developed countries they are generally less than ten per 100,000 infants under one year old. France is an interesting example in this respect. During the second half of the nineteenth century, the level of infanticide was consistently around 15 to 20 per 100,000. However, France was the country with the lowest birth rate in the world (in 1850, the average number of children per woman was only 3.5, as against five to six in the majority of other countries), and the proportion of unwanted pregnancies therefore must have been lower than anywhere else. The French infanticide rate decreased progressively to the level of one per 100,000 during the 1970s. Thus, even in this particular case, distinguished by the early prevalence of contraception (infanticide is often connected with getting rid of unwanted children), the decrease recorded is very great. However, there is every reason to assume that the figures do not show the full scale of the decrease since in the rural societies of yesteryear, a number of infanticides were not known about and therefore not recorded as such, but were disguised under the heading of "accidental deaths" (most usually by suffocation or drowning).

The ways of our ancestors

Old village societies practised actual physical violence rather than symbolic violence. Life was primitive and subsistence precarious. They knew no forms of punishment other than private vengeance, and applied no rules other than the *lex talionis*, carried out in the coldest of cold blood. Law was non-existent, or without executive force. Words were harsh, rivalries dogged, often bloody and at times murderous. There was no, or scarcely any, substitute for violence. Evidence of this harshness was manifold. One has only to see films from the period between the two World Wars, the reports of debates in parliament or the political controversies in the press up to about the middle of the century to see to what extent language itself has become milder. The spoken word has become less crude, more euphemistic, and conflicts more subdued.

In the developed countries, corporal punishment is nowadays excluded from education. What could be more natural, one might think! This is to forget that in times past the cane was the schoolmaster's most essential tool. The old principles of the clerical teaching of years gone by are clear. It was a case of taming the demon who suggested "bad habits" to the child, of domesticating the devil slumbering in him. The right of correction of the *pater familias* has, for a long time, been called into question and the Swedes, descendants of the fearsome Vikings, have even passed a law prohibiting the smacking of children.

Although a feeling of insecurity still exists, the insecurity is no longer of the same kind. Gangs of peasants no longer haunt our country lanes. Who therefore today, in order to escape from pillage and massacres, has to take refuge regularly in his cellar or loft or, like the villagers of the Middle Ages, barricade himself behind walls or flee into the mountains? Who still has to fight to defend his property? Those times are past. There are now land registries and title deeds.

As with all structural changes, these have been slow, but profound. They have permeated, little by little, all countries and all social strata. They began with behavior and then reached the language itself.

Gentleness is becoming more and more characteristic of the first relationships of human beings with the world. Childbirth without violence is gaining widespread acceptance, and breast feeding is once again prevalent. The phenomena of children put out to a wet nurse, exposed or abandoned, or where all were destined for slaughter, have disappeared from the European countryside. The bands of wandering children, wild, orphaned and unloved, always ready for violence, have long disappeared. The street urchin is now a literary rather than a social type. Never has respect for children been as high, never has parental anxiety about education been as acute. The slightest act is measured and weighed up. In the intimacy of the family, the child, who has become a rarity, is given every attention and pampered. Society itself is not to be outdone. From conception to death, it monitors the individual, surrounds him and protects him. Aside from a few miscellaneous obtrusive events on which the current affairs searchlights are trained, this discreet, daily, continuous solicitude persists.

And would they have us believe that the present age is about to succumb to barbarism? Have we forgotten that the best known civilizations practised bloody rites at which our sensibilities can only quake in horror? Since the dawn of time, human sacrifices have been performed for all kinds of reasons, economic, magical, and religious. The gods, it is believed, are thirsty. To appease their anger (or to atone for one's misdeeds) people periodically immolated one of their own. To ensure the fertility of the earth, they soaked it with blood.

Our violence exists, undeniably, but it is nothing as compared to ancient, feudal or even classical violence. The fear is there, however, irrational, and fostered by the sensationalism of the media.

In the industrialized world, the United States stands out through a wholly exceptional frequency of violence. In the Soviet Union, homicide increased dramatically during the 1980s but nevertheless remains approximately only half as widespread as in the United States, and this appears largely related to the current situation, with the greater scarcity of food and the disorganization of the state. What could be the reasons for this specific American condition?

The great American fever

The United States is in the grip of a real crisis of violence. The number of persons murdered increased from 8,000 a year during the 1950s to more than 20,000 in the mid-1970s and has scarcely changed since then. The phenomenon primarily concerns the black population, but if the coloured population is more violent, it is also more often a victim of violence. The risk of being killed is six times greater than in the white population, itself five times more exposed than European populations. Violent crime is more murderous today than in the depths of the economic depression of the 1930s.

The turning-point dates from the start of the 1960s and was extremely sudden. Between 1960 and 1972, the homicide rate doubled and two years later exceeded the sad record of 1933. However, the United States was the most affected by the great economic crisis (13 million unemployed, i.e. 25 per cent of the active civilian population in 1933). The consequences were terrible. Millions of families sank into poverty overnight. Bankruptcies followed each other in quick succession. The social pyramid was shattered. For tens of thousands of migrants or children of migrants, deeply attached to the American model of social success, their lives collapsed. There was a cruel and inevitable loss of social status. Suicides and homicides multiplied. America recovered only slowly from the ordeal, with the world economic recovery and the social experiment of the New Deal.

Around 1960, American society toppled. The age of all-conquering optimism marked by successive epic events (the New Deal, the Allied victory, the post-war economic boom) was succeeded by the age of disenchantment. Economic progress had not fulfilled all expectations. It did not bring any "greater caring." All the social indicators broke down, one by one, almost at the same time. Puritan morals yielded ground. Premarital sex became the norm. Extra-marital sex itself was no longer the exception and, above all, its social significance changed profoundly. Punished in certain states most severely, adultery was no longer considered a crime, scarcely a fault, rather a chance mishap. Fertility plummeted. American families, consisting usually of three or four children until the end of the 1950s, henceforth had an average of two. Divorce, which had been increasing slowly for decades, increased abruptly, to the point where more than one third of marriages being entered into were liable to end in divorce. The broken marriage assumed the dimension of a social phenomenon, and the number of single-parent households continued to increase. The great social projects for the elimination of poverty, the reduction of ghettos and the assimilation of minorities, were over-ambitious and did not achieve what had been hoped. The American model came to grief on urban problems. The great messianic and all-conquering faith was succeeded by individualistic and skeptical withdrawal. The Viet Nam war also helped to shake certainties and led to some serious soul-searching. The moral crisis was a serious one.

Violence showed itself first of all in the coloured population and was more intra-racial than inter-racial. More than half the people arrested for murder are black although the black population represents only 10 per cent of the population of the United States. Statistics relating to states with a large Hispanic population show that at the end of the 1980s the number of murder victims amongst that population was around 3,000 a year. This was half the figure for the black population but three times greater than for other population groups (Whites and Asians).

The very high increase in the sales of arms (since the beginning of the 1960s) certainly plays a great part in this American fever and in the apparently inexplicable fact that violence in the 1970s could be more murderous than in the 1930s. It is doubtful whether American citizens today are more dangerous than those of 1930. They are perhaps more selfish, less inclined to stick together. They are above all better armed. Current legislation relating to the purchase, ownership and use of firearms is notoriously inadequate. *Gun control* is only a theme for election campaigns. It yields to the cult of the hand gun, engraved in the national culture. In the United States, to a great extent, individual liberty cannot be conceived without a well-stocked rack of weapons at home. It is such a burning issue that no government dares to tackle it head-on. In the eyes of Americans, "a weapon is a work of art, a jewel, the source of power and a symbol of virility. Nothing deserves more respect."

This socio-technical change has certainly amplified the effects of the moral crisis (as illustrated by the increase in drug abuse in marginal populations, in particular the black minority, unintegrated, closeted in its ghettos) which is sweeping across the country. It explains, to a great extent, the sudden bout of widespread violent crime seen there. It has, in fact, been established that homicide tends to increase with the density of the ownership of weapons per inhabitant. In general, in the various states of the United States of America, the greater the proportion of owners of firearms (and therefore the less restrictive the laws) the higher the homicide rate.

The extreme case of the United States thus usefully shows the dangers inherent in an over-liberal approach to the social control of individual behavior. The heritage of direct action, of immediate justice through arms, is still alive. Often, all it takes is a small argument between friends, lovers or spouses—since violence is first and foremost a family matter—for one of the protagonists to seize a weapon and shoot. The majority of murders are impulsive.

Crime in the family

The family is a place of paradox. A center of affection, a refuge against adversity, it is also the foremost centre of violence, the only place in which everyone can discover their true face, undisguised. Violence in this context is strong, stronger than in any other environment, but violence between members of the same family is a thing which is not usually discussed. It is secret and shameful. By its very nature, it escapes public knowledge. The only witnesses to it are the members of the family. The existence of family ties impels them to keep silence, both out of concern for their own image and out of fear of reprisal. Only the obvious cases of violence, i.e. the most horrifying or the most visible (the discovery of a corpse, or the marks of blows) are detected. The family when all is said and done, has become the last refuge of the instincts; it is both the most loving place and the most violent. It is as it were, the only place where the natural state survives. Within the framework of the family, everything is permitted. There is one single exception—sexual abuse—which is severely condemned. In all societies, incest is loathed.

The majority of murderers are to be found within the family circle or, more widely, the circle of relatives. This is a long-established, universal fact. In general, it is estimated that one-quarter to one-third of all homicides are domestic murders in which one member of the family kills another. According to some research, in the United States, one couple out of six has a physical altercation at least once a year, ranging from throwing objects to the use of a knife or hand gun. There is more risk of being killed within the family circle than in any other social group, except perhaps the army or police. Family crime is the least well-known, and no doubt the least well-recorded, but it is the most common. The lesson is disconcerting but clear: if anyone needs, for his own safety, to be wary of anyone, it is primarily of his own family rather than the passing stranger.

2. HISTORY OF THE DUEL

In addition to prohibited violence, there is a violence which is permitted and at times esteemed. This is ritual, lawful violence, the violence of duels and judicial executions.

The duel is a special custom. It is the institution which, *par excellence,* is symbolic of the customs of the governing classes in centuries past. People were then very punctilious about the Code of Honor. As in the heyday of the feudal system, any affront, or any act felt to be such, was expiated in blood. Suicide or murder? It was neither and the duel does not fall into any modern categories. It relates to another ethic, that of private vengeance, and to another mystique, that of truth through arms.

For centuries, violence has been the favored means of settling individual disputes or conflicts. Amongst our forefathers, everything was judged by the force of arms and every hierarchy was the hierarchy of force. The army and the nobility revered those who excelled in the duel.

Around 1830 in France, for example, in civilian society, taking one year with another, duels were still causing the deaths of between 20 and 30 men. Although prohibited since Richelieu's edict of 1626, this bloodthirsty institution did not then disappear. The duel, in fact, did not figure in the penal code. Legally, it did not exist.

3. SUICIDE TRENDS

The study of suicide is an important part of criminology. For centuries, in fact, suicide was considered to be a crime against God and man. A sin of vanity, a revolt against the divine, an admission of guilt, an act of cowardice—it was all this simultaneously.

Nowadays, suicide is in actual fact often only a strategy for avoiding shame or dishonor and, in this sense, it is a substitute for the murder or duel of yesteryear.

Historical overview

In traditional societies, suicide was rare. In the middle of the nineteenth century, there was no country—outside the Germanic cultural area of Central Europe— in which the frequency of death by suicide was greater than 10 per 100,000 inhabitants. Denmark, which was then considered to have the strongest propensity towards suicide in the world, had a rate lower than the current rate (25 rather than 30 per 100,000). Death by suicide affects, as a general rule, far fewer than 10 persons per annum per 100,000 inhabitants in the less developed countries and more than this in the developed countries. The only advanced countries which are an exception are the Catholic countries of Southern Europe (Italy, Spain, Portugal and Greece) and the British Isles. At the end of the 1980s, the suicide rates in the principal developed countries were as follows: USSR 20; United States 15; Japan 19; unified Germany 20; France 22; England and Wales 9; Italy 8. The majority of the rates are thus between 10 and 20 per 100,000.

Let us return to trends observed over many years. According to Swedish data, which cover 240 years, the conclusion is similar to the one drawn from observations

Current suicide rates are
~~was~~ 6-7 x higher than
at the end of the 18th
century.
(no doubt due to
improvements in gathering
statistics)

ALSO - a major cause
was industrialization

concerning Austria, ays than
it was in the past. T her than
those at the end of t due to
improvements in th ng been
concealed), but the 1e factor
alone.

The causes of the

In all countries by a style
of harmonious fam heteenth
century. The rise w explain
this are many and v l in very
diverse ways depend e phrase:
the industrial revolution. Industrialization turned living conditions upside down,
broke up old structures—family and village communities—and created a syndrome
of adaptation, opening up the process of individual disintegration. It was accompanied
by disordered urban development and pitiless exploitation of the workers driven
from the countryside. The anomie, described by Durkheim (1897) as a lack of
moral standards by society, is here closely akin to Marxist class analysis. The suicide
rate is a social representation of the human cost of the transition from agricultural
civilization to industrial civilization. The most striking current example of anomie
is the micro-society of the Greenland Eskimos, some groups of whom remained
closed in on themselves and had no contact with Western civilization until the
end of the last century. In a few decades, they changed from an autarkic way of life
based on food gathering and fishing to a wage-earning tertiary society. The abrupt
shock was accompanied by an uncontrollable increase in alcoholism and violence.
During the 1980s, the suicide rate there reached a record level of 125 per 100,000
and the homicide rate 25 per 100,000.

In the least developed countries, the suicide rate is around two or three per
100,000, and sometimes even much less, as in the traditional societies of Africa
before the eruption of modernity. Aggressiveness is more frequently turned against
others than against oneself. In these societies. with a greater degree of solidarity,
where poverty is shared, people become accustomed to bearing the harshness of
existence. They adapted to it, aided by fatalism and religious superstition.

It is not, however, possible to ascribe the increase noted to economic
development as such. Suicide is not a defect of modernity. In the process of
development, it is not becoming prosperous itself which kills but the psychological
inability to shoulder the hazards and new complexity of life. Even the same social

transformations are borne better by one society and less well by another. Finland and Norway absorbed the shock of the industrial revolution without an epidemic of suicides. Italy adapted admirably to the economic "miracle" of the post-war years, and to the latent political instability which was characteristic of that period. In both cases, there is a whole attitude to living which comes into play—flexibility in behavior, and the solidarity of family ties.

4. A CASE-STUDY: ENGLAND FROM THE THIRTEENTH CENTURY TO THE PRESENT DAY

A systematic analysis of violent deaths since the Middles Ages is possible only in Britain.

Violence as a way of life

In previous centuries, violent death was common in the life of peasant societies. Although the homicide rate varied from one country to another, the incidence of murder was everywhere very high in comparison with the rates which prevail today. Homicide rates greater than 20 per 100,000 were altogether common. In the rural area of Warwick, for example, in the thirteenth century, the homicide rate was 47 per 100,000 inhabitants. The rates were not as high in cities like London or Bristol. During the period 1244–76, the rate was between eight and 15 in London and remained around four in Bristol. The élite were less violent than people in country areas. The urban population was divided socially. At that time, violence was above all collective, being committed by organized groups on the basis of close relationships of interdependence, such as ties of blood or marriage, membership of a village community, or ties with friends or neighbours.

People had scarcely any contact outside a small circle of relations or friends. It was this circle, in the event of aggression, which provided natural, unconditional allies, vital to survival. In the event of a quarrel or conflict, there were only a few social institutions in a position to serve as an arbiter or mediator. Authority and justice had to be administered by oneself. Violence was, above all, the struggle of the poor against other poor people. Robbers had nothing to lose, neither horse, nor land, nor property. Organized gangs stole animals from stables and clothes or money from houses. Country communities had to defend themselves against these bands of criminals. There being no police, they had to organize themselves collectively to protect themselves. The authorities were incapable of dealing with rural banditry. In small rural communities, everyone carried a knife to cut bread or wood or for other uses. If necessary, this knife could serve as a weapon in a fight; axes also served as tools or weapons. Brawls often resulted in someone's death and in the absence of effective medical care, the wounded often died as the result of infections. Violence was considered acceptable and often even necessary in everyday life. Outside the large towns, there was neither a police system nor any guarantee of justice. Death formed part of life. It was a way of life, often even a condition for survival. Because of the great impact of illnesses and epidemics, life was short and precarious. Men were accustomed to spending their lives fighting against animals; they were brutal and incapable of controlling their emotions. In short, they had to fight to survive and to provide their own justice.

The "civilizing" of manners

This high level of criminal violence diminished century by century. At the end of the seventeenth century, the death rate from homicide was, in Britain, around five per 100,000. Four centuries earlier, according to observations relating to various localities, the rate was very much higher, probably around 20. Even if this figure is only a rough estimate, there is no doubt that homicide was much more extensive than during the following centuries. The records, through the large number of murders which they reveal, offer the image of a brutal and violent society. Many victims were "found murdered" in fields, by paths or at the roadside. Whilst in recent centuries murder has primarily been the death of a person following an altercation between two individuals, in the eighteenth century, homicide was often carried out by groups, several innocent victims being found lying on the ground, killed by gangs of robbers.

With the progressive emergence of the modern state, another important phase in criminality appeared in the nineteenth century. The forms of primitive violence, in fact, predominated until the centralized states began to include the inhabitants in a political life extending beyond the local context. This change took place in the nineteenth century. Police forces were organized and came into being as official institutions responsible for seeking out and arresting criminals. It was from the state that the victims of violence gradually came to seek assistance. The exodus to the towns finally produced a type of man who was more civilized and less rough than his forebears. Schools also played a role in this great transformation, They took children off the streets and were an instrument of social transformation, teaching a new code of conduct and a new collective morality, better suited to modern urban civilization.

Violence therefore only decreased when the state of law replaced the natural state. Until the eighteenth century, torture was commonplace in all Western countries, Capital punishment, considered to be quite legitimate, was preceded by the most horrible tortures.

13

5. HISTORY OF THE DEATH PENALTY

Executions in the UK

According to the London Bills of Mortality, from the middle of the seventeenth to the middle of the nineteenth century the execution rate was higher than the homicide rate. This is perhaps related to the fact that prisoners were taken to London to be executed, but the documents on the functioning of justice at that time show that the death penalty was frequent, even for minor crimes such as the theft of cattle or larceny. In England in the eighteenth century, the death penalty was the main weapon in the arsenal of punishments, being considered a prime deterrent; capital punishment was therefore imposed for the most diverse crimes and offences. At the end of the eighteenth century, the death rate by execution was five per 100,000 inhabitants. Even children were condemned to death and executed. Capital punishment was considered to be the only means of preventing an explosion of crimes. Life expectation was brief and haphazard; life had scarcely any value. Thus there were scarcely any scruples about putting an end to it.

From the eighteenth century to the present day, the number of criminals condemned to death and subsequently executed has decreased, decade by decade, in both absolute and relative numbers. At the beginning of the twentieth century, in England, it had become negligible. In France, the trend observed is similar. The mean annual number of executions fell from 72 in 1826–30 to 31 in 1851–5 and to only two in 1901–5. It could be said that the death penalty fell into disuse. Similar observations are valid for the majority of other European countries.

The ceremonial of the public execution

For the death penalty to serve more successfully as an example, executions were held in public in order to add shame to the punishment. The ceremonial was skillfully prepared and meticulously ritualized. It was a genuine national event which attracted considerable crowds, drawn by a morbid curiosity. For many people, coming from remote parts of the countryside, it was the great pilgrimage of their life, a kind of journey to Hell.

The event was the occasion for excesses of all kinds. For some it was like a trade fair. The entrance fee was high, with wild speculation, nearby balconies being rented out at exorbitant prices. In England, "the *hanging days* were, during the eighteenth century and the first half of the nineteenth century, the equivalent of national holidays, and more frequent." Stands were put up as if for football matches. People squeezed in everywhere to find a place.

These enormous gatherings took place in a climate of real collective hysteria. Passions were unleashed, riots broke out, insuppressible panics seized hold of the crowd. A number of people died, suffocated or trampled under foot. It was a gigantic communal frenzy, a quasi-mystical celebration of death and the supernatural. In London, in 1807, 40,000 people were present at the execution of a murderer. When the performance came to an end, almost a hundred corpses lay on the ground.

Hangings were individual or in groups of 12, 16 or even 20. The condemned prisoners were often drunk, and the hangman no less so. Sometimes horrifying incidents took place. It could happen that the hangman and the condemned man came to blows. It could also happen that the gallows did not work properly, that the rope broke or the victim survived strangulation. The proceedings then began again until death ensued.

All sorts of superstitions surrounded hanging. The rope was cut into pieces and sold at a high price to people who wanted to ward off harm, and the clothes of the hanged men were sold at an astronomical price. A gigantic purification ceremony, the public execution was a symbolic rite of the extermination of the Devil. Capital punishment, in fact, assumed a religious significance.

The dawning of clemency

Everywhere, the transition from the era of the dogma of capital punishment as a corner-stone of the penal system to the era of its total decline took place gradually. The falling off in the number of death sentences took place at different times depending on the country. Generally speaking, the more advanced the socio-economic development of the country, the less the tendency to carry out executions there.

The countries which were the first to abandon capital punishment were those of Northern Europe. Everywhere there, the death penalty fell into disuse before the First World War. Finland set an example, as early as 1826, with a good half-century start on the neighboring countries (Norway 1875; Denmark 1892; Sweden 1910). *De jure* abolition followed quite closely on *de facto* abolition. In all these countries it took place before the Second World War (Norway 1915; Sweden 1921; Denmark 1933). In the Netherlands and Belgium, the change was even more remarkable. In the Netherlands the authorities were particularly bold, *de facto* abandonment being sanctioned in 1850 and legal abolition taking place around the same time.

The example did not stop in Northern Europe, however. In Portugal, abolition took place more than a century ago (1867). In Switzerland, similarly, abolition goes back to 1874; although the death penalty was re-established in some backward cantons in 1879, abolition was finally extended to the entire country in 1942. Even the young democracies, such as Italy or West Germany, were no exception.

The United States remains atypical with respect to crime as with respect to the death penalty. The pro-slavery legacy, the Darwinist tradition and the cult of the firearm have no equivalent in any European country. The debate on the death penalty is still topical. It keeps interminable controversies alive, especially among economists. It suffices, however, to reread Beccaria (1738–1794), a criminal lawyer and economist, to spare oneself futile speculation. Two centuries ago, he revolutionized the ideas of his age by asserting that the entire penal law ought to be based on one humanistic principle—that of the *minimum* effective punishment. According to this concept, it is not the cruelty of the punishment which has a deterrent effect on the criminal, but its certainty.

6. THE CAUSES OF THE REDUCTION OF VIOLENCE WITH THE PASSAGE OF TIME

Many factors have contributed to this centuries long lessening of violence:

The strengthening of the state with its enforcement machinery (the police and the courts) and the establishment of its social moulds—the school and the army. There is no freedom without laws and without a state arbiter to ensure that they are observed, as Locke (1691) proclaimed three centuries ago. In Europe itself, at the beginning of the last century, the nation state existed only in England and France. In France, in particular, the process of state control is very old, with urban police forces in existence for centuries. The country has one of the most heavily manned, best distributed and most effective police forces in the world, and this is a long established situation. If, at the beginning of the nineteenth century, the comparative level of private violence, as measured by the murder rate, was incredibly low in this country, it is because behind the history of violence, looms the history of the state. Conversely, the United States, whose history is dominated by violence, is characterized by a continuous rejection of public power, any intervention by the state being quickly condemned as socialism or even communism.

The slow disappearance of want. The barbarity of some crimes is explained by poverty. Medieval chronicles abound in accounts of famines which degenerated into cannibalistic slaughter. Until the nineteenth century, European social history was punctuated by food riots which soon turned into murderous frenzies. "The starving belly has no ears," goes the proverb.

The demographic revolution, or the decrease in mortality, has resulted in an unprecedented enhancement of the value of human life. When death is omnipresent, when it strikes every day, life is cheap.

The rise in the standard of education. Violence denotes a failure of dialogue, and begins where the power of the word ends. Fist fights and brawls are, through compensation, the necessary mode of expression of those who, in order to make their mark, have no substitute other than brute force. The illiterate expresses himself only by gestures or by means of a restricted vocabulary, whose limits he reaches very quickly; the universe of symbols and signs passes him by. As a practical man, it is his physical strength which provides him with his living and gives him value in the eyes of other people; it is his strength which, on occasions, can serve as an argument in a dispute. In primitive societies, with a low level of mechanization, physical strength is admired and is a cult object. This is because in daily life it guarantees employment and respect. In bureaucratic tertiary societies, this cult is replaced by the cult of intelligence. Woe betide the person who fails tests and examinations. Individual violence is absurd and is becoming nonsense. Much more importantly, it condemns or stigmatizes a person in the eyes of others. The use of force—except within a few extremist circles or a few poor environments where it is still prized—is rejected with horror. It becomes shameful and unworthy. It denotes, amongst those who employ it, conduct amounting to failure, a return to primitive and regressive behavior.

7. THE MYTHOLOGY OF VIOLENCE

Actual violence is decreasing, but the sense of insecurity, on the other hand, is tending to increase. How can this apparent increase in the sense of insecurity, as evidenced by opinion surveys, be accounted for?

The paradox of insecurity

Several factors can contribute to this:

The increase in criminality, a phenomenon which is by nature inflationary as soon as a society becomes affluent, diversifies its trade and increases its rules and regulations. But, in this increase in crime, everything is a question of weighting and the usual indicators are deceptive. Burglaries and car thefts, which are particularly becoming more and more frequent, are taken very badly by the victims. Perceived as an attack on personal privacy, these offences are among those which generate the most insecurity.

The increasing intrusion of the media into individuals' private lives, particularly television, whose effect is great on elderly and retired people, who are more vulnerable and often isolated. The "news" is often a selection of events in which, because of their attractive and assessable nature, violent occurrences occupy a disproportionate amount of air time and are suddenly brought very close by the television screen. Attacks such as those perpetrated against Presidents Reagan and Sadat or against Pope John Paul II caused tears in the most obscure cottages and helped to give credence to the idea of insecurity, even if, as with any terrorist act, they were aimed only at the most highly visible international figures. The news creates the event.

The provision of safety nets in all areas of daily life (social security, unemployment insurance, life insurance etc.) has resulted in the creation of new demands for security. Physical security is considered to be a right; the desire for it increases as other hazards of life are covered.

The increase in the democratic spirit which, over the centuries, has resulted in a narrowing of social differences and an increased liking for liberty. In addition, with the overall improvement of standards of behavior and the development of medical techniques (such as anaesthetics and the relief of pain), sensitivities have become more refined and the violence tolerance threshold has been lowered considerably. A new consciousness of violence has thus arisen, based on the principle of reciprocity. We do not do to others (since they are similar to us) what we do not do to ourselves.

The very decrease in violence which, by increasing actual security decreases subjective insecurity. It is the famous paradox of de Tocqueville: the more something unpleasant diminishes, the more what remains of it become unbearable.

An eternal myth

The divergence between fact and opinion about violence is not new. It is well known to the historians of crime. Thus, Cockburn wrote: "The majority of Englishmen in the nineteenth century were convinced that crime was increasing as never before . . . the authors of the eighteenth century, likewise, were terrified at what they considered to be the advent of a wave of violent crime." Tobias, a nineteenth-century expert in this field, had the impression, taking only the evidence of the age into account, that he was facing an unprecedented crime wave, especially among young people, and this in the very period of a decrease in actual violence. Just as clear are the observations of the report of the American Commission on Violence (1969). In it, it was simply remarked that, without going back any further, the eighteenth and nineteenth centuries had witnessed horrors which would make the leaders in this latter part of the twentieth century tremble. Revolutions and civil wars followed each other in America and Europe. In 1910, again, with the violent strikes that were breaking out across the country, what was most feared by the English and American public was the imminence of a new revolution.

The market of fear

In our times, the force of pessimistic prejudice about violence is more difficult to resist because it is powerfully sustained by the major media. There is an undeniable convergence of interest in the survival of such a myth. In addition to the obvious, but marginal, interest of the security industries (locks, armor plating, alarm systems, firearms, security companies etc.) there is the interest, infinitely more powerful, of two spheres that are increasingly interacting—the political world and the world of information. Every government is tempted to make use of fear in order to extend its means of enforcement (recruitment of police officers, magistrates and prison officers, increasing penalties etc.). In addition, competition between the media encourages pandering to viewers and readers and therefore encourages sensationalism. The editorial policy of the majority of daily and weekly publications is dependent upon commercial needs. Banner headlines about horrible crimes attract readers and bloodthirsty news sells well. The public loves sensational events and needs thrills. The financial structure of the press in Western countries is such that serious newspapers survive only with difficulty.

CONCLUSIONS

From morning till night, modern man is bombarded with information. Scarcely has he got out of bed when he listens to the news, and there is the most astonishing diversity, abundance and incoherence. The most varied events, totally alien to his daily life, abruptly enter his mental universe. This ceaseless explosion of messages changes his view of the world. It reshapes his perception, his opinion and his feelings. As a result, he apprehends the social, abstract universe only through these scraps of reality thrown his way haphazardly by current events. The reason is, in this great information lottery, that in order to get through, the message has to undergo several tests: selection, simplification, exaggeration etc. Violence passes all of them. It is always there, because it attracts, intrigues and fascinates.

But reality is confused, and in order to overcome this confusion, people need to take the time to analyze, reflect and put things in perspective. This was the very purpose of this article—to reposition recent history *vis-à-vis* longer-term history. It can thus be seen that progress is accompanied by a slow reduction in violence directed against others and that, on the other hand, suicide, which was rare or almost non-existent in primitive societies, where the individual did not have primacy over the group, is becoming more frequent. However universal it may be, this trend does not rule out reversals, nor a diversity of paths from one nation to another. The forms of violence retain an effect which varies according to the culture.

The Frequency of Homicide

JAMES B. GIVEN

So violent and motley was life, that it bore the mixed smell of blood and roses. The men of that time always oscillated between the fear of hell and the most naive joy, between cruelty and tenderness, between harsh asceticism and insane attachment to the delights of the world, between hatred and goodness." The glittering paradoxes of Johann Huizinga have for long summarized the tenor of life in medieval Europe. Late nineteenth- and early twentieth-century historians in particular saw the Middle Ages as a period when the iron rules of a Hobbesian state of nature held undisputed sway in Europe. For the French historian Achille Luchaire, the medieval period was the age of the war of all against all: "Imagine a social state in which security for property and person does not exist; no police, and little justice, especially outside of the larger cities; each one defends his purse and his life as best he can." Across the Channel in England, T. F. Tout, the pioneering historian of the medieval English administration, wrote, "Not only were medieval criminals more numerous than their modern counter-parts, but by reason of their numbers and importance they excited much more general sympathy than they do nowadays, and were as a rule dealt with by society in a more lenient manner.... It is hardly going too far to say that homicide was the special misdeed [of the knightly class] and forgery the particular peccadillo of the [priestly class]. Few self-respecting gentlemen passed through the hot season of youth without having perpetrated a homicide or two."

More recently, the judgment of historians has become more sober and less gracefully expressed. But most still perceive the Middle Ages as a period peculiarly prone to violence and brutality. For Marc Bloch "violence [was] the distinguishing mark of [the] epoch and [the] social system." He portrayed medieval men as emotionally unstable, given to violent outbursts of rage and equally extravagant displays of repentance and contrition. And he wrote of the "despairs, the rages, the impulsive acts, the sudden revulsions of feeling" of the men of the time and of the "constant acts of violence" that these unstable characters perpetrated.

English historians have agreed with their French counterparts. Looking back from a society in which interpersonal violence is remarkably rare to the time of their forefathers, they have been struck by the prevalence of violence. Gwyn Williams, having surveyed London politics in the thirteenth century, concluded that "violence was endemic." He found a seething city where trivial quarrels often ended fatally, where ill-paid and often idle private chaplains itched for a fight, where tournaments could stop all work in the city for a week, and where a wrestling match could result in the destruction of one of Clerkenwell priory's walls. For Williams, the "most immediate and vivid characteristic" of thirteenth-century Londoners was their "capacity for reckless violence." The foremost modern historian of rural England, R. H. Hilton, has agreed with this view of medieval English life. For Hilton, the society that existed in the West Midlands in the thirteenth and fourteenth centuries was one "where violence, bribery and corruption were normal means of settling the issues which arose between men," a society where "the expectation of life was short and…death in all its forms was always present."

These opinions, perceptive as they may be, are almost all founded solely on impressionistic evidence. Medieval chronicles and letters are indeed filled with stories of murder and rapine. But chroniclers and other writers, like most people, were interested in recording the unusual and the dramatic. Literary sources may testify to a preoccupation with violent death, but they cannot reveal how common in reality such phenomena as violence and homicide were. For this purpose, the eyre rolls with their virtually complete lists of murder victims are indispensable. Simply to sum the number of bodies, however, is insufficient. If the relative incidence of homicide in the different regions of thirteenth-century England is to be grasped, the proportion that the victims of homicide constituted of the entire population of each area must be determined. In modern sociological and criminological literature this is usually expressed as the number of people in every 100,000 of the population who were murdered in a year. Accordingly, rates calculated on this basis have been derived for each of the twenty eyres under study here. The results of these calculations are in Table 1.

**Table 1. Estimated homicide rates
(per 100,000 population per year)**

County	Eyre	Number of Victims	Rate			
			Author's estimates	Russell's estimates	1801 figures	Per 20 settlements
Bedford	1202	22	13	12	8.9	0.8
	1227–28	58	15	15	10.6	0.9
	1247	69	23	22	15.7	1.4
	1276	172	28	26	18.9	1.6
All		321	22	21	15.0	1.3
Bristol	1227	11	4	—	—	—
	1248	5	4	—	—	—
All		16	4	—	—	—
Kent	1227	173	20	16	6.8	1.0
	1241	112	21	16	7.1	1.1
	1255	209	28	22	9.8	1.5
All		494	23	18	7.9	1.2
Norfolk	1250	127	7	11	9.0	0.7
	1257	193	9	13	10.9	0.9
	1268–69	399	11	17	13.5	1.1
All		719	9	15	11.7	0.9
Oxford	1241	59	12	17	9.2	0.5
	1247	116	20	29	15.9	0.9
	1261	134	18	26	14.5	0.9
All		309	17	25	13.5	0.8
Warwick	1221–22	158	38	18	9.0	1.0
	1232	114	64	30	15.0	1.6
	1247	104	48	22	11.2	1.2
All		376	47	22	10.9	1.2
London	1244	54	8	—	—	—
	1276	145	15	—	—	—
All		199	12	—	—	—

Obviously these rates are, at best, only approximations. The population estimates on which they are based are vague. Despite their crudity, these estimated homicide rates are nevertheless interesting. If the population estimates made by the author are used as the basis of calculation, it is found that the homicide rate varied from a high of 64/100,000 per annum reported at the 1232 eyre of Warwick to a low of 4/100,000 per annum reported at the 1227 and 1248 eyres of Bristol. Of the rural areas, Warwick consistently had the highest homicide rates, with an overall rate of about 47/100,000 per annum for the 25 years covered by the three eyres. Norfolk had the lowest rate, 9/100,000 per annum for the 23 years covered by the eyres. If the estimates based on J. C. Russell's figures are used as a basis for calculation, some differences appear. Although the highest homicide rate still remains that of the 1232 Warwick eyre, it is much reduced, being only 30/100,000 per annum. And the overall rate for Norfolk is found to have increased to 15/100,000 per annum. If we assume that the counties in question had the same population in the thirteenth century as they did in 1801, the homicide rates found are still high. The highest, however, is that for the 1276 eyre of Bedford, 18.9/100,000 and the lowest is 6.8/100,000 for the 1227 eyre of Kent.

Because the population estimates upon the basis of which these homicide rates have been figured are very imprecise, homicide rates have been calculated on yet a fourth, and considerably different, basis. Instead of using population as a basis for estimating homicide rates, I have used the number of settlements within the county. Homicide rates have been calculated in terms of the number of homicides per twenty settlements per annum. For example, in the four years covered by the 1202 Bedford eyre there were 22 homicides reported. Since there were about 146 settlements in Bedfordshire, this means that for every twenty settlements in the county the figure was 0.8 for homicides committed every year. Similarly, in the eleven years covered by the 1268–69 Norfolk eyre, 399 homicides were reported. Since there were 698 settlements in Norfolk, this means that for every twenty settlements there were 1.1 killings every year. With calculations on this basis, the 1232 Warwick eyre and the 1276 Bedford eyres show the highest rate, of 1.6 homicides committed every year for every twenty settlements. The 1241 Oxford eyre now shows the lowest homicide rate, with only 0.5 in every twenty settlements each year.

Unreliable as they are, these homicide rates gain further meaning when they are contrasted with those in other societies. The most reliable figures come from the modern industrialized nations with their statistical habits of mind and their elaborate police bureaucracies. It appears that, for the most part, modern industrial societies, especially European ones, have low homicide rates. Since 1930 the homicide rate in Great Britain has remained fairly stable at the low figure of 0.4/100,000 per annum. In 1974 the rate in the United States was 9.7/100,000. Homicide rates in various American cities fluctuate rather widely. In the years between 1948 and 1952, Philadelphia had a rate of 5.7/100,000 per annum and Miami had a rate of 15.1/100,000 per annum.

Estimating homicide rates for modern agrarian societies presents many of the same problems that are encountered in estimating them for medieval England. Population size is often unknown and many homicides are unreported. The problem is further confused by the fact that some writers compute homicide rates in terms of victims, the practice followed in this essay, and some in terms of offenders. However, in broad outline it is possible to gauge the amount of homicide in many rural societies. Homicide rates range from a low of 0.7 per 100,000 for offenders among the BaLuyia of Kenya to the nearly incredible rates of more than 200 victims per 100,000 in some Mexican villages.

Cross-cultural comparisons of the frequency of murder are in some ways an exercise in comparing apples and oranges. Homicide rates are influenced heavily by the types of weapons available and the quality of health care. A study of homicide in Chicago has shown that guns are five times as likely to inflict fatal wounds as knives. However, despite the lethalness of the techniques available in industrial societies for taking human life, the advanced methods of treating major traumatic injuries and handling infection have lowered homicide rates. Bearing in mind the uncertainty of the estimated rates for the thirteenth century and the difficulties of making cross-cultural comparisons, it is nevertheless clear that England in the thirteenth century was a violent country. If the streets of medieval England did not run with blood, and if thirteenth-century Englishmen did not murder each other with the same frequency as Mexican peasants today, nonetheless, they were more violent than their modern descendants, and more violent than many modern agrarian peoples.

One may not choose to put much trust in homicide rates based on what are no more than informed guesses about the size of thirteenth-century populations. Yet a consideration of the number of homicides committed in every twenty settlements per annum makes it clear that murder was a frequent phenomenon in medieval England. As has been pointed out above, the number of homicides in every twenty settlements oscillated between a high of almost 1.6, reported at the 1276 Bedford eyre and the 1232 Warwickshire eyre, and a low of 0.5, reported at the 1241 Oxford eyre. In other words, there was a good possibility that there would have been a homicide in every settlement in these counties once every twenty to forty years. Therefore, it is possible that every person in England in the thirteenth century, if he did not personally witness a murder, knew or knew of someone who had been killed. There was an even greater chance that an Englishman would have encountered someone who had killed a man. The eyre rolls give the names of 2,434 victims. They also list 3,492 people accused of having participated in a homicide in some fashion. But these 3,492 people represent only a fraction of the total number of people who committed murder. In many cases when the jurors reported a killing, they claimed that they did not know the identity of the slayers. Indeed, 531 of the victims, 21.8 percent of the total, were stated to have been killed by unknown assailants. It is therefore certain that experience of homicide in one form or another was widespread in thirteenth-century English society. In studying the patterns of homicide, we are concerned with one of the major social phenomena of the age.

Homicide in the
Twentieth Century United States

MARGARET A. ZAHN

This article is a review of extant information on homicide in the United States from 1900 to 1979. This descriptive review is seen as a necessary prelude both for a historically grounded theory of homicide and for a set of workable social policies to deal with this type of interpersonal violence. This review establishes not only the changing trends but also a portrait of the dominant types of homicide existing in different periods of American history.

METHODOLOGICAL CONSIDERATIONS

Establishing a portrait of homicide through an entire century, using existing studies, poses a variety of problems. The first is lack of comparability across studies. Studies on homicide lack comparability in a number of ways. One way is in how homicide is defined. In some studies, homicides include those cases killed by officers of the law or those occurring in self-defense, that is, justifiable. In other studies they do not. Those studies in the 1920s, for example, seem more likely to include justifiable homicides than do those in the 1960s. Further, in some periods abortion and/or infanticide are included as separate types of homicide, while at other times they are not included or defined as criminal homicide. Further, while many studies discuss victim-offender relationships, there is no consistent definition across studies of the various types of victim-offender relationship, for example, what constitutes an acquaintance or a stranger. In fact, in many studies, there is no definition at all. Further, in some studies only cases in which the offender is known are included while in others those with both known and unknown offenders are included. Additionally, some studies use offenders as their research base, while others use victims and sometimes the two are confused with each other. In all, there are many ways in which the available studies are not comparable and thus difficult to use.

Additional problems revolve around data sources, their availability at different time periods, and biases and difficulties specific to each source. There are, for example, no fully national homicide statistics prior to the early 1930s. Thus, data in the early part of the twentieth century are essentially local in character. The major types of data sources available for use include arrest, conviction, or execution data from local units of government; coroners' data also from local units of government; and newspaper accounts. A brief nonexhaustive review of some of the kinds of problems with two of these data sets follows.

POLICE DATA

It has generally been concluded that police data are more useful than correctional system data for studies of crime since the police have first contact with the original criminal events upon which the statistics are based. While this may be true in establishing trend data, it may be less valid for victim-offender relationship, motive, or manner of death. In effect, initial police reports may convey a different motive from either subsequent police reports or court reports. Further, manner of death and presence of alcohol and drugs are more accurately reported by a Medical Examiner than a police report. This kind of data may be especially important in tracing the impact of illegal substance use and laws governing it on homicide types and rates. The point is that, while "experts" agree that police reports are most useful, they do not specify for what and it seems that the usefulness depends on the question about homicide that we want answered.

Despite this caveat, review of the literature on police statistics indicates that these statistics may reflect as much about the activity, size of the police force, ability to do detective work, and tolerance level of the community as they do the actual criminal phenomenon itself. A victim-offender relationship may remain "unknown" as a result of police inactivity, inadequate police work, or lack of interest in the victim. Lack of interest, in turn, may stem from the social characteristics of the victim (a skid rower or junkie in modern urban America; an Indian or black in earlier American towns) or from organizational restraints on police investigative departments. For example, lack of systematic investigation may result from assessing that the community does not want the investigation done or from low morale occurring when the police feel that their work will not result in prosecution. A systematic review of how police organization and police practice impinge specifically on homicide has not, to my knowledge, been done. It certainly seems credible that official police data may be fairly accurate on the actual occurrence of a homicide event. Our understanding of the types of homicide or of motives, however, may directly reflect the size of the force, the connections its investigative units have to the community, the priorities of the departments, and other organizational variables.

Other problems such as changes in legal code also may affect police data. At the present time, people dying as a result of faulty car design would not be classified as murder victims. While their cases might be investigated by accident investigation units, they would not likely be investigated by the homicide unit. Should pending court cases establish that deaths due to faulty design intentionally put out by a car company are homicide, a new type—that is, corporate homicide—would emerge as would changed police organization to investigate and report it.

CORONERS' DATA

Mortality data are produced also by coroners and/or medical examiners' offices who forward their results, via death certificates, to the Division of Vital Statistics of the National Center for Health Statistics. While this article does not review all problems with data at the local coroners level, it should he noted that, as with police departments, patterns and practices of the coroners' offices will affect data collected by them. Some examples support this. The coroner, an appointed or elected official, is responsible for determining cause and/or manner of death. Coroners, as opposed to medical examiners, require no medical training. In some places the only requirement for holding office is that they be of legal age to hold office, and be living. Early in the century, and in the late nineteenth century, there was a fee-for-service system among coroners which directly affected their reporting of homicides. Coroners received a set fee for each death that they investigated and for which they established cause of death. The fee paid was the same no matter how much difficulty the case involved and the fee was, in cases of murder, often to be collected from the convicted offender. If, then, it was likely that the offender could not be found, as when a victim was found with a slit throat on the highway, or if the victim was of low social value, for example, an infant, these deaths were not likely to be reported as homicides but rather as a ruptured aorta in the case of the slit throat and suffocation for the infant.

Further, the thoroughness of the investigation and detailed determination of cause of death is directly affected by the size, training, and funding of coroners' and medical examiners' staffs. Doing autopsies and establishing and maintaining toxicology units is expensive. Some offices, for example, large Medical Examiner (ME) offices, have such equipment and thus can tell actual cause of death, drugs in the blood stream, and the like. Many other smaller units cannot.

The factors noted above affect data collection at the local level; additional ones affect its reporting at the national level, that is, in the Vital Statistics reports. Changes in definition and coding affect the reports. For example, the ME determines intent of death during the course of investigation. If he/she calls it a homicide, it is; otherwise, it may be called an accident. If the medical examiner cannot determine which cause this suspicious death is, he/she can then call it undetermined. Prior to 1968, however, there was no possibility for calling a case undetermined. If an ME was unsure, the case was assigned, through a series of complex procedures, to either the accident or homicide categories. The impact of such shifts in coding schemes on homicide rates is unclear but it is certainly plausible that such changing classification procedures have a decided effect on the data produced.

Added to this problem is the fact that states entered the national reporting system at different times. While Vital Statistics were available for some states from around 1900, they did not become fully national until the 1930s. Prior to the 1930s, the data available depended on which states and cities were included. Boston was the first entrant and, in general, there were data from East Coast cities very early. Boston had death data in 1880, Pennsylvania in 1906, and Washington, D.C., in 1880. Other states, however, for example, Georgia and Texas, entered the registry much later, in 1922 and 1933, respectively. In establishing the homicide trend, then, we have difficulty with obtaining national data prior to 1930 and, throughout the century, there are the forementioned data-reporting difficulties which affect the quality and the nature of the data.

In general this rather extended discussion of police and coroners' data has been included since almost all studies of homicide are based on one or the other of the two. While there are numerous problems with the data at both the local and national levels, it is somewhat reassuring to note that when comparing Uniform Crime Reports (UCR) and Vital Statistics rates of homicide through time, they are consistently in the same direction. In general, vital statistics rates are usually somewhat higher than the UCR for the same year. This is due largely to the fact that Vital Statistics use a medical definition of homicide, that is, the intentional taking of another's life and UCR uses a legal definition, that is, the willful killing of another. Justifiable homicides, then, for example, police officers killing felons, are included in Vital Statistics while they are not in the UCR.

In the following sections all major studies of homicide from 1900 to 1979 are reviewed. The review attempts to establish a clear pattern of both the volume and type of homicide existing in each time period.

HOMICIDE: 1900–1930s

Despite the limitations of Vital Statistics noted earlier, these data were the basis for two major studies of early twentieth century homicide: Brearly, *Homicide in the United States* (1932) and Hoffman, *The Homicide Problem* (1925). Brearly and Hoffman were concerned with rates and showed that there was a steady increase in homicide rates from 5.0 in 1906 to 8.5 in 1929 (8.8 in 1926 and in 1928 were the highest years reported in their studies). Higher victimization rates existed among blacks, among the young, and among men in certain regions of the country. The South and its northern neighbors (Ohio and West Virginia) had the highest rates while the New England states and the northern part of the Midwest had the lowest. The majority (71.46%) of the homicides were completed with a gun with the general tendency being toward an increase in the use of guns throughout the early 1900s. Brearly explains part of the increasing homicide rate by inclusion of the western and southern states into the mortality data, and perhaps to some extent the impact of prohibition.

Local studies of specific cities using police and court data support the general trend established by Brearly. Sutherland and Gehlke, based their arrest data from Baltimore, Buffalo, Chicago, Cleveland, St. Louis, and the state of Massachusetts, show increasing homicide rates from 1900 to the late 1920s with the peak for the five cities occurring in 1928. For Massachusetts the peak was in 1925.

Boudouris's study of Detroit 1926–1968 using police records also shows the late 1920s to have a higher homicide rate than any of the other periods he studied. Boudouris's is one of the few studies for this time period that classified data into victim-offender relationships. Based on police record data for both victim and offender, Boudouris classified homicides into (1) domestic and love affairs; (2) friends and acquaintances; (3) business relationship, for example, landlord-tenant and prostitute-pimp; (4) criminal transaction, that is, homicide resulting from violation of the law, for example, bootlegging; (5) noncriminal, that is, killing of a felon by police or private citizen; (6) cultural-recreational-casual; (7) subcultural-recreational-casual; (8) other; and (9) unknown. He found that for the years 1926–1933, the largest percentage of homicides were noncriminal or justifiable, that is, killing of a felon by a police officer or a private citizen. When these were removed from the analysis, there were almost equal proportions of homicide involving domestic relations (18.2%), friend and acquaintances (18.2%), and criminal transactions (16.6%).

Many of the criminal transactions during this period (up to 1933 and the repeal of prohibition) were related to gang wars to control bootlegging. Forty of the 130 criminal transaction homicides in 1926–1929 or 71 out of 236 in 1926–1934 were of this variety. An additional 18 of the homicides were police killed in the line of duty, often in the process of enforcing prohibition law.

An analysis of 883 homicides in Chicago for the years 1926–1927 showed a somewhat similar pattern to that shown in Detroit. Like Detroit, a large percentage of homicides during this period were justifiable. While these Chicago data do not specify criminal transactions as a type of homicide, the data do suggest that when justifiables are removed from the analysis, the two major categories of homicide were gang and criminal related (approximately 33.3%) and altercations and brawls (30.4%). Domestic homicides were quite low being only 8.3% of the total.

These two sources, then, suggest that to speak of one modal type of homicide for the 1900–1933 time period would be inaccurate, for there were a number of types. The occurrences of friends or acquaintances killing each other in arguments were frequent; however, homicides resulting from criminal transactions and those considered justifiable took on equal if not paramount importance. These latter two types, furthermore, were both apparently highly related to bootlegging and to the attempted enforcement of prohibition laws. The extent to which family-related homicides were of importance varied with the city studied. It shared almost equal importance with criminal and friend homicides in Detroit but was of lesser importance in Chicago.

In sum, when we look at available data for the period of 1900 to the early 1930s, we find there was an increasing rate of homicide from 1900, peaking in the late 1920s and early 1930s. While the friend-friend homicide persisted as a major category, the category of criminal transaction and justifiable homicides became of equal or sometimes greater importance in terms of the amount and type of killing that was going on. The repeal of prohibition affected the rate, and the mid–1930s began to see a decline in rate and change in type which became pronounced in the next period of history.

HOMICIDE: THE MID–1930s TO THE MID–1960s

The mid–1930s began to see collection of fully national data on homicide both in the Vital Statistics and the UCR. These data reveal a steady decline of the homicide rates from the high of the late 1920s and early 1930s (Vital Statistics data) to a low and fairly steady rate of 5.6 in the 1940s and 4.8 in the 1950s. The low rate of the 1950s persisted until the mid–1960s.

In terms of the relationships in which people were killed, there were a number of studies of this period representing both southern and northern cities. All of the studies seem to show that during this period, domestic and love-related homicides became a more important category than in any preceding time and that males killing males in quarrelsome situations continued to be an important form of homicide, while homicides related to criminal transactions decreased to a small percentage.

Bullock, using police records for the 489 cases of criminal homicide in Houston 1945–1949, found the highest rates of homicide clustered among low-income, black, and Hispanic people, 67% of whom were laborers and domestic servants. The homicides occurred most frequently between people who knew each other (in 87% of the cases the victim and offender were acquainted with each other) and arguments were the prime precipitating factors. Bullock does not indicate the number killed in domestic quarrels but indicated marital discord as a third most important reason for death. The three most frequent patterns precipitating homicide were: (1) arguments originating out of a variety of situations; (2) love triangles produced by jealousy between friends; and (3) marital discord. The most frequent place of death was a rooming house (42.1% of the victims were killed there) followed by a tavern (28.6%) and the street (21 .1%).

Birmingham, Alabama, was studied by Harlan during this same period. In his analysis of 500 cases of criminal homicide in that city from 1937 to 1944, he found that the majority of the victims were black males (67.8%) and that 45.2% of the cases were black males killing other black males. In all but 4.7% of the cases, the victim and the offender knew each other. The modal category was a black male killing a black male while arguing in a private residence. Murders stemming from such arguments (e.g., arguments over dice or money) were the prime circumstance surrounding homicides in Birmingham; marital discord, jealousy, and quarrels over lovers ranked next in frequency as the basis for murder.

In northern cities of that time, Cleveland and Detroit, a similar pattern prevailed. Bensing and Schroeder, using 662 cases of homicide from 1947 to 1953 in Cleveland, found that the majority of homicides involved black males who knew each other. In only 4.5% of the cases were the victim and offender unknown to each other. While Bensing and Schroeder's study does not permit establishing the predominant motive for homicide, they do list the following three motives as important: (1) quarrels of a petty nature; (2) marital discord; and (3) love or sex disputes in which the deceased is slain by one other than a spouse or common law mate.

The importance of marital and love disputes is further documented in Boudouris's study of Detroit. He examined police reports on homicide in Detroit

33

from 1926 to 1968. Analysis of his data shows the 1940s and especially the 1950s to be a time when domestic relations and love affairs claimed most of the homicide deaths. Recomputing his data to combine domestic relations and love affairs into one category indicate that in the 1920s, 21.9% of the homicides were domestically related; that figure rose in the 1930s to 29.3%; to 32.6% in the 1940s; and to a high of 38.4% in the 1950s. The friends and acquaintance category remained in a steady second place to domestic and love relations as lethal during the 1940s and 1950s.

Criminal transactions, which were of importance in the late 1920s and early 1930s, declined to a total of 19.2% of Detroit's criminal homicides in the 1940s and 9.2% in the 1950s.

Wolfgang's classic study further demonstrates the importance of close relationships in homicide during the 1940–1960 period. Wolfgang examined the universe of 588 criminal homicides in Philadelphia which occurred in 1948–1952. He used primarily police records which included the investigation reports of the Police Homicide Unit, witnesses' statements, and the like. The data for the 1948–1952 period indicated an overall criminal homicide rate of 5.7 per 100,000. The homicide rates for blacks and males were many times greater than for whites and females. The rate was 22.5 for blacks; 1.9 for whites; 9.0 for males; and 2.6 for females. Taking race and sex together, black males had a rate of 36.9 per 100,000; black females 9.6; white males 2.9; and white females 1.0. Further, a significant association was found between age and homicide. Those in the age group 25–34 were most likely to be victims, and offenders were likely to be in the 20–24 age group.

In terms of homicide setting, Wolfgang found that the single most dangerous place in Philadelphia in 1950 was inside a home (50.5% of the victims were slain there). Furthermore, the methods used to kill varied, with stabbing being the major means of death (38.8%) followed closely by shooting (33%), beating (21.8%), and other means (6.4%).

Wolfgang classified the cases both in terms of the victim-offender relationships and in terms of motive recorded by the police for the slaying. The relationships were coded into those of family; close friend, that is, frequent direct intimate contact over time; acquaintance, that is, direct contact as a result of personal knowledge but devoid of intimacy or frequency; stranger; paramour, mistress, prostitute, that is, a love object other than a spouse; sex rival; enemy; paramour of offender's mate; felon or police officer; innocent bystander; homosexual partner. (In 38 of the cases, the offender remained unknown.)

When adding together those involving a love object or sexual relationship, that is, family, paramour, and homosexual partner, we find that 35.1% of the victims were in a close love or sexual relationship with the killer. Further, when adding close friend and acquaintance, 28.2% and 13.5%, respectively, we find an additional total of 41.7% of the victims knew their killer.

Motives were classified as being the ostensible police recorded motive and included alterations of a "relatively trivial origin" (35.0%); domestic quarrels (14.1%); jealousy (11.6%); altercations over money (10.5%); robbery (6.8%); revenge (5.3%); accidental (3.9%); self-defense (1.4%); halting a felon (1.2%); escaping arrest (1.0%); concealing birth (1.0%); other (3.4%); and unknown (4.8%).

In sum, the 1940s and especially the 1950s were a time with a relatively low and stable homicide rate. It was a time, further, when two types of murder seemed most prevalent, that between family members—usually husband and wife or lovers—and that between two males known to each other who were arguing at the time. In some cities, for example, Detroit, the family and love relationship murder was predominant, while in other places the male killing a male was the more frequent. But in all instances these two types were the dominant ones and, unlike an earlier period, the family and love relationship murder became a more highly dominant form in relationship and motive.

HOMICIDE: THE 1960s AND 1970s

The trend of homicide in the 1960s and 1970s, as indicated by UCR data, shows the rate to remain fairly low and stationary from 1960 to 1965 (4.6, 4.8, 4.8, 4.8, 5.1, respectively). The rate began to increase in 1965 and 1966 (the rate was 5.6 in 1966) and continued steadily upward throughout the latter half of the 1960s and into the 1970s with a peak rate occurring nationally in 1974 at 9.7. (The average UCR rate in the 1960s was 5.5, and in the 1970s 8.9.)

In terms of specific studies of homicide there are more studies in this period than was true of earlier times. The most comprehensive study during this time was the Violence Commission Report (1969).

The Violence Commission Report and subsequent analyses by Curtis was a national survey, using a 10% random sample of 1967 arrest reports, of 17 large U.S. cities. The Commission found criminal homicide to be intrasexual in nature (63% of the cases where the victim-offender relationship was known involved a male killing another male) and intraracial (when race of both the victim and the offender is known only 10% of the murders are interracial). It is suspected, however, that the increase in stranger killings represents also an increase in interracial murders, especially black on white. In terms of victim-offender relationships, the 17 American cities in 1967 showed husband and wife killings to account for 15.8% of all criminal homicides; 8.9% were other family members; 9.0% were other primary relations, that is, close friends and lovers; 29.8% were nonprimary but known to each other; 15.6% were strangers; and in 20.9% of the cases the offender remained unknown (thus likely to be a stranger).

Regarding motive, the survey revealed that minor altercations were the most frequent reasons for the death (35.7%); followed by unknown reasons (21.0%); other reasons (10.6%); and robbery (8.8%). Family quarrels accounted for only 7.7% of the homicide deaths. In terms of weapon, 46.6% were killed with a firearm, 29.2% with an knife, and the remainder by other means.

Other local studies reveal similar homicide patterns although with some variation based, apparently, on differences between northern and southern cities.

Block, using police records, studied 7045 criminal homicides occurring in Chicago from 1965 to 1974. He found that the homicide rate doubled in that period of time from 11.4 per 100,000 in 1965 to 29.2 in 1974. The number of homicides in which the victim and offender did not know each other increased dramatically from 95 to 410 and, in fact, the most common offender is one whose identity remains unknown to the police. Much of the increase in homicide could be accounted for by an increase in the number of homicides related to robbery. There are, according to Block, essentially two patterns of homicide, one of altercation homicide based on domestic feuds or arguments with friends and the second based on robbery. The second increased much more rapidly than the first in the time period studied. Further, there was an increase in homicides using guns.

Riedel and Katzenelson, using arrest data for 3411 homicides in Washington, DC, from 1957 to 1974, found an increasing rate for the time period, from 12.2 in 1957 to 31.3 in 1974. They found an appreciable decrease in the age of offenders. Homicide remained an intraracial event, primarily between nonwhite offenders and victims. While they did not do an analysis based on victim-offender relationship, they do note a decrease in the percentage of homicides occurring in homes. In 1957, 58.0% of the homicides occurred there, while in 1972, 32.7% did. One of the largest changes was in method used to kill: In 1957, 35.9% of the homicides were committed by firearm, by 1974 this had increased to 82.8%.

The findings for Chicago and for Washington, DC, are similar to those in Cleveland and in Philadelphia. Hirsch, using coroners' records, found that the homicide rate in Cleveland rose gradually in the early 1960s and then dramatically in the latter half of the 1960s. The rate of increase was great for both nonwhite and white males, although the increase for white male victims were much greater, 600% compared to 200% for nonwhites. While they do not study victim-offender relationships, they note a higher percentage of homicides occurring by firearms than in the preceding time periods.

Zahn, also using medical examiners' records, studied 1935 homicide victims in Philadelphia from 1969 to 1973. When comparing her results with those of Wolfgang, who studied Philadelphia in the late 1940s and in the 1950s, she found a much higher rate of homicide in 1970, 19.2 per 100,000. There are more offenders in the youngest age groups. Data showed that over half (50.4%) of the homicides occurred with a gun, and 35.3% occurred at home. Further, in terms of reasons for the homicide, the most frequent category was arguments: 34.9% of the homicides resulted from such circumstance. This was followed by unknown (fully 24.3% of the homicides occur for unknown reasons, usually by unknown offenders) and this was followed by domestic quarrel (15.4% of the homicides occurred for domestic reasons). In general, while the dominant form may be an acquaintance killing another acquaintance in an argument, it is closely followed by a stranger killing someone, with the circumstances immediately surrounding the event remaining unknown.

Findings from studies of northern cities, then, show a consistent picture of an increasing homicide rate in the late 1960s and into the 1970s; an increase in homicides by gun; and an increase in homicides with unknown assailants who may be murdering for money or for reasons other than direct argument. The stranger is, indeed, a more fearful figure in northern American cities in the 1970s than he was earlier.

Studies of southern and southwestern cities for the same time period show a somewhat different pattern. Mumford et al., using police and medical examiners' records for 591 victims in 1961–1962 and 1971–1972, found that there was an increasing rate of homicide, increasing for both black and white males. The pattern of homicide varied somewhat, however, for the blacks and the whites. While most blacks and whites were killed at home by relatives or acquaintances, more blacks were killed in such a situation than whites. Whites were more likely than blacks to be killed in a public place and this tendency seemed to increase from the 1960s to the 1970s. In both situations, however, firearms were the main mode of attack and there was an increase in the use of firearms from the 1960s to the 1970s.

Lundsgaarde, studying 300 murders in Houston in 1969, found murder was largely intraracial, with only 6% of Houston killers crossing racial boundaries. The categories of relationship and kinds of situation have not, he claimed, changed significantly over the past 40 years, with the exception of a slight increase in the number of killings involving strangers (in 17.5% of the cases the killer was a total stranger to the victim). In his sample the vast bulk of victims knew their killers— in 31% of the cases they were in the family group. In Houston most were killed by guns (86%) and more were killed outside the home (60%) than inside.

Zahn and Snodgrass, studying 202 homicide victims in Dallas, found, as in Houston, that most victims were males; that 33.6% of the killings were family related; and 24.5% involved acquaintances, 17.3% strangers, and 13.4% unknown. About equal numbers were killed inside as outside the home, and the primary motive for killing was domestic quarrels. Of the murders, 38% were a result of domestic quarrels. As in all other cities, the gun was the main instrument of death.

Taking all studies from the 1960s and the 1970s there is some commonality. There is a higher rate of homicide than in the time period immediately preceding it. By and large homicide is, as in other time periods, intraracial and intrasexual, although there is some slight increase in interracial (black on white) homicide and guns are the most frequent mode of attack. There is an increase in stranger murders and in cases where the offender remains unknown, although this increase is much more pronounced in northern cities. In southern or southwestern cities domestic violence remains a significant category while in the North the stranger and the unknown assailant homicide is now a dominant (if not the dominant) murder relationship.

SUMMARY

From a review of the foregoing information, it seems warranted to suggest the following regarding homicide in twentieth century America.

The Homicide Rate

The homicide rate has fluctuated through time. The trend was relatively low at the turn of the century but started to increase in the early twentieth century, reaching one peak in the 1920s and early 1930s. The course went down, with occasional exceptions, in the 1940s and remained low and stable during the 1950s and early 1960s. A sharp and steady rise began to occur around 1965, peaking in 1974 (the rate was 9.7 in that year). The rate for the final two years (8.8) remains high, however, and is the same as the high rates found in the 1920s (8.8 in 1926; 8.7 in 1927, and 8.8 in 1928).

The Sexual Character of Homicide

Homicide has remained intramale in character through time. Generally speaking, when comparing across studies, approximately 60% of the cases involve a man killing another man. Very few women kill another woman. In cross-sex killings, while men and women (usually husbands and wives) have been killing each other for some time, it seems that there is more likelihood for men to kill women than the reverse. (Research which I am currently beginning will determine whether this is true even during times of increasing attempts at female liberation.)

The Racial Character of Homicide

The extent to which homicide is intraracial or interracial is somewhat difficult to assess, since white frontiersmen killing Indians and the Ku Klux Klan killing blacks may not be generally contained in information on homicide. Using conventional sources on homicide, however, it seems that homicide is consistently an intraracial rather than an interracial event. While the predominance of homicide within racial groups is consistent through time, there has been some increase in interracial homicide since the mid–1960s. In 1967, 10% of the homicides were interracial with the percentage being higher than that in some cities.

The Victim-Offender Relationship

The comparison between studies on victim-offender relationship is the most difficult to accomplish. This is due to the fact that there is no consistent definition of what constitutes an acquaintance or a stranger relationship and, further, many studies use motive as the basis of classification, for example, criminal transaction, but do not indicate whether the criminal transaction involved an acquaintance or stranger relationship.

After trying to make the data comparable, however, the following seems supportable. Throughout the century a male killing another male with whom he is acquainted is a regular and persistent form of homicide. During the time of greatest homicide, however, the stranger or economic relationship murder predominates. In the late 1920s the murder related to prohibition and in the 1960s and the 1970s the murder by unknown persons for unknown reason and/or the murder for profit (robbery) are of importance. In contrast, when homicide rates are low such as in the 1950s, family and acquaintance homicides are dominant, with family murders especially so.

In general it seems that the percentage of family-related murders does not fluctuate dramatically through time. The stranger and unknown categories of relationship and so-called economically motivated homicides, however, do. They are the main contributors to the times of highest rates. In all events, while some categories of victim-offender relationship remain throughout time, the prominence of these types varies in different time periods.

Manner of Attack and Homicide

Many current researchers point to the increasing use of guns as the reason for the increase in the homicide rate generally and, more specifically, for the increase in homicides where the victim's assailant remains unknown. The data from existing studies suggest that deaths by firearms do not show continuous progressive rise throughout the century, but rather that a high percentage of deaths by gun occur at the same time as high homicide rates. Since we have seen that the homicide rate fluctuates decidedly, so, too, does the use of guns.

Prior to the twentieth century. Lane indicates that a person in Philadelphia was as likely to have been killed by a gun (25%), a sharp instrument (25%), or fists and feet (21%). In the 1924–1926 period, the overall rate of firearms used in homicides rose sharply. Brearly reports that 70.2% of the nation's homicides were gun related. Boudouris, writing of Detroit 1926–1929, also indicates high use of firearms, with 60.9% of the victims killed that way. His figures, interestingly, almost duplicate those of the most recent UCR which show 62.5% killed by guns, 19% by a sharp instrument, 12.9% by a blunt instrument, and 5.5% by the body. The findings from the 1920s and from the 1970s contrast sharply with Wolfgang's findings in the 1950s in Philadelphia where the major means of death was a knife.

Time series studies, further, support the notion of the fluctuating use of guns. Riedel, for instance, traced death by guns in Washington, DC, from 1957 to 1974. The percentage killed by guns remained low and steady from 1957 to 1966 (e.g., 35.9% were killed by firearms in 1957). These percentages jumped to 82.8% by 1974, with the percentages for each year since 1966 being the following (52%, 60%, 70%, 73%, 66%, 65%, 76%, and 82%, respectively).

Block also reported an increase in killings by guns as it attended an increase in murder during robberies and by unknown assailants. Interestingly, however, in Chicago, killings of women victims were about equally likely to he killed by gun or other method, while gun killings of black and Latin males increased especially fast.

The point is that guns do bear a relationship to the murder rate; in times of highest homicide rates, the 1920s and early 1930s and since 1968, the percentage of people killed by gun is also high. Yet it would not seem that availability of guns alone is the answer to the high U.S. homicide rate. It seems unlikely, for example, that the number of guns available were appreciably less in the 1950s than in the 1920s, or that the number changed drastically in Washington, DC, from one year, 1968, to the next, 1969. What may change is not only availability but also the readiness to use guns and the definition of when and for what purpose the use of firearms is desirable.

From the foregoing we might ask of what importance it is to know these facts; to know that the rates of homicide fluctuate with very high peaks in the late 1920s and early 1930s and the mid–1970s; to know that the major types of victim-offender relationship are somewhat variable with the high rate times being characterized by more guns, more stranger, and unknown homicides; and that, while family killings and males killing their male acquaintances remain types, the importance of family-related homicide is relatively stable through time and significant when the overall homicide rate is low. The importance lies in two areas: the research questions they trigger and their implications for social policy.

While a complete statement of new research directions and all the policy implications derivable from them is beyond this current attempt, a few beginning statements may prove helpful.

In terms of research directions, this historical review would suggest that closer attention be paid to the connection between markets for illegal goods and the overall rate of homicide violence. It seems possible, if not likely, that establishing and maintaining a market for illegal goods (booze in the 1920s and early 1930s; heroin and cocaine in the late 1960s and early 1970s) may involve controlling and/or reducing the competition, solving disputes between alternate suppliers, or eliminating dissatisfied customers. The resolution of such problems in illegal markets is not easily done by resorting to use of legal sanction (although payoffs may occur). There may, then, be more likelihood of resorting to force to settle differences. This resolution has the added advantage of silencing the victim and thus preventing unwanted information from leaking to official sources.

The use of guns in illegal markets may also be triggered by the constant "fear" of being caught either by a rival or by the police. Such fear may increase the perceived need for protection, that is, a gun, thus may increase the arming of these populations and a resulting increased likelihood of use. For the overall society this may mean a higher homicide rate.

All of this supposition, of course, begs the larger questions of why substance use is sanctioned at certain times and why so many people at certain periods want these substances. Both questions may also be related to research foci necessary for understanding homicide.

If this historical survey might prompt different research directions, so, too, might it prompt new considerations of policy issues. For example, these findings have direct implications for the deployment of criminal justice resources. The very allocation of resource systems may be affected by such knowledge, for with careful monitoring of types of homicide that are occurring, differing allocations to solve the problems associated with these types might occur. As robbery-related homicides increase, for example, the allocation of resources to improve robbery detection equipment in stores or on the streets and educating the citizen in self-protection (without arming himself/herself) might result. Further, additional resources to increase crime lab work, for example, ballistics, would seem a reasonable approach. Because of the prohibitive cost of such labs, they might be set up on a county or regional base, thus allowing not only better detection but cost-effective detection as well.

When family homicide is dominant, additional resources to family courts; more training to help people solve domestic disputes; educating people to not reach for a gun if they argue; or, if they have guns in the house, to make sure they are not loaded, might be done. And, if homicides are linked to illegal market activity, attempting to draw people out of the illegal markets and into legal ones would seem necessary.

Further, gun control has often been proposed as a way to reduce the homicide rate. Since the data here indicates a correlation between a high homicide rate and a high use of guns, this approach seems justified. However, those persons using guns and their reasons for doing so must also be closely examined. Perhaps, if my previous analysis has any validity, taking profit out of illegal substance markets would also reduce the use of guns in some populations and, thus, the homicide rate overall.

Many more research and policy considerations suggest themselves. I hope that these few illustrate sufficiently, however, the direct relevance of history to our current endeavors and that they provide some illustration of why a firm grounding in history is necessary for both the understanding of and the solution to the problem of homicide.

Revised Code of Washington, Title 9A, 1996

CHAPTER 9A.32 RCW
HOMICIDE

RCW 9A.32.010 Homicide defined.

Homicide is the killing of a human being by the act, procurement or omission of another, death occurring within three years and a day, and is either (1) murder, (2) homicide by abuse, (3) manslaughter, (4) excusable homicide, or (5) justifiable homicide.

non criminal homicide.

RCW 9A.32.020 Premeditation—Limitations.

(1) As used in this chapter, the premeditation required in order to support a conviction of the crime of murder in the first degree must involve more than a moment in point of time.

RCW 9A.32.030 Murder in the first degree.

(1) A person is guilty of murder in the first degree when:

(a) With a premeditated intent to cause the death of another person, he or she causes the death of such person or of a third person; or

(b) Under circumstances manifesting an extreme indifference to human life, he or she engages in conduct which creates a grave risk of death to any person, and thereby causes the death of a person; or

(c) He or she commits or attempts to commit the crime of either (1) robbery in the first or second degree, (2) rape in the first or second degree, (3) burglary in the first degree, (4) arson in the first or second degree, or (5) kidnapping in the first or second degree, and in the course of or in furtherance of such crime or in immediate flight therefrom, he or she, or another participant, causes the death of a person other than one of the participants: Except that in any prosecution under this subdivision (1)(c) in which the defendant was not the only participant in the underlying crime, if established by the defendant by a preponderance of the evidence, it is a defense that the defendant:

(i) Did not commit the homicidal act or in any way solicit, request, command, importune, cause, or aid the commission thereof; and

(ii) Was not armed with a deadly weapon, or any instrument, article, or substance readily capable of causing death or serious physical injury; and

(iii) Had no reasonable grounds to believe that any other participant was armed with such a weapon, instrument, article, or substance; and

(iv) Had no reasonable grounds to believe that any other participant intended to engage in conduct likely to result in death or serious physical injury.

(2) Murder in the first degree is a class A felony.

RCW 9A32.040 Murder in the first degree—Sentence.

Notwithstanding RCW 9A.32.030(2), any person convicted of the crime of murder in the first degree shall be sentenced to life imprisonment.

RCW 9A.32.050 Murder in the second degree.

(1) A person is guilty of murder in the second degree when:

(a) With intent to cause the death of another person but without premeditation, he causes the death of such person or of a third person; or

(b) He commits or attempts to commit any felony other than those enumerated in RCW 9A.32.030(1)(c), and, in the course of and in furtherance of such crime or in immediate flight therefrom, he, or another participant, causes the death of a person other than one of the participants; except that in any prosecution under this subdivision (1)(b) in which the defendant was not the only participant in the underlying crime, if established by the defendant by a preponderance of the evidence, it is a defense that the defendant:

(i) Did not commit the homicidal act or in any way solicit, request, command, importune, cause, or aid the commission thereof; and

(ii) Was not armed with a deadly weapon, or any instrument, article, or substance readily capable of causing death or serious physical injury; and

(iii) Had no reasonable grounds to believe that any other participant was armed with such a weapon, instrument, article, or substance; and

(iv) Had no reasonable grounds to believe that any other participant intended to engage in conduct likely to result in death or serious physical injury.

(2) Murder in the second degree is a class A felony.

RCW 9A.32.055 Homicide by abuse.

(1) A person is guilty of homicide by abuse if, under circumstances manifesting an extreme indifference to human life, the person causes the death of a child or person under sixteen years of age, a developmentally disabled person, or a dependent adult, and the person has previously engaged in a pattern or practice of assault or torture of said child, person under sixteen years of age, developmentally disabled person, or dependent person.

(2) As used in this section, "dependent adult" means a person who, because of physical or mental disability, or because of extreme advanced age, is dependent upon another person to provide the basic necessities of life.

(3) Homicide by abuse is a class A felony.

RCW 9A.32.060 Manslaughter in the first degree.

(1) A person is guilty of manslaughter in the first degree when:

(a) He recklessly causes the death of another person; or

(b) He intentionally and unlawfully kills an unborn quick child by inflicting any injury upon the mother of such child.

(2) Manslaughter in the first degree is a class B felony.

RCW 9A.32.070 Manslaughter in the second degree.

(1) A person is guilty of manslaughter in the second degree when, with criminal negligence, he causes the death of another person.

(2) Manslaughter in the second degree is a class C felony.

CHAPTER 10.95 RCW
CAPITAL PUNISHMENT—
AGGRAVATED FIRST DEGREE MURDER

RCW 10.95.020 Definition.

A person is guilty of aggravated first degree murder if he or she commits first degree murder as defined by RCW 9A.32.030(1)(a), as now or hereafter amended, and one or more of the following aggravating circumstances exist:

(1) The victim was a law enforcement officer, corrections officer, or fire fighter who was performing his or her official duties at the time of the act resulting in

death and the victim was known or reasonably should have been known by the person to be such at the time of the killing;

(2) At the time of the act resulting in the death, the person was serving a term of imprisonment, had escaped, or was on authorized or unauthorized leave in or from a state facility or program for the incarceration or treatment of persons adjudicated guilty of crimes;

(3) At the time of the act resulting in death, the person was in custody in a county or county-city jail as a consequence of having been adjudicated guilty of a felony;

(4) The person committed the murder pursuant to an agreement that he or she would receive money or any other thing of value for committing the murder;

(5) The person solicited another person to commit the murder and had paid or had agreed to pay money or any other thing of value for committing the murder;

(6) The person committed the murder to obtain or maintain his or her membership or to advance his or her position in the hierarchy of an organization, association, or identifiable group;

(7) The murder was committed during the course of or as a result of a shooting where the discharge of the firearm, as defined in RCW 9.41.010, is either from a motor vehicle or from the immediate area of a motor vehicle that was used to transport the shooter or the firearm, or both, to the scene of the discharge;

(8) The victim was:

(a) A judge; juror or former juror; prospective, current, or former witness in an adjudicative proceeding; prosecuting attorney; deputy prosecuting attorney; defense attorney; a member of the indeterminate sentence review board; or a probation or parole officer; and

(b) The murder was related to the exercise of official duties performed or to be performed by the victim;

(9) The person committed the murder to conceal the commission of a crime or to protect or conceal the identity of any person committing a crime, including, but specifically not limited to, any attempt to avoid prosecution as a persistent offender as defined in RCW 9.94A.030;

(10) There was more than one victim and the murders were part of a common scheme or plan or the result of a single act of the person;

(11) The murder was committed in the course of, in furtherance of, or in immediate flight from one of the following crimes:

(a) Robbery in the first or second degree;

(b) Rape in the first or second degree;

(c) Burglary in the first or second degree or residential burglary;

(d) Kidnapping in the first degree; or

(e) Arson in the first degree;

(12) The victim was regularly employed or self-employed as a newsreporter and the murder was committed to obstruct or hinder the investigative, research, or reporting activities of the victim.

RCW 10.95.030 Sentences for aggravated first degree murder.

(1) Except as provided in subsection (2) of this section, any person convicted of the crime of aggravated first degree murder shall be sentenced to life imprisonment without possibility of release or parole. A person sentenced to life imprisonment under this section shall not have that sentence suspended, deferred, or commuted by any judicial officer and the indeterminate sentence review board or its successor may not parole such prisoner nor reduce the period of confinement in any manner whatsoever including but not limited to any sort of good-time calculation. The department of social and health services or its successor or any executive official may not permit such prisoner to participate in any sort of release or furlough program.

(2) If, pursuant to a special sentencing proceeding held under RCW 10.95.050, the trier of fact finds that there are not sufficient mitigating circumstances to merit leniency, the sentence shall be death. In no case, however, shall a person be sentenced to death if the person was mentally retarded at the time the crime was committed, under the definition of mental retardation set forth in (a) of this subsection. A diagnosis of mental retardation shall be documented by a licensed psychiatrist or licensed psychologist designated by the court, who is an expert in the diagnosis and evaluation of mental retardation. The defense must establish mental retardation by a preponderance of the evidence and the court must make a finding as to the existence of mental retardation.

(a) "Mentally retarded" means the individual has: (i) Significantly subaverage general intellectual functioning; (ii) existing concurrently with deficits in adaptive behavior; and (iii) both significantly subaverage general intellectual functioning and deficits in adaptive behavior were manifested during the developmental period.

(b) "General intellectual functioning" means the results obtained by assessment with one or more of the individually administered general intelligence tests developed for the purpose of assessing intellectual functioning.

(c) "Significantly subaverage general intellectual functioning" means intelligence quotient seventy or below.

(d) "Adaptive behavior" means the effectiveness or degree with which individuals meet the standards of personal independence and social responsibility expected for his or her age.

(e) "Developmental period" means the period of time between conception and the eighteenth birthday.

CLASS A FELONIES:

i) murder in the first degree

Premeditated or extremly indifferent to human life, otherwise murder in 2nd degree

Aggravated First degree murder (worst) (p45-47)

SENTENCES:

1st Degree ~Life

Aggravated - Death sentence (Baring Mental Illness)

ii) Homicide by Abuse:
Victim is: i) 16 or under
ii) disabled
iii) dependant adult

MUST SHOW RECORD OF ABUSE

CLASS B FELONIES:

Manslaughter 1st Degree
Recklessness or killing of unborn child by injuring of mother

CLASS C FELONIES:

Manslaughter in second degree
Criminal Negligence.

CHAPTER 2

Data Sources & Measures

I n order to know as precisely as possible how many murders have been committed, by whom, with what kinds of weapons, under what circumstances and motives, in what types of locations, and so on, the most accurate information possible is necessary. The measurement of murder poses unique problems for criminologists, because it is a relatively less frequent but more serious crime than most, and two of the primary measurement techniques that criminologists rely upon are not viable.

In general, the volume and nature of crime are typically measured with either available official-record data sources (e.g., police and court records) or with surveys of either victims (victimization surveys) or of offenders (self-report surveys). Data on murder is impossible to collect in victimization surveys, simply because the victim is dead. Information could be collected in a self-report survey, but because murder is so rare among the general population, a huge sample would be required to capture any killers, and respondents might be much less likely to admit to and tell you about their murders than their larcenies. Some researchers, instead, ask convicted killers about their offenses, but the truth of their responses is in doubt, and that kind of information is limited to small-sample case studies and anecdotal data from which it is difficult to generalize to the broader community of potential killers.

For murder, it seems that the best available data sources are the official records of the criminal justice system, even with all of their recognized problems and limitations. The difficulties in producing accurate measures of the magnitude of the problem are illustrated in the work of Hotaling and Finkelhor on simply estimating the number of child abduction murders by strangers. Across multiple data sources there is substantial discrepancy in reported numbers, for a crime for which one would guess there would be extremely accurate counts.

Riedel focuses on the differences in the national estimates for all murders produced by law enforcement agencies compared to the vital statistics on mortality compiled by public health agencies. Simply put, they do not match, and one is left again to ponder the reasons why.

Keppel and Weis describe an alternative official data source on murder, a multi-state, regional computerized information system that includes a wealth of specific data on every murder committed (solved and unsolved) in the region since 1980. Case information, which is submitted by local homicide investigators, is used for both investigative and research purposes. This type of data base has many advantages over other sources of information about murder, particularly detailed, comprehensive data on every murder case in the participating jurisdictions over an extended period of time.

Estimating the Number of Stranger-Abduction Homicides of Children: A Review of Available Evidence

GERALD T. HOTALING & DAVID FINKELHOR

The American public from time to time has been gripped by the fear that large numbers of strangers are poised to abduct and murder its children. Such panics typically intensify in the wake of particularly grisly, nationally publicized crimes. In the 1920s and 1930s, for example, the notorious abduction murders of Blakely Coughlin, Bobby Franks, Marian Parker, and Charles Lindbergh, Jr., among others, each triggered intense public reactions and political pressure across the country to introduce the death penalty for ransom kidnapping. Similarly, in the early 1980s the nationally publicized tragedies of Adam Walsh and Etan Patz led to public outcry, followed by the passage of the Missing Children's Assistance Act, the founding of the National Center for Missing and Exploited Children in 1984, and new efforts to locate missing children through pictures on milk cartons and billboards and through telephone hotlines.

In the face of this kind of public concern, it is remarkable that there are so few reliable statistics about the scope of the problem. The number of children thought to be kidnapped by strangers each year in the United States has been estimated at anywhere from "less than 300" to "up to 20,000." Child Find of America, a missing children's information center, has contended that as many as 5,000 children are kidnapped and murdered annually. These are crude estimates. Unfortunately, more precise estimates are hard to obtain. The official source of national crime statistics, the Uniform Crime Reports, do not publish statistics that specify the number of persons under 18 killed by strangers in total, let alone the number killed by strangers in the course of abductions.

Other sources of information are equally inadequate. Public health officials have recognized that homicide (of all sorts, not just stranger homicide) is one of the five leading causes of death among children in the United States, yet the subject has been badly neglected by researchers. Most of the available studies are limited to fatal child abuse of infants and preschoolers, where the perpetrators primarily were parents or other caretakers. Very little has been written about stranger homicides.

This article is a small effort to remedy this situation. Because of the seriousness of this crime and the anguish it provokes, there is a need to fill the statistical void on stranger-abduction homicides of children. This article first reviews five previous studies to try to derive estimates about the number of stranger-abduction murders of children that occur each year in the United States. Second, it presents the results of a special analysis the authors conducted of the *Comprehensive Homicide File,* concerning the number of abduction murders of children during the nine-year-period 1976–1984.

Six estimates are presented in Table 1. Five of them come from police records or police statistics. Three general, preliminary points need to be made about these analyses. First, the terms kidnapping and abduction are used interchangeably here. The line between the two crimes has grown quite murky since the 1930s. Statutes on kidnapping have expanded to such an extent that they now cover behavior considered to constitute abduction. Secondly, though kidnapping is defined differently in different states, in general the legal definition represented in the statistics is broader than people's common-sense definition of the crime. The offense of kidnapping statutorily requires the following elements: (1) an unlawful taking of the victim accomplished by force, threat, or deception, or without consent of the appropriate guardian if the victim is incompetent or under the age of 14, (2) removal of the victim from his or her place of residence or business, or a substantial distance from the vicinity where he or she is found, or confinement of the victim for a substantial period in a place of isolation and (3) proof that the actor proceeded with one of four evil purposes: (a) to hold the victim for ransom or as a hostage, (b) to facilitate a felony or flight therefrom, (c) to terrorize or physically injure the victim or another person, or (d) to disrupt governmental or political functions. It should be noted that a victim (in this case, a child) does not necessarily have to be missing for an extended period of time to have been abducted. A child who

Table 1

Summary of estimates and revised estimates of stranger-abduction homicides of persons 17 and younger from six data sets

Study	Original Estimate			Revised Estimate	
	Data Source	Annual Estimated Number	Rate per 100,000 Children	Annual Estimated Number	Rate per 100,000 Children
Illinois Criminal Justice Information Authority (1987)	FBI data (1980–82)	1,250	1.98	250	0.39
National Center for Missing and Exploited Children's Police Record Study (1986)	Police Records in Jacksonville, FL and Houston, TX (1984)	578	0.93	318	0.42
Wilbanks (1984)	Police Records in Dade County, FL (1980)			123	0.19
National Center for Missing and Exploited Children Reporting Data	Missing Child Cases Reported to National Clearinghouse (1984–87)			46–88	0.11
Best (1987)	Supplemental Homicide Report for State of California (1984)	170–280	0.36	210	0.33
Hotaling and Finkelhor (1988)	Comparative Homicide File (1976–79, 1980–94)			52–158	0.17

was taken forcibly into a vehicle, driven somewhere, raped, and murdered usually would be counted as an abduction murder even if that child's absence was never noted.

Third, as in many reanalyses of existing data, the numbers utilized in this study were not necessarily collected for the purpose at hand. This was somewhat compensated for through use of several data sets, which enabled generation of a number of estimates that could then be compared. The goal of this exercise was to produce a range of estimates of stranger-abduction homicides and to try to understand the reasons behind differences in these estimates. Each data set is described in terms of its original focus and, when applicable, the modifications made to construct an estimate for purposes of the present study.

ILLINOIS CRIMINAL JUSTICE INFORMATION AUTHORITY AND ILLINOIS DEPARTMENT OF LAW ENFORCEMENT (ICJIA-IDLE)

Estimate: 250 Children

The original ICJIA-IDLE annual estimate of children who are victims of stranger-abduction homicide was 1,250. This estimate was based, upon FBI Uniform Crime Report data for 1980–82 on the total number of children murdered under any circumstances. The authors of the ICJIA-IDLE study took the rounded average of 2,500 child homicides yearly in the U.S. and estimated that half (or 1,250) are committed by strangers. This is an extremely liberal, upper-bound estimate of possible stranger-abduction homicides. First, this estimate considers 18- and 19-year-olds to be children, even though most studies of children are limited to persons 17 years of age and younger. The inclusion of 18- and 19-year-olds inflates the estimate considerably since the number of murders by strangers of 18- and 19-year-olds is roughly equivalent to the total number of murders by strangers of all children aged 17 and younger. Second, the assumption that half of all murders of children are by strangers is grossly inflated. The ICJIA-IDLE made the generous but erroneous assumption that in all homicides in which the victim-offender relationship is unknown, all the unknown offenders were strangers. Other data have shown that less than 20 percent of all child homicides are by strangers. For example, Williams and Flewelling reclassified unknown victim-offender relationship murders from the *Supplemental Homicide Reports* as family, acquaintance, or stranger, based on the circumstances surrounding homicides in which the victim-offender relationship was known. This statistical adjustment resulted in an estimate that 38 percent of all homicides of persons 17 and younger are by family members, 45 percent by acquaintances, and 17 percent by strangers. Finally, this estimate assumes that all murders by strangers involve abduction. This is not likely, as the study authors themselves pointed out, since deaths resulting to a child when a stranger burns a building down or kills the occupants of a household during a burglary probably would not qualify as stranger abduction even under the broadest criteria. All three of these factors greatly inflate this estimate.

The ICJIA-IDLE estimate can be corrected at least in terms of the first two problems. The 18- and 19-year-olds can be removed and the figure modified through a more accurate estimate of the percentage of children killed by strangers. This yields an estimate of 250. This is really an estimate of the number of children killed by strangers, not an estimate of the number killed in stranger abductions. Thus, it represents an upper bound.

NATIONAL CENTER FOR MISSING AND EXPLOITED CHILDREN'S POLICE RECORDS STUDY (NCMEC-I)

Estimate: 318 Children

The National Center for Missing and Exploited Children (NCMEC) conducted a search of police records for all crimes committed against children in 1984 in Jacksonville, Florida and Houston, Texas. This study was designed to record all instances of attempted and actual kidnappings of children aged 17 and younger by nonfamily members. For the purposes of the police record check, kidnapping was defined by the study designers as behavior involving the seizure, confinement, enticement, taking, concealment, or abduction of one person by another. Under this definition, any movement of the victim from one place to another qualified as a case of kidnapping. Overall, the study found 269 cases of attempted and actual kidnapping by nonfamily members. Almost two-thirds of these cases involved sexual molestation episodes, and only three percent of the kidnapped children actually were missing for a period of more than twenty-four hours.

Of particular interest here is the finding that six of the nonfamily abductions in these two cities resulted in murders. The two cities contained slightly more than one percent of the nation's total child population of 62,688,000, so an extrapolation to the U.S. as a whole would lead to an estimate of about 578 children abducted and murdered by nonfamily members that year. This estimate is certainly high, given the unusually high rates of serious violent crime in both cities. Actually, the child-homicide rate in these two cities was almost twice the national average (the national child-homicide rate for persons 14 and younger was 1.32, compared to 2.42 in Jacksonville and 2.21 in Houston). Taking this into account reduces this estimate by 45 percent, to 318 abducted/murdered children.

This revised estimate of 318 nonfamily-abduction child homicides requires one further clarification. The NCMEC study designers chose to count "non-family," not just "stranger" abductions. Since no specific information in the report is given about the victim-offender relationship, there is no way to determine how many victims actually knew their abductors. Some of these abductors may not have been strangers, but other nonfamily members like babysitters or parents' girlfriends or boyfriends. Thus, the 318 figure is not truly an estimate of stranger-abduction homicides of children since it may include murders involving very different dynamics and motivations. However, the 318 figure may be a good yearly estimate of the number of children abducted and murdered by both strangers and acquaintances.

HOMICIDE IN DADE COUNTY, FLORIDA (DADE)

Estimate: 123 Children

In an analysis of homicide patterns and trends in Dade County, Florida, Wilbanks examined several forms of murder data from 1917–1983. An appendix in his book contains summaries of all homicides committed in Dade County, Florida during 1980. These data allow calculation of the number of children killed in the course of abductions. Each case record of the murder or non-negligent manslaughter of a person 17 years of or younger was abstracted. Using criteria for kidnapping developed by drafters of the *Model Penal Code*, cases were coded as involving abduction if any forced movement, confinement, or detention of the victim by the offender had taken place prior to the homicide. This method yielded three homicides classified as stranger abduction out of the nine homicides of children by strangers in 1980.

Extrapolation from these data to the U.S. as a whole is, of course, very speculative. Based on the nation's child population of over 63 million in 1980, the three stranger-abduction homicides in Dade County (with a child population of 386,000 in 1980) would translate into about 490 stranger-abduction homicides annually nationwide. As in the earlier NCMEC-I extrapolation, however, this is certainly an overestimate, given the very high overall homicide rate and child-homicide rate in Dade County compared to the U.S. as a whole. The homicide rate for persons aged 14 and younger for Dade was four times higher than the national average during 1980–1984. Factoring this in, the estimated number of stranger-abduction homicides occurring nationally would be 123.

NATIONAL CENTER FOR MISSING AND EXPLOITED CHILDREN CLEARINGHOUSE REPORTING DATA (NCMEC-II)

Estimate: 46–88 Children

Another crude estimate of stranger-abduction homicides can be made from cases of missing children known to the National Center for Missing and Exploited Children. The NCMEC is a national agency that tries to assist families and law enforcement in locating missing children. As such, it is informed about many of the most serious, long-term, criminally motivated cases; but it clearly is not informed about all such cases. If a child is kidnapped, sexually assaulted, and killed, and the body is found within a matter of hours, it would be unlikely that anyone would contact the NCMEC. Still, since most of the kind of stranger abductions that fit the public image are reported to the NCMEC, it is of interest to know approximately how many abduction homicides this organization is made aware of on an annual basis.

For the forty-three-month period between June 1984 and January 1988, the National Center had reports of 445 children who were abducted by strangers. The known status of these children as of March 1989 was as follows: 130 were found alive, 75 were found dead (for purposes of this study, presumed murdered), and 240 were still missing. Comparison of the first two numbers shows that of those children found, 37 percent were found dead. Thus, of the children who were still missing, it is likely that somewhere between 37 percent and 100 percent of them also will eventually be found dead. This suggests an additional 89 to 240 from among those still missing. This computation would yield an estimate ranging from 164 to 315 stranger-abducted children murdered during this forty-three-month period or between 46 and 88 children annually.

CALIFORNIA SUPPLEMENTAL HOMICIDE REPORT DATA (*SHR*-CA)

Estimate: 210 Children

Best analyzed FBI *Supplemental Homicide Reports* records for 1984 in the state of California to derive an estimate of abduction homicides. The FBI *Supplemental Homicide Reports* computer file contains detailed information on homicides committed in the United States on an annual basis. The major advantage of these data over the usual FBI statistics is the information on the relationship between victim and offender. Moreover, a summary circumstance code is assigned to each homicide, which describes the context and/or precipitating event in which the homicide took place (for example, whether it was connected to a robbery, burglary, arson, lover's triangle, etc.). Cases in which there is no evidence about the set of circumstances that led to the homicide are labelled "undetermined." Unfortunately, kidnapping/abduction is not one of the thirty-two circumstances used to classify homicides.

Best tried to estimate the number of cases of child-abduction murder by eliminating relationships and circumstances that had little or no probability of involving a stranger abduction. Thus, he eliminated all homicides by family members and acquaintances and all stranger homicides in which the context was a burglary, larceny, arson, robbery, an alcoholic brawl, etc. This process left twenty-eight homicides of children by strangers in California in 1984 that could have occurred in conjunction with an abduction/kidnapping. These homicides occurred in conjunction with rape (14), other sex offenses (1) other felonies (2), or suspected felonies (11). From this total, Best estimated the number of stranger-abduction homicides occurring nationwide: between 170 and 280, depending upon the multiplier that is used to extrapolate from California to the U.S. as a whole. California contains 10 percent of the nation's population but 16.5 percent of the nation's homicide victims under age 18. Best put the best estimate within that range, at 210.

COMPARATIVE HOMICIDE FILE FOR THE YEARS 1976–1984 (CIIF)

Estimate: 52–158 Children

The same kind of data that Best used for California, the *Supplemental Homicide Reports,* are available for the U.S. as a whole and for an extended time period, 1976–1984. The *SHR* for this period contain victim- and offender-level information on 156,624 homicides. The *Comparative Homicide File,* however, is a transformation of the *SHR* data and contains more refined information on the victim-offender relationship, the circumstances under which the homicide occurred, and the type of weapon used, as well as the age, sex, and race of both victim aid offender.

Following Best, the present authors counted all homicides by strangers of persons aged 17 and younger in which the precipitating event was either rape, other sexual offense, other felony-type, or suspected felony. However, there was also a fairly large category of homicides in which the precipitating event was undeterminable. It is difficult to say whether homicides in the undetermined category typically involve abduction/kidnapping circumstances. Best, in his analysis of *SHR,* excluded all of these undeterminables because the majority of murders classed as undetermined are probably not felony-related. However, more information is sorely needed about the nature of homicides of children that get classified as undeterminable. To be conservative, the present authors calculated two estimates from the *CHF:* one that excludes and another that includes these determinable cases.

For the most recent *CHF* period, 1980–1984, according to the *CHF* there were 260 homicides of persons under 18 by strangers involving circumstances of rape, other sexual offenses, other felony types, or suspected felonies. This works out to an average of fifty-two such murders annually. This number increases to 158 per year when homicides with undetermined circumstances are included. Table 2 presents these counts broken out by circumstances for the years 1980–84.

Like the other estimates presented here, the one based on the *CHF* is still quite crude. First, it is doubtful that all of the homicides in these five circumstance categories involved a kidnapping, even under the most liberal of definitions. It is easy to imagine sexual assaults and felony murders that have no abduction component. Second, it is possible that some abduction homicides were included in some of the other excluded circumstance categories, since police were required to select only one of thirty-two categories. Still we are inclined to think that the figure is more likely on the high side than on the low, that the first problem is bigger than the second. We especially think that the estimate that includes homicides of undetermined circumstance (158 per year) is likely to be high, since not all the undetermined circumstances are likely to involve abduction.

Table 2

Annual estimated counts and rates of stranger-abduction homicides of children by circumstance for 1980–1984 (average per year)

Circumstance	1980–1984	
	N	Rate per 1,000,000
Rape	15	0.24
Other sexual offenses	4	0.06
Other felony types	7	0.11
All suspected felonies	26	0.41
Undetermined	106	1.69
Total (excluding undetermined circumstances)	52	0.83
Total (including undetermined circumstances)	158	2.52

SUMMARY OF INCIDENCE ESTIMATES

The various estimates and revised estimates of the number of child-abduction homicides are presented in Table 1. They range from a low of 46 to a high of 318. Although the low differs from the high by a factor of about seven, all are still far below Child Find of America's estimates of 5,000. These estimates are, of course, crude, but they are most likely to represent "upper bounds." Three of them (ICJIA, SHR-CA, CHF) count large categories of events that probably, on inspection, do not involve an abduction. The ICJIA-IDLE estimate is, in effect, an extreme upper bound because it counts all children murdered by strangers (abduction or not). The ones based on the *SHR* and *CHF* count all murders involving rapes and other felonies (abduction or not). Two others (NCMEC-I and DADE) extrapolate from high-crime areas of the U.S. to the country as a whole. Of all the estimates, we are inclined to see the one from the *CHF* as the best guess. It is based on national data over an extended historical period. The Miami and the Jacksonville–Houston (NCMEC-I) estimates are also valuable because their counts are based on events that are known to be abductions. The fact that they are somewhat higher than the *CHF* is amenable to explanation. Extrapolations based on urban areas would be expected to generate rates that are higher than those for the whole country. Even though the NCMEC-I estimates were corrected for the high urban crime rates, stranger-abduction homicide probably is a more urban phenomenon even than child homicide in general.

Another confirmation of the *CHF* estimate comes from the Dade County study. In the Dade County study, the three abductions constituted 33 percent of the stranger homicides of children during the study year. This is close to the ratio between total stranger homicides and the midpoint estimate of stranger-abduction homicides found in the *CHF* data.

In spite of the convergence around an estimate of 52–158, there are some important caveats about any figure derived in this manner. In all studies reviewed in this article, the estimates of stranger-abduction homicides were based on cases that were recorded in police or agency records. It is possible that some abduction homicides never become part of those records. There are children who disappear and whose whereabouts never become known, and the circumstances surrounding their disappearances are never determined. It is very difficult to know how many of these children there are, but at least three categories of this type should be noted: 1) children whose bodies are recovered but never identified, 2) children who are reported missing for unknown reasons whose bodies are never found, and 3) children who are never reported missing and whose bodies are never found. What we know about these populations is extremely limited.

1. The unidentified remains of juveniles. A 1984 survey of members of the College of American Pathologists found evidence that there were fewer than 100 bodies or skeletons of young persons remaining unidentified at the end of 1983. The actual number was 68, but extrapolating to the entire population of pathologists places this number around 100 (reported in College of American Pathologists. 1986). It is not known how many of these 100 juveniles were murdered or how many were accident victims (drownings, etc.) or, of those murdered, how many were abducted by strangers. Many of these remains may be unwanted infants.

2. Children who are reported missing for unknown reasons whose bodies are never found. Among the 269 nonfamily abductions found in the NCMEC police records study in Jacksonville and Houston are three cases of children missing for unknown reasons. There was not sufficient information in the files on these children to determine whether they had been kidnapped, met with accident, or left home voluntarily. When children simply disappear, abduction is generally considered a possible reason, but there are a variety of other likely explanations, including running away or accidental death. If all three children in the NCMEC study defined as "unknowns" were murdered (very unlikely), it would be possible to extrapolate to a national number of 132 children in this category (1/2 of the original NCMEC estimate of 269 nonfamily abductions). But there is no reason to assume that all of these children were abducted. There are many other reasons why these children might be missing.

3. Children never reported missing whose bodies are never found. A third group of children could avoid official statistics completely. Some children may be abducted and murdered but never be reported as missing, or they may never show up in homicide statistics. These might include throwaway children, illegal aliens, and children abducted after having run away. There is no known estimate of how many children would meet these criteria and little basis for venturing a guess.

It is virtually impossible, given available information, to say whether these three groups are sizable enough to make any substantial difference in efforts to estimate the number of stranger-abducted and murdered children. However, readers should bear in mind that until more is known about these groups, the question needs to be considered unresolved.

SUMMARY AND CONCLUSION

This article has reviewed six different estimates of the level of reported stranger-abduction murders of children in the United States. These estimates range from 46 to 318, with our best guess being 52–158. This is substantially fewer than what the public has perceived and what a few expert "guesstimates" might have led people to expect. In further contrast to public perceptions, the available data suggest that there has been no recent upsurge of such cases and that the prime targets of such murders are teenagers, not young children. This is not to argue that public concern about stranger abduction and stranger-abduction murder is misplaced. Although these crimes are rare, when they do occur, they are horrendous, leaving terrible scars on families and communities. If this public concern leads parents and children to take rational precautions and if it leads law enforcement to improve its ability to find victims and capture perpetrators, then the concern is positive.

There is undoubtedly some component of exaggeration to the public concern as well. Because of the enormous emotional investment parents make in their children, the loss of children through abduction is all too easy to imagine. Some research has suggested that disproportionate emphasis is put on stranger danger. In a 1981 survey, Finkelhor found that 84 percent of parents talked to their children about kidnapping whereas only 29 percent had talked to children about sexual abuse, an event that is far more common. Parents may have been concerned about molestation, but the topic is uncomfortable to discuss and popular formulas make it easier to discuss kidnapping. In another study, a 1986 survey in a large midwestern city, 44 percent (of 315 fifth-grade children) believed it was likely that they would become missing children and 59 percent were afraid to be friendly toward people they did not know. When asked to rank five life concerns, fully one-half of the students ranked someone grabbing them as their primary concern. Being taken from their families is a kind of primal fear that children might have even in the absence of alarmist publicity, but it is easy to believe that this preoccupation with kidnapping is in part fueled by media attention.

It is important for parents and the media to put the various kinds of dangers to children in better perspective. Compared to our best estimate of 52–158 children killed in stranger abductions, for example, we have fairly reliable data showing that over 1,100 children die each year through abuse or neglect by their parents and caretakers. Over 7,000 children die in motor-vehicle accidents, and almost 2,000 children are victims of suicide every year. If people were as concerned about motor-vehicle safety as about stranger-danger, we might have many fewer children killed in accidents.

Deaths of children are truly tragic events, and the United States is a society in which their violent deaths are unacceptably high. The United States ranks first in the world in homicide rates for 1- to 4-year-olds and fourth in the world (and second among developed countries) for 5- to 14-year-olds. Children being killed by strangers who abduct them are terrible and properly feared tragedies, but they are a small portion of children who die in tragic and preventable circumstances.

Nationwide Homicide Data Sets:
An Evaluation of the Uniform Crime Reports and the National Center for Health Statistics Data

MARC RIEDEL

B ecause there is general agreement that most homicides find their way into a reporting system, it is easy to assume that there are few problems with homicide data sets. That there are other dimensions of the problem is implicit in what has come to be referred to as the "Sellin dictum:" "the value of a crime for index purposes decreases as the distance from the crime itself in terms of procedure increases." While this dictum is usually meant to emphasize the greater value (for index purposes) of data gathered from police rather than from sentencing agencies, the dictum also suggests that what and how data are reported is affected by the reporting organization. As O'Brien indicates, reporting systems are "filters" which affect the kind of information that is ultimately used as data by researchers. Thus, while homicide may be a highly reported crime, an examination of the reporting systems indicates undocumented variations, errors in classification, and difficulties with missing cases and values.

Unlike other crimes, homicide is the only offense in which there are two nationwide reporting systems that gather detailed information on the entire population of events. The present chapter describes and assesses the homicide data provided by these two reporting systems. One of these reporting systems is the Federal Bureau of Investigation's (FBI) Uniform Crime Reporting Program (UCR Program) for which the most detailed source of information is the Supplementary Homicide Reports (SHR). The other reporting system is the

National Center for Health Statistics (NCHS) through which information on homicides is collected as part of mortality data.

Two types of comparisons will be made: intrasystem and intersystem. Intrasystem comparisons focus on similar variables collected at different times by various organizational levels within the same reporting system. An example of an intrasystem comparison is the relative level of agreement between frequency distributions of victim-offender relationships for several cities as reported (1) by the SHR and as recorded (2) by local police departments. Intersystem comparisons, on the other hand, examine the extent of agreement between two different homicide reporting systems. At a national level, intersystem comparisons contrast information available from the SHR or the UCR with that available from the NCHS. State and local intersystem comparisons focus on the extent of agreement between police departments and the offices of medical examiners in reporting.

THE UNIFORM CRIME REPORTING PROGRAM

According to the UCR definition, criminal homicide is composed of two categories: murder with nonnegligent manslaughter, and manslaughter by negligence. Murder and nonnegligent manslaughter are defined as "willful (nonnegligent) killing of one human being by another." As a general rule any death due to injuries received in a fight, argument, quarrel, assault or commission of a crime is counted as a murder or nonnegligent manslaughter. Suicides, accidental deaths, assault to murder, attempted murders, justifiable and excusable homicides are not included in the category of murder and nonnegligent manslaughter.

Manslaughter by negligence includes the killing of another person through negligence. Traffic fatalities are excluded. While manslaughter by negligence is part of the definition of criminal homicide, it is not included in the Crime Index. In the research reported here, the focus will be on murder and nonnegligent manslaughter.

One of the early critics of the UCR indicated that, with respect to definitions of crime, the United States "is in effect 50 separate sovereign countries rather than one." The definitions provided by the UCR Program are meant to be sufficiently general so that information about the relevant act could be collected under the various state statutes. However, as Wolfgang has indicated, there is no assurance that these definitions will be applied correctly or consistently.

In addition, when multiple crimes are committed by the same person at the same time, only the most serious will be reported in the UCR. Because homicides are considered the most serious offense, the UCR reports the large majority of homicide occurrences.

Methods and Measures

The methods used by the UCR Program have been subject to extensive evaluation and criticism. While some of these criticisms are applicable to homicide data, many of the problems that beset homicide data are peculiar to it. To understand these problems, it is necessary to point out how the UCR Program collects information on homicides. Each of the three forms used to gather homicide data is procedurally independent from the others. Since there is no identifier for the same event on more than one form there is no way to determine which cases are represented by more than one form. Comparisons, therefore, cannot be made by individual case, but must be made on aggregations of cases.

FBI Estimates

The extent of coverage for reporting homicide is a function of the number and population of jurisdictions. The extent of Return A coverage has increased over the years.

Incomplete coverage on Return A necessitates estimation. Historically, methods to estimate the total number of homicides have varied considerably. According to Cantor and Cohen, various methods were used to arrive at estimates of total homicides prior to 1948. From 1948–1958 all such estimates were based on the aggregate percentage change for comparable reporting areas in adjacent years. Even though the pre-1958 figures were later revised numerically, the percentage changes used to obtain the original estimates were preserved.

From 1970 through 1975, the UCR Program annually revised past homicide figures. These six series were different because each year the UCR Program revised previous estimates on the basis of additional information from newly acquired reporting areas.

For their analysis, Cantor and Cohen examined two series. The first, from 1935–1976, consisted of estimates reported in each of the annual editions of the UCR. The second series, available from 1933–1972, was published by the Office of Management and Budget. The latter revised the UCR series to adjust the pre-1958 series so that they would be compatible with the post-1958 series. According to the authors, inspection of the eight series over the period from 1960 through 1970 indicated that none of these series differed in their estimates by more than one-tenth of a homicide per 100,000 population. Because of problems with revisions, Cantor and Cohen (1980) suggest that the UCR series not be used as source of data to study homicides prior to 1958. For homicides prior to that date, the Office of Management and Budget series appears to provide the best available FBI estimates.

Finding a reliable series of the total count of homicides for the nation does not necessarily mean that the same data source can be used for geographical subsets. The completeness of the Return A data varies for states, regions and cities in terms of quality and coverage. The completeness of a national data series when compared to other sources may hide large sources of error when smaller units are tabulated. Researchers are generally sensitive to this problem, however, the author knows of no research whose purpose is to generally assess underreporting of the Return A for different geographical subsets.

Supplementary Homicide Reports (SHR)

Return A forms and their estimates represent an aggregated total number of offenses from a law enforcement agency for a given month. In 1961, the SHR of the UCR Program began requesting detailed information on each murder and nonnegligent manslaughter case. For that year, information was collected on 3,008 murders (primarily from cities) out of a national estimated total of 8,600 murders. Although national coverage was attempted in 1962, until 1965 most of the information on murders and nonnegligent manslaughters came from large cities. For 1962 through 1975, the SHR was primarily a record of the age, race and sex of victims, weapon and the circumstances of the offense. Beginning in 1976, information about the offender and additional information about the homicide event were requested.

Until 1976, the various editions of the UCR Handbook provided general directions to law enforcement personnel for completing each form. Although computer processing was used, there was little effort to give clear unequivocal instructions which could be easily translated into computer codes. For example, the 1965 UCR Handbook gave the following written instructions for completing information on three variables: "Provide the data requested as to age, sex and race of the victim." When the SHR form was received by the UCR Program, codes were assigned and used to prepare tapes that are currently made available to researchers. From the perspective of a user who is accessing an SHR computer tape, what is needed is an understanding of major changes in categories of the coding guides as well as the handbook

The instructions given in the UCR Handbooks do not vary in content during the 1962 through 1975 period. With respect to the coding guides, sex, as expected, was not changed from the inception of the form to the present. Similarly, age codes have undergone minor changes, and this is primarily at the younger ages. Codes for race of the victim and offender remained the same: White, Negro, Indian, Chinese, Japanese, Other, Unknown.

The major changes occurred in the codes given for weapon and circumstances. For the period 1962–1967, weapons were divided into firearms, stabbing and piercing instruments, other dangerous weapons, personal weapons, strangulation, and unknown; no more detailed breakdowns were given. Beginning in 1968, the weapons breakdown became more specific. Handguns, rifles and shotguns, for example, were distinguished from each other as well as from other types of guns.

From 1962–1975, the "circumstances" records were broken into three major categories. They were: (1) murder and nonnegligent manslaughter occurring within the family unit, (2) altercations outside the family but usually among acquaintances, and (3) felony or first degree-type murders where the death penalty may result. Beginning in 1968 each of the categories were further refined. For example, "altercations outside the family, but usually among acquaintances" were divided into lovers and triangles, drunken brawls, altercations over money, and other arguments.

From 1973 through 1975 an additional refinement was added to the circumstances code. Where the SHR indicated a crime-related murder, a set of sub-circumstance codes relating to the type of crime were provided.

It is very difficult to develop a usable variable or variables from the circumstances data for the period 1962–1975. In his research, Curtis was able to develop a distinction between family murders, murders involving friends, neighbors and acquaintances, and non-primary relationships using the circumstances variable. For the friends, neighbors and acquaintances categories, he used the SHR categories of "romantic triangles," "lovers' quarrels" and "other arguments." For the non-primary relationships, characterized as "mostly strangers," he used the categories of "known felony type" and "suspected felony type." This effort probably represents the best approximation of a usable variable, given its nature during this period.

The major problem with the circumstances category was that it represented a combination of several variables. For example, crime related murders may also occur among family murders. What was needed, and provided beginning in 1976, was a distinction between victim-offender relationships and circumstances.

For the period 1976 through 1985 beginning with the data reported in 1976, the SHR underwent an extensive revision which substantially improved its utility as a nationwide source of homicide data. The handbook and the coding guides became more congruent with each other because some of the codes used in preparing the data were given to the law enforcement personnel completing the form. While Return A and the estimates remained a victim-based reporting form, the SHR became an event based system. In other words, when the murder or nonnegligent manslaughter involved multiple victims and offenders, information was collected on each of the offenders and victims who participated in the same event. Codes were provided in such a way that users were able to disaggregate the data and create a victim based system. Second, as has been mentioned earlier, information was collected on both the victim and offender.

Rather than confusing victim-offender relationships with other aspects of circumstances, a separate victim-offender relationship variable with a series of detailed codes was used. Circumstances were divided into codes for types of felonies, codes for circumstances that did not involve felonies, and one code for suspected felony type.

Intrasystem Comparisons of SHR Data

Research on the SHR and NCHS can be conveniently divided into three groups: (1) agreement between the SHR and city police records, (2) studies of corrections for missing data and (3) studies of the problems of classification.

Police Reports and the SHR

Three studies examine the amount of agreement between SHR and city police information with respect to both case and variable completeness. As part of a larger project, Riedel and Zahn collected detailed information from police records for one year (1978) on seven United States cities selected for geographic representativeness. The information on the number of cases and distributions on several variables for each of the cities was compared to similar distributions found in the SHRs of the same city and year. Table 1 reports the overall amount of agreement between the number of cases found in police departments and those reported by the SHR.

The greatest agreement was found in Dallas in which the SHR reported one less murder than the city police. In five of the seven cities, there was a slight tendency for police departments to record more murders than the SHR. In St.Louis and Newark, the tendency was reversed, with the SHR reporting more murders than the police department. While it is not known what accounts for these discrepancies, the comparisons support the hypothesis that, at least for large cities, the SHR is reasonably complete with respect to the number of cases.

Zahn and Riedel also examined the amount of agreement between police department records and the SHR for sex, race and age of murder victims, weapon and victim-offender relationships. For male victims in the seven cities, the agreement ratio ranged from .95 in Oakland to 1.02 in Newark, indicating high agreement. For female victims, there was much less agreement—generally in the direction of

Table 1
Total number of murder cases as reported
by police departments and SHR in seven cities

City	City Frequency	SHR Frequency	Agreement Ratio*
Philadelphia	362	353	.97
Newark	102	109	1.07
St. Louis	207	210	1.01
Memphis	116	114	.98
Dallas	233	232	1.00
Oakland	98	96	.98
Ashton	90	88	.98

*The amount of agreement is measured by dividing the SHR frequency by the frequency recorded by city police

overreporting by the SHR. The agreement ratios ranged from .96 in St. Louis to 1.29 in Newark; three of the cities had ratios larger than one. Because of classification difficulties, only data on black victims were used in comparing police records to SHR. The range of differences was from one case in Ashton to nine cases in St. Louis, where the SHR reported more black victims than were recorded in police records.

Although age classifications are somewhat arbitrary, age was grouped in ten-year intervals for making comparisons among the seven cities. In general, there was less agreement in reporting age than in reporting any other victim variable. In addition, there was no clear pattern that characterized the comparisons across cities. For example, in Oakland there was almost complete agreement in the youngest ages (1–19) and a fairly linear progression in discrepancy as age increased. On the other hand, Ashton had fairly high rates of agreement, with the greatest discrepancy in the 60–69 and 70–79 age groups.

For weapons, the level of agreement was more than 90 percent in five of the seven cities. Except for Newark, reporting between the two series was consistent across cities when the weapons were knives or guns. The discrepancies between the two series were greater when data for other types of weapons were compared across cities.

These comparisons support the lack of a systematic reporting pattern. For example, Newark city police frequently reported fewer murders than the SHR: however, this was not always the case. There was some tendency for city police departments to record more murders than the SHR, but the pattern is not consistent.

One variable, victim-offender relationships, shows a consistent pattern of underreporting for city police departments as compared to SHR data. The distributions of victim-offender relationships for city police and SHR data are given in Table 2.

As shown in Table 2, among the three types of victim-offender relationships, the city police consistently record more stranger murders than the SHR. For six of the seven cities, (excluding Dallas) the agreement ratios were smaller than for either of the other two types of victim-offender relationships.

For the individual cities the agreement ratios ranged from .07 in Oakland to .97 in Dallas. In other words, while the Oakland SHRs only reported about 7 percent of the stranger murders, the Dallas SHRs reported almost 97 percent of them.

While agreement for the stranger murder category is less than agreement for the other two categories, the greatest agreement for family murders occurred in Dallas, Oakland and Ashton. For the within family type, the ratios ranged from a low of .74 in St. Louis to a high of 1.06 in Ashton (excluding Memphis). For unknown reasons, the Memphis SHR reported many more family murders than city police.

In terms of agreement ratios, Table 2 illustrates that for three cities, murders of friends and acquaintances had the highest agreement ratios. For Philadelphia, the SHR reported slightly more murders of friends and acquaintances than by the police (1.06). For the remaining cities, the SHR reported as few as 35 percent of the murders of friends and acquaintances in Oakland to as many as 97 percent of these murders in Newark. The SHR uniformly reports a larger number and more unknown relationships than the police. The range in agreement was from 1.58 in Philadelphia to 3.04 in Oakland. In an analysis of Chicago Police Department records and SHRs for the years 1976–1981, Riedel found that stranger homicides were also underreported.

It appears that the underreporting of stranger homicides in Memphis is the result of a reporting lag between local police departments and the UCR. In the original study of this problem, Riedel used a computerized data base of all homicides in Memphis from 1974–1978 and compared the distribution of victim-offender relationships with a similar distribution from the SHR. The pattern of agreement among the three victim-offender categories was similar to that reported in the seven cities and Chicago.

Table 2
Victim-offender relationships as reported by
seven city police departments (PD) and SHR (1978)

City	PD Freq.	SHR Freq.	Agreement Ratio
Philadelphia			
Within Family	46	40	.87
Friends & Acquaintances	138	147	.94
Strangers	106	52	.49
Unknown	72	114	1.58
TOTAL	362	353	.98
Newark			
Within Family	13	10	.77
Friends & Acquaintances	32	32	1.00
Strangers	28	21	.75
Unknown	29	46	1.59
TOTAL	102	109	1.07
St. Louis			
Within Family	27	20	.74
Friends & Acquaintances	92	68	.74
Strangers	37	17	.46
Unknown	51	105	2.06
TOTAL	207	210	1.01
Memphis			
Within Family	16	23	1.44
Friends & Acquaintances	68	64	.94
Strangers	23	12	.52
Unknown	9	15	1.67
TOTAL	116	114	.98
Dallas			
Within Family	44	39	.89
Friends & Acquaintances	95	78	.82
Strangers	63	61	.97
Unknown	31	54	1.74
TOTAL	233	232	1.00
Oakland			
Within Family	11	10	.91
Friends & Acquaintances	51	18	.35
Strangers	14	1	.07
Unknown	22	67	3.04
TOTAL	98	96	.98
Ashton			
Within Family	19	19	1.00
Friends & Acquaintances	38	32	.84
Strangers	21	12	.57
Unknown	12	25	2.08
TOTAL	90	88	.98

Riedel also found that stranger homicides took a longer time to clear by the identification and arrest of one or more offenders in Memphis in comparison to other types of victim–offender relationships. Because of the longer time, when SHRs were completed by police departments each month, the victim–offender relationship information was not available and the relationship was recorded as "unknown." These records were then forwarded to the UCR. If an arrest was made later, the victim–offender relationship was recorded in police records, but an updated report was not forwarded to the UCR.

Missing Values

Probably because of funding reductions in recent years, researchers are using secondary data and official statistics more frequently. This has led to more concern with the problems of missing cases and missing values in these data sets.

However, for researchers who are interested in studying patterns of murder, the concern is one of unbiased reporting rather than a complete count. In other words, the variable may be incompletely reported, but that does not mean that what is available is reported in a biased fashion.

Williams and Flewelling have developed an interesting and useful approach to the problem of missing data in the SHR. The authors developed three alternative rate calculation procedures to take account of missing values, using a sample of 83,007 incidents of murder and nonnegligent manslaughter in the U.S. from 1980 through 1984. Only murder and nonnegligent incidents that involved one offender and one victim were used. The geographic areas included 168 cities with more than 100,000 people, their respective metropolitan areas (N = 125), the 50 states, and nine geographic regions.

The first rate calculation procedure, which accounted for non-reported cases in the SHR, is a ratio of the number of victims reported on Return A to the number of victims reported in the SHR. The adjusted counts are derived by multiplying the unadjusted counts in the SHR by the weighting factor.

The second and third rate calculation procedures developed by Williams and Flewelling focused on victim–offender relationships, although other offender characteristics could be used. The second procedure extrapolates from the known composition of a category of victim–offender relationship to the unknown one. Thus, if 40 percent of the known events involve stranger murders, the 40 percent of the unknown cases are added to the calculation of the adjusted rate of stranger murders.

The difficulty with the second approach is that it assumes that the distribution of known characteristics is the same as the distribution of unknown or missing values. Because proportionately more of the unknown cases involve stranger murders, the adjusted rates tend to overestimate the rates of murder among family members of friends and acquaintances and underestimate the rates of stranger murders.

To address this issue, Williams and Flewelling developed a third procedure in which an additional variable, circumstances of the offense, was added to the calculations if it was related to the victim-offender relationships. This variable indicated whether the murder was felony-related. The effect of the procedure was to adjust family and acquaintance murders downward and stranger murders upward, as theoretically expected.

After constructing unadjusted, adjusted, and circumstance adjusted rates, the authors calculated bivariate correlations among the three types of rates for the cities, metropolitan areas, and states. The correlations for the three methods were high, ranging from a low of $r = .936$ to a high of $r = .996$.

The authors also used percent poor and percent black in a regression analysis to determine if parameter estimates were altered by the estimation procedures. The correlations changed to some extent; however, the greatest changes occurred in the expected directions for the origin (a) and the regression coefficient (b). The authors concluded that:

> To the extent that an investigator's analytical purpose is to determine the absolute amount of change in rates of family, acquaintance, or stranger homicide associated with changes in theoretically relevant variables, these findings suggest that the use of an adjustment procedure is necessary. Moreover, descriptive statistics pertaining to the absolute and relative amount of specific types of homicide are affected in important ways by the adjustment procedures used (e.g., the absolute and relative amount of stranger homicide becomes higher than family homicides). The circumstance adjustment procedure appears most appropriate because it uses an extensive range of data in the SHR to guide the adjustment process, and analyses using the resulting rates reveal predictable empirical patterns. Nonetheless, if an investigator's purpose is merely to determine patterns of association (i.e., direction, significance, or magnitude of an association), then the choice among the rate calculation procedures is not so consequential.

Problems of Classification

In addition to a reporting lag, the SHR is hampered by a lack of knowledge concerning the validity of its classification categories. In one of the few studies of its type, Loftin compared the homicide circumstances classification for the SHR to a classification generated by examining narrative summaries of each of 196 cases from the files of the Baltimore City Prosecuting Attorney and the Public Information Office of the Baltimore Police Department. An initial inspection of the two classifications indicate a high degree of consistency. The Baltimore SHR classified 14.3 percent of the homicide circumstances as robbery while Loftin's coders classified 17.3 percent of the homicide circumstances as robbery. However, when the cases are grouped and cross-classified, 42 cases were classified as robbery-circumstance in one or both of the studies, but only 20 of them were so classified in both studies. If the three categories are considered (robbery, not robbery, and undetermined), the two classifications agreed in only 93 out of 196 cases; only a 47 percent agreement.

Loftin concluded that the classification of robbery-related homicides was not very reliable. He suggests that there are three problems with the SHR classification. First, categories used by the SHR are mutually exclusive which forces coders to place a case in only one category when, logically, it could be placed in two or more. Second, there are no clear rules for coding cases with ambiguous motives. Third, the SHR coders placed many more cases in the "undetermined" category than did the coders used by Loftin. The failure to use an appropriate "other-than-robbery" category can have a major impact on studies of the correlates of robbery-murder.

Loftin, Kindley, Norris and Wiersema extended the analysis of classification to an examination of victim-offender relationships. In developing and testing the utility of a classification based on attributes of the victim and of the offender, Loftin, et al., used homicide and SHR cases from the earlier study. Forty of the Baltimore homicides were classified as stranger homicides by either the SHR or attribute classification, but only 16 (40 percent) were classified as homicides with stranger involvement by both classification approaches.

SHR Summary

Evaluation of the research comparing SHRs to police department records on murder suggest the following conclusions. First, with respect to missing cases, the comparisons suggest that the SHR reports the majority of cases. In comparisons of the seven city data and Chicago, the agreement with respect to the total number of cases was very high. These results are, however, based on comparisons in large cities; the amount of agreement in rural areas and small towns is unknown.

Second, in comparing distributions of variables, with one exception, the nature of the relationship between the two data sets is unclear. While there is a tendency for city police to record more cases than the SHR, there is no clear pattern. Furthermore, with respect to the amount of discrepancy, there are large variations among cities.

Third, there is substantial evidence that stranger murders are underreported in the SHR. The difficulty is that they are not underreported by any consistent amount. The research suggests, however, large variability across cities and over time in the same city. In the seven cities noted previously, the number of stranger murders reported by the SHR may be incorrect by as little as 3 percent (Dallas) or as much as 93 percent (Oakland). In Chicago, depending on the year, the SHR may report as many as 95.1 percent (1978) or as few as 60.0 percent (1980) of them.

Fourth, given this pervasive problem of missing values, the alternative method of rate calculation using information about the circumstances proposed by Williams and Flewelling is important. The construction of circumstance-adjusted-rates is more important in determining the absolute amount of change in offender variables than in descriptive studies or studies attempting to determine the magnitude or direction of association.

Finally, the SHR appears to have errors and problems of classification. The research by Loftin and his associates indicates a considerable lack of agreement between the classification used by the UCR and that constructed by the authors.

THE NATIONAL CENTER FOR HEALTH STATISTICS (NCHS)

Unlike the UCR Program, homicide data from the Vital Statistics Division of the NCHS is part of a nationwide collection of mortality data. In this discussion, the U.S. refers to the 50 states and the District of Columbia.

Information on mortality, including homicide, is collected through the use of a standardized death certificate which is completed by a medico-legal officer, such as a medical examiner, in the case of a violent death. The death certificate, or a state approved variation which contains relevant NCHS information, is then given to the funeral director who gives the certificate to the local registrar and secures a burial permit. The local registrar, who may be the county health officer, verifies the completeness and accuracy of the death certificate, makes a record of it and sends it to the state registrar. The state registrar reviews it for incomplete or inconsistent information, makes a copy and forwards a copy to the National Office of Vital Statistics. There, coders prepare the case according to categories given by the *International Classification of Diseases* and enter the case into the national mortality data published as Vital Statistics of the United States.

Because NCHS assumes complete coverage since 1933, no estimates are used and all published data is considered final and not subject to revision.

While all states have adopted laws that require the registration of deaths, NCHS maintains on-going quality control measures to examine and analyze demographic and medical items on the death certificates, as well as coding errors. By 1985, national officials concluded "that over 99 percent of the births and deaths occurring in this country are registered."

Definition and Classification

The classification categories of homicide used by NCHS are established by the *International Classification of Diseases* (ICD), a publication of the World Health Organization which supports a world wide vital statistics reporting system. This classification is revised decennially in a meeting of participating nations. The various ICD causes of death are given three digit codes and, in recent revisions when more detail is needed, four digits are used.

Since the series of homicide data examined here began in 1933, classification categories are governed by the fourth through the ninth revision of the ICD. Table 3 summarizes the major categories used in each revision.

What makes general comparisons of NCHS and FBI definitions difficult is that the ICD versions of homicide are expressed solely in terms of the classification categories–which vary every ten years.

One major source of incompatibility between the two series is that prior to 1949, NCHS classified justifiable homicides under the category of "other means." Since most justifiable homicides involve legal intervention by police and legal executions, comparisons with the murder and nonnegligent series of the FBI are difficult because police killings and executions cannot be extrapolated from the NCHS series. However, beginning in 1949, separate categories were established for legal interventions and executions. Cantor and Cohen suggest that the latter changes "allow comparison of these two homicide indicators with, what appear to be, roughly equivalent definitions."

Examination of Table 3 indicates that the one category which remains identical through the various revisions is homicide in which the cause of death was a cutting or piercing instrument. Causes of death by homicide that were classified as "other or unspecified means" in early revisions sometimes acquired separate codes in later revisions. For example, homicides by poisoning became a separate category in 1949.

Beginning with the eighth revision, several other new categories were introduced: homicides due to fights, brawls or rape, and corrosive and caustic substances were listed as a cause distinct from poisoning. Hanging and strangulation

Table 3

Homicide-cause-of-death categories showing ICD revisions (3 digit codes)

1930–1938 4th (1940)	1939–1948 5th (1940)	1949–1957 6th (1948)	1958–1967 7th (1957)	1968–1978 8th (1967)	1979– 9th (1977)
Firearms	Firearms	Firearms and Explosives	Firearms and Explosives	Firearms and Explosives	Firearms and Explosives
Cutting or Piercing Instruments	Cutting or Piercing Instruments	Cutting or Piercing Instruments	Cutting or Piercing Instruments	Cutting or Piercing Instruments	Cutting or Piercing Instruments
Other Means	Other Means	Other Means	Other and Unspecified	Other and Unspecified	Other and Unspecified
Infanticide (Under 1 year)	Infanticide (Under 1 year)			Fight, Brawl, Rape	Fight, Brawl, Rape
				Corrosive or Caustic Substance	Corrosive or Caustic Substance
		Poisoning	Poisoning	Poisoning	Poisoning
				Hanging and Strangulation	Hanging and Strangulation
				Drowning	Drowning
				Pushing from High Places	
					Child Battering and Other Maltreatment
				Late Effects of Injury	Later Effects of Injury

and late effects of injuries which led to the victim's death, as well as pushing the victim from high places were also added.

For the ninth revision (See Table 3) explosives and firearms were distinguished as to type. In addition , a new category, "Child battering and other maltreatment" was added. In one sense, the addition of this category is reminiscent of the "Infanticide" category that was used from 1930 through 1948. However, this new category is a more legally specific category and the four digit codes request additional information in order to determine whether the act was done by parents, other specified or unspecified persons.

NCHS Data Set Variables

Unlike the UCR Program, NCHS data contain no information on the offender. While NCHS reports time and location information, it is limited to victim characteristics. Also unlike the UCR, there is a three-year lag in making the NCHS data available to users. The UCR information on 1986 crimes was available mid-1987. The most current homicide statistics available from NCHS in 1987 are from the calendar year 1984.

The NCHS documentation of each variable and each reporting year is detailed and extensive The sex, age and race of the homicide victim is recorded. The age reported is the age on the death certificate as of the last birthday. Homicides are also classified by the race of the victim: white, black, Indian, Chinese, Japanese and other races. Beginning in 1979, the additional categories of Filipino and other Asian or Pacific Islander were used to classify the homicide victim. NCHS has consistently made a distinction between classifications of race and ethnicity, although it does not provide an ethnicity classification. Thus, the "white category includes, in addition to persons reported as white, those reported as Mexican, Puerto Rican, Cuban and all other Caucasians."

Information is given for the place of residence of the victim and the place of the incident's occurrence, SMSAs, metropolitan and non-metropolitan counties, and for urban and for rural areas. Before 1970, homicide victims who were nonresidents of the U.S. were classified by place of death in the residence data. Beginning in 1970, these victims were not included in the residence data. Because these nonresident United States victims were always classified in the place of occurrence data, but not place of residence, beginning in 1970, the total number of homicides by place of occurrence will always be slightly larger than the total number of homicides by place of residence. The month in which the homicide occurred has been regularly reported for the NCHS series. The date of death was first made available in the 1972 data.

Intrasystem Comparisons of the NCHS

Reviewing the research on the NCHS reporting system must proceed differently from that done in examining the UCR. The small body of available research examines problems at either the national or the local level. National level research focuses on problems that exist from the time the death certificate leaves the possession of the local registrar to the time the results appear in annual editions of vital statistics. Research on local problems examines the classification of homicides at the local level.

Decennial revisions of the ICD raise questions of comparability between the homicide series of different revisions. To determine the effect of classification revisions, NCHS uses comparability ratios. Comparability ratios are based on dual coding of a single set of death certificates. For example, to construct comparability ratios for the seventh and eighth revisions, a sample of death certificates coded by the classification categories of the seventh revision is coded by the classification categories of the eighth revision. This procedure is done for a sample of deaths for one seventh revision year and for each of the major cause of death categories.

The ratios are obtained by dividing the numbers of deaths assigned to particular cause of death category according to the eighth revision, by the number of deaths assigned to the most nearly comparable causes under the seventh revision. The resulting ratios measure the net effect of changes in the classification, changes in rules for selecting the underlying cause of death, and changes in procedures used by NCHS.

These comparability ratios can be used by researchers to correct the series from the previous revision to make it comparable to that given by the later revision. For example, Israel and Klebba show how the asthma rate decreased from 2.0 to 1.4 in the 1967 seventh revision data when multiplied by the comparability ratio of .696.

At the national level, there were two isolated events which had an impact on NCHS homicide data. First, in 1964, approximately 6,000 deaths registered in Massachusetts were not received by NCHS. NCHS indicates that figures for this year for the U.S. and the New England Division were "somewhat affected." Second, data on deaths for 1972 were based on a 50 percent sample of all deaths occurring in the 50 states and the District of Columbia.

No matter how carefully the data are treated at the state and national level, the accuracy and utility ultimately depend on classification of the cause of death by the medical officer completing the death certificate. Highly critical of the NCHS procedure at the data collection stage, Sherman and Langworthy point out several significant flaws.

First, they point out the poor quality of medical diagnosis at the time of death. They cite a study by Moriyama, Baum, Haenszel and Mattison which indicates that 39 percent of a Pennsylvania sample of death certificates was based on "sketchy" diagnostic information. Another study was done by James, Patton and Heslin of 1,889 autopsied deaths in Albany, New York. The authors reviewed clinical information, autopsy protocols and laboratory reports and concluded that 57 percent of the homicide and suicide deaths could have been misclassified as to the circumstances of the death.

Sherman and Langworthy contend a second flaw is that there is "apparently widespread lack of the coroners' awareness of, support for, and legal obligation to comply with the system's request for the full information necessary to code the causes of death according to ICD categories." In a telephone interview with the authors, the then chief medical examiner of New York City claimed that most of his colleagues around the country are generally "turned off" by the ICD categories, particularly where stigma may result from the use of the categories. In another interview, a board-certified forensic pathologist indicated that individuals with his qualifications should be more aware of ICD categories.

A third flaw pointed out by Sherman and Langworthy is that the instructions for completing the standard death certificate are vague. While it is especially true in trying to distinguish a civilian-caused homicide from a death caused by legal intervention, the subject of the Sherman and Langworthy study, the implication is that the statement holds for other kinds of homicides as well. In response to how the injury occurred, a very small space is made available on the death certificate. In addition, the handbook on death registration for medico-legal officers urges users to be complete in their reporting while "using as few words as possible."

NCHS Summary

It is clear that the mortality reporting system of NCHS, which includes homicides, is much simpler than that of the UCR. With state bureaus of vital statistics enforcing death and birth registration requirements and with complete reporting since 1933, it is a system which is probably about as well and simply organized as could be expected for such a heterogeneous collection of people, jurisdictions and states.

From the researchers viewpoint, the addition of four digit categories in the ninth revision of the ICD contributes much to the utility of the NCHS dataset. The major advantage is that criminal justice researchers can now manipulate the three and four digit categories to create a data series which more closely approaches the requirements of specific criminal law and criminological categories.

The availability of comparability ratios affords the research user the opportunity to evaluate the effect of various revisions on a lengthy homicide series. A review of the comparability ratios for the total number of homicides over the many revisions suggests that changes in classification have had a minimal effect on the series. However, most of the comparability ratios have been limited to assessing the effect of revisions on the total number of homicides; very little information is available on the changes in classification with respect to three or four digit codes.

The most serious criticism of the NCHS data is the limited reliability and validity of death certifications. Other than one or two studies and some anecdotal evidence, of limited utility, there is no adequate empirical research. The quality of death certifications is a particularly critical issue, because no matter how sophisticated the remainder of the NCHS reporting system becomes, death certifications are the initial essential input. Without validity and reliability at this point, all other efforts have little value.

INTERSYSTEM AGREEMENT: NCHS AND UCR

The present section examines the amount of agreement between the NCHS and the UCR at the national and state or local levels. Despite the fact that police departments generally have long term cooperative relationships with the offices of medical examiners or coroners, neither of their national reporting counterparts have capitalized on that relationship to establish case identifiers that would be common to both reporting systems. Thus, like comparisons between police department and SHR data there is no way to compare, on a case-by-case basis, homicides reported to NCHS by a coroner or medical examiner to homicides reported by the police to the UCR. With respect to studying intersystem agreement, researchers are left with aggregate comparisons defined by time and location.

National Comparisons

In comparing Return A, FBI estimates, and SHR figures to NCHS figures, there are two problems. First, there is a problem of comparability in terms of specific reporting areas. The UCR receives reports from law enforcement agencies while NCHS receives reports from county level medical examiners or coroners. The jurisdiction of law enforcement agencies, except for county Sheriffs, does not always coincide with the county level jurisdiction of NCHS data. While it is possible in some instances to make the two data sets comparable with respect to reporting agencies, it requires detailed knowledge of the boundaries of the law enforcement reporting agency and how that knowledge can be matched with county level data. For national and state comparisons, this issue is not a problem.

The second problem, that of similarity in definition, has been alluded to in earlier sections. NCHS reports data on homicides, which include justifiable homicides. While homicide data are available, most of the research using data from the UCR has used murder and nonnegligent manslaughter. While a major category of justifiable homicides, police killings and executions, can be removed from the NCHS data series beginning in 1949, at best, the results represent only general comparability. This general comparability may be adequate for nationwide comparability studies, but represents a problem if smaller geographical units are used. It is possible that NCHS data may be made more comparable to the murder and nonnegligent manslaughter category beginning in 1979 because of the addition of four digit codes. However, no research examining that problem has been done.

One of the earliest studies of the agreement between homicides as reported by the UCR and the NCHS was done by Hindelang. He compared murder and nonnegligent manslaughter and NCHS annual totals for the nation from 1935 through 1970. In examining the graph of rates for the two series, Hindelang concluded that agreement between the two series from 1940 through 1970 was "generally good. Indeed the similarity in the shapes of the curves is striking."

Cantor and Cohen did a more extensive investigation of the agreement between UCR data and the NCHS data. For all intersource comparisons, Cantor and Cohen used the national murder and nonnegligent manslaughter estimates available from the Office of Management and Budget (OMB). Estimates from the annual UCR reports were not comparable before and after 1958.

From 1949, when the authors were able to eliminate police killings from the NCHS series, to 1973, comparisons of the two series indicated close agreement. However, in the period from 1960 through 1963, the two indicators moved in opposite directions for reasons that were unknown to the authors. They recommend that any analysis which is primarily concerned with that time period be conducted with both indicators to assess the effect of discrepant trends in those years.

Assessing the amount of agreement for the entire series (1933–1975) raises many more problems. In order to examine the entire series for both data sources, Cantor and Cohen used the NCHS series which included police killings; these data were compared with the OMB estimates of murder and nonnegligent manslaughter. They found that the correlations between the two series varied from .85 to .98 depending on whether the 1933–1970, 1936–1975 or 1933–1975 periods was selected. The correlation was affected most dramatically by whether either the 1933–1935 or 1970–1975 period was excluded from the entire series. With the former period removed, the correlation for 1933–1975 is increased from .92 to .98. When the 1970–1975 period is eliminated, the same correlation drops from .92 to .85.

To demonstrate the different results that would be obtained with independent variables, the authors intercorrelated the two series with such explanatory variables as percentage of homicides cleared by arrest, percentage of resident population between the ages of 15–24, and the unemployment rate. They found different results depending on the time period and, sometimes, the homicide series analyzed. They further indicated that the point in time at which the analysis begins and ends may substantially effect the results of the analysis and strongly recommended that researchers consider the time frame under study in planning the analysis. Cantor and Cohen further suggest that a critical evaluation is particularly important in studies which depend on the analysis of homicide time series data of the deterrent effect of the death penalty.

Using data from a previous project of nationwide homicide patterns, the author examined the amount of agreement between FBI estimates, Return A counts, SHR counts, and NCHS counts of homicides. Local intervention and execution homicides were excluded from NCHS series and murder and non–negligent manslaughters were used for the FBI series. Figure 1 gives the rates of each measure by reporting year.

The differences in the rates for FBI estimates and NCHS data are small and they parallel one another closely. The curves for SHR counts and Return A counts also cluster together, but are some distance from the other two rates. In addition, Figure 1 indicates a very close relationship between Return A and SHR rates after 1974.

To explore the amount of agreement in more detail, agreement ratios were calculated for each year of the series and a mean agreement ratio was calculated for a series of comparisons. For example, SHR frequencies were divided by FBI estimates for each of the eleven years. The mean of the series range and difference between the highest and lowest annual agreement ratio is given in Table 4.

Table 4 indicates that, with one exception, the highest mean agreement ratio is for the comparison of FBI estimates for murder and nonnegligent manslaughter with NCHS counts of homicides for the eleven year period; the FBI estimates account for .97 of the homicides reported by NCHS. Given that NCHS data probably contain some justifiable homicides, this result suggests that there is very close agreement between the national series. The range of agreement ratios ranges from .95 in 1968 to .98 in 1975.

According to Table 4, the highest mean agreement ratio is for the comparison between Return A counts and SHRs (.99). There are, however, several reasons to believe this mean agreement ratio may be higher than would be the case if data were available for the entire eleven year series. First, examination of the annual

Figure 1
Homicide rates in the United States(1968–1978) according to four sources

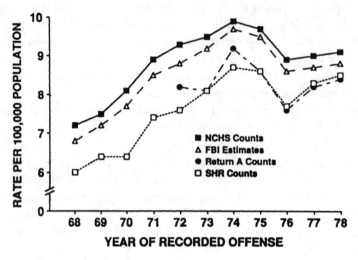

Table 4
Mean agreement ratios comparing four sources
for the total number of homicides (1968–1978)

	SHR vs. FBI Est.	SHR vs. Return A	SHR vs. NCHS	NCHS vs. FBI Est.	NCHS vs. Return A	Return A vs. FBI Est.
X̄ (agreement) N = 11	.89	.99ᵃ	.86	.97	.89ᵃ	.92ᵃ
Range	.83–.97	.92–1.01	.79–.94	.95–.98	.89–.93	.89–.96
Diff.	.14	.09	.15	.03	.03	.08

ᵃN = 7

agreement ratios derived from the data in Table 4 indicate that the lowest agreement ratios are always found earlier in the series, whereas the highest are found late in the series. Thus, in comparing Return A counts to SHRs, the series from 1968–1971 would probably have low agreement ratios which would depress the mean agreement ratio. Second, unlike any other comparison, there are three years (1976–

1978) in which the SHR reports more homicides than Return A which serves to bring the mean agreement ratio closer to 1.00.

Nevertheless, the agreement between SHR and Return A is impressive. It is the only comparison in which the total numbers agree completely for two years (1973 and 1975) and for four of the remaining five years, there is no more than a five percent difference.

The high agreement ratios between Return A counts and the SHR data suggest a growing congruence between the two forms. Although there are other plausible explanations, the close agreement for these two measures suggests that law enforcement agencies that provide the UCR with Return As also tend to provide them with SHRs for each homicide. Consideration of this point, along with the research reported earlier which found that the total number of cases reported by the SHRs agreed well with those recorded by the large city police departments, suggests that most underreporting of homicides may be occurring in rural areas and small towns.

There is more agreement between FBI estimates and the NCHS data than between FBI estimates and other measures within the UCR. According to Table 4, the mean agreement ratio for the SHR data and FBI estimates is .89, while for Return A counts and the FBI estimates, the mean agreement ratio is .92. As with the comparison between Return A counts and the NCHS data, the latter mean agreement ratio may be lower than reported here.

State and City Comparisons

The only study of comparisons between homicide measures reported by the UCR and the NCHS at both the state and city level was done by Sherman and Langworthy. Rather than focusing on homicide or murder, these authors examined homicides committed by police officers.

To determine whether NCHS measures could be used as a measure of police killings of civilians, the authors used thirteen jurisdictions for the years 1970–1976 and gathered comparable data on police homicides from NCHS data and police generated sources. The latter included data reported by the police to statistical analysis centers, data from SHRs, and data compiled by the police. The jurisdictions were two heavily urban states (California and New Jersey), six less urban states (Alaska, Nebraska, Oregon, South Carolina, Vermont and Wisconsin), and five New York city counties.

In nine of the thirteen counties, the death counts from police-generated data exceeded those compiled by the NCHS. The authors found that 51 percent of the police homicides were underreported by NCHS; the latter number held not only for the total, but also for the heavily urban and less urban clusters of jurisdictions.

According to NCHS national data, the jurisdictions used accounted for 25 percent of all deaths by legal intervention from 1971–1975. Considering the amount of underreporting, and the fact that some years were omitted in some jurisdictions, the authors conclude that the total national incidence of police homicides was about 26 percent higher than reported by the NCHS. Sherman and Langworthy also concluded that NCHS data cannot be used to measure the national incidence of police homicides. Since the police generated data does not cover the entire country, it is clear, the authors suggest, that the number of police homicides nationwide are simply unknown.

The authors also attempted to determine whether available data sources could be used to measure the relative incidence of police homicide from one city to another or one police department to another. To address this question, NCHS data and a combination of several sources of police killings were used. Information was complied on the latter alternative source of police homicides, as well as the NCHS, for a total of 133 city-years from 36 jurisdictions of over 250,000 population. The correlation between the two data sources was .64 for the raw data; when the death counts are standardized by population, the correlation drops slightly to .53. As the authors point out neither correlation accounts for even half the variance.

While the data were not accurate enough to measure relative incidents from city to city, similarities in the pattern of relative incidents make it possible to use either data set as a measure of the pattern of variation in police homicides in relation to a set of independent variables. To examine that possibility, the authors developed measures of theoretically relevant independent variables. Among the cluster of community characteristics, they included such variables as population density, gun density, unemployment and suicide rates, violent index crime and UCR homicide rates. The cluster of police organizational structure variables included such variables as geographic decentralization, span of control and self regulation. Examples of police organizational policy variables were disciplinary formalism measures and disciplinary pressure measures.

The seventeen measures were correlated with the two measures of police homicides. Despite the diversity of procedures employed with the data, the researchers found that the two data sources generated similar results. The alternative data sources produced stronger correlations and most were in the theoretically predicted direction. The authors concluded that the two measures can be used to gauge patterns of variation in police homicide rates.

Focusing on homicide in the seven cities mentioned earlier in the chapter, Riedel and Zahn compared the number of homicide cases reported by the police department to that recorded by the medical examiner in each of the seven cities. In general, the degree of agreement was high with five of the seven cities having a 95 percent or better agreement figure for the total number of homicides.

Data from police departments and medical examiners offices were also compared for victim's sex, race, age and victim-offender relationship. The agreement for victim's sex was very high, ranging from 99.5 percent in Philadelphia to 100.0 percent in the other six cities.

The agreement on race between the two local sources ranged from 75.6 percent in Ashton to 100.0 percent in St. Louis. In general, discrepancies in the area of race occurred in the coding of Hispanics, Mexicans or Puerto Ricans. In Newark, over half of the discrepancy on this variable occurred because the police department coded the victim by the specific ethnic group while the medical examiner coded the victims race as "other races."

For victim's ages, when the criteria of agreement included differences of ages by only one year, the range of agreement was from 80.1 percent in Newark to 99.0 percent in Ashton. Five of the seven cities had 90 percent or higher agreement.

Not surprisingly, the poorest agreement occurred for victim-offender relationships. The range was from 52.2 percent in Ashton to 80.6 percent in Newark. No data was available on this variable from the medical examiner's offices in St.Louis.

The reasons for the poor agreement on the relationship variable are a result of the medical examiner's concern for the victim and lack of data on him or her. Subsequent investigation and apprehension of the offender is the concern of the police department. Consequently, whatever data on victim-offender relationships are available at the *time* of the event is what finds its way into the medical examiner's files. In support of this view, agreement was high between offices on domestic slayings for which offenders are quickly apprehended. It was poor for stranger and acquaintance slayings, which require more time to clear by arrest.

Intersystem Summary

Research on national, state and city comparisons of the amount of intersystem agreement between homicide measures used by the UCR and NCHS data support the following conclusions.

There is greater agreement between the two series with recent data in contrast to older data. This is true not only for comparisons of FBI estimates and NCHS counts, but also for comparisons of Return A counts and SHR counts with FBI estimates and NCHS measures. While it is difficult to give an answer which would be appropriate for all uses and occasions, it appears that with respect to a report of total homicides from the UCR, data prior to 1960 will present greater difficulties than data from that point to the present. From 1960 onward, many of the revision problems that characterized early estimates were resolved and the agreement with NCHS data appears to be very high.

For the NCHS, the data appears to be usable beginning in 1949 when police killings and executions were given separate codes. However, with regard to specific variables, this data generally has less utility because it is limited to the victim and some of the cause-of-death categories were not refined until 1979.

There is a kind of schizophrenic character to the results of national comparisons. On the one hand, very close agreement between FBI estimates and NCHS data are found; on the other hand, much lower agreement occurs between FBI estimates and other measures of murder and nonnegligent manslaughter. SHR counts and Return A counts, for example, seem to agree very well with each other from 1974 to 1978, but neither agree closely with FBI estimates. There is something paradoxical about a reporting system in which intersystem measures agree better than intrasystem measures.

The problem seems to reside in the agencies that do not report to the UCR. What is needed is a more careful examination of which agencies are not reporting, or are underreporting, to the UCR. A more careful review of these agencies' practices would allow us to assess both their relative contributions to the number and character of homicides and whether additional efforts should be made to bring them into the reporting system.

With respect to the intersystem comparison at the state and local levels, it appears that the NCHS seriously underreports police homicides. The research by Sherman and Langworthy indicates that the NCHS may underreport police homicides by as much as 51 percent.

Comparisons of case completeness and variable completeness at the level of city police departments and county medical examiners offices indicate a high level of agreement between the two organizations. Most of the discrepancies in the total number of homicides were small and occurred because of jurisdictional disagreements and conflicts over the definition of the crime. For specific variables, such as the victim's sex, race and age, the agreement was generally high. The lack of agreement for victim-offender relationships was mainly for stranger relationships for which information is more difficult to collect and less important to medical examiners.

For the researcher who is examining variations in homicides or police homicides, the results are encouraging. The efforts of Cantor and Cohen to relate variations in homicide to independent variables and those of Sherman and Langworthy with police homicides indicate that FBI estimates and NCHS data provide similar results. Of course, as both sets of authors indicate, they have not included all possible independent variables, nor, in Cantor and Cohen's case, did they consider how the two dependent variables behave with other than national level data. In light of Cantor and Cohen's study many cautionary statements about the time period covered by a proposed analysis, it is important that the researchers attempting to use either FBI homicide data or NCHS data examine very carefully how the two reporting systems behave in the time period and at the geographical level of aggregation needed.

SUMMARY

Perhaps the most unequivocal conclusion that can be made about the two nationwide homicide data sets is that both provide, consistent with their definitions, a reasonably accurate count of the annual number of homicides for approximately the past 25 years. While an accurate national count of homicides may extend back to 1949 for NCHS, the research does seem to indicate that their count of legal intervention homicides substantially under-reports the number of police homicides.

When questions of variable completeness are considered for SHRs, it is clear there is a substantial amount of disagreement between national and city police sources. Whether a similar pattern of disagreement exists for national and local NCHS sources is unknown because of an absence of research.

Where the concern focuses on whether the data can be used for studying variations in the offense, the results are somewhat more positive. However, the available research is limited. Cantor and Cohen's analysis, Sherman and Langworthy's results and Williams and Flewelling's comparisons of rates suggest that the two data sets may have considerable research utility without being complete with respect to the number of cases or variables. However, the research by Loftin and his associates indicates that there may be numerous classification errors.

Considering the enormous amount of resources that have been expanded over the years to obtain a complete record of the most highly reported offense, murder or homicide, the record of achievement for either reporting system cannot be described as enviable. Where the major claim for success rests in only being able to count reasonably accurately the number of times the event occurs nationally in a time period, it appears to this author that the expenditure of resources has been disproportionate to the amount of achievement

The single greatest problem for both reporting systems, as well as research criminologists, has been the unwillingness to focus research on the basic first step—

how the murder or homicide is initially reported at the level of reporting officer or medical examiner. There is very little research at the local level with respect to how judgments are made with respect to the SHR, how reports of investigating officers are transferred to SHRs, the qualifications of police personnel who do this task or how recording inconsistencies are resolved. Neither data set is going to be better than the quality of the data at this first step.

In reviewing the two nationwide homicide reporting systems, the reader may be more impressed with the simplicity and rigorous detail of the NCHS reporting system in comparison to the UCR. However, the two reporting systems operate with different sets of constraints and confront slightly different reporting problems.

As an organization, the NCHS has expended more resources on resolving the problems of their reporting system, especially at the state and national level. But that is, after all, part of the major mission of NCHS as an organization. The UCR, on the other hand, is a rather small part of a much larger organization that is devoted to the practice of nationwide law enforcement. In other words, given the greater amount of resources available to the NCHS, more quality and completeness of data should be expected for the NCHS than for the UCR.

In addition, the data collection and reporting tasks of the two reporting systems cover different problems. NCHS is primarily concerned with collecting information on the age, race, sex and cause of death of the homicide victim. One of the most important sources of victim information for the NCHS— the dead human body—is the most available and is sometimes the only indication that a homicide has occurred.

Data collection problems for the UCR are more difficult. While information is available on the victim, the UCR also collects additional and detailed information about the offender, who may or may not be available. Since murder and nonnegligent manslaughter clearance rates are about 75 percent, about 25 percent of the offender information will be missing at the time of the event and, frequently, for some period thereafter.

The well-organized NCHS reporting system is impressive. The system entails mandatory reporting at the state level for all 50 states. The organization of reporting from local medical officers to the state level is well defined; only one form is completed; classification categories are relatively clear and are periodically updated. Returns are carefully monitored, and great care is taken in assembling the final collection of homicide data.

On the other hand, for the UCR, only part of the reporting agencies fall under a mandatory system, several forms need to be completed, classification categories have only recently been clarified, and there is no well-developed system of monitoring returns and updates. Given the considerations that have been discussed, what is surprising is not that the NCHS data are of high quality, but that the FBI homicide data are as good as they are.

Finally, in recent years, the UCR has become an organization that is more open to the requests and suggestions of researchers. In its responsiveness to requests and criticisms, the UCR has recognized that criticisms that go unanswered by the reporting organization tend to be self-reinforcing and lead to stereotypes.

In working with the research community, the UCR currently follows practices similar to the NCHS, an organization that has had a long and successful history of working with researchers. In part, the greater sophistication of NCHS data stems from a recognition that making data available to researchers is not a one-way street; because researchers make extensive and detailed use of the data, they find deficiencies which are not apparent to the more casual user. Thus, cooperation with the research community pays dividends to the reporting organizations by making them aware of shortcomings and problems that they otherwise would not have found.

Improving the Investigation of Violent Crime: The Homicide Investigation and Tracking System

ROBERT D. KEPPEL & JOSEPH G. WEIS

I n conducting investigations, detectives need methods and tools that will help
them do their jobs as effectively and efficiently as possible. Ready access to
information about the crimes being investigated is one of their needs. Armed
with such information, detectives will be better able to develop good leads and in
turn to solve the cases. The Homicide Investigation and Tracking System
(HITS), a program that began in Washington State, is helping investigators work better by allowing them access via computer to a wide range
of information about serious crimes and to resources that can help
solve them.

HITS is a computerized murder and sexual assault investigation program
that collects and analyzes information pertaining to specific serious criminal
offenses. The system relies on law enforcement agencies in Washington
State to voluntarily submit information to HITS investigators on murders,
attempted murders, missing persons cases in which foul play is suspected,
unidentified persons believed to be murder victims, and predatory sex
offenses. The information is stored in the seven data files that compose
the HITS system.

HITS provides three major services to law enforcement agencies. First, it
supplies information related to a murder or predatory sexual assault case, including
the following:

- Incidents with similar characteristics involving murder, attempted murder, suspected murder, or predatory sexual assault and persons missing as a result of suspected foul play.
- Evidence, victimology, offender characteristics, offender's method of operation, associates, geographic location of the case, weapons, and vehicles.
- Identification of known murderers and sex offenders living in a particular community.

Second, HITS permits analysis of murder cases to identify:

- Factors that may help solve a particular murder case.
- Possible links between a single victim, offender, or case and other incidents of violence.
- Verification of statements provided by informants, offenders, or both, in which the information relating to an alleged murder is incomplete or questionable.

Third, HITS provides investigators with the following resources:

- Names of experts who can assist with a murder or sexual assault investigation.
- Advice and technical assistance on the various steps to be followed in a murder or sexual assault investigation.

Prior to HITS' use in Washington State, the only way to obtain this type of crime information was through time-consuming, labor-intensive personal visits, interviews, telephone calls, teletypes, and letters.

Most cases listed in HITS occurred from 1981 through 1986, and data on these cases were compiled under a 1987 National Institute of Justice (NIJ) grant. Subsequently, HITS has been funded through the Washington State attorney general's office, and some agencies have begun adding murder and rape incidents reported prior to 1981 to the system.

SETTING UP THE SYSTEM

As part of the NIJ project, researchers first wanted to determine the number of murders that occurred in Washington State from 1981 to 1986. Each of the following agencies were contacted for information:

- Police and sheriffs' departments covering 273 jurisdictions.

- Medical examiners' and coroners' offices in 39 counties.
- Prosecuting attorneys' offices in 39 counties.
- Washington State Department of Vital Statistics.
- Uniform Crime Report unit of the Washington Association of Sheriffs and Police Chiefs.

To date, every police and sheriff's department in Washington State has cooperated in developing the HITS system.

Initially, more than 1,300 murder files were located in police agencies across the State. Virtually every department had investigated one or more murders in the 1981–1986 period. After all known cases had been identified by name, case number, and investigating jurisdiction, each police and sheriff's department was asked to voluntarily complete the HITS data collection instrument, a 54-page form containing 467 fields of information, for each murder file. In addition to salient characteristics about the murder event, victim(s), and offender(s), the HITS form also asked questions about the quality of the murder investigation and its solvability. Investigators spent an average of 2.3 hours completing each form.

After 1986, a shorter version of the HITS form, containing 250 fields of information, was developed. This form asks much of the same information as the original form, but omits questions related to the NIJ research project. The shorter form takes approximately 30 minutes to complete.

The short version of the HITS form has been evaluated by homicide investigators in all the larger police and sheriffs' departments in Washington State as well as by investigators in Arizona, California, Florida, Georgia, Iowa, New York, Oregon, and Texas. They concluded that it is the most comprehensive application of homicide information for investigative purposes ever developed.

USING THE HITS PROGRAM

The HITS program uses a relational-based data management system to manage the data files. The most important feature of HITS for murder and rape investigations is its interactive search capability. By choosing among 250 fields of information, HITS analysts can ask for single- or multiple-field information in any order or combination.

For example, if a detective were investigating the rape and murder of a white female prostitute, he or she could use HITS to discover whether similar crimes had been committed in the previous 2 years. Using information provided by the detective, a HITS analyst could query the data base for any combination of data: victim's gender, race, or lifestyle; date and cause of death; location of the body;

presence or absence of clothing; concealment of the body; or date of body discovery. In this way, the analyst could identify other cases with common elements and supply the detective with the names of victims murdered in similar ways, date of body discovery, investigating agencies, case numbers, and primary investigators' names and telephone numbers. This type of search would take only a few minutes to perform.

DATA ORGANIZATION

The HITS program contains information from at least six sources and is stored in seven different data files: murder, sexual assault, preliminary information, Department of Corrections, gang-related crimes, Violent Criminal Apprehension Program (VICAP), and timeline. Because of the diversity of sources, three master data files were constructed to aggregate information about persons, addresses, and vehicles so that any one query could search all seven data bases at the same time. The fields available for analysis range from 20 to more than 250.

HITS Murder File

The data base created with the NIJ grant is the HITS murder file, which contains information about victims, offenders, and methods of operation for more than 4,000 murder investigations. When a murder is committed, law enforcement officers complete the HITS murder form, which is then keyed into the murder file. The murder file also includes information on 49 cases from the Green River Task Force. A series of murders involving prostitutes in the Seattle/Tacoma area, the Green River murders began in July 1982 and ended in March 1984. To date the Green River murder count is 41 dead and 8 missing.

The following three cases demonstrate how HITS has helped Washington's law enforcement agencies in their murder investigations. For these and other cases discussed in this report, names, locations, and related facts have been withheld in cases where investigations are ongoing.

Random railroad killings. A Spokane detective filed a HITS form for the murder of a male vagrant found stabbed to death in a railroad yard. When analysts checked the HITS system, a similar case involving a male vagrant in Cowlitz County was identified. The HITS investigation revealed that a person previously considered a possible witness in the Spokane case was listed as a suspect in the Cowlitz County case. When HITS information was communicated to other law enforcement agencies, investigators from Thurston County reported a third case involving a male vagrant to HITS. The witness is now listed as a suspect in a Midwestern State for a similar murder.

Double murder. When a Federal under-cover agent overheard someone bragging about killing two people in Washington State and being enroute to the Western United States to kill someone else, the agent requested information on double murders in Washington State. The agent was referred to a law enforcement agency in Washington that had cases similar to those mentioned by the potential suspect. The suspect is currently under investigation.

Victim location. A police informant from the Eastern United States told a police detective in Western Washington that an acquaintance had murdered two people in the same area—one victim from the detective's own jurisdiction and another from an unknown location. After spending 4 days contacting numerous police agencies trying unsuccessfully to locate the second victim and coordinate investigations, the detective called HITS and was given the information needed within seconds.

HITS Sexual Assault File

The HITS sexual assault data file contains information about victims, offenders, and methods of operation for more than 2,000 rape investigations. The HITS sexual assault file form asks investigators to provide data on serial rapists, stranger rapists, and predatory sex offenders. Two cases show how HITS data have helped detectives solve sexual assault investigations.

Tracking known sexual offenders. After an extremely brutal rape and attempted murder, the investigating detective requested HITS information about offenders with a particular physical description and method of operation, HITS staff provided the detective with a list of known sexual offenders who had been released from prison during the past 5 years and the areas to which they had been released. The detective was also provided photographs of suspects, one of whom was immediately identified by the victim as her assailant.

Victim identification. A western Washington police agency was trying to identify a female victim who had been raped and murdered at an unknown location east of the Cascade Mountains about 5 years earlier. The HITS unit provided the name of the victim and the investigating officer to the inquiring agency.

HITS Preliminary Information File

The preliminary information file stores information about crime classification, chronology, victims, offenders, methods of operation, weapons, vehicles, geographic locations, and other pertinent information. The file also contains more than 4,600 sex-offender registrations. Information for the file is gathered from the following sources:

- Teletypes.
- Newspapers.
- Crime bulletins.
- Sex-offender registration files.
- Requests for information from investigators.

Violent crime information transmitted via teletype through the Washington State Patrol's access system is automatically entered into HITS' preliminary information file. No other State system stores this type of data for retrieval and use in investigations. In addition, every week a clipping service provides newspaper articles containing information about murders and rapes that have occurred in Washington State. This information is also entered into the file. The teletype and newspaper data are particularly valuable because they are usually the first information given to HITS about the occurrence of a violent crime.

Every inquiry from a police investigator, whether it receives a response or not, is stored in the preliminary information file. This allows investigators to keep their inquiries active in the event that information becomes available in the future. For example, if an investigator asks whether an adult male named Joe Smith has been found murdered, a negative answer might be given, but the inquiry is stored in the file. Later, if another investigator reports Joe Smith as a murder victim, the two items are matched and the appropriate authorities informed of their mutual interest in the case.

The preliminary information file stores data about murder and sexual assault cases only until completed HITS reports have been submitted by the investigating agency. The following case illustrates how this file has been used in the field.

Suspect analysis. During an investigation of a rape, the victim described the suspect's appearance and vehicle, which matched those of someone the investigating officer had stopped only minutes before being detailed to the rape case. The officer notified other agencies by teletype to be on the lookout for the suspect. When the teletyped information was entered into the HITS preliminary information file, another teletype was found describing a similar rape that had occurred in another jurisdiction several months earlier. Both the physical description and the method of operation matched, and the prior address of the suspect was located in the same city as the agency that had issued the earlier teletype. HITS staff notified both police agencies that they both had cases involving a similar method of operation and known offender.

Department of Corrections File

The more than 189,000 records stored in the Department of Corrections data file offer immediate access to the identification of current and former inmates who have been convicted of murder or sexual assault. Updated bimonthly, the file can be used to check the physical description of a convicted felon against the description of an unknown suspect in investigations involving sexual assault. The following case illustrates how the file has been used.

Suspect and method of operation. When HITS received a teletype summarizing a second-degree rape incident, physical description of the suspect, and method of operation, HITS staff identified a convicted rapist with a comparable physical description and method of operation who had been released from prison in the previous 3 months. The subject was living only a few blocks from the location of the rape. HITS released all of the information to the investigating detective.

Gang-related Crime File

A separate data file for gang-related crimes and driveby shootings contains more than 76,000 records from the Los Angeles County sheriff's department and police agencies within Washington State. The data from Los Angeles were received after investigators discovered that numerous gang members had migrated from California and had committed crimes in Washington. The file is routinely used to search for aliases or nicknames and physical descriptions of potential offenders.

VICAP File

Prior to implementation of the HITS system, the State attorney general's office helped local police agencies participate in VICAP, a national serial murder tracking program run by the Federal Bureau of Investigation (FBI). Approximately 350 of the State's murder cases, entered into the VICAP system before HITS was created, have subsequently been merged into the HITS murder file. Now, when data from a HITS form are entered into the HITS system, the computer automatically reformats the information and creates a report to be submitted to VICAP.

Timeline File

Another data file used for analysis is a timeline file that records chronological activities of known murderers. The file contains information about times and places of offenders' movements. As of January 1993, the file had information on 9,083 locations for 73 known murderers.

Data for the file are gleaned from employment records, arrest records, banking records, traffic tickets, and any other record collected during a murder investigation that reveals the location of a possible offender. These times and places can be cross-checked against the dates and locations of murders. The file is another way to determine if a known murderer could have been the perpetrator in other murders. The following two cases illustrate how detectives have made use of the timeline file.

Travel pattern analysis. When an alleged serial killer from Minnesota was arrested in Texas, his travel pattern was examined, and investigators determined that he had spent a considerable amount of time in Washington State. Minnesota authorities contacted the HITS unit, and an analysis was conducted by HITS staff. A murder case involving a woman who had been beaten, strangled, and raped was located in the files. Further investigation revealed that the suspect had been released from a jail in Western Washington the day before the murder and had hitchhiked along the same thoroughfare where the body was discovered. The case is under continuing investigation.

Methods of operation. A Kansas detective contacted the HITS unit when he discovered that an identified multiple murderer from Kansas was known to have visited Washington State. The detective described in detail what the killer did to his victims and how he disposed of their bodies. When a similar case was found in the files, HITS analysts contacted the police agency that had reported the case. Currently the suspect is under investigation.

COST OF HITS

Since 1986, after initial NIJ support, ongoing operational costs have been borne by the Washington State Legislature, which in 1990 awarded $1.2 million for the 11-member HITS staff in the attorney general's office to operate the program for 2 years.

The only cost to local agencies has been the 30 minutes it takes an investigator to fill out the HITS form. This is negligible compared to the time an investigator would spend trying to obtain information that HITS can supply in a matter of minutes.

Time is also saved by the automatic integration of HITS with VICAP. Investigators are not required to complete two questionnaires because the HITS computer automatically generates VICAP data from the HITS form. HITS staff also routinely verify leads, telephone contacts, and other information that VICAP requires concerning a murder.

SIGNS OF SUCCESS

As of January 1993, HITS staff had received more than 800 requests for investigative assistance in violent crime cases. Most of these requests had been received since 1988, when the Washington State attorney general announced that the HITS system contained investigative information on more than 1,600 murder cases. The rate of response to requests has been extremely high; assistance has been provided in more than 850 murder and rape investigations.

A 1990 survey of 495 police chiefs, sheriffs, and homicide investigators indicated that 90 percent of respondents had heard of HITS and that 86 percent of respondents who had used the system found it ranged from "somewhat useful" to "extremely useful" in their investigations.

National recognition. HITS is known as a computerized information system that is used in the field as an effective investigative tool. Recently HITS won two national awards for outstanding achievement—one from the Council of State Governments and another from the National Association of State Information Resource Executives.

EXPANSION BEYOND WASHINGTON

Offenders recognize no State boundaries. With that in mind, in October 1991 Kenneth Eikenberry, then Washington State attorney general, and Reginald Madsen, superintendent of the Oregon State Police, signed an agreement to allow Oregon access to the HITS system. Oregon State investigators can now electronically transfer information about violent crimes committed in their jurisdictions into the HITS computer. As of January 1993, data from more than 700 murders committed in Oregon in the past 6 years have been entered into the HITS program. As a result, police and sheriffs' investigators have violent crime information from two States readily accessible for use in their own investigations. In addition, law enforcement officers from California, Idaho, Kansas, and Canada have submitted information about selected violent crimes to HITS for analysis.

BENEFITS OF HITS

Small law enforcement agencies that do not encounter murder cases frequently or that have investigators inexperienced in specialized murder investigation techniques have found the HITS program to be especially beneficial. HITS analysts can offer guidance, based upon years of experience, on how to organize a murder investigation and provide access to information not available in any one department's files. Other benefits include the following.

HITS' prioritization of solvability factors helps investigators identify avenues of proper and logical followup. Through HITS, analysts have discovered that different types of murder cases reflect critical solvability factors—such as the likelihood that a friend, lover, or spouse committed the crime—unique to each category of murder. Such information is particularly useful to a detective in a small jurisdiction where there are few murder cases to be investigated.

HITS' methods improve the criminal justice training curriculum for law enforcement investigators. For example, the Washington State Criminal Justice Training Commission has redesigned its basic homicide investigators training curriculum to reflect changes initiated because of HITS.

HITS complements Federal research and programs against violent crime. In addition to the automatic link between HITS and VICAP, the data collected on homicides in Washington State are useful for the FBI's Uniform Crime Reporting Program. But because the information collected by HITS is more comprehensive and richer in detail, it is even more valuable in answering questions from legislators, elected officials, and government staff about the characteristics of victims, offenders, and murder incidents.

The information HITS provides enables other government agencies to better understand the complex process of murder investigation and its accompanying costs. Using data from HITS files, law enforcement agencies can help educate other government bodies about the needs that must be addressed in agency budgets.

HITS is a model that other states can replicate and adapt to their own needs. The creation of computer programs and methods for data collection and routine analyses could assist other jurisdictions in coordinating and sharing violent crime investigation information.

CHAPTER 3

The Characteristics & Distribution of Murder

There are many "facts" about murder that need to be established and confirmed through scientific research. They are the critical building blocks to a better understanding of an abnormal act that is very difficult to comprehend. After all, how could anyone kill someone else? We need to identify the personal and social characteristics of the killers and their victims, as well as other important correlates of murder. For example, how does murder vary by age, sex, race, and social class?

Two papers on the characteristics and distribution of murder, one by Schmid (a sociologist at the University of Washington) focusing on Seattle between 1914–1924, and the other by Monkkonen examining New York city between 1800–1874, both show the consistent patterning of the personal, social, and ecological features of murder. The characteristics of killers, victims, and their murders were essentially the same in the first quarter of the 20th century as they are today in Seattle. Murder was and still is more typical of the young, males, economically marginalized, socially isolated, racial and ethnic minorities, who live in the most unstable neighborhoods in the city. Illuminating the complex role of race and ethnicity in murder, one of the most interesting findings is that the Chinese residents had one of the highest murder rates at that time, surpassing the white and black murder rates, which is the opposite of what one finds today in Seattle. Monkkonen observes a similar complexity in the role of race and ethnicity in murder for New York during the

19th century. Contrary to today, it was European ethnic groups, particularly the Italians and Irish, who accounted for most of the violence, including murder, which over the course of the century, declined substantially. The small black population had a relatively high murder rate, but, contrary to today, a higher rate of victimization by white killers. Of course, all of these findings beg the question, just what is the effect of race and ethnicity on murder? It seems that it is secondary to the effects of recent immigration, socioeconomic status, and neighborhood influences.

There are other aspects of murder that have been addressed by many researchers. Recently, the involvement of gangs in murder, particularly drug-related murders and drive-by shootings, has received a lot of media and research attention. Maxson and her associates have compared gang and nongang homicides in Los Angeles, and have come to some startling conclusions about the discrepancy between what people believe and what the data show about gang involvement in murder. Of course, gang killings are often viewed as motivated by drugs—scores are being settled on the street and the shooters are high on drugs.

Parker focuses on the effect of another drug—alcohol—on occurrence of criminal homicide. The consumption of alcohol can act as a catalyst or disinhibitor, increasing the odds that volatile social relationships may lead to murder. And the distribution patterns of alcohol sales are directly related to differences in murder rates across communities. It has also been observed that murder is related to other high risk and reckless behavior.

Once again, the interesting scientific question, for all of the correlates of murder, is "How come?" Why do males commit around 90% of all murders? Why is the murder rate so much higher among the young? Why are the black murder rate and victimization rate so much higher than the white rates? What is it that links suicides and accidents with murder? And so on. Those types of questions should be addressed and, hopefully, answered by the theories of murder. The theories need to explain the correlates or apparent "facts" of murder.

A Study of Homicides in Seattle, 1914 to 1924

Seattle had the majority of the murders

CALVIN F. SCHMID

I. SOURCE AND COLLECTION OF DATA

The data used in this study of homicides in King County, Washington, for the ten-year period, 1914 to 1923, inclusive, were taken from the death records at the coroner's office. Needless to say, the task of collecting the material was fraught with much difficulty and labor. The paucity of the data along with their imperfections, inadequacies, and limitations are the inevitable obstacles one has to encounter in attempting a study of this kind. Thanks to the new system of death records established at the coroner's office a little over a decennium ago, we are enabled to get much valuable information concerning homicidal deaths that would, otherwise, either have remained obscure or unknown.

II. TERRITORIAL DISTRIBUTION OF HOMICIDES

The period covered in this study is that of 1914 to 1923, inclusive, or ten years. Of the total of 252 homicides for this period, 186 were males and 66 were females.

(a) King County in general. A very noteworthy yet expected fact is that the overwhelming majority of homicide is concentrated in the densely populated area of Seattle. It will be observed that there is a marked difference between the number of homicides and the rate per 100,000 of population in the above enumeration; although Seattle had 84 per cent of the homicidal crimes yet its rate of 6.7 is the

lowest. It should be noted, however that because of extremely small population and the large base upon which the rate is computed, the results for some of the minor civil divisions may be some what illusory and exaggerated. Considering the county as a whole, with its population of 389,273 and 252 homicides for the ten-year period, we have 6.5 as the rate per 100,000 of population. Among the larger civil divisions which apparently had a clean record for this period are: Redmond precinct 1,172 population, Oak Lake precinct 1,459, Warren precinct 1,564, Enumclaw precinct 1,993, and Renton city 3,301.

(b) Distribution of homicides in Seattle. Almost 25 percent of the crimes are concentrated in a very small area, about four blocks wide and ten blocks long. This territory can be divided roughly into two districts viz., the *upper* (east) and the *lower* (west). The *upper* part is characterized by a motley number of cheap hotels and rooming houses, old frame residences, many of which are now used as houses of prostitution, and a large variety of retail stores. This section also includes Seattle's "Chinatown," typified by its "joss" houses and commercial establishments. The permanent denizens of this district consist chiefly of foreigners, of which the majority are Japanese and Chinese. Many of the migratory workers and dispossessed transients of various types room in this section, but spend most of their time in the lower section.

The *lower* section still possesses the same stigma, and not without some reason, which it carried during the old "red-light days." In area it is comparatively small— about two blocks wide and about three blocks long. It is a community within a community, isolated and apart, for the conventionally proper never visit this district save under exceptional circumstance, possibly for sight-seeing or changing of street cars. This section is characterized by its ubiquitous vampire establishments seemingly designed for the exploitation of the migrant worker, for it is he who is the chief habitué of these parts. Pool and card room, gambling dens, cheap hotels with their quotas of courtesans, sex practitioners, dance halls, burlesque vaudeville shows, restaurants, employment offices, pawn shops, drug stores with their window displays of venereal disease nostrums and sex specifics, social welfare institutions, and missions of various denominations constitute the organizations, both for good and for bad, of this section.

Directly northwest of the above designated section, extending in length for a distance of about fifteen blocks, and, in width, measured from the harbor line, about six blocks, is situated the important business district of Seattle. In this section, it will be observed there are approximately twenty homicides. To the north and east of this section, varying in distance from ten to twenty squares, are the old residential districts in which are now located a large number of hotels, apartment houses, retail stores, garages, schools, and churches. The districts designated as Madrona, Capitol Hill, North Broadway, and Queen Anne contain the largest sections of the fashionable residential areas of the city. In the extreme west of this portion of the city, we have Fort Lawton, a government barracks, and Magnolia Bluff, a district comparatively new and not thickly settled. It should be noted that all along the waterfront there are docks, wharves, and warehouses of various kinds. To the north of the section just described is located Ballard, characteristically known as the home of the workingman; there are also several shingle and lumber mills within this area. East of this section are situated Phinney, Green Lake, Fremont, Wallingford, University, and Laurelhurst, which are predominantly residential in character, although along the shores of Lake Union are located a number of industrial plants, chiefly lumber mills.

Coming back to the central part whence we started and going southward along the waterway to the city limits, taking in practically all of South Seattle and Georgetown, then crossing to the west side and including all of Youngstown and Harbor Island, we have within this area the most important industrial establishments of Seattle. Beacon Hill, Mt. Baker, and part of Rainer Valley constitute the better residential sections in the southern part of Seattle. Most of Rainer Valley, Rainer Beach, Colombia, and South Park contain residential sections along with many truck gardens operated chiefly by Japanese and Italians. West Seattle and Fautleroy, which include many recently settled areas, are exclusively residential.

In conclusion, we may summarize the salient points in this discussion concerning the territorial distribution of homicides in the city of Seattle as follows: First, about 25 percent of the homicides were concentrated in a district less than ten blocks long and four blocks wide; with a population of 6,863 people of whom less than 20 per cent are females, this district had 40 homicidal crimes, or relative to 100,000 of population, 58.0. Secondly, there is a fairly large percentage, about 20 in number in the business district. Thirdly, computing the homicide rate of the residential sections north of Lake Union and the Lake Washington Canal with a population of 81,800 people, of whom over 50 per cent are females, and 12 homicidal deaths during the decennium, 1914 to 1923, inclusive, we have the very low figure of 1.5 per 100,000 of population. Fourthly, in the industrial and residential sections in the southern part of Seattle there are about 52 homicides, which may well be considered disproportionate.

III. YEARLY AND RACIAL DISTRIBUTION OF HOMICIDES

The yearly number of homicides occurring during this period shows a marked variability—a minimum of seventeen in 1918 and a maximum of thirty-five in

Excessive death rates of Black? Oriental

1915. To attribute this variation to any specific cause or causes would, I believe, be unwarranted. The average annual number of homicidal crimes is 25.2, or a rate of 6.5 per 100,000 of population.

A most noteworthy fact is the excessive homicide death rate of the Oriental and Negro elements. The greater homicidal frequency, relative to the general population, of these races can possibly be explained on the following grounds: First, the environmental conditions, most notably of the Chinese and Japanese, and in some instances of the Negros, are more conducive to crime than those of the average population. A great number of the Orientals in Seattle live under bad conditions in the "worst" part of the city, and often pursue such occupations as keepers of cheap hotels and lodging houses, pawn-shops, second-hand stores, gambling dens and the like. Secondly, the Negros and Orientals consist of a large percentage of unmarried adult males, in such a group we find not only a high homicidal death rate, but also a high rate of criminality. Thirdly, tong wars, exclusively among the Chinese, have claimed several of the homicidal victims. Fourthly, due to the comparative smallness of the population, the homicide rate as noted above tends to give a somewhat exaggerated view of the actual number of homicidal deaths both among the Negros and Chinese.

IV. SEASONAL DISTRIBUTION OF HOMICIDES

One of the most significant facts shown by the study of homicidal crimes in King County is the exact antithesis of the commonly stated generalization that crimes against the person almost invariably reach their ascendancy during the warmer months of the year. The smallest number of homicides occurred during months of June and July, while the largest number occurred during the months of December and January.

Weather conditions may be an important factor in determining the extent and kind of crime, i.e., crimes against the person or property, but there are other more potent factors in this area that explain the apparent discrepancies. First, the temperature is comparatively low and equable—a difference of less that 2.4 degrees between the maximum 63.7 and minimum 39.9. Secondly, the great influx of seasonal and migratory workers into Seattle from October until May with consequent widespread unemployment, produces conditions prolific of crime.

V. DISTRIBUTION OF HOMICIDAL VICTIMS BY AGE AND SEX

First, it will be observed that the per cent of males killed by homicide, as compared with females, increases with the age, while the per cent of females killed by homicide decreases with age. Secondly, the age-graph presents a fairly smooth curve of normal

A Study of Homicides in Seattle, 1914 to 1924

distribution, the peak being between the ages of thirty and forty years. Thirdly, the homicidal frequency among the males far exceeds that among the females.

VI. HOMICIDES BY MANNER IN WHICH DEATH WAS EFFECTED

Perhaps the most striking fact is that 191, or 75.8 per cent, of the 252 homicides during this decennial period, resulted from the use of firearms. Fracturing the skull, most often with an axe or hammer, claimed 26, and stabbing, 19 victims during this period. Strangulation, employed predominantly in infanticidal crimes, asphyxiation, poisoning, and drowning were the other means used.

APPENDIX

Disposition of the first and second degree murder cases adjudicated by the Superior Court of King County, Washington, during the decennium, 1914 to 1923, inclusive. Ancillary, and, in some respects, adventitious to the main study of homicides, is appended herewith, a study of the first and second degree murder cases adjudicated by the Superior Court of King County for the decennial period, 1914 to 1923, inclusive. The material presented below, which was copied from the criminal dockets at the prosecuting attorney's office, necessarily possesses certain limitations and imperfections, and, in consequence, this cursory study makes no pretense to correlate the homicides committed and the cases tried during the period under consideration, nor does it warrant the reading of finer details into the data herein presented. This inquiry is merely suggestive.

The first thing to strike the attention is the large percentage of women found not guilty, and the relatively light penalties received by the remainder. Of the fifteen women tried for first and second degree murder, three were sentenced to the state penitentiary at Walla Walla for the following terms respectively: 10 to 20 years, 2 to 20 years, and 1 to 10 years; of the remaining 12, one was given a sentence for one year at the county jail, one was fined $1,000, one had her sentence suspended, and the rest, nine in number, were found not guilty! Whether these verdicts and sentences exemplify "leniency" or "justice," one cannot definitely assert.

Of the eighty-one men tried for first and second degree murder during this ten-year period, 1914 to 1923, inclusive, 18 or 22.2 per cent were found not guilty; 2 had their cases dismissed, 8 had to serve terms in the county jail varying in length from four months to one year, five were sentenced to the state reformatory, three of which for one to twenty years, and the remaining two for two to twenty years; 28 were sent to the state penitentiary for periods varying from one to twenty-five years, 18 were given life imprisonment, and 2 were hanged.

109

Racial Factors in New York City Homicides, 1800–1874

Eric Monkkonen

It is important to examine issues of race, ethnicity, and violence in a historical setting so that we may establish a perspective from which to view contemporary problems. We may look back to a time when guns were rarer, when poverty was more widespread, and when racial discrimination was more intense, and ask what differences this made. There is more than an antiquarian interest that propels this quest: Gurr has surveyed a large body of research that indicates that our current high homicide rates and rates of other criminal violence are a relatively recent phenomenon. He shows how there is good evidence to believe that homicide and violent crime rates have been declining since the middle ages.

Lane's research on Philadelphia suggests that these patterns were not the same for African-Americans. After the Civil War, white homicide rates declined, while black homicide rates increased. Lane shows how racial discrimination created what was a structurally different city for blacks as opposed to the one for whites including immigrants. He argues that these structural features account for the crime differences.

In particular, we can compare various newly arrived immigrants to African Americans. We know that African Americans faced increasing hostility from immigrants around the time of the Civil War and that all evidence points to their declining opportunities in the late 1850s.

Although the data limitations frustrate fine grained analysis, a historical analysis makes clear some of the differences between the nineteenth and twentieth centuries. These differences serve to remind us that broad historical change effects interpersonal behavior and conflict. That they are effected suggests that such patterns can continue to change, that criminal offense sometimes considered to be beyond the reach of social control is not beyond the reach of social and historical circumstance. In some ways, the exact nuances of change are less significant than that there is change at all.

The data base used here, constructed for an ongoing quantitative study of homicide in New York City, provides us with an opportunity to examine race, ethnicity, and homicide in the nineteenth century.

SETTING

It is essential to understand some of the relevant features of nineteenth century New York City even before describing the data. Though very important, New York has never been a typical American city. In the first three quarters of the nineteenth century, it grew dramatically from a city of about sixty-thousand to become a metropolis of over a million. This astonishing growth made it America's largest metropolis, with a polyglot immigrant population after 1840. Its early size alone makes the city worth studying, for while atypical, it was by any kind of definition, the major American metropolis.

Because most of the homicides analyzed below occurred after the 1830s—95 percent in the half-century between 1834 and 1874—this description will focus on this mid-century period. By 1834, the city's population had reached a quarter-million, but it would not be until the last years of the 1840s that the demographic event occurred: the flood of immigration from Ireland and Germany. In 1850, the city reached a half-million, and on the eve of the Civil War, over 800,000.

In 1845, when the census began reporting birthplace tallies, the city had 135,000 foreign born residents, about one-third of its population. By 1850 the figure had reached over a quarter-million; in 1860 it grew again to well over a third of a million—almost one half of the city was foreign-born.

Yet for the city's African-American population, there was a very different history—one of declension in size from 16,000 in 1840, to about 12000 in 1860, and perhaps less than 10,000 in 1865. New York state had abolished slavery by 1827. Thus, by mid-century, less than 2 percent of the city's population was black. This demographic trajectory, so different for the rest of the city's people, tells us much. Traditionally, African-American men had worked on the city's docks, in its shipyards, and in various service occupations. The new immigrants competed vigorously, and sometimes violently, for these jobs.

III

Riots & Racism

& death rates in NY.

This story had a tragic culmination in 1863, in the New York City draft riots. No matter how one interprets these riots, they always contain a base element of racism. Triggered by the efforts to draft poor and immigrant workers, the city's white immigrant youth quickly turned their initial political protest into a race war against African-Americans. A large but never reliably established number died—many victims of vicious public lynchings, not too surprisingly, after the riots, the city's black population decreased even faster.

The personal violence of the riots horrified New Yorkers. But personal violence had been an increasing feature of city life well before 1863. The estimated per-capita homicide rate had been increasing for several decades, reaching heights that would not again be reached until 1970. This grim feature of the nation's largest metropolis went undiscussed in the nineteenth century media.

Data and Sources

1831–1874
95% of 1,559 murders.
76 occurred < 1831 fragmentary sources —

The data consist of 1,559 murder cases. Ninety-five percent of these cases occurred after 1831 and before 1874. The small number (76) of pre-1831 cases are a result of fewer real homicides and more fragmentary sources. Variables include weapon, relationship of the killer to victim, and subsequent outcomes affecting the killer—arrest to execution. For both killer and victim, variables include gender, age, and race or ethnicity. Seemingly obvious inferences have been avoided, which has created more missing variables: for instance, a person mentioned as a *youth* has not been assigned an age, or seemingly ethnic names have not been given an ethnic code. The reason for this seemingly excessive caution is that Lane's Philadelphia study used German names to indicate ethnicity, when it was equally possibly that in Pennsylvania the person could have been fifth-generation American born. The one place I have made an interpretive leap is for some Irish-named people who were involved with other Irish born.

19th century vital stats are very poor.

The data sources used here required detailed discussion, as their provenance suggests where the biases may lie. The data used for this study have been generated in the context of a long-term, comparative study of annual homicide rates in New York, Liverpool, and London. Outside Massachusetts, nineteenth-century vital statistics for the U.S.A. are very poor. There are no *official* sources. The closest to such would be the coroner's reports, which begin with detailed annual reports in 1866.

The coroner was required to investigate and call a jury to examine all nonnatural deaths. These individual reports are available in the city archives. Prior to about 1823, they are fragmentary. Homicides comprise only a tiny part of these reports. After 1866, the summaries of these investigations were available in annual reports.

When the jury decided that the cause of death was not one man hitting another in a bar, but rather the fall to the floor or that the victim had a weak heart, the case would be tallied in the annual reports as an accidental death or as due to heart failure.

In this world, gun murder could be interpreted as a duel; the beating to death of a senator as a *caning*. Coroner's juries reflected their world, and as a result, they found no murder where juries today would.

To gather data on homicide then, requires supplementing the coroner's reports. An initial check on the completeness of the 1866 homicide counts compared with those reported in the *New York Times* indicated some discrepancies, and further name comparisons have shown that for the pre-1870 years, the lists of homicide victims in the newspapers and in the coroner's records overlap but do not match completely. There was, in other words, an undercount by the coroner.

Most of the data analyzed here have come from newspapers. After the 1820s and prior to the late 1870s, the press of New York City reported homicides with some vigor, if not with the constancy we might have wished. Typically there would be a notice of a fight or killing, which gave some detail of the event, the weapon, and the people involved. All the killings reported here are those which the newspaper report stated as a fact that the person was dead.

Using the newspapers is complicated by several other factors as well. While by far the most consistent and reliable newspaper, the *New York Times,* began publication only in 1853. Compared to the other papers, the *Times* exhibited less race bias than was typical for the era, in part because of its Republican leanings. For the era between the late 1820s and the late 1850s, there are several newspapers that daily reported local news, like homicides: these included the *Daily-Tribune.* Prior to the mid-1820s, the reporting of what we called news was practically nonexistent. Even so, careful searching has revealed homicide mentions do occur, and so my research continues to scan these early newspapers, including the *Commercial Advertiser, Evening Post,* and *Daily Citizen.*

There is with these data a question that has plagued all criminologists: unreported offenses. While we know today that murders are the crime most often cleared by arrest, we are treading on more speculative ground in the past. A more difficult issue remains the nonreporting of details of importance to us today: race, ethnicity, and age.

Sometimes historians have been forced to guess at ethnicity by names, but I have avoided that here, except when there is a very strong contextual as well as textual probability that the person's ethnicity can be inferred. Such a case would occur when an Irish-named person was involved in a conflict with another, and the second person, in another article, was identified as Irish.

? of interest in nature of interracial homicides data gives insight into nature of social relations.

Race and Ethnicity

A question of initial interest is the nature of interracial homicides. These can give some insight into race relations and the nature of social relationships in nineteenth-century New York. It must be noted that even here relationships cannot be unambiguously inferred: a low level of interracial violence could simply be the result of high degrees of social segregation. Killer and victim races can first be examined under the assumption that all African-American killers of victims were noted as such, while native-born whites, or persons who appeared to be, would likely go unnoted. Beginning with the least restrictive definition of race and ethnicity: Less than 4 percent of all killers or victims were black. Black victims were as likely to be killed by blacks as whites, while black killers were slightly more likely to kill blacks. This suggests some degree of racial motivation in the killings of blacks, dealt with further below.

In order to look more closely at ethnic and race relations between killer and victim, those victims and killers with ethnicity or race identified have been paired. Missing information reduces the total number of cases to 282 or about 20 percent of all killings.

These figures can be interpreted several ways, but the most straight-forwarded has to do with opportunity—killers and victims usually knew one another, were relatives, friends, workmates, or casual acquaintances. Even an interracial killing, the murder on Oct. 20, 1844, of James Chapple (probably white) by Samuel Riley (black), is best understood this way: Chapple was a sailor and Riley the cook on board the docked brig the *Francis P. Beck*. The most clustered, the Irish, has 83 percent of their victims from the same ethnic group, blacks had 61 percent from their group. Germans 56 percent, and Italians 42 percent. Irish killers and victims cluster strongly, suggesting their stronger degree of ethnic clustering. And, in this context, African-Americans were no different from other sociocultural groups.

At-Risk Populations

While the data analyzed here include over eighty years of New York City's history, 1750–1874, three-fourths of the cases are for the two decades 1854–1874. During these years, the city's population grew from about 600,000 to just over a million. Its African-American population, on the other hand, grew only slightly from 13,000 to about 14,000. If we take an imaginary population figure at the mid-point, about 800,000 and 13,500, we can contrast the homicides black and white in the ratio to populations—the black homicide rate equaling about twice the white one.

With only 13,500/1 million people African American.

A.A homicide rate is 2x white homicide rate

The corresponding mid-point estimates of native-born whites, Irish, Germans, and Italians are 414,000, 160,000, 109,000 and 1000. Assuming that native-borns were the least likely to be so noted in homicide reports, in contrast to the foreign-born and blacks, a crude ratio of homicides by group at-risk setting native-born whites to 1, yields .8 for the Irish, .9 for the Germans, 2 for the African-Americans, 15 for Italians, and .7 for all foreign-born. The foreign-born ratio to the native-born white ratio is almost certainly a vast underestimate, the foreign-born white homicide victims simply not being noted in the sources. The best both sets of comparative at-risk estimates can give us is a sense that the black homicide rates probably ranged from 1.6 to 2 times the white homicide rate.

Even this range of estimates may need to be modified by the notion of population at-risk, for homicide was both gender and age asymmetrical. Of the 1,397 nonblack victims where sex is mentioned, 78 percent were men: for blacks alone, the figure is 90 percent (for both killers and victims). Of the 555 victims where age is mentioned, 90 percent were between the ages of 17 and 50, 50 percent between 23 and 40: for 18 blacks alone, the figure is similar, 90 percent between the ages of 22 and 51, 50 percent between 26 and 40, although the low numbers of reported ages may bias these values.

The 1860 census of population reported age and sex distributions by race for the New York county. Of these whites, 23.5 percent were males between 20 and 49; as contrasted with 23.3 percent of the black population. Yet one wonders about the believability of these data: by the 1910 census 25.2 percent of the total white population were males between 20 and 49 years old, as compared to 30.9 percent of the black population. The 1910 age/sex distribution makes a notable difference: it alone would reduce the ratio of black to white homicides from 2 to 1.4. Changes of similar magnitude could occur for the other ratios. For the 1860 data, the question occurs of whether the decreasing population had been young men, or whether they had been miscounted.

Given that the homicide rate is sensitive to how the population at-risk is defined and measured, the demographic composition of the New York City African-American population remains an important, unresolved, and perhaps even insoluble, issue.

Race and Weapons

Homicide notices often mentioned weapon type. Because their high cost and low quality no doubt cut down on their prevalence, guns were used far less often than today. The Civil War caused a step upward in the using of guns, though compared to today, guns were still relatively rare in homicides. Of the 1,323 cases with information on weapon, 18.7 percent were gun murders and 27 percent knife murders. Dividing these cases at 1861 gives 634 post-1861 cases; 25 percent were gun murders and 26 percent knife murders; the pre-1861 gun percentage drops to 13.

Race also made a difference in weapon use. Twelve percent of black killers used guns, and 48 percent used knives. For whites the figures were 19 percent and 26 percent. Most interesting is the Civil War impact: prior to 1862, no black killers used a gun; all six incidents occurred after 1862. These differences suggest that blacks were less likely to own handguns, possibly due to cost.

Race and Gender

As in the examination of race and age, our understanding of race and gender relations depends in some part on the population at-risk. That is, should the gender ratio of the African-American population differ dramatically from that of, say, the Germans, then this alone might account for differences in homicide.

Although there is no clear warrant to say so, I hypothesize that the African-American population was more adult and more male than the white population. This would result in more black victims and killers being men. Interestingly, this was the case for victims but not for killers. For killers, the race-gender distributions were similar enough to show no statistical significance. For victims, the differences were statistically significant: 90 percent of the black victims were men, as opposed to 77 percent of the white victims.

Aside from the plausibility of differing but unmeasured at-risk populations, which would still leave unaccounted the differences between victims and killers, other possibilities can only be raised as questions. Were African-American men more in public than women? Did their work on and near docks put them at-risk relative to African-American women, who worked in safer locations? Did white men attack spouses and women companions more? Were there cultural differences in the tolerance of violence against women? A comparison of noted ethnicity and race of men who killed women shows some apparent differences: 21 percent (10) of the victims of black offenders were women, as opposed to 39 percent (45) of Irish, 32 percent (24) of German, and 15 percent (3) of Italian. Note that all the cautions apply to interpreting these data: gender balance, the probable underreporting of ethnicity versus the probable higher reporting of race. The results nearly disappear when all killer victim relationships are examined: 24 percent (296 of the 1,211 pairs where gender is positively known) of all the killings were a man killing a woman. We are left with a conundrum— Was there in fact a cultural difference, did the apparently lesser degrees of

Table 1
Race and Gender

	Victim Race		
Victim Sex	White	Black	Total
Male	1044	43	1087
	78%	90%	78%
Female	304	5	309
	22%	10%	22%
Total	1348	48	1396
	100%	100%	100%

Pearson chi2(1) = 3.9603 Pr = 0.047
likelihood-ratio chi2(1) = 4.6544 Pr = 0.031

	Killer Race		
Killer Sex	White	Black	Total
Male	1116	46	1162
	94%	90%	94%
Female	74	5	79
	6%	10%	6%
Total	1190	51	1241
	100%	100%	100%

Pearson chi2(1) = 1.0547 Pr = 0.304
likelihood-ratio chi2(1) = 0.9204 Pr = 0.337

femicide reflect demography and opportunity, or is the difference a consequence of poor reporting?

Racial Attacks

At least three killings of blacks could be identified in the media as having possible racial motivations. These exclude the dozens of racially motivated killings during the draft of 1863. These three cases were identified by examining, where possible, the twenty-two cases where the victim was black and the killer was not identified as black. It is easy enough to guess that these cases are not representative, but I present them to give an idea of the information available.

The first of the probable race murders in New York City took place on August 8, 1847, when an unknown person murdered a sailor named James Steele, who was returning to his barge. Although absolutely no mention is made of possible racial motives, one cannot help but wonder. Six years later, on December 22, 1853, James Crumbly murdered 29-year-old Edward Matthews. This happened when "a terrible conflict took place in the Fifth Ward, between a party of white men, who are of notorious character, and a gang of colored persons." This "riot" occurred after an African-American had been assaulted by three of the white men, took shelter in a black oyster and liquor saloon run by Matthews, from whence a group of blacks returned to avenge his injuries. According to the paper, Matthews "was a sort of leader among the colored residents of the Fifth and Eighth Wards, in consideration of his pugilistic abilities."

In 1867 William Higgins and a gang of white men murdered Christian Bostwick in Higgin's liquor store. Higgins testified that Bostwick, a cook on a coastal steamer, refused to leave the store, so he beat him. According to the article, Bostwick was well known among the "numerous colored population in the Eighth Ward."

All of these cases carry in common the elements of a racial attack. Typically, the killers were backed up by the other white men, and typically victim's noted occupations hint that there could have been latent conflicts over occupations involved. Since all the secondary literature for this era indicates how job "turf" formed an important part of antiblack aggression in northern cities, these incidents seem to support that notion. On the other hand, the high number attacks that did not carry racial overtones requires that we be very cautious. The dichotomized race distribution of victims and killers contains little to support to a strong pattern of race-motivated killings. Therefore, I conclude that race motivation played a secondary role in homicides. Yet in such a small black community, the impact of even a few unpredictable racial attacks must have been very deep.

An Issue of Justice

The study of the role played by racial bias in the justice system is fraught with complexity, even in the present era. During the period under examination here, New York City changed from a slave to a nonslave to a fairly vigorous pro-Reconstruction political atmosphere. But ethnic and racial hostility ran high, and most New Yorkers were white, especially after the antiblack draft riots.

Immigrants, particularly the Irish and Germans, were more heavily involved in homicides than their numbers warrant, but as the city continued to fill with immigrants in the post-Civil War era, homicides per capita decreased.

The ways in which race mattered were complex and shifting, and my discussion here is based on the assumption that while ethnicity (and class) played a highly important role, the experience of blacks contrasted with all nonblacks is a fundamental starting point. Here the question is about treatment by the justice system: Were there differences in arrest, trial, and punishment of blacks and nonblacks?

Blacks had about the same likelihood of arrest and trial for homicides as nonblacks. It is possible that missing information about trials—quite common—biases these results, just as it is possible that there was an underreporting of murders by nonblacks. The data collection strategy for this research, using all suspicious deaths, whether or not called a homicide by a coroner's jury, was deliberately designed to overcome such events, however.

A precise analysis of the past is even more difficult, although one can guess that a society with fewer claims to evenhanded justice might have less to hide. Because we have good records on executions, it is possible to examine at least the outlines of the role race played in the heaviest and rarest punishment meted out to killers in nineteenth-century New York. For this portion of the analysis, the data on the beginning and end of the individual level processes are better than those on the middle. That is, the original counts of murder and any executions are more accurate than are arrests, trials, and sentences.

Nineteenth-century New Yorkers tended to be against capital punishment, in contrast to our perception of that era. Out of over 1,560 murderers, only 2 percent, 31 were executed for their crime. And the proportion being executed was diminishing over time—every year between 1800 and 1875 decreased the probability of execution by 3 percent. Even though a high proportion of arrests was made, there was erratic follow-up. Basically, it was easy to get away with murder, in part because when cases came to trial, juries were apt to give the offenders the benefit of the doubt. In a city filled with bars, rowdiness, and a good deal of physical violence, the all important coroner's juries often placed themselves in the offender's situation and found the deaths to be accidental, the result of a friendly fight. Beginning in the decade of the 1820s, the loosely parallel relationship between executions and homicides ended— executions remaining at the same level, even as homicides spiraled upward.

The one exception to such leniency for capital offenses came for African-American offenders, who were twice as likely to be hanged as their white compatriots. Surprisingly, the race of their victims did not seem to matter much, however.

And even this clearly biased system allowed 90 percent of the black offenders (51 of 58) to escape the gallows. Executions became substantially less frequent every year.

CONCLUSION

There are several conclusions to be drawn from the probe, based on still fragmentary data. New York was a violent city, even if not as violent as today. Perhaps more important is what it was not: a city with violence coming from people of color. It was a violent city of principally white persons, many of them recent immigrants. Had guns been as prevalent as today, how much more violent would this city have been?

The rate at which homicides occurred fluctuated considerably through this period, but it is important to note that it often dropped as precipitously as it rose: immigrants did not necessarily produce violence, as though by some law of pressure cooking. Persons of color participated in this violent society. In the few specifically racial incidents, African-Americans were the victims of racially-motivated attacks. None of these incidents compared to the draft riots, of course, but they do illustrate that African-Americans were in a dangerous city.

Finally, there are two broader implications to be drawn. First is a message of hope: rates of violence can come down, even if we cannot yet identify mechanisms causing that to happen. Second is a message about research: we can learn a great deal from the past that will help us think about the present, if we are willing to commit the energy to the task.

Differences Between Gang
and Nongang Homicides

CHERYL L. MAXSON, MARGARET A. GORDON,
& MALCOLM W. KLEIN

In this paper we have two purposes in mind. The first is to fill the gap in the criminological literature on how gang-related homicides differ from other homicides. The second is to address whether gang-related homicide warrants distinctive public concern as well as specialized law enforcement responses. Using bivariate and discriminant analyses, we can assess how different the two types of homicides are from each other, the nature of the differences, and the relative effect of each of the variables in producing these differences.

METHODS

The following analyses utilize data collected from law enforcement investigation files on over 700 gang- and nongang-designated homicides within the jurisdiction of the Los Angeles Sheriff's Department (LASD) and the Los Angeles Police Department (LAPD) between 1978 and mid-1982. Due to differences in sampling procedures as well as jurisdictional differences in investigation and recording practices, it was necessary to treat the LASD and the LAPD cases as separate samples. To maximize the comparability between gang and nongang incidents, all homicides included in these analyses have at least one named suspect between the ages of 10 and 30.

FINDINGS

The homicide incident descriptors can be roughly divided into characteristics of the setting (broadly defined) and characteristics of the participants. In both categories, major gang/nongang differences emerge.

Turning first to the LASD data, the setting descriptors indicate that the where and how of homicide is clearly related to gang/nongang distinctions. Gang killings are far more likely to take place in public settings, particularly on the street. They are somewhat more likely to involve automobiles and shooting out of a vehicle. They are more likely to involve guns and more weapons overall in the incident.

Gang murders are more likely to include additional offenses, particularly attempted homicide and assault with a deadly weapon. Note, however, that the number of additional offenses among such cases does not differ between gang and nongang events. Gang cases are more likely to inflict injuries in addition to the homicide, although the difference in the number of injured victim companions per injury case does not reach statistical significance. There are more gang cases with unknown suspects (again, the number of unknown suspects among these cases does not differ) and more cases involving intimidation or fear of retaliation. The only other exception to the pattern of gang/nongang setting differences among the LASD cases is the time of day. The majority of both gang and nongang homicides occur at night, between 10 P.M. and 6 A.M.

In sum, most setting variables differentiate between gang and nongang homicides. Gang homicides appear to be considerably more visible and more violent. Yet the differences are not so striking as one might have expected. For example, drive-by shootings, presumably the quintessence of gang killings, occur in only 48 of 226 cases. Similarly, fear of retaliation is noted in 33% of the gang cases—one might have anticipated a higher figure—but also in 10% of the nongang cases. The difference in presence of various weapons is also less striking than might have been expected.

Variables not typically examined by researchers, such as presence and type of associated offenses, injuries to other victims, and unknown suspects also emerged in this analysis (admittedly with low coefficients of association) and help to fill out a picture of the gang homicide setting. As compared to the nongang setting, it is less dramatically different than is often depicted, but more broadly different than is generally recognized (that is, more gang/nongang differences, but smaller than commonly assumed). This finding suggests a generally qualitative as well as quantitative difference.

The second aspect of possible differences is in the characteristics of the homicide suspects and victims. The participant variables even more clearly distinguish gang from nongang cases, a point easily illustrated by reference to the measures of association. Gang homicides involve two and a half times as many participants. Participants in gang incidents are twice as likely never to have had known prior contact between victims and suspects, and are less than one third as likely to have had a clear prior relationship. Homicide victims and suspects charged with homicide are about five years younger in gang incidents, despite the age restrictions placed on the sample (10 to 30 years). Gang suspects and victims in the LASD jurisdiction are far more likely to be Hispanic and almost never white, in contrast to the more even ethnic breakdown in nongang cases.

The ethnicity difference is not surprising; Los Angeles has long been known for its Hispanic gangs in contrast with the white ethnic gang activity observed in cities such as Chicago or Boston. The relationship difference may be surprising to some, because in decades past, gangs were generally portrayed as preying primarily on well-known adversaries. The presumption that warring gang members know each other at least by reputation, if not by sight and name, seems untenable. Among gang-designated homicides with clear gang-on-gang motives or behavior during the incident, 54% show no evidence of any prior personal contact. In these gang homicides, the relationship between opponents appears to be based on gang affiliation rather than enmity between familiar individuals. In spite of rising public concern about innocent bystander victims, we found mention of only four such cases (all gang-related).

Turning now to the LAPD data, a number of setting factors differentiate between gang and nongang incidents. However, it is notable that the distinctions are not as uniform nor as large as those observed in the LASD data. Presence or type of associated offense are not differentiating factors in the LAPD data, and consequently the presence of other victim injuries does not separate gang from nongang cases. As in the LASD data, street location and presence of firearms and automobiles are more likely in gang killings.

To a greater extent than was the case with the setting variables, the LAPD participant characteristics do differentiate between gang and nongang cases. Victim ethnicity is the only exception. In contrast with the LASD, LAPD homicides have a preponderance of black participants as well as high proportions of Hispanic participants, but very few white suspects or victims, even in nongang cases. The participant variables show a general pattern of lower coefficients of association in the LAPD data than is true in the LASD tables, but the jurisdictional difference in the participant data is nowhere near as striking as it is with respect to setting characteristics.

Discriminant analysis was utilized to assess the differentiation between designated gang and nongang cases in a multivariate context. This technique produces a linear combination of discriminating variables (a discriminant function) that best separates the groups from each other. In both the LASD and LAPD data, the proportion of variance in the discriminant function (eta^2) accounted for by the two groups (gang and nongang) is surprisingly high (.48 and .38), given the complexity and ambiguity of the file materials and the exploratory nature of the research. Classification based on the discriminant function is successful in 82% of LASD cases and 79% of LAPD cases.

All coefficients are statistically significant; the direction is relative to the signs of the group centroids. In the LASD data, two participant variables—mean age and ethnic status of suspects—are clearly the most important, followed by street location, number of participants on the suspect side, and presence of a gun; variables pertaining to characteristics of the suspects, rather than of the victims, predominate.

Results from the LAPD and LASD analyses are generally similar. Confirming the observations made from the bivariate tables, the LAPD discrimination between gang and nongang cases is lower. Both sets of analyses indicate a strong overall capacity for the participant variables to discriminate between gang and nongang cases, and this is particularly true of variables describing designated suspects and other participants on the suspect side. The characteristics of the homicide setting tend to be of secondary importance to the participant characteristics.

CONCLUSIONS

Both the cross-tabular and discriminant analyses display substantial differences between gang and nongang homicides; several items of particular interest may be highlighted. For instance, some may be surprised by the relatively common instances of gang homicides involving participants on each side with no prior personal contact, but also by the relative absence of "innocent bystander" victims. Greater automobile involvement fits the general picture of modern mobile street gangs, as do the preponderance of intra-ethnic relationships between opposing sides and the preponderance of minority group and male involvement. Finally, while gang suspects and victims are, as expected, considerably younger than their nongang counterparts, they are older than might be expected of "youth gang" members. In the absence of good historical data, it is nevertheless our impression that gang homicide participants described here are older than their counterparts of two or three decades ago.

There can be little doubt, given the data presented here, that gang homicides differ both quantitatively and qualitatively from nongang homicides. Most distinctly, they differ with respect to ethnicity, age, number of participants, and relationship between the participants, properties clearly related to the *group* nature of the events.

Gang homicide settings also differ from those of other settings. They are more likely to involve public areas, automobiles, firearms, and, in the LASD data, associated nonhomicide offenses and injuries to other victims. The contribution of group processes to the higher incidence of these features is well worth further research.

Finally, given these differences, gang incidents seem to present unique problems to investigators and may well benefit from the specialized skills and experience of experts on gangs. The public nature of gang homicides, reluctance of victims, witnesses, and informants to provide information (either through fear of retaliation or gang loyalty), and the lack of prior contact between victims and offenders suggest that investigators might profit from knowledge about the character of such offenses and access to relatively sophisticated gang intelligence (territories, rivalries, membership rosters, and descriptions). Location, automobile involvement, and gun presence suggest potential points of intervention. While the data presented here refer to homicide, analysis of nonhomicide violent incidents indicates marked similarities between the two offense types regarding the nature of gang/nongang differences. Therefore, the implications of the differences between gang and nongang homicides for specialization in law enforcement can be more broadly drawn as gang/nongang *violence* differences. Given the nature of these differences, investigative specialization may be justified in police departments of cities having large gang populations.

Implications for public concern regarding gang homicides are less clear. It is evident that gang incidents are generally more chaotic, with more people, weapons, offenses, and injuries out in the open, among people less familiar with each other. However, the small number of "innocent bystander" victims suggests that the potential threat of gang violence to the general public is not substantial.

Bringing "Booze" Back In:
The Relationship Between
Alcohol and Homicide

ROBERT NASH PARKER

The purpose of this article is to test a number of hypotheses derived from a theoretical analysis of the relationship between alcohol and homicide using U.S. state-level data for homicide rates in the early 1980s, with additional specification involving specific types of homicide. Five types of homicide are examined, based on circumstances or on the prior victim/offender relationship: robbery, other felony, family intimate, family other, and primary nonintimate. After a discussion of underlying assumptions, the theoretical arguments are summarized. Additional theoretical analysis derives predictions about specific types of homicide, and the data and measures are described. After a discussion of the results, including a consideration of which predictions are supported by the analysis and which are not, a concluding discussion is offered on the importance of theoretically based empirical analysis for the homicide/alcohol relationship, for homicide and violence in general, and for social science research.

This is by design an ambitious effort, but there is much to be gained by the approach taken here. Homicide research in general has suffered from "one theory" approaches, that is, from studies in which one theory is developed extensively and tested with a standard list of control variables that do not include indicators of concepts from other theories. Researchers can always come up with new theories, but the test is whether these new ideas prove to be an advance over previous perspectives. The approach taken here is to bring four theories into play, each augmented by a consideration of alcohol, and simultaneously to test them empirically. The result is that not only are competing hypotheses compared and contrasted, but the utility of the newly developed hypotheses are also more severely tested than would be the case in the typical "one theory" approach.

UNDERLYING ASSUMPTIONS:
ALCOHOL, HOMICIDE, AND DISINHIBITION

How might alcohol be related to homicide? Pernanen identifies at least four important possibilities; first, alcohol consumption could have a direct effect on homicide. Although most analysts reject such a simplistic assessment, there is little direct research evidence including alcohol use with measures of concepts from theories of homicide. Here, alcohol consumption will be used as a control in each model specified, so that the effects of consumption can be directly assessed.

Second, alcohol may mediate or intervene between homicide and its other major causes. The results presented here are in reduced form and do not allow for a full examination of intervening relationships. However, with alcohol consumption as a control in each model, the implications of such hypotheses can be examined in a reduced form and are discussed below with regard to southern region, racial composition, and economic deprivation.

A third possible role for alcohol is an interactive one, in which alcohol is related to other important causal factors. Interaction hypotheses will be examined here in two different forms. First, dummy variables are used to define categories of alcohol consumption and then multiplied by a continuous variable to test two interactions involving alcohol consumption. The second form, in which a set of dummy variables is used to examine all possible combinations of two variables, is used here to test the interaction of alcoholic beverage regulation and social control.

A final possibility is that alcohol and homicide are not related, that the evidence in support of this relationship is spurious. In this "common cause" model, alcohol and homicide appear to be related because of some third variable, which has been excluded unintentionally. The way to minimize this possibility is to conduct a thorough theoretical analysis, with the goal of logically identifying factors to be included (and excluded). The common cause or spuriousness model can be directly examined in the analysis presented here. If the relationship between alcohol consumption and homicide is partially or mostly spurious, then examining models in which alcohol consumption, regulation, and several interactions involving these variables are specified, along with indicators from the four major theories, will provide an appropriate empirical test.

What is the general impact that alcohol has on human behavior? One answer to this question that has been thoroughly discussed in the alcohol research literature is the *disinhibition approach.* The disinhibition approach suggests that the impact of alcohol on behavior is to remove the effect of social inhibitions that otherwise restrict or prohibit behaviors contrary to important social norms. The underlying assumption made here is somewhat different: Despite the existence of moral, religious, and legal arguments and statutes to the contrary, violence has widespread normative support in Western culture. The popularity of violent professional sports, violent television programs and movies, and books portraying extreme forms of violence, and evidence from research on topics such as family violence contribute to the notion that violence is normatively supported in U.S. society. Norms vary in the degree to which institutional support exists for their enforcement and for the application of sanctions to violators. In situations of normative conflict, alcohol can be seen as a disinhibitor of those norms with the weakest institutional support.

It is also clear that violence has the potential to be a successful tool in interpersonal disputes. If people were removed from all constraints of normative structure, violence would be an attractive and effective method for dealing with some types of disputes. For example, if someone is making verbal remarks that are insulting and annoying, violence could be an effective method for silencing such attacks. This is a common scenario in homicides, but it is also clear that many verbal insults are launched in day-to-day interaction, with few of these being responded to with violence. Situations in which alcohol may be most likely to disinhibit normative proscriptions against the use of violence are those in which violence would be effective. To refrain from violence in such situations requires what could be called *active constraint,* that is, an unwillingness to use what is perceived to be a very effective alternative for dispute resolution because the normative structure prohibits or limits such actions. A rational-choice perspective would suggest that in most cases people select responses to the behavior of others from the perspective of perceived success at achieving objectives or goals; active constraint requires people to select nonviolent methods that they perceive to be less effective in achieving their goals. Further, Pernanen suggests that the behavior of people under the influence of alcohol is consistent with a rational-choice model of behavior. Although people under the influence of alcohol may not be very good at rational choice, there is no evidence to suggest that such individuals do not attempt to systematically choose their behavior from among perceived alternatives, based on perceived information, in a manner consistent with their perceived goals. The normative structure is reasonably powerful, and everyday life suggests that it is generally successful at preventing violence.

In the active-constraint situation, however, the disinhibiting effect of alcohol may be most pronounced. Passive constraint of violence, in which violence is perceived as less effective than alternatives, is likely to be unaffected by the disinhibiting effects of alcohol; in most cases, the small and physically weak person will not attack a larger, stronger adversary unless aided by effective weapons. However, the larger, stronger person may be willing to use violence under the influence of alcohol when advantages over the opponent make such a strategy an effective one, despite powerful normative strictures against such behavior. The disinhibiting effect of alcohol on norms that proscribe violence, especially under the condition of active constraint, is an important assumption on which the theoretical analysis used here is based. The general role of alcohol in violent behavior is to enhance the rate of violence, all other things being equal.

Passive constraint is less likely than active constraint to be disinhibited, because even an individual under the influence of alcohol cannot fail to see the disadvantages of violence in a particular situation. Evidence supporting this argument is found in many cases of alcohol-involved homicide, where one of the participants leaves the initial scene of the confrontation only to return a short while later with some additional weapon designed to make their violence more effective. Such efforts, designed to transform the situation from one of passive constraint to one of active constraint, do not always result in success; alcohol may disinhibit active constraint, but it still has a negative impact on judgment and information processing, so that the actor who returns armed with a better weapon, and/or the actor who initiated the violence, can still end up the victim of the incident. Regardless of the complexity of the processes involved, the argument here, and one that is consistent with a number of the detailed case summaries provided by Wilbanks, is that alcohol makes the disinhibition of active constraint more likely.

Economic Deprivation, Homicide, and Alcohol

Socioeconomic approaches focus on the economic structure of society and the disadvantaged position of many individuals. The link between homicide and poverty is based on conceptions of poverty and its impact. Perhaps violence is one of the few options available to those without the economic means to deal with the problems and crises of everyday life. Absolute deprivation may also produce emotional situations that escalate into violence that, again, is directed at those close at hand—spouses, children, friends, and so on. The absolute deprivation approach suggests that violence can occur among such individuals because everyday life is difficult to deal with. Early conflict approaches identified such a link, and more recent discussions have also suggested the importance of absolute deprivation.

In addition, a number of studies that compare absolute to relative economic deprivation almost all conclude that absolute deprivation, rather than relative deprivation, is one of the keys to understanding how economic deprivation affects homicide. Although a more extreme version of this measure is often used in homicide research, the relationship between poverty, alcohol consumption, and homicide may be somewhat different. The more skewed measures that have found favor with homicide researchers may be less relevant when alcohol is considered because the absolute poorest do not constitute the most important group of alcohol users. A much larger class of alcohol users, whose economic status hovers at or below the poverty line but who are not the absolute underclass, are more relevant here because they have sufficient resources to regularly use alcohol and are much more likely to be in "situated transaction" situations—that is, in social settings where the type of disputes arise that can lead to homicide—than are the real underclass.

What role does alcohol consumption play in the deprivation/homicide relationship? Alcohol consumption may interact with deprivation in the causation of homicide. If alcohol serves to enhance violence, the effect of poverty on homicide would be greatest where alcohol consumption is also highest. If alcohol consumption were low, the poverty/homicide relationship might disappear or turn negative, because poverty rates might remain constant while homicide could decline to zero. Alcohol consumption conditions the way in which poverty and homicide are related.

Subcultures of Violence: Southerners and African Americans

Subculture of violence approaches focus on the diversity of cultural and normative behavior and on expectations that exist in a large, diverse society. This diversity suggests that certain groups may exist in which members commit homicide as a legitimate, alternative method of dispute resolution. The notion that a subculture exists in U.S. society in which violence is a legitimate means of interaction and problem solving was developed by Wolfgang and Ferracuti. Their argument is that among a certain segment of the population, values are held that legitimate the use of violence in some social situations.

In the United States, empirical investigations of violent subcultures have focused on southerners and African Americans. Historical evidence links the development of a subculture of violence for both groups with the institution of slavery and with post–Civil War accommodations to the dejure elimination of the slave-based economic system. Two studies that make this argument with regard to homicide, Gastil and Hackney, present evidence of a link between state homicide rates and measures of regional location or the degree to which a state's population had southern origins. Despite a number of studies that have failed to find empirical support for this notion, researchers continued to be struck by the plausibility of the Gastil-Hackney thesis as applied to both the South and to African American urban populations. Researchers continue to find empirical evidence in support of the Gastil-Hackney argument, using various time periods and/or specifications of independent variables. Messner suggests that racial composition and the southern region are the dominant predictors of homicide, contrary to results presented by Loftin and Hill. Huff-Corzine et al. also find support for the subcultural perspective.

Evidence from research into regional differences in drinking patterns suggests that the southern region homicide relationship may be explained in terms of the nature and pattern of southern drinking. Although overall rates of alcohol consumption are lower in the South than in other regions of the United States, southerners who drink alcohol have significantly higher rates of consumption than those from other parts of the country. These data suggest that southern drinking patterns differ from those in other regions, with the South containing a greater number of both abstainers and heavy drinkers. The pattern of high consumption per occasion in the South would not only be consistent with one important category of homicide—acquaintance killing acquaintance in a public or semipublic setting—but would also present direct evidence of a cultural difference between the South and other regions. Direct cultural indicators are almost universally missing from empirical research on the impact of subculture of violence, so not only does alcohol as a concept lead to greater understanding of the causes of homicide, but it also helps provide a more appropriate test of subculture of violence theory. Alcohol plays the role of an intervening variable in this argument, and the direct association between region and homicide would disappear if alcohol consumption per drinker is controlled.

Arguments concerning the role alcohol may play for African American subcultures of violence are complicated by evidence concerning drinking patterns by race and by evidence on the racial composition/homicide relationship. Research on racial differences in drinking patterns has shown that Whites drink more than African Americans, although there is evidence of an interaction by socioeconomic characteristics. Lower class African American drinking patterns, as reported in ethnographies, may be more problematic than the drinking behavior of more affluent African Americans, with the former involving heavy weekend binge drinking. Recent evidence from a national survey that contained an oversampling of African American respondents suggests an inverse relationship between income and drinking, such that among those with lower incomes, African Americans report heavier drinking patterns, whereas for those with higher incomes, Whites report heavier drinking.

These results suggest the possibility that alcohol consumption intervenes between a racial composition/social class interaction and homicide. If a place has a larger population of poor African Americans, consumption should be elevated, resulting in higher rates of homicide. If a substantial affluent African American population resides in a particular place, consumption rates should be lower, thus producing lower homicide rates.

Capital Punishment, Alcohol Regulation, and Social Control

A third approach focuses on the relationship between rates of crime and rates of punishment, arguing that the death penalty is a deterrent to murder in those places were it is carried out with appropriate frequency and speed. Empirical research has led to increased rather than decreased controversy about the impact of the death penalty on rates of homicide, with a number of contradictory studies appearing.

The deterrence approach specifically links the observed rates of any offense such as homicide to the actions taken by authorities to punish those who have committed the offense. Discussions of deterrence theory often involve distinctions among at least four aspects of capital punishment: (a) certainty, or the likelihood that an offender will be executed (indicated by the number of executions divided by the number of murder); (b) severity, or the relationship between those executed and those who receive alternative punishments for murder (indicated by executions per prisoner in the penal system serving time for this offense); (c) celerity, or the length of time between conviction and execution; and (d) public knowledge of the execution. If certainty, severity, and public knowledge are high, and if the application of the punishment is swift, homicide rates should reflect these facts over time by lowering as deterrence is increased. Most studies, however, have failed to find such an effect, and in some cases homicides were seen to increase following executions.

There are at least two distinct approaches to integrating alcohol conceptually with deterrence theory. First, from a sociolegal control point of view, the willingness to have a capital punishment statute in a particular locality, and the further willingness to actually implement such a law by means of executions, reflects a tendency in favor of strong social control by government of individual behavior. Strict control of alcohol sales and distribution can also be seen in this same light. If both capital punishment and alcohol control are related to an underlying dimension of social control, their joint presence in a community could lead to an enhanced effect of social control such that one type of control enhances the impact of the other. If a locality has both types of laws, we would expect the lowest rates of homicide; in those places where neither law exists, the highest homicide rates could be expected. Places in between, with one form of social control and not the other, should have intermediate levels of homicide.

Death Sentences, Alcohol Consumption, and Deterrence

A second approach to the relationship between deterrence and alcohol is based on a "rational choice" perspective and, as such, depends on the ability of individuals to reliably calculate the relative values of rewards and punishments (as well as the likelihood of each) for any contemplated action. Alcohol consumption can be seen as interacting with the deterrent effect of capital punishment, because consumption would affect the ability of actors to calculate rationally. This leads to the prediction that in places with capital punishment and high levels of consumption, deterrence theory would be short-circuited, resulting in little or no deterrent effect of capital punishment and perhaps in higher homicide rates. In places where capital punishment and low levels of consumption exist, the deterrent effect would be more likely to operate, thus leading to lower homicide rates. Here, alcohol changes the causal pros by which deterrence is related to homicide.

Alcohol consumption and Routine Activities

Finally, the "routine activity" or "lifestyle" approach has become the focus of many recent efforts to understand violence in general and homicide in particular. This approach suggests that we should expect increasing rates of violence because the pace, tempo, and style in which people live has increased their exposure to potential violence and at the same time reduced the ability of traditional guardians to protect people from violence. Cohen and Felson look at the decreasing size of households, the increasing propensity of people to live alone, and the increase in nighttime activities outside of the home such as eating, seeking entertainment, and shopping. In addition, they point to the increased likelihood that families are composed of two wage earners and will thus have the increased financial resources to pursue such activities.

This approach suggests that the causes of homicide may be independent of the social, cultural, economic, and legal contexts of behavior stressed in the approaches previously discussed. Hindelang et al., Cohen and Felson, and Cohen et al. argued that increases in homicide could be explained by social and economic trends that bring together suitable targets—that is, potential victims, motivated offenders, and an absence of effective guardians. Cohen and Felson, define a "household activity ratio," essentially a measurement of the number of U.S. households likely to be unoccupied during the day and to be composed of members who spend substantial amounts of time away from home. They argue that increases in this indicator reflect lifestyle changes that have resulted in higher crime rates. Their findings for the United States show a significant relationship between this ratio and the homicide rate between 1947 and 1974.

The key to understanding how alcohol is related to routine activities depends on the role alcohol plays in those activities. Routine activities theory directs attention to where an activity like alcohol consumption takes place, and under what circumstances. If most drinking takes place in bars, restaurants, and other public places, this behavior is likely to be part of a set of routine activities that involve going out of the house, often at night, for leisure-related pursuits. Nighttime activity is a key indicator in tests of routine activity theory, and it has been found to be an important predictor of victimization. Therefore, higher rates of consumption in on-site facilities like bars and restaurants should lead to higher rates of homicide, because more people would be exposing themselves to risk with higher levels of nighttime activity related to alcohol consumption. If alcohol consumption is done mostly at home, this would imply less exposure to risk of homicide because of lower levels of nighttime activity related to alcohol consumption. Patterns of alcohol consumption can be seen as indicators of routine activity and, as such, alcohol consumption patterns are predicted to directly affect homicide rates.

DATA, MEASURES, AND ANALYTICAL APPROACH

This study involves the estimation of a complex model—a number of theoretical hypotheses have been identified and a number of indicators need to be included for these hypotheses to be simultaneously evaluated. In this type of modeling, the strongest justification for inclusion of an indicator is its link to the theoretical hypothesis being tested.

To evaluate these hypotheses, a data set was assembled for U.S. states including the District of Columbia, circa 1980. For these 51 cases, poverty is measured by the percentage of the state's population below the official U.S. poverty line income level for families in 1980, and alcohol consumption is measured by 1980 spirit sales per adult drinker, measured in gallons. To measure the interaction of poverty and alcohol consumption, a dummy variable was created equal to 1 if the state's rate of consumption per adult is greater than the U.S. mean of 1.2 gallons pure ethanol equivalent per adult, and zero if the state's consumption rates is below the national mean. This measure of high versus low consumption is then multiplied by the poverty indicator to create a term that is equal to the poverty indicator when consumption is above the national mean, and equal to zero when consumption is below the national mean.

The selection of "above average" as the cutoff for the high-consumption interaction term is based on the notion that a large percentage of the drinking population, many of whom would not be diagnosed as having a drinking problem using the standard diagnostic instruments, are nonetheless at risk of being involved in an alcohol-related violent incident. This notion is also related to the single distribution of consumption theory, which also suggests that consumption all along the range of total consumption is related to problems such as violence. These ideas are in contrast to the more conventional notion that it is the extremely intoxicated person who is most likely to combine alcohol and violence. The approach taken here is based on the argument that alcohol's role in violence is to enhance the regular, normal, everyday violence that is caused by a number of other factors. If alcohol use enhances these everyday occurrences of violence, places with above-average consumption should also be places in which violence is enhanced; that is, arguments are more likely to become violent, and violent incidents are more likely to involve serious injury and death, thus leading to greater homicide rates.

The African American poverty measure is a ratio of the percentage of African American families below the poverty line divided by the percentage of African American families above the poverty line for 1980; as this ratio increases, so does consumption and thus the homicide rate. Similarly, if a state is in the southern region, consumption per drinker increases, and so should the homicide rate. These two hypotheses are examined here in reduced form so that if the African American poverty or southern regional hypothesis is supported, consumption will have a significant positive impact on the homicide rate, whereas the African American poverty ratio and the southern regional dummy will have insignificant net effects on the homicide rate.

The social control indicator was constructed so that if the state had a capital punishment sentencing law for homicide in effect in 1980, the social control status of the state would be either mixed or high, depending on how alcoholic beverages were regulated. Alcohol-related social control was measured by three dummy variables, according to an analysis of state-level alcoholic beverage control laws. State regulations most often deal with how the retail sales and wholesale distribution of alcoholic beverages are organized and regulated. In states where both wholesale and retail systems are directly run and "owned" by state agencies, alcohol regulation was classified as "strict" by Janes and Gruenewald, and if those states also had a capital punishment statute in force, the high-social-control dummy variable was given a score of 1 (11 states). In states where both systems were under the control of private business enterprises and no capital punishment statute was in effect, alcohol regulation was considered "weak" by Janes and Gruenewald, and a score of 1 was assigned on the low-control dummy variable (13 states). The remaining states (27) either had no capital punishment law and strict alcohol control regulations or had relatively weak alcohol control laws with capital punishment laws in effect; these "medium" control states were the excluded comparison category.

The direct effect of capital punishment on homicide rates consists of more than the simple fact of having a statute in effect; as the controversy over the moral and legal implications of the death penalty grew in the 1960s and 1970s, there were many jurisdictions that had statutes in effect but in which no death sentences were ever handed down by local courts, or were overturned on appeal in state appellate courts. Beyond simply having a statute on the books, the actual application of the death penalty in cases is a further implementation of a deterrence approach to homicide. Using data reported by Bowers, a measure of the main effect of capital punishment was created by dividing the total number of death sentences issued by local courts by the total number of homicides in each state during the period 1973 through 1982. This measure is the death sentence rate, with the population at risk being approximated by the number of murders. It might be more appropriate from a theoretical point of view to calculate an execution rate by dividing the number of executions by the number of death sentences issued, but this measure would be misleading, especially over the period under consideration, because of the legal requirements in death sentence cases (i.e., the various appeals) that often delay the implementation of a death sentence. Thus the death sentence rate is a more appropriate indicator of the use of capital sentences.

The capital punishment/alcohol consumption interaction, like the poverty/consumption interaction described previously, was created by multiplying the death sentence rate by a dummy variable scored 1 for alcohol consumption below the national mean of spirits sales per adult drinker. When consumption is above the mean, the rational process through which capital punishment is thought to operate may be short-circuited; when consumption is low, the impact of alcohol on rational processes is minimized, and it may be that capital punishment acts as a deterrent in such conditions. Of course, alcohol is not the only substance available that might reduce the ability of a population to act rationally; legal and illegal drugs of various types remain unanalyzed here.

The final independent variable is derived from the routine activity perspective. The proportion of alcoholic beverage licenses that allow on-site beverage sales (e.g., bars, restaurants, nightclubs), divided by the total number of licenses of all types, is an indicator of the pattern of drinking-related behavior within the state.

The greater the ratio of on-site licenses to the total, the more likely it is that people in that state routinely seek entertainment, food, and companionship outside the home. Alcohol consumption is one of the predominant activities in such settings, and the combination of consumption and the "time out" nature of the social and entertainment-related activities sought by patrons of such establishments makes violence and homicide more likely. Data on police service calls show that for violent offenses, bars, restaurants, and other alcohol outlets account for a significant majority of such calls in major metropolitan areas. Because these activities are much more likely in our society to take place at night, a higher score on this measure reflects greater levels of nighttime activity, which is a key indicator in the routine activity perspective.

The dependent measures used here—homicide rates per 1,000 people for the years 1981, 1982, and 1983—are taken from Federal Bureau of Investigation (FBI) Supplemental Homicide Report data. Five types of homicide rates are used, based on the circumstances and/or the victim offender relationship: (a) robbery homicide; (b) homicides committed along with rapes, burglaries, arson, and other felony crimes; and three types of "primary" relationship homicide including (c) family intimate, or homicides occurring between spouses, lovers, and ex-lovers; (d) homicides occurring between other family members not known to be sexually intimate; and (e) primary nonintimate, or homicides that take place between friends, neighbors, and acquaintances. Because three consecutive years of homicide data are available for each type, the dependent variables are unmeasured constructs estimated simultaneously with the structural equation model, allowing for the control of random and nonrandom measurement error in the dependent variable at the same time effect parameters are estimated. Although the independent variables in the model are single indicators or constructed interaction terms, most of the independent measures are measured with reasonable accuracy, whereas official crime data, including homicide rates, are well known to suffer from measurement error problems. The use of full information maximum likelihood models allows for the effects of measurement error in the homicide data to be controlled, although this approach provides no particular advantage for the independent variables.

A number of the hypotheses to be tested here apply differentially to the different dependent measures. Based on a combination of previous research on the relationship between the types of homicide examined here and the independent variables discussed previously, specific expectations can be identified. Considering the poverty and high-consumption effect, which in general is predicted to be more strongly related to homicide than either poverty or alcohol is directly, the effect should be strongest for homicides occurring between family members and lovers; poverty has had stronger effects on primary types of homicide than it has had on robbery and other felony homicides. However, Parker found that poverty had a strong positive effect on robbery homicide rates in U.S. cities with a population over 50,000 in 1980, suggesting that the poverty/alcohol consumption interaction may have a positive effect on this type of felony homicide.

Concerning the southern regional and racial composition hypotheses, results of prior research suggest that these effects would be most relevant for primary homicide rates including family intimate, other family, and primary nonintimate. In previous research, these effects were strongest for primary types of homicide and largely insignificant for felony types. Concerning the social control and capital punishment/alcohol consumption interaction, based on rational-choice arguments, it is most likely that robbery and other felony types of homicide rates will be significantly affected by these variables.

Finally, concerning the routine activities hypothesis, a greater proportion of on-site licensed alcoholic beverage establishments is most likely to affect primary nonintimate homicides. Although it is often the case that spousal homicides occur in similar contexts to those in the primary nonintimate category (i.e., at or near public or semipublic places like bars or clubs), many of these crimes also occur at or near home; if a higher proportion of on-site establishments means that people go out more often, this indicator could be unrelated to or even negatively associated with primary intimate homicide. Robbery and other felony homicide rates could also be increased by higher levels of nighttime activity because the potential targets of such crimes may be more vulnerable and less likely to be guarded effectively.

Table 1 summarizes, by theory, the alcohol-related hypotheses derived here, the role of alcohol vis-à-vis the relevant variable(s), the predictions in terms of strength and direction, and the types of homicide that are hypothesized to be most applicable in each case.

THE LIMITS OF MACRO- AND MICROSTUDIES OF HOMICIDE

Before presenting the results of the analyses, some discussion of the limits imposed by the macrodesign of this study is relevant related to the standards of proof used in the social sciences, the impact of those standards on micro-and macrostudies, and the relationship between theory and theoretically driven research.

An appropriate criterion for deciding whether a hypothesis should be tested at the micro- or macrolevel is the location of the variation to be explained by the causal relationship, and the underlying process being examined. In the case of alcohol and homicide, the assumption is often made that these are microlevel

Table 1
Summary of major interaction and
intervention hypotheses and derived predictions

Theoretical Perspective	Hypothesis	Prediction for Homicide	Effect Stronger for Types of Homicide
Economic deprivation	High alcohol consumption enhances poverty's effect	++	Robbery; other felony
Subculture: Southern	Alcohol consumption intervenes	0	Family intimate; family other; primary
Subculture: African American	High rates of African American poverty lead to higher consumption	0	Family intimate; family other; primary
Social control: tolerance for formal control	Capital punishment laws and strict alcohol control combine	–	Robbery; other felony
Social control: deterrence	Capital punishment rates in the presence of low consumption	–	Robbery; other felony
Routine activity	On-site licenses cause more nighttime activity	+	Primary; robbery; other felony

++ = Effect is enhanced and much stronger than main effects.
+ = Effect is positive and not necessarily stronger than main effects.
0 = Main effect is nonsignificant when hypothesis is included in the model.
– = Effect is negative and not necessarily stronger than main effects.
— = Effect is negative and stronger than main effects.

phenomena, but an examination of the research literature on homicide, which is almost entirely macro in nature, suggests otherwise. The same is true of the literature on the causes of alcohol consumption—among the most important factors are such macrolevel phenomena as alcohol regulation and the geographic density of alcohol outlets.

Any individual study of alcohol and homicide would be flawed in a number of ways. If a representative sample of individuals is taken, the number of homicide victims or offenders included would be too small for analysis. If a design that includes only homicide victims and/or offenders is used, sample selection bias, as well as an inability to measure macrolevel factors that have been found to be important causes of homicide, would be major shortcomings.

The present study, like every other study of homicide in the research literature, is dependent in part on assumptions about how groups of individuals are likely to act in a given set of circumstances. The particular set of assumptions used here, under the rubric of selective disinhibition and active versus passive constraint, is clearly delineated. It might be argued that the ideal design would be one in which micro and macro are combined, and there are at least two ways in which microdata are folded into the macromodel being examined here. By including alcohol consumption and theorizing about its role in homicide, an additional behavioral factor that is well known to co-occur with homicide has been brought back into homicide research. The individual nature of the prior victim/offender relationship is the basis for construction of the five dependent variables examined here. Given the weaknesses of individual studies described here, and given the fact that few such studies, if any, have contributed to the literature on homicide, there is no reason to prefer such studies over the present design. Macrostudies are superior to microstudies in this particular substantive area. One notable exception is the research of Luckenbill, but the emphasis on the nature of the dyadic interaction, and on the importance of bystanders, makes Luckenbill's analysis structural rather than individual.

A number of possible alternative specifications that are found in the homicide deterrence literature remain unaddressed in this study. Some designs have incorporated lagged effects of deterrence measures on crime outcomes, but the best studies employing such lags find little evidence of a deterrent effect. Arguments have also been made for the simultaneity of the crime and punishment relationship, but again the best studies examining this relationship have found little evidence of this effect. The focus of this study is on the way in which alcohol might affect processes of deterrence and social control; given the lack of easily identified instruments necessary for identification, a reciprocal causation model is beyond the scope of this effort.

RESULTS AND DISCUSSION

Table 2 lists the independent variables, including interaction and main effects and the standardized coefficients for each hypothesis, and gives alternative goodness-of-fit indicators for each equation. The first column, which gives results for robbery homicide, shows that the poverty/high alcohol consumption interaction term is positively and significantly related to robbery homicide rates, net of the main effects of poverty and alcohol consumption as well as the other independent variables. The combination of poverty and high alcohol consumption leads to even higher rates of robbery homicide and although the main effects of alcohol consumption

Table 2
Empirical evaluation of alcohol and
homicide hypotheses, U.S. states, circa 1980

Independent Variable	Type of Homicide				
	Robbery Homicide	Felony Other Homicide	Family Intimate Homicide	Family Other Homicide	Primary Nonintimate Homicide
Poverty/high consumption	0.352[a]	0.391[a]	–0.152	–0.005	–0.056
Poverty (main effect)	0.051	–0.171	0.123	0.158	0.110
Alcohol consumption	0.116	0.065	0.287[a]	.089	0.244[a]
African American poverty ratio	0.210	–0.001	0.267[a]	0.321[a]	0.335[a]
High social control	–0.235[a]	–0.271[a]	–0.085	–0.043	–0.159[a]
Low social control	–0.025	–0.071	0.039	0.001	–0.040
Death sentence rate	0.321	0.219	0.493[a]	0.039	0.339[a]
Death sentence/low consumption	–0.262[a]	–0.161	–0.275	0.085	–0.185
On-site license ratio	–0.143	–0.033	–0.028	–0.269[a]	–0.066
South	0.227	0.484[a]	0.384[a]	0.438[a]	0.417[a]
R^2	.460	.492	.636	.737	.687
Chi-square probability	.544	.619	.847	.967	.994

[a]Coefficient at leat 1.6 times Standard Error.

and poverty are positive, neither reach significance in this equation, which is an indication of the distinctive pattern of robbery homicide rates among states that have both high consumption and poverty. The hypothesized interaction between the death sentence rate and consumption is also found, as the effect of the death sentence/low consumption term is negative, indicating that in states with below average spirits consumption, the higher the death sentence rate the lower the rate of robbery homicide. In addition, these results show that in states with both strict control of alcohol sales and capital punishment statutes, robbery homicide rates are significantly lower than in states with either type of social control alone; states with low levels of social control (i.e., neither type) are not significantly different from states with one type or the other.

The results for robbery homicide rates also reveal that a number of hypotheses previously described were not fully supported. Although alcohol consumption was not a significant predictor of robbery homicide, controlling for this variable did cause the impact of the southern regional variable to be insignificant. Similarly, the impact of the African American poverty ratio was insignificant for robbery homicide, net of consumption. Finally, the routine-activity hypothesis was not supported by results for robbery homicide.

The second column of Table 2 gives results for the felony other homicide rate, revealing a similar pattern to that of robbery homicide. The effects of the poverty/high consumption interaction and the high social control indicator were significant, as predicted, and the African American poverty ratio was not significant net of alcohol consumption, also as predicted. However, the death sentence and consumption interaction was not a significant predictor of felony other homicide, nor was the on-site license indicator. The southern regional indicator was significant and positive in the equation for the felony other homicide rate, disconfirming the consumption-as-intervening-variable hypothesis in explaining high southern regional rates.

The middle column of Table 2 gives results for the family intimate homicide rate, revealing a different pattern from the two types of felony homicide. None of the predicted hypotheses are supported by these results, although several interesting findings emerge. For example, the death sentence rate has a significant and positive impact on family intimate homicide, consistent with the "brutalization" effect of capital punishment found by Bowers and Pierce. Alcohol consumption has a significant, positive net effect, although this is consistent with the predicted role of consumption as an intervening variable in the southern regional and racial composition/poverty hypotheses; in both cases, the effects that consumption was predicted to eliminate were significant and positive net predictors.

The fourth column of Table 2 gives results for the family other homicide rate. Only one of the predicted hypotheses is supported—the negative and significant impact of the on-site establishment ratio. This finding suggests that as people engage in higher rates of nighttime activity, family other homicides decline as people spend less time at home with family members, thus resulting in fewer homicides among nonintimate family members. Like the results for family intimate homicide, the African American poverty ratio and the southern regional indicator have direct, positive, and significant effects on other family homicide, despite control for alcohol consumption.

Finally, the fifth column of Table 2 gives results for the analysis of the primary nonintimate homicide rate. These results are in some ways similar to those discussed previously for the two primary types of homicide and are in some ways like those for the two types of felony homicide. As was the case for robbery and felony other homicide, states that have both strict control of alcoholic beverage sales and distribution, and also have capital punishment, have lower rates of this type of homicide than do states with one type of control or the other or states having neither type of social control. However, similar to primary intimate homicide, alcohol consumption has a direct, positive and significant impact, as do the southern regional indicator and the African American poverty ratio, the latter effects contrary to predictions. The on-site routine activities indicator, predicted to be most important for predicting the primary nonintimate homicide rate, was not a significant net predictor of this type of homicide.

Goodness-of-fit indicators reported in Table 2 show that the set of hypotheses considered here forms the basis of an effective prediction of these five types of homicide. Explained variances range from just below .5 to a high of .74 in the equation for the family other homicide rate. Chi-square-based goodness-of-fit indicators are relatively poor for the two types of felony homicide, but improve substantially in equations for the three types of primary homicide.

CONCLUSIONS

The results of this study are summarized in Table 3, which shows the results in terms of the important interaction and type of homicide predictions stated in Table 1. These results demonstrate the utility of the theoretical work set forth in Parker concerning the way in which alcohol consumption and its regulation affect homicide and the relationship between alcohol, homicide, and the causes of homicide. Among the hypotheses discussed in Parker, the impact of poverty on homicide was found to be enhanced in combination with above average rates of alcohol consumption, particularly for robbery and felony other homicide rates. The social control hypothesis, in which the combination of capital punishment and strictly regulated alcoholic beverage systems was predicted to lower rates of homicide, was also supported in three of the five types of homicide considered here. The death sentence and low rate of consumption interaction hypothesis was also found to be supported in the case of robbery homicide, an important finding for a number of reasons. Robbery homicide is in some ways the most "rational" type of homicide considered here, because it occurs during an economic crime. However, the effect of the death sentence rate on even this type of homicide is nonsignificant. Thus this finding in support of a deterrence-based hypothesis may give a clue as to why

Table 3
**Summary of results, interaction and
intervention hypotheses, and derived predictions**

Theoretical Perspective	Prediction for Homicide	Effect Stronger for Types of Homicide	Results Summary	Hypothesis Supported
Economic deprivation	++	Robbery; other felony	Robbery (++) Other felony (++)	Yes
Subculture: Southern	0	Family intimate; family other; primary	Family intimate (+) Family other (+) Primary (+)	No
Subculture: African American	0	Family intimate; family other; primary	Family intimate (+) Family other (+) Primary (+)	No
Social control: tolerance for formal control	—	Robbery; other felony	Robbery (—) Other felony (—)	Yes
Social control: deterrence	—	Robbery; other felony	Robbery (–) Other felony (0)	Mixed
Routine activity	+	Primary; robbery; other felony	Primary (0) Robbery (0) Other felony (0)	No

Note: see Table 1 for symbol key.

most research fails to find support for deterrence hypotheses; the relatively high rates of substance abuse, both of alcohol and other legal and illegal drugs, may in fact be the reason that in the face of ever increasing criminal penalties for violent crimes, such crimes have not shown corresponding declines.

Considering alcohol consumption as a potential cause of homicide has also yielded additional benefits. Despite the pessimism expressed by some, alcohol consumption had direct effects on two of the three types of primary homicide analyzed here. Alcohol consumption should become a regular part of models designed to analyze homicide rates, especially because these findings occurred in the context of models that contained measures of poverty, the southern region, and racial composition. The failure of the on-site routine activities indicator may also be important in showing the limitations of this theoretical approach; until these results, almost every test of routine activity theory has had nothing but positive results.

Finally, like a number of recent studies on violent crime, the importance of race-specific measures, both dependent and independent, is revealed by the fact that despite controls for consumption and the other major causal factors in homicide included in the analysis, the African American poverty ratio was a significant predictor of all three types of primary homicide rates. It would be particularly interesting to include this variable along with alcohol consumption in an analysis of African American homicide rates; the process in which consumption intervenes between African American poverty and homicide might be more pronounced for African American homicide rates than for White rates.

A further test of this hypothesis would be greatly facilitated by a measure of African American alcohol consumption rates; no such measure is currently available at the state level. It might be possible to estimate the African American fraction of the total consumption rate, using a combination of national and local surveys.

Finally, these results underscore the importance of theoretically driven research in which interaction effects are specifically examined. Much research in criminology and sociology in general can be characterized as an attempt to find the intervening variable in causal processes. In this case, the hypotheses of this type were not strongly supported.

CHAPTER 4

Types of Murder

The general public knows the various types of murder by such terms as mass, serial, sexual, juvenile, domestic, and stranger. Each term has derived its meaning primarily from the popular news media. Unlike theories that focus on the causes of crime, the types of murder have not been classified empirically by those who should, namely behavioral scientists and criminologists. In fact, no credible source has defined these terms. Consistently throughout professional journals, definitions of these words appear haphazardly and with different meanings depending on the author's preference.

MASS AND SERIAL MURDER

Until thirty years ago, mass murder referred to any murder event in which more than one murder was committed at the same time by the same person. Mass killers, like Charles Whitman in the Texas Tower, James Ruppert of Ohio, and Howard Unruh of New Jersey, were highlighted on the front pages of most major newspapers. The Federal Bureau of Investigation defines mass murder as the killing of four or more victims at once, but without any apparent empirical basis. They add to the typology confusion by declaring that the killing of two victims at once is a double murder and, consequently, the killing of three people at once is a triple murder.

Since the early 1980's, definitions of serial murder have also reflected what any particular author arbitrarily declared. Fox and Levin in their book, *Mass Murder*, place serial murder as a sub-category of mass murder. Many contemporary references, including those which cite the FBI definitions, refer to serial murder as three or more victims killed over time and mass murder as a category unto itself. It's only in the 1990's that the FBI has diminished the confusion by defining serial murder as two or more victims killed over time, the definition most police investigators have used anyway, despite the FBI's earlier efforts to create an official definition of serial murder.

A killer like Patrick Kearney, a hospital nurse who committed euthanasia on over 40 elderly people in a hospital setting, frequently appears as an example of a serial murderer in the popular media and professional journal articles. For the purposes of this work, the killings of Patrick Kearney are more appropriately classified as a multiple murder (viz. a multiple-victim murder). We use a more classical and conventional definition of serial murder, one that is consistently held among most serial murder investigators: *the killing of two or more people over time with the primary motivation of sexual assault.*

The opening essay in this section, Dietz's "Mass, Serial, and Sensational Homicides," describes the sensational nature of mass and serial homicide in today's society. Those types of murder are always noted on the front pages of local newspapers and on the 5 o'clock TV news, and their stories are the focus of best selling books and novels.

The second paper, by Stote and Standing, addresses an important question about both serial and mass murder—has there been a relatively recent upsurge in these types of murder? There is certainly a common public belief that there are more multiple-victim killers in contemporary society than in the past. Their careful research shows that there is no indication of a specific swing toward serial and mass murders. Rather, they have increased only as much as the overall homicide rate.

A team of British psychologists, Canter, Missen, and Hodge, examine the characteristics of an international sample of hundreds of serial killers in their paper "Are Serial Killers Special?" Again, the common belief, as well as much of the academic literature, that supports the view that serial killers are abnormal, flawed individuals who are even substantially different from ordinary killers, are called into question. They conclude that serial killers are *not* so special.

An important aspect of understanding serial murder is the motivation of the killer. The last paper in this section, "The Serial Murderer's Motivation: An Interdisciplinary Review," offers explanations from the sociological, psychological, and biological perspectives. It should be noted here that these are "explanations" based on motivations identified with other types of criminal behavior that have been studied empirically. An in-depth, scientific study of the motivations of serial killers has never been undertaken.

SEXUAL MURDER

Sexually-motivated murder comprises only about five percent of the known motivations for murder, but occupies more than its share of space on the front pages of newspapers and in the minds and fears of the public. The sexual psychopath's characteristics have been the main focus of attention when studying such sexually-motivated serial killers as Ted Bundy, The Hillside Stranglers, and John Wayne Gacy. As noted above, sexual murder is an important feature of serial murder. The central question regarding sexual murder is, are all sexual murderers capable of serial murder? To illuminate this question, we have included papers from different fields of emphasis.

The paper by Geberth and Turco, an experienced detective and psychiatrist, respectively, examines the extent to which apparent sexual components in a murder case are characteristic of "classic" serial murder. They examined over 300 cases of serial murder, with the objective of examining the extent to which criteria of antisocial personality disorder and sexual sadism are evident, in order to assess the proposition that serial killers are "psychopathic sexual sadists."

We have waited over twenty years for improvements in what is known about sexual killers. Grubin, a forensic psychiatrist, presents an insightful discussion of the components of sexual murder. His data were gathered from his experiences with British sexual killers, but, as you will quickly realize, these killers mirror their American counterparts. The reader will also notice that the sexually-motivated serial killer's characteristics are very similar to those who are caught after one murder. The question, then, is: Will a single-victim, sexual murderer kill again, and if convicted, should he be released from prison to kill again?

JUVENILE MURDER

Juvenile murder has a twofold meaning. It has been used to refer to anyone under the age of eighteen who has killed someone else or who is a victim of murder. One paper focuses on the juvenile killer, the other on the juvenile victim. The first is representative of the multitude of psychological studies about kids who kill. Most juvenile killers range in age from 14 to 17 years, with most in the 16 to 17 age category. Rarely will you find anyone under 12 years old who chooses to kill another human being.

Unfortunately, there is a small group of predatory criminals who prey on children, abducting them and then killing them. The paper by Weis, Keppel, and

Hanfland, "Profile of a Predator," is drawn from the only national study of child abduction murder by strangers. It focuses on the personal and social characteristics, motivations, and post-offense behavior of the killers in over 600 child abduction murder cases. This type of killer is described as a predatory, sexually-motivated, social marginal who has a history of crime and violence, most of it directed toward child victims.

DOMESTIC MURDER

Domestic violence definitions are as varied as the number of state and federal agencies that are funded to control or study domestic violence. Some states have enacted laws relating to domestic violence to prevent greater violence after the police leave an initial call to a family fight. Many of the domestic violence laws are pointed at violence between marital partners. And the meaning of domestic murder is, likewise, ambiguous. Goetting delineates the differences between women and men who kill their spouses. In many circles, domestic murder has been split into another category called "spousal murder." In the study by Straus, "Domestic Violence and Homicide Antecedents," he reveals those causative factors that propel family members to kill family members in domestic conflicts.

STRANGER MURDER

The act of killing by strangers is the most misunderstood type of murder. Because the media highlight that type of murder, it gives the impression that they occur frequently. The reality is that less than 20 percent of all murders occur between strangers. More important, the primary motive for stranger murder is not sexual assault, but robbery. The final paper in this chapter is Zahn and Sagi's exceptional study, "Stranger Homicides in Nine American Cities." At the heart of their study is robbery, the most frequent motivation for stranger murder.

—————

Mass, Serial and Sensational Homicides

PARK ELLIOTT DIETZ

My task today—that of conveying information about three understudied classes of offenses—compels me to speak to you without the quantitative cloak of social science with which I would prefer to dress this gruesome subject. Of necessity, I rely on case examples and fragments of research, because no quantitative data are available on most of the topics addressed here. My approach is to describe the elements common to these three classes of offense, to describe examples of each class, and to suggest the subtypes most often observed for each class.

COMMON ELEMENTS OF MASS, SERIAL AND SENSATIONAL HOMICIDES

Mass, serial and sensational homicides all evoke a high degree of publicity. The predictably high publicity attending these crimes is among the motives of their perpetrators. Like John Hinckley, offenders in each of these categories see headlines as one of the predictable outcomes of their behavior, which they pursue in part for this purpose. The American preoccupation with celebrity is no secret. A recent issue of *TV Guide,* the weekly index to American preoccupations, offers the following network and cable experiences: *Eye on Hollywood, Hollywood Insider, Star Search, Celebrity Chefs, Lifestyles of the Rich and Famous,* and *You Can Be a Star.* The celebrity industry is of such compelling interest to the public that it has even spawned a secondary industry of celebrity "news" programs in the form of *Entertainment This Week*, *Entertainment Tonight*, *Showbiz Week*, *Showbiz Today* and *This Week in Black Entertainment*. In the midst of such strong cultural endorsement of the goal of becoming famous, only one show, *Fame*, regularly carries the message that becoming famous requires work.

Offenders vary in the degree to which publicity is a motivator. At the one extreme are those whose suicide at the conclusion of the offense precludes seeing themselves in the news, but even they, like other suicides, may expect to witness the aftermath. (Some suicide notes refer to the joy the decedents expect to experience in watching the mourners suffer.) At the other extreme are those who enhance the probability of apprehension for the sake of publicity. Lust murderers whose victims have not been discovered have been known to return to the scene of the murder and move the body to insure its discovery. Having followed newspapers and media broadcasts carefully and heard nothing of the crime, the killer is disappointed. His crime is incomplete: a woman died, but the community escaped. By insuring publicity for the crime, he reveals his desire to terrorize the community as a whole.

Publicity can aid or hinder the investigation of these crimes. The fingerprint identification of Richard Ramirez and broad dissemination of his photograph as a suspect in the Nightstalker murders led to an earlier arrest than might otherwise have been expected. Unknown to the public, however, are those instances in which politicians under fire from the press to produce results in headline cases have revealed investigative information and police strategies, thereby hindering investigations or destroying promising operations.

Mass, serial and sensational homicides are understudied because the frequency of these offenses is too low to permit the desirable research—requiring interviews, primary source documents or both—to be conducted within a single institution or city. That difficulty is remediable only through collaborative research or centralized data collection. The latter approach is the basis for work at the FBI Academy's Behavioral Science Unit, where studies of lust murder, sexual homicides, autoerotic fatalities and other low-rate phenomena have already been completed, and within the unit's recently developed National Center for the Analysis of Violent Crime, which Mr. Geberth discusses. Headquartered at the FBI Academy in Quantico, Virginia, the Center makes it possible for low-rate offenses to be studied by systematically interviewing offenders and collecting offense, offender and victim data from the nation as a whole. Current studies focus on serial killers and serial rapists.

Mass, serial and sensational homicides tend to elicit a premature conclusion that the offender must have been mad. The tendency of the press, public, and public officials to regard such individuals as mad solely on the basis of their crimes reflects widespread needs to attribute such behavior to alien forces. As with the mythical werewolves and vampires and the demons of the middle ages and of contemporary Pentecostals, the attribution of unacceptable human conduct to possession by madness reassures the believer that people like him are incapable of such evil. Even those with a greater factual basis for judgment—such as evaluating clinicians, jurors and judges—are at unusually high risk of drawing the wrong conclusions in these cases.

MASS MURDER

The term "mass murder" has been applied to events as dissimilar as the Whitman Texas Tower shootings, the series of lust murders attributed to Jack the Ripper, the mass poisonings in Jonestown, the current abortion policy in the United States, the Holocaust and the Bhopal industrial disaster. Without taking issue with any of the political or metaphoric uses of the term, I would adopt a narrower meaning for purposes of behavioral science approaches to criminal homicide. For these purposes, mass murder should be defined as offenses in which multiple victims are intentionally killed by a single offender in a single incident. For the definition to be operational, we must also specify the meanings of "a single incident" and of "multiple victims."

In specifying that the killings occur within a single incident, we seek to distinguish mass murder from serial murders in which murders occur in separate incidents, sometimes separated by long time intervals and great distances. Thus, both time and distance are possible limiting criteria for the concept of a single incident. With respect to time, we can achieve the desirable distinction by limiting mass murder to offenses occurring within a 24-hour interval. With respect to distance, however, we encounter greater difficulty. Surely a murderer who kills half the requisite number of victims at one site and then travels directly to another site where the other half are killed ought to qualify as a mass murderer, as would one who killed a sufficient number of victims while shooting from a moving vehicle or traveling aboard a train, ship or aircraft. I would therefore ignore location or distance in the definition of mass murder.

The number of victims required for the designation mass murder is a more arbitrary matter, but one with important implications for the characteristics of the class so defined. For example, the proportion of mass murder victims who are relatives of their killers is determined by the number of victims required in the definition. If the cutoff point is set at 10 or more victims killed in a single incident, the cases become rare and the majority of victims are strangers, as in Charles

Whitman's Texas Tower killings (two family members and 14 strangers killed, 30 others wounded) and James Huberty's MacDonald's massacre (21 strangers dead, 19 wounded). Indeed, by this definition the only mass murder in American history in which most of the victims were family members was the killing of 13 people in Wilkes-Barre, Pennsylvania, by former prison guard George Banks. Banks had had children by four women and lived with three of them and their children on a rotating basis, making it possible for him to kill enough family members to set such a record.

Given the small number of cases in which there have been 10 or more victims, the cutoff point should be fewer than 10. One way to select a lower cutoff point is to choose one that will maximize the number of cases defined as mass murder (so that there will be enough to study) while minimizing the odds that the cases so defined will be murders occurring as a byproduct of other crimes (which would otherwise confound research findings). The Bureau of Justice Statistics publishes annual survey data on criminal victimization other than homicide, including the number of victims per incident up to the category of four or more victims. For all violent criminal incidents in 1983, 88.5% involved one victim, 8.9% two victims, 1.7% three victims and 1.0% four or more victims. A threshold for mass murder of three victims would exclude the possible byproducts of more than 95% of violent crimes. A threshold of five victims would exclude the byproducts of more than 99% of violent crimes. We can take notice of these data without unnecessarily restricting the definition if we define mass murder as the willful injuring of five or more persons of whom three or more are killed by a single offender in a single incident.

Paranoid symptoms of some kind have been evidenced by all of the men who have killed 10 or more victims in a single incident in the United States. James Huberty and his wife, who routinely abused one another, treated their home as an armed fortress. Mrs. Huberty once threatened neighbors with a gun, and James Huberty, an admirer of Hitler, blamed President Carter for the economic conditions that caused his unemployment. Depressive symptoms predominate among those who kill more than three but fewer than 10 victims in a single incident. The commonest of these cases are those in which depressed men, sometimes drinking excessively, kill their families and sometimes themselves. In any community in America, ask an old timer if there's ever been someone in the area who has killed his whole family. More likely than not, he'll say something like this: "There was a time this man I knew, a regular guy—hard worker, wife, kids, went to church— sudden-like up'n killed the whole family. They say he was drinkin' real heavy, but I always thought he must've went crazy. Seems he even killed the dog. It was all in the papers, but then you never heard no more about it." These cases rock the local community and create lifelong memories that something terrible happened there. In the less migratory years of American history, the houses where such things occurred sometimes came to be regarded as haunted—if they were not burned to the ground, as was George Banks' house. If these cases make the national news, it is a brief appearance. Even when the man does not kill himself, thereby allowing for his story to become public at the trial, these cases do not capture the national imagination. I think they are regarded as family business. They are too close for comfort.

The Banks case is familiar to me and less familiar to most than Whitman or Huberty, so I describe it briefly here as an illustration of mass murder. Although he had served time for armed robbery, Banks was employed as a correctional officer at the correctional facility at Camp Hill, Pennsylvania. One day he told coworkers that he was thinking of shooting inmates from the tower. He was taken to a mental health center which recommended that he take some time off from work and referred him to a mental health center in his home town of Wilkes-Barre. He went to the mental health center with one of his women, whom he presented as his wife without acknowledging his unusual living arrangements. He did not become engaged in treatment.

Unbeknownst to those who evaluated him, Banks had long been fascinated by weapons and survivalist themes. In his home was a collection of *Soldier of Fortune, Commando* and *Gung Ho!,* three magazines devoted to the imagery of warfare and glamorous portrayals of military and paramilitary weapons. He had purchased equipment and materials of the kind advertised and promoted in these magazines, including a Colt AR-15 semi-automatic rifle, the civilian equivalent of the M-16 and a manual offering instruction on the crafting of silencers in home workshops. Over the years he had devised plans for the protection of his family in the event of warfare or civil disaster. While working in a state job that gave him access to such information, he had charted the locations of mountain sites of fresh water where he might take his family in the event of disaster.

One day in September 1982 Banks drank alcohol at a party, napped, awakened and ordered the two women with whom he was then living to retrieve his AR-15 magazine and ammunition from the two locations at which they were stored. He had them dress him in a fatigue-like jumpsuit, and he donned a Civil War cap. In the course of the next few hours he shot and killed eight women and children in his home, killed one bystander in the street and wounded another, commandeered a car at gunpoint, and drove to a trailer where another of his women and their son lived, and at the trailer killed their son, the woman, her mother and another little boy who was spending the night. He eventually locked himself in an abandoned house and held the police at bay for seven hours before surrendering.

Five psychiatrists testified at his trial, including Dr. Robert Sadoff, and each of us diagnosed him as suffering from paranoia. The defense and its witnesses contended that Banks' paranoia caused him not to know the nature and quality of his act and not to know that what he was doing was wrong. The state and its witnesses contended that Banks' behavior and statements at the time of the offenses showed that despite his psychosis, he knew the nature, quality and wrongfulness of his acts. Banks himself testified—over his attorneys' objections—that the police had tried to make it look bad for him by moving the bodies and inflicting additional gunshot wounds on his victims. He even circulated to the jury the full-color scene photographs of his dead children—which the defense had managed to keep out of evidence—to prove to the jurors the depravity of the police conspiracy. Banks was convicted and sentenced to death.

I have seen no typologies of mass murder that I think warrant review. The mass murderers of which I am aware have fit unambiguously into one of the following three categories: *Family annihilators,* usually the senior man of the house, who is depressed, paranoid, intoxicated or a combination of these. He kills each member of the family who is present, sometimes including pets. He may commit suicide after killing the others, or may force the police to kill him. *Pseudocommandos,* who are preoccupied by firearms and commit their raids after long deliberation. James Huberty carried a rifle, a shotgun, and a pistol and hundreds of rounds of ammunition. Charles Whitman hauled to the top of the tower a footlocker containing a rifle, a shotgun, two pistols, a revolver, 700 rounds of ammunition, food, water, a radio and toiletries. The murderer may force the police to kill him. *Set-and-run killers,* who employ techniques allowing themselves the possibility of escape before the deaths occur. Examples include those who bomb buildings or vehicles on which they are not traveling, who set arson fires, or who tamper with food or products, as in the Tylenol poisonings. While the offender may have one or more particular victims in mind, he considers the indiscriminate killings of bystanders an unimportant cost in relation to the enhanced probability of escape provided by these methods. As with bombings generally, the most common motives are anger or revenge toward people or institutions, but extortion, insurance fraud and ideological motives are also observed.

SERIAL MURDERS

As in the case of mass murder, the most homogeneous class of offenders results from a definition limited to the most extreme cases. Those who kill others in 10 or more separate incidents, without exception, kill more strangers than familiar people. This fact is almost tautologic, however, because it is nearly unthinkable that one could kill 10 family members, one at a time, without someone noticing a pattern. Serial killers who are able to reach the 10-victim level are able to do so because they manage not to be caught, which generally requires either careful execution and an acceptable public persona (as in the John Wayne Gacy case), or high mobility (as in the case of Lucas and Toole), or both (as in the case of Ted Bundy). While every serial killer is mentally disordered, nearly all are psychopathic sexual sadists, and few, if any, are psychotic. Psychotic offenders rarely have the wherewithal repeatedly to escape apprehension.

In contrast to murder generally, the victims of serial killers are most often strangled, beaten or knived, rather than shot. I attribute this to the greater intimacy of contact weapons over projectile weapons, reflecting the sexual component of the killers' motivation. Like other sexual sadists, they often pursue occupations and hobbies that bring them in contact with injured and suffering people or people over whom they have control. Ambulance services, hospitals, mortuaries, correctional facilities, police agencies and specialized military combat units prove attractive to them but sometimes have standards that they cannot meet. The single most prevalent job is probably that of a security guard. Their interest in police-related activities and their inability to become legitimate police officers (due to a criminal record, lack of discipline or other factors) reveals itself in such behavior as collecting police paraphernalia, using police badges or equipment to gain access to victims, monitoring police radio frequencies and, most strikingly, inserting themselves into the investigation of their own crimes. Many of the elements common to serial killers are illustrated in a case that has been described in greater detail elsewhere.

A white man in his mid-30s was charged with approximately a dozen murders in several states. His father, whom he had never known, had been executed for murdering a police officer and had also killed a correctional officer during an escape. Shortly before being executed, the father wrote: "When I killed this cop, it made me feel good inside. I can't get over how good it did make me feel, for the sensation was something that made me feel elated to the point of happiness...." Often told of his resemblance to his father, he came to believe that his father lived within him.

His mother, who had been married four times and brought home a succession of short-term extramarital sexual partners, frequently told her son that she had been raped by her father when she was nine. She ridiculed her son's bedwetting, which persisted to age 13, by calling him "pissy pants" in front of guests; he was beaten for the bedwetting and night terrors. For as long as he could recall he had

had recurrent nightmares of being "smothered" by nylons and being strapped to a chair in a gas chamber as green gas filled the room. One of his stepfathers beat him relentlessly. For leaving a hammer outside, he was awakened by this stepfather burning his wrist with a cigar. For playing a childish game while urinating, he was forced to drink urine. When his mother once intervened, the stepfather pushed her head through a plaster wall, after which she, too, actively abused the children. His hostility toward her was unconcealed, as he said: "Sometimes I [think] about blowin' her head off.... Sometimes I wanta' put a shotgun in her mouth and blow the back of her head off...." For years, his favorite sexual fantasy was of torturing his mother to death.

He had been knocked unconscious on multiple occasions and had remained comatose for over a week after a head-injury at approximately age 20. A CT-scan of the brain showed abnormally enlarged sulci and slightly enlarged ventricles. Results of the Halstead-Reitan Neuropsychological Battery and the Luria-Nebraska Neuropsychological Battery were interpreted as showing damage to the right frontal lobe.

He had juvenile police contacts for vandalism, malicious acts, running away and multiple burglaries. Apprehended for lewd contact with a seven-year-old girl at age 13, he was sent to reform school for a year. At age 16 he was arrested for armed robbery. At age 18, two weeks after the birth of his first child, he married the child's mother. Despite subsequent arrests for armed robbery, beating his wife, assault, burglary, auto theft, theft, parole violation and other offenses, he was awarded custody of his daughter after divorcing his first wife. His second and third marriages ended in divorce after he beat his wives, and his fourth marriage ended in divorce for unknown reasons.

After many more arrests and a jail escape, he was eventually sentenced to prison on conviction of armed robbery. He initiated sexual contact with his seven-year-old daughter during a conjugal visit on the prison grounds. Prison records from his early 20s document a psychotic episode with paranoid delusions and suicidal ideation following the death of a brother. After he was paroled from prison he impregnated one woman and married another (his fifth wife). He separated from her after he was released from parole. His second through fifth wives appeared young enough to pass as teenagers.

In his early 30s he lived as husband and wife with his 13-year-old daughter, whom he impregnated. The pregnancy was aborted. He continued to molest his daughter, who reported one of his rapes. He also sexually assaulted one of her girlfriends. He celebrated one of his birthdays by sodomizing his then 14-year-old daughter. Eventually she moved to her grandparents, and he began living and traveling with another woman, who became his sixth wife and his partner in a two-year series of rapes and murders.

His wife knew of his fantasies of torturing young girls and his desire for women he could control and abuse, and she assisted him in each of his known murders by selecting the victim, orchestrating the abduction and concealing the evidence. He beat, tortured and raped his victims, whom he forced to play the role of his daughter in fantasy scenarios that he directed. Although he would not describe this scenario, he did reveal that his favorite sexual fantasy involved the killing of a woman. In the early years in which he employed this fantasy, the woman killed was his mother, which he associated to her having turned his father in to the police after a prison escape: "I was gonna' string her up by her feet, strip her, hang her up by her feet, spin her, take a razor blade, make little cuts, just little ones, watch the blood run out, just drip off her head. Hang her up in the closet, put airplane glue on her, light her up. Tattoo 'bitch' on her forehead...." This fantasy gradually changed and came to include forced sexual activity and other forms of abuse and torture. After his first wife left him, she replaced his mother in the fantasy; eventually their daughter replaced her.

His early victims were all teenaged girls; his later victims included adults. After his initial murders, he again raped his daughter and her friend. They reported these offenses, and an arrest warrant was issued. The offender changed his identity, as he had on previous occasions, using falsified identification papers. A gun enthusiast, he bought and sold various firearms; shortly before his last arrest, he possessed two revolvers, a semiautomatic pistol, a derringer, and a semiautomatic assault rifle. Those of his victims whose bodies have been located died by gunshot wounds or blows to the head. Some of the bodies were still bound.

Masturbation he regarded as shameful, dirty and unmanly. The first sexually explicit pictures he could recall having seen were photographs of his mother with a man he did not recognize. He had never been to an "adult book store" or an X-rated movie "because I didn't want anybody to think I was in that category." He considered *The Exorcist* and *Psycho* influential in his life. He mentioned "sadism-maschotism" (*sic*), but denied that he was sadomasochistic, saying, "sadism-masochism is where you like to be hurt while you hurt, and I don't think that's it. Maybe one half of it, 'cause I think I've been hurt enough." The imagery characteristic of bondage and domination pornography disgusted him: "That ain't me.... The ball in the mouth, the excess rope, I think what they've done is taken a fantasy and overdo it. The mask makes somebody look like out of Mars... You're in a room and a girl walks out with a rubber suit or whip and she's subject to get shot." The covers of detective magazines were the source of fantasy material most congruent with his preferences.

He insisted on representing himself at trial and fired his attorneys. He was sentenced to death for the first two murders for which he was brought to trial. Out of concern for the fact that the state in which he was sentenced is slow to execute its death-row inmates, the citizens of one area in which he had murdered made private contributions to the prosecutor's office in another state known to execute death sentences more rapidly to facilitate his extradition and prosecution there. He currently awaits trial in the second state for additional murder charges.

Highly inflated estimates of the number of serial killers and their victims have appeared in the press. Claims to the contrary notwithstanding, there is no empirical evidence that the frequency of serial killers is increasing or is higher in the United States than in other countries. Improved communications among police agencies, new recognition of the phenomenon, and centralized reporting to the FBI Academy Behavioral Science Unit in recent years all increase the probability that a series of murders will be attributed to a single offender, leading to increased detection. The true rate of occurrence is not known for any country at any time, so it is not yet possible to study temporal trends or to make international comparisons.

A requirement of 10 murder victims and 10 killing incidents for inclusion in the category of serial killers is good for the purpose of looking at one extreme and conceptually homogeneous group of offenders, but is too high a threshold for certain other purposes, such as alerting law enforcement agencies to a series of crimes in progress or learning why some similar men get caught earlier. Offenders who have killed a smaller series of victims are more heterogeneous. Offenders who have killed five or more victims in five or more killing incidents fall within five categories:

Psychopathic sexual sadists, the type illustrated by the above case history. Every individual known to me who has killed a series of 10 or more victims in 10 or more separate killing incidents has been male and diagnosable as suffering from antisocial personality disorders and sexual sadism. Although these men have oddities of fantasy and worldview that lead some psychiatrists to label them "borderlines," it is my impression that this most often reflects the psychiatrists' unwillingness or inability to face the fact that these men enjoy killing people, as in the older tendency to label men like Albert Fish "ambulatory" or "latent" schizophrenics. Examples include Ted Bundy, Edmund Kemper, Dean Corll, John Wayne Gacy, Wayne Williams and Henry Lee Lucas.

Crime spree killers, who kill repeatedly during a series of crimes motivated by the search for excitement, money and valuables. The most famous cases in this category are those of Bonnie Parker and Clyde Barrow and of Charles Starkweather.

Less familiar examples occur among men who kill repeatedly during robberies less sensational than those of Bonnie and Clyde.

Functionaries of organized criminal operations, including traditional organized crime (La Cosa Nostra), ethnic gangs, prison gangs and street gangs. Contract killers, illegal mercenaries, and terrorists are subsumed by this category.

Custodial poisoners and asphyxiators, most of whom are caretakers of the debilitated, of children or of both. On ample evidence, physicians and nurses have been suspected of serial killings of patients in hospitals in New Jersey, Michigan, Texas and Ontario, occasioning some fascinating applications of hospital epidemiology. The recent cases in which cause of death has been established have involved the administration of curare-like agents, digitalis compounds and insulin, but analogous cases that would pose greater postmortem detection problems may involve administration of potassium or other electrolytes or various forms of mechanical asphyxiation. Similar cases have occurred in the homes of babysitters, foster parents and, of course, the baby farms of 19th century England.

Supposed psychotics, who claim to be acting at the direction of command hallucinations or under the influence of compelling delusions. I temper this category with the word "supposed" because I have not yet had occasion to examine a truly psychotic serial killer and because of the contested facts in some of the best known cases. For example, David Berkowitz (known as Son of Sam or the .44 Caliber Killer) was said by some commentators to have maintained that he killed his six murder victims at the direction of a dog and in keeping with the interpreted content of delusions of reference, but by others to have been malingering mental illness. Angelo Buono (the Hillside Strangler), John Linley Frazier and Herbert Mullin are additional examples.

SENSATIONAL HOMICIDES

With respect to the topic of sensational homicides, I am not bound by any customary use of the term. Perhaps a suitably operationalized definition would be that sensational homicides are those that have a higher than chance probability of receiving coverage in tabloids such as the New York *Daily News* and the *National Enquirer* or in the detective magazines such as *Detective World, Front Page Detective, Homicide Detective, Official Detective Stories* and *True Detective.* My impression, based on informal scanning of the headlines of tabloids for the past two years in connection with my research on celebrity victimization and a formal study of detective magazines, is that five types of homicides are overrepresented among those selected for feature-length articles in these periodicals. These five types may fairly be said to represent the five types of sensational homicides other than mass and serial murders: sexually sadistic homicides involving sexual assault, torture, kidnapping or sexual mutilation; homicides followed by significant postmortem injuries, such as decapitation, amputation or disarticulation (for example, the case of Ed Gein) or involving vampirism or cannibalism (for example, the killings by Albert Fish and by Richard Trenton Chase); homicides with elements of occultism, satanism, cults or religious ritual (for example, the Manson Family killings); homicides in which either the offender or the victim is socially prominent or famous (for the example, the killings by Fatty Arbuckle and by Claudine Longet and the murders of Ramon Novarro, Sal Mineo and John Lennon); and infanticide, matricide and patricide.

The first three of these categories are demonstrably overrepresented among the homicides described in detective magazines. Dr. Bruce Harry, FBI Supervisory Special Agent Robert R. Hazelwood and I recently reported the results of a content analysis of 18 detective magazines. In a random sample of articles, we found that 38% of homicides involved torture of the victim, a far higher percentage than is true of homicide generally. Killings of strangers, binding and gagging of victims, stabbings and sexual mutilations accounted for a much larger share of the homicides described in these articles than of homicides as they occur in the United States. Women victims in the articles were almost universally sexually assaulted prior to being murdered, whereas fewer than 2% of all homicides occur in the context of felonious sexual conduct. One fourth of the cover headlines promoting articles in the magazines we studied included some sexual reference, such as: "Grisly Revenge of the Gay Ripper," "Riddle of the Dead Nude in a Closet," and "Fiend Who Raped and Hung His Victims."

Mutilation themes often appear on the cover of detective magazines, even though the proportion of all homicides involving mutilation is low. Illustrative titles include, "Mutilations on Mulberry Street" and "Texas Manhunt for the Knife-Wielder who Mutilated the Pretty Artist in Lovers' Lane." Suggestions to the potential buyer that an article may be about vampirism or cannibalism are highlighted, as in "The Holy Vampire Drank His Victim's Blood," even though most of the titles that suggest these acts refer to something else (for example, use of the word "roast" to refer to burning of victims in "Roast A Family of Six"). Elements of occultism or satanic ritual, even if irrelevant to the crime, are stressed in the promotional material, as in "Case of the Voodoo Hit Man" and "Satanist Smiled as He Snuffed the Snitch."

Homicides of and by the famous and prominent do not occur with sufficient frequency to support the sensational journalism industry. The industry adapts to this through three strategies. First, those cases which do occur are worked and reworked until the last reader has tired of the story. Second, misleading headlines are used to suggest that such a murder has occurred, when the article really refers to the death of a contract, the celebrity's dog or the character portrayed in a new film. Third, noncelebrity cases are used to illustrate the hungered-for themes that overly successful people meet bad ends, powerful people abuse their power to harm others and even the most respected members of the community are evil. Two examples from detective magazines in our study are: "Church Sexton Electrocutes Bride" and "Trail of the Slaying Deacon."

Infanticide, matricide and patricide occur with sufficient frequency to be standard fare for tabloids, but are curiously unexploited by detective magazines, perhaps because the cases are so readily solved that there is not much of a detective story to unfold or because the sexual elements are too subtle. The central element uniting these homicides with the other types that are regarded as appropriate grist for the sensationalism mill is that they are emotionally arousing, which is by definition the essence of sensationalism. Given the frequency with which the public is bombarded with sensational events of all kinds, one might wonder how anything remains emotionally arousing. We should be thankful that even as so many of our cultural sensitivities erode, we at least do not experience extinction of our aversion to cruelty, mutilation, the diabolical, the fall of angels or the taking of life between parent and child.

SUMMARY

Mass, serial and sensational homicides share several common features. First, they occur with a frequency too low to permit the ordinary research habits of psychiatrists or criminologists to elucidate their characteristics. Second, they typically evoke a premature and sometimes erroneous conclusion that the offender must have been mad. Third, they generate an extreme degree of publicity, leading to unusual media influences, both beneficial and detrimental, on criminal investigation, the processing of cases through the criminal justice system and the behavior of offenders, would-be offenders and others. The most common varieties of mass murder can be described as family annihilators, pseudocommandos and set-and-run killers. Serial killers can be classified as psychopathic sexual sadists, crime spree killers, functionaries of organized criminal operations, custodial poisoners and asphyxiators and supposed psychotics. While the possibilities for sensational homicides through innovations might seem limitless, the varieties observed in the sensational press involve sadism, mutilation, the occult, prominent offenders and victims, and infanticide, matricide and patricide.

Serial and Multiple Homicide: Is There an Epidemic?

ROBERT STOTE & LIONEL STANDING

In the last few years, considerable public attention in the USA has focused on dramatic reports of serial and multiple homicide, which are commonly taken to mean a number of murders by one person, committed respectively over a period of time or all at the same time. Various recent highly publicized cases in the mass media have each involved several dozen victims, the ultimate being the nearly two hundred victims attributed by some investigators to Henry Lee Lucas, and acknowledged by him. Egger discusses this case and the credibility of the victim count.

Books on the topic of serial murder have recently appeared with sensational titles, involving terms such as "epidemic." These works, and corresponding newspaper reviews, may give the impressions that these forms of murder are largely a new phenomenon that is unique to our times, or at least have recently shown a sudden increase in frequency, as compared with the past. The opposite viewpoint has not been publicized.

While there is evidence that the absolute numbers of US serial homicides and multiple homicides have increased sharply over the last 200 years, the question remains open regarding these rates when corrected for population increases, and possible increases in all types of homicide over time.

The notorious problems of reliability and completeness for crime statistics are well known. These are particularly acute in the case of serial homicide. The compilation of the Uniform Crime Reports is based on victims rather than cases, which makes them useless in studying serial homicide and multiple homicide. There is also the problem of linkage blindness which often prevents officials from seeing that several crimes over a period of time and often in different regions are related, and the problem of people who simply disappear. Altogether it is not surprisingly that different writers have given estimates for the number of currently active serial murderers ranging from 30 to 500.

Accordingly it was decided to survey the entire issues of the major US newspaper for each of two decades (1951–1960 and 1981–1990), to obtain a listing of serial homicide and multiple homicide for these years. As with many archival data, these figures depend on the accuracy of police reports and the possible vagaries of newspaper editing. However, the sensational nature of serial/mass murder renders it unlikely to be ignored in the media. It is hoped frequencies in the two decades, assuming that the factors involved in the reporting and editing of news stories remain fairly constant over time.

METHOD

The authors took the 1951–1960 and 1981–1990 sections of the *New York Times Index* as the most trustworthy available database with a national coverage, and examined these sections in detail for reports of possible serial homicide and multiple homicide, using the keyword "Murder," with cross-references to new sub-headings where warranted.

Serial homicide was defined here as two or more homicides over a period of time, in different incidents. Homicides were excluded if they involved robbery for gain or for personal revenge, etc. Multiple homicide was defined as involving two or more people deliberately killed in a single incident. Data were compiled on the basis of number of cases, rather than the number of victims. Population estimates for the years involved were taken from the *Statistical Abstract of the United States (1980/1991)*.

RESULTS

1. The data show a sharply higher absolute level of serial homicide for the 1980's than the 1950's. The absolute level of multiple homicide is also higher in the 1980's (see Table 1).

2. Comparing types of murder, there are more multiple homicides than serial homicides, within each decade. The total of both represents about a quarter of one percent of total homicides, in either decade.

Table 1
Frequencies of serial, mass and all homicides (cases),
with rates per 100,000 population, 1951–60 and 1981–90

	1951–60		1981–90	
	Number	*Rate*	*Number*	*Rate*
Serial	39	.024	139	.059
Mass	168	.102	374	.158
Total	207	.126	513	.217
Total homicides per decade	78041	47.3	206842	87.1

3. There is no consistent trend over time for either type of crime within each decade.

4. Corrected for population, the 1980's serial homicide rate is 2.48 times higher than would be predicted from the rate in the 1950's. The multiple homicide rate for the 1980's is 2.65 times higher than expected from the 1950's.

5. All other homicides (i.e., non-serial and non-multiple) have increased 1.84 times in this period.

6. Corrected for the increased rate for (other) types of homicide, the observed rates of serial and mass killing in the 1980's are close to the expected rates (calculated as the 1950's rates multiplied by 1.84). For serial homicide, the observed rate in the 80's is 0.059 per 100,000, which is slightly higher than the expected rate of 0.044. However, for multiple homicide, the observed rate of 0.158 per 100,000 is slightly lower than the expected rate of 0.188.

7. Predictions of serial homicide and multiple homicide rates in the 1980's made from the growth of all violent crime, 1955–1985, would be almost twice as high as the predictions made using the increase in general homicides, thus greatly exceeding the rates actually observed in the 1980's.

8. The data of Hickey, reanalyzed to yield rates per 100,000 of population, show an increase of 4.5 fold in serial murder during the last 50 years, for cases. The twofold increase (1950–1988) is roughly parallel to the growth in other homicides during this time. It is likely that Hickey's data in fact underestimate the rates for the earlier years; modern technology and information sharing imply less linkage blindness today (the failure of the authorities to see the connection between a series of victims).

DISCUSSION

The present data indicate that an overall increase in serial homicide and multiple homicide has occurred from the 1950's to the 1980's, but this is attributable to the rise in population and in homicide generally. On a per capita basis, the frequencies of serial and mass murder also are within the bounds of US historical trends for the last 200 years.

It should also be noted that data complied by Gurr show three great waves of violent crime starting in 1850, 1900, and 1960, rather than progressive growth over time. Even more strikingly, Gurr found that the rate of homicide in Great Britain has dropped by a factor of more than ten to one, from the thirteenth century to the present.

Though this does not detract from the seriousness of the social problem involved, it therefore appears that serial and multiple murder today represent not an abrupt "epidemic," but rather a proportionate reflection of an increase in violent crime and homicide in general. We can find no sign of a suddenly emerging social pathology. Public concern is warranted, but should not be focused excessively on these forms of homicide.

On the basis of the broad trends viewed in the hundreds of cases examined here, which fit with the general picture presented by other commentators, there is a characteristic pattern for serial homicide and multiple homicide.

The author's view of the cases examined is that serial homicide typically involves white males (20–40) who repeatedly kill young women or girls (but males if the killer is homosexual), by hand or knife, and generally mutilate them. Weeks or months elapse between successive kills. Killers are "respectable," not overtly criminal, psychotic or retarded, and seem quite normal to associates.

Multiple killers are males of comparable age and occupational level, who again kill innocent victims. However the pattern is quite different, since the killer (often a hostile or aggressive individual, though some are over-controlled) here performs a spectacular public act of self-and-other destruction. Also, the victims are of all ages and both genders (often acquainted with the killer), guns are employed, and the killer frequently commits suicide on the scene.

Though it is the more common social problem, the mass murderer represents a fairly understandable momentary personal crisis, in comparison to the insatiable killing drive of the serial murderer. The mass murderer is driven to a cathartic act of retribution by life-pressures, rage, and personality problems. Serial killing, by contrast, represents a remorseless pursuit of sexually based gratification, a perverse form of ritual hobby. Both types of homicide are "senseless" in that material gain is not involved. Neither act resembles the broad pattern of homicide in general.

Are Serial Killers Special?

DAVID CANTER, CHRISTOPHER MISSEN & SAMANTHA HODGE

In 1936 H. Russell-Wakefield contributed a chapter to a book on "The fifty worst crimes of the last Hundred Years." The chapter was about Henri Landru, a Frenchman who was guillotined in 1922 for the murder of at least 11 women. In the chapter H. Russell-Wakefield refers to ". . . serial murderers such as Landru who made homicide their career. . . ." and in so doing established a term that gained currency over the subsequent 50 years. Along the way, the US law enforcement agency that usually only has jurisdiction in homicide cases if they can be shown to be part of a series, the FBI, started to take a special interest in the characteristics of men who had committed a number of sexually related homicides.

Through their many lectures worldwide the FBI Behavioural Science Unit encouraged the notion that serial killers were a special breed of offenders that required special systems to be set up to investigate their crimes. A centralized record of violent crimes (VICAP) was established in the USA with the intention of dealing with this "growing menace." A new clutch of "experts" was also hatched to "profile" this specific set of criminals. Furthermore, despite the lack of any systematic assessments of the efficacy of VICAP, or its Canadian descendant VICLAS, and the luke warm support for "profiling" as anything more than a useful second opinion, international examination of the possibility of introducing centralized record keeping systems and "profiling teams" into many other countries and even of cross-national networking of the systems is currently being actively considered. It is therefore essential to consider the nature of serial killing and to question what the most appropriate investigative strategies are for dealing with it.

THE DATA SET

Defining a "serial killer" simply as anyone who has committed more than two murders over a period of time, perhaps more technically "episodic homicides," Missen has collected and collated information over a ten year period on serial killers world-wide, from every source he could identify. He has examined newspaper reports, accounts in books and magazines and, where ever possible directly contacted the law enforcement agencies involved in investigating these crimes, By cross checking information from various sources it has been possible to build dossiers on 3,532 serial killers from over 30 countries, who were identified from 1860 up to the present day. Of course, much of the information in the sources available has to be treated with caution, accounts of child rearing practices in the killers' infancy, or the personalities of his parents may owe more to journalistic imagination than to actuality. But other information such as the locations in which bodies were found, the date of birth of the offenders, their convictions prior to the murders, and many of the details of how the murders were carried out, which tend to be a matter of public record, are found by corroboration to be reasonably accurate. This *corpus* of information is the basis for the present study.

ARE SERIAL KILLERS ON THE INCREASE?

By examining the frequencies of serial killers for each decade since 1860 a clear picture of their changing numbers can be established. By far the largest number of such murderers have been found in the USA, 2,617 and so it is appropriate to consider the frequencies for that country as the bench mark against which to examine the situation for the UK. The figures make it clear that serial killers increased in number steadily until the 1970's when the rate of increase climbed considerably. Assuming that about 70% of all the USA serial killers we have identified (i.e. 1,832) have been active in the last 25 years, that means that in any year about 73 (1,832/25) are active.

There can be little doubt then that the phenomena that has grabbed public attention and become the staple diet of Hollywood thrillers has indeed increased considerably over the last quarter of a century in the USA. However, there has been no similar comparison for other countries. For although it has been possible to identify 164 serial killers in the UK since 1860 the trend in these numbers is directly analogous to those for the USA. It is worth noting also that the 144 serial killers for France follow a similar pattern over the same period. The 165 such offenders for Germany also show the recent upsurge, but the figures for the earlier part of this century do not show the same steady increase, presumably because of the chaos of two world wars.

Using parallel calculations to those for the USA indicates about 5 such individuals a year may be active in each of Britain, France and Germany at the present time. This is an important number, but it does need to be set against the current annual homicide rate for England and Wales of around 600 a year.

RELATIONSHIP TO GENERAL HOMICIDE FIGURES

When looked at in isolation the inflation in serial killings over the last two decades can lead to the vision of the emergence of an entirely new form of killing and killer that requires new forms of investigation to combat it. Yet comparison with the general pattern of homicides is most instructive. The frequencies of homicides for the USA and for Britain have been broadly on the increase since the middle of the last century. Indeed the figures follow each other closely with there typically being 40 US homicides for every British one. As many have noted the frequency of murders grew in both countries during this century up until the second world war when they dipped to the levels of the previous century. Then they started to climb at an increased rate up until the present day.

What is clear from the homicide frequencies is that the number of serial killers closely parallels the number of homicides in general. In order to gauge some index of the relationship between serial killer and general homicide figures the number of serial killers for every decade since 1860 were compared with the number of homicides in the first year of that decade. Although these comparison are only approximations and various other calculations can be made the relative similarity of the year on year homicide figures and the close correlation between the number of serial killers and the numbers of their victims does mean that however these comparisons are calculated they give similar results.

Up until the second world war, in broad terms in the USA, for every 800 homicides that took place in a year there was one serial killer active in the decade in which that year fell. In Britain the figure is closer to 400 homicides for one serial killer in the decade. After the second world war the rate increases, for the USA to 250:1 and for the UK to 100:1.

These figures deserve much closer attention and more detailed analysis, but three points can be drawn from them as they stand at present: 1) The serial killer rate is a direct reflection of the general homicide rate; 2) The proportion of serial killers to homicides has increased since the second world war; 3) Most curiously of all, the proportion of homicides in the UK that can be related to serial killings is distinctly higher than in the USA.

At first sight these comparisons may appear to challenge the view that the USA is a more violent society. In such a context if it is assumed that Serial Killing is seen as an indicator of "motiveless" violence against strangers then it would have been expected that a higher proportion of killings would have been committed by these extremely "alienated" individuals. However the figures do make sense and accord with the existing understanding of the differences between US and UK murder if serial killing is seen as little different from conventional murder. Within this perspective a distinction needs to be drawn between violence and those particular aggressive acts that result in murder. If aggression breaks out within a violent society where weapons and demonstration of coercive control is more acceptable then there is an increased probability that aggression will lead to a killing, but those forms of aggression that are at the heart of premeditated murder may be similar in most societies. If such is the ease, then serial killing will be a standard, albeit small, component of this form of aggression. This leads to the proposal that there are a higher proportion of serial killers per homicide in the UK than the USA because there are fewer outbursts of emotional violence that turn into murder in the UK than in the USA.

CHARACTERISTICS OF THE VICTIMS

In order to consider the characteristics of serial killers a sub-sample of 217 US serial killers was identified on which reasonably full information was available. This allowed examination of the relationship with their victims that existed prior to the murder. The common assumption is that homicide in general grows out of a pre-existing relationship between victim and perpetrator but that serial killers are essentially killing strangers in a more random way. The analysis shows that 68% of the victims were known to the offenders prior to the offence. In 45% of the cases the victim knew the offender either as an acquaintance, associate, neighbour or family member. Indeed it is common for at least one of the victims of a serial killer to be a close associate or family member.

These bald figures hide a whole range of scenarios from offenders secretly targeting victims, giving unknown victims lifts as hitch-hikers, accosting prostitutes, taking casual acquaintances home and then killing them, through to killing their own tenants and family members. The central point though, is that this range of contacts is typical of all murder. Perhaps one difference is that there is a tendency for the victims to be female, unlike homicide in general where the majority of victims tend to be male, but as Hickey has pointed out, from his sample of 200 offenders 48% killed both males and females, figures paralleled in our sample. So there is no obvious focus for the targets of serial killers that clearly distinguish them from other forms of homicide, other than a tendency towards more obviously vulnerable victims and people who also tend to have less obvious direct contact with the offender. They can therefore be looked upon as typical of those murders in which an obvious culprit may not be immediately apparent and which therefore pose some special difficulties of investigation.

CHARACTERISTICS OF THE OFFENDERS

If there are no very obvious distinguishing characteristics of the victims of these murderers or of their relationship to them, other than that they may be such as to make the crimes more difficult to solve whether or not they were the victim of an offender who had not killed anyone else, then are there some obvious, special aspects of the offenders that mark them out from other offenders?

Age

Wilson and Herrstein show that the peak age for violent crime in the USA in 1980 was in the late teens to mid-20's. There are many sociological and anthropological explanations of these results, but when compared with the 205 serial killers for whom we have details of their age at the onset of their series it can be seen that the distribution does overlap considerably with that well attested "dangerous age." The mean value of 28 years is little older than would be anticipated purely on the general figures for violent crime, but it does accord with the dominant age of British murderers as reported by the home office and is actually very close to the mean of 32 years old for 239 murderers in a sample of British cases that initially proved problematic to the investigators.

Criminal History

Furthermore, serial killers are clearly drawn from the general criminal population. Three-quarters of our 217 US serial killers had previous convictions, 24% of the full sample having convictions for burglary and theft, 22% for violence and 17% for drug related offences with 16% having history of sexual offence convictions. Many of them had started their life of crime early, with 45% having a juvenile criminal history. Thus although the emphasis of their crimes is more towards violence and sexually related crimes than would be true for the criminal population as a whole they are certainly not law-abiding citizens prior to their killings. They thus share much with the criminal fraternity that finds its way into other forms of serious crime.

Family Circumstances

The domestic setting out of which they grow also is typical of most criminals. In a quarter of the cases it was known that the offender's immediate family had a history of criminality. Their families were typically dysfunctional in a variety of recognizable ways, an absent father, frequent moves, institutionalized mother known for her promiscuity, and much violence in the family (48%). These experiences left a sizable minority of these men physically handicapped (18%), scarred (13%) or with a stutter or similar disorder (13%). Indeed, as has been noted for many sub-groups who are involved in violent crime, a high proportion (45%) had suffered some serious head injury or other physical trauma at some point in their life prior to killing. This seems to reflect their life-styles rather than being a distinct cause of their crimes. They relate to the high proportion (64%) who had been physically or sexually abused during their childhood, many by family members (48%).

Educational History

The disruptive early years are also shown in the educational background of these offenders. The great majority of them (87%) dropped out of school many without any qualifications at all (78%), some illiterate (10%). However, the general pattern does not indicate completely incompetent, "drifters." A notable proportion of them (37%) had held some sort of skilled manual occupation and a handful (4%) had professional level occupations. In fact court assessment of the IQ's of these individuals do indicate that a remarkable proportion (56%) scored in the high range (above an IQ of 120). This does not support the popular belief (implicitly fostered by FBI claims) that these offenders are often near geniuses, indeed many of them are of the low intellectual ability associated with most criminals.

It is therefore reasonable to think of these murderers as often drawn from the more capable levels of the criminal population. They are less likely to be the totally incompetent offender who gets caught through obvious "errors," but they are certainly not some sort of "super-criminal" as favored by Hollywood. Many of them (47%) drink heavily, or take drugs (29%) around the time they commit their crimes and thus cannot be regarded as studious intellects set on some determined mission.

DISTANCES OFFENDERS TRAVEL

Competent criminals may be the simplest way of describing people who manage to kill a number of times without getting caught. But the picture does not emerge of some very special sub-group that will only be detected by means not normally available to police investigations. Of particular importance in these considerations is the locations in which the crimes are committed and the relationship this has to the location at which the offender is based around the time he is carrying out his offences.

The idea that criminals are active at locations that bear a distinct relationship to where they live has been established for common crimes such as burglary for a considerable time. However the possibility that this is also true for more serious, serial crimes of an apparently impulsive nature such as rape has only recently been established. Deriving from that work has been the hypothesis that offenders have a natural *range* over which they operate. This is likely to be a function of their resources and capabilities. The simplest test of this hypothesis, proposed by Canter and Gregory was that offenders would tend to live within an area defined by a circle that was drawn with a diameter either end of which were the two offences furthest from each other. In their study of 45 serial rapists living in the area of London they found that 86% did indeed live within the area defined by the circle.

Taking the sample of US serial killers for whom there was reliable geographical information on 121 it was found that the same "circle hypothesis" accounted for 87% of the offenders. There is thus strong evidence that serial killers, like other criminals, tend to operate in an area that can be defined in relation to where they live. The difference between such offenders is therefore also likely to be the scale of area over which they operate. This further hypothesis that there is some range that is typical for any particular offender implies that there is strong relationship between both the maximum distance the offender is likely to travel and the minimum distance. This can be directly tested and does indeed show strong correlations for the US 121 serial killers and for the 29 UK serial killers on whom information was available.

These results add further support to the view that these are not highly devious, specially gifted offenders who roam far and wide, but that like other offenders they seek out targets a comfortable distance from their base within the limits of their own resources and capabilities. The average distances involved also show how the scale of these ranges is a reflection of the life style mobility of the country.

These findings are important both for individual investigations and for policy decisions about the systems that should be put in place in preparation for any major investigation. They suggest that intensive local effort should be the prime basis of any investigation with only minimum recourse to national or cross-national systems.

IMPLICATIONS FOR INVESTIGATIONS

Serial Killers have been considered in terms of their general statistical patterns. There has been no examination of the patterns of their behaviour nor any speculation on their "motivations." It is quite possible that such considerations would reveal these offenders both to be distinguishable from criminals at large and also to have large variations between each other. This, however, is mainly of relevance to the explanation of these crimes and is only of relevance to investigations when the details can be shown to require different approaches to conducting an enquiry than is true for any other murder enquiry. At present the results indicate that serial killers do indeed pose particular demands on police investigators but this is mainly because like many other murderers they have found ways of killing that make detection difficult.

The figures presented have been largely drawn from US serial killers, however, making allowances for the increased violence and mobility of the USA there do appear to be many parallels with the British situation. Indeed, there is some intriguing evidence that serial killing may be some what more typical of UK murder in general than US murder in general.

There is a clear sense in which serial killers emerge because one-off [single-victim] murders are not solved. The results of this study also demonstrate there is a great deal in common between serial murderers and those people who have yet to commit a second or third murder. They are of a similar age, kill a similar range of victims, and come from similarly dysfunctional family and criminal backgrounds. As a consequence the best strategy for tackling serial killings is to ensure that the investigation of all murders is as thorough and effective as possible. As in all types of crime a small sub-group of offenders do travel some considerable distance and therefore are particularly challenging to an investigation. But the results of the current study indicate that the majority have a preferred range of operation that tends to be within a few miles of where they live. Rather than set up special systems that are likely only to be relevant once such individuals have been identified and therefore most of the time will be of little value, it is better to use established findings to identify whether or not an offender falls into this sub-group and then put resources specifically into that investigation.

The Serial Murderer's Motivations:
An Interdisciplinary Review

DANA D. DeHART & JOHN M. MAHONEY

The recent deluge of media attention to the phenomenon of serial murder has led many to believe that the serial murderer is a "new breed of killer"; these crimes, however, have existed throughout the ages. Historical examples include fifteenth-century child murderer Gilles de Rais, nineteenth-century serial killer "Jack the Ripper," and Wisconsin necrophile and cannibal Ed Gein who was apprehended in the nineteen-fifties.

The present article is intended to offer a summary and expansion of diverse and often conceptually-elusive motivational explications of serial murder. Contemporary theoretical perspectives concerning serial murder will be drawn from a variety of disciplines, and integrational approaches will be emphasized.

A RECENT SURGE?

The misconception that serial murder is unique to contemporary times may be the result of a recent surge in the incidence of serial killings. Jenkins notes that only two cases of murders of ten or more victims are known in the United States between 1950 and 1970, in contrast to 39 known multiple murder cases since 1970. In the late 1980s, the Federal Bureau of Investigation estimated that there were about forty-five multiple murderers active in the U.S. at any one time, and estimates of the number of annual U.S. serial murder victims range between 1 percent and

25 percent of the total number of homicide victims, with some sources estimating as many as 5,000 serial murder victims each year.

Despite the social impact of serial murder, many rudimentary aspects of the phenomenon remain unresolved, and existing research containing serial murder is not easily accessible. Although a number of theorists have addressed etiological and motivational aspects of serial murder, a psychological literature search of *serial murder* currently yields only two citations. Considering the paucity of research, further theoretical and empirical exploration appears warranted.

A DEFINITION OF SERIAL MURDER

For the present authors' purposes, a serial murderer is defined as an individual who murders two or more victims over a period of time which entails breaks or "cooling off periods" between some victims; the length of these intervals may range from a few days to several years.

Serial murder, in part, is defined by the nature of the killer's motivations. The murderer's motive, often sexual in nature, has an *intrinsic* locus and commonly involves gratification derived from the act of murder itself. Those individuals who murder in a serial fashion, yet whose primary goals are extrinsically derived, seem to be a more heterogenous than homogenous group. Investigation of such killers may be accomplished more fruitfully from an extrinsic primary goal perspective. For instance, murderers who kill as a result of jealous rage (an extrinsic goal) are likely to be psychologically different from those individuals who murder for material gain (another extrinsic goal). The present authors' focus on intrinsic motivation is paramount for exploration of the origins and development of killers' motivations. For these reasons, such extrinsically-motivated murderers are excluded from the present definition of a serial killer.

Jesse has discussed six motivations for murder, including *elimination, jealousy, gain, revenge, ideological conviction,* and *lust of killing.* For the purposes of the present definition, motives of elimination and of jealousy are not among the serial killer's goals. The killer is not attempting to work for the cause of some group. Neither does the killer seek to eliminate or retaliate against a specific victim who intentionally or unintentionally provokes conflict or who is a physical threat. The serial killer who wants revenge does not pursue revenge against an individual; the murderer generalizes his or her hatred to an entire category of individuals and retaliates by victimizing that group somewhat randomly. The ideological conviction of the serial killer is, again, intrinsically-derived; the killer acts to achieve his or her own ideals, not to work toward goals sought by exterior sources. The killer's behavioral orientation is expressive, rather than instrumental, with the murderer seeking enhancement of a personal psychological state rather than material gain.

INFERRING MOTIVE

Motives, by definition, are inferred constructs. Several methodological constraints are relevant to inferences made about the serial killer's motivations. Because information about the crimes often must be garnered from a serial killer's personal narrative, reliability of the data may be suspect. That is, in the case of serial murder, as with any deviant behavior, there exist substantial reasons for the murderer to dissimulate his or her account. Some killers deny any involvement in the crimes, while others gradually reveal the nature and extent of involvement apparently to "buy time" while awaiting judicial processing. Additionally, murderers may alter or exaggerate claims for egocentric or status reasons. Due to these reliability and validity problems in assessing the killer's report, motivational inferences may be complicated.

Furthermore, if researchers choose to distinguish between one-victim murderers and serial murderers, ambiguities in scientific and legal classification of serial killers may diminish the validity of data. For instance, even though a serial may be intended, the murderer might fail to actually kill a second victim, and hence, would not be legally adjudicated as a serial murderer. Alternatively, the serial killer may be found guilty of only one murder, though many more victims existed.

It should be borne in mind that any given person may have more than one reason for committing serial murder, and that only general similarities among killers can be drawn because each killer is unique. With these *caveats* in mind, we will explore some hypotheses regarding underlying motives of the serial killer.

PROFILES OF THE KILLER

Holmes and DeBurger describe differences among serial killers with respect to the murderer's behavioral background, victimology, modus *operandi,* and geographic mobility. Based on such differences, the researchers have specified four general profiles of serial murderers, with each of these types deriving from a differing motivational orientation.

Visionary serial killers are typically motivated by psychotic delusions or hallucinations. Herbert Mullin, for instance, was a paranoid schizophrenic who heard "voices" commanding him to kill thirteen people in order to avert natural disasters . In contrast, *mission-oriented* murderers consciously seek to rid society of an "undesirable" group of people. Jack the Ripper's murder of prostitutes, for example, might be construed as mission-oriented murder. Holmes and DeBurger also describe the *hedonistic* serial murderer, who kills for thrills, pleasure, or contentment, and the *power/control* serial murderer, who compensates for a lack of social or personal mastery by exerting control over victims.

These researchers have proposed general profiles of four types of differentially-motivated killers, yet from what sources do the motivations arise? In the quest for hedonism, power, or ideological commitment, how has the serial killer come to defy social mores in order to achieve personal goals? While Holmes and DeBurger provide a convenient nosology of motives, a more extended classification is suggested by examination of theories of deviance and aggression.

MOTIVATIONS FOR MURDER

Personal Motivational Model

Psychophysiological Approaches

The possibility of a biological or genetic basis for serial murder is an unresolved issue at present, however, several biologically-based theories of the phenomenon have been proposed.

Paleopsychology—A recent and controversial model, paleopsychology, postulates that human aggression derives from the hierarchical functioning of sociobiological, ego-psychological, sociological, philosophical, and spiritual influences on the individual. This phylogenetic model asserts that behaviors involving human violence reflect the consequences of a neurologically-regressed pattern of behavior. Bailey's paleopsychological model is an extension of the concept of the *triune brain,* first advanced by Maclean.

According to Maclean's triune brain principle, the human brain consists of three distinct structural components. The most fundamental and primitive structure of the brain is the neural chassis, or Reptilian-complex (R-complex), which regulates maintenance functions in the body, such as breathing and consciousness. The limbic portion of the brain, which encloses the R-complex, regulates subsequently-evolved neurological functions, such as emotions, hunger, pain avoidance, and pleasure seeking. The most advanced component of the triune brain is the cerebral cortex, which, according to Maclean, contributes the human capacity for rational thought and logical analysis.

Bailey has theorized that human action is heavily linked to the functioning of the limbic system and the R-complex. According to Bailey, the behavioral impulses from the more primitive structure of the brain are stronger and more urgent than those of the cerebral cortex; yet, the relative influences of biology, culture, and rational thought may differ depending upon the state of the organism and upon situational factors. Bailey asserts that most individuals engage in phylogenetic regression and progression, and that humans actually have a preference for regressive activities. The human neocortex acts as an inhibitory filter for powerful impulses from the lower brain, and aggression results from deficient or failed neocortical inhibition of basal impulses. The serial killer's behavior, in Bailey's view, arises from a basic reliance upon the functioning of the repetitive and unemotional processes of the R-complex, and from reliance upon the emotion-oriented limbic system. The serial killer, then lacks or fails to respond to behavioral constraints imposed by more advanced neocortical functions.

Bailey posits that the murderer's brutal aggression is an atavistic expression that is reptilian, protoconscious, automatic, and instinctual in nature. Such extreme phylogenetic regression may have origins in 1) abnormality of the murderer's neurological structure, such as genetic abnormality or brain damage, 2) predisposing developmental or environmental factors, such as learned behavior or prolonged physical stress, or 3) immediate situational elicitors, such as intoxication or recent trauma.

Sensation seeking—Another physiologically-based theory that may explain the serial murderer's motivations is that of sensation seeking. The sensation-seeking hypothesis is similar to paleopsychology, in that impulsive behaviors are said to relate to reduced cortical functioning. Certain individuals, called "sensation seekers," are posited to have lower levels of cortical arousal, and hence would have lessened inhibition over lower-brain functioning. Sensation seekers purportedly attempt to "augment" this low level of arousal with a profusion of stimulus-laden activities. Thus, according to a sensation-seeking perspective, the serial killer's state of physiological arousal is such that a high level of stimulation is required for gratification—the killer's antisocial behavior is dictated by stimulus starvation. The murderer seeks the thrill of murder because such activity is stimulating; the excitement of pursuing the victim and the subsequent elusion of authorities serve as motives. There are some circumstances in which serial killers even seem to engage in narcissistic "games" with civil authorities in order to outwit these potential captors in the search for the killer. The still unidentified "Zodiac Killer," for example, teased authorities with generous correspondence, mocking the efforts of law enforcement personnel and including clues regarding the killer's identity.

Hormonal variations—Another provocative perspective on aggression also relates to sensation seeking, but focuses on psychopharmacological variations within the individual. Numerous researchers have found that normal and enzymatic activity corresponds with sensation seeking, dominance, delinquency, and other excessive behavioral tendencies. Particularly, testosterone and a related enzyme, monoamine oxidase (MAO), have been linked to unprovoked violence and victimful crimes. Some researchers posit that these chemicals relate directly to aggression, while others hypothesize that testosterone and MAO merely mediate a relationship between antisocial behavior and sensation-seeking tendencies. Still others suggest that the influence of such chemicals on neurotransmitters, such as serotonin, mediates aggressive behavior. MAO, for instance, affects the serotonin concentration surrounding axon terminals. Because MAO metabolizes excess serotonin between synapses, a deficiency of MAO could result in serotonin surplus, thereby increasing the number of "false" nerve transmissions taking place. Such discharges may facilitate antisocial behavior, in that serotonin has been empirically linked to irritability, impulsiveness, and aggression. Several researchers, however, have considered that MAO activity may simply reflect existing levels of neuro-transmission, and thus relationships between aggression and MAO or MAO's hormonal associate testosterone may be spurious correlates to neurotransmitter-aggression relationships. Nevertheless, heavy concentrations of MAO occupy the brainstem and portions of the limbic system. Hence, hormonal theories of violence are not incompatible with Bailey's paleopsychological model of lower-brain-mediated aggression, but the causal linkage remains ambiguous.

Some theorists have expanded upon hormonal models of aggression via the *organization-activation hypothesis.* This hypothesis states that embryo-logical or neonatal steroid activity influences formation of certain neurological structures. These permanently-altered structures then respond differently to adult hormonal infusion. According to these researchers, both adult hormonal activity and the behavioral responses to such steroid variation are affected by social contexts within which neurological operations take place. Hence, neonatal experiences of certain individuals, combined with learning history and certain adult hormonal variables, may provide a context for murder.

Psychological Models

Psychodynamic approaches—The classical psychodynamic model reflects the principles elaborated by Freud, who believed that human behavior is instinctual, irrational, and unconscious. Freud classified human instincts into two broad categories: 1) life (sexual) instincts, and 2) death (aggressive) instincts. The energies that provide impetus for these instincts purportedly arise from the *Id.* The Id is Freud's term for a basic and unstructured component of personality which functions upon the *pleasure principle,* that is, upon the reduction of pain and the enhancement of pleasure.

Death instincts, or *Thanatos,* are postulated to be driven by self-destructive energies, which are kept in check by survival-driven libidinal energies of *Eros,* the collective life and sexual instincts. Because, according to Freud, Eros blocks direct expression of death instincts, some of the natural Thanatotic energy is left undischarged. In the course of self-preservation, the individual may use unconscious defense mechanisms, such as projection or sublimation, to dissipate undesirable Id impulses. Alternatively, the individual may direct destructive energies outward, with Thanatos being *displaced* and expressed as aggression toward others.

In the "normal" individual, psychic energies from the Id are controlled by the rational Ego and the morally-ingrained Superego. In certain individuals, however, the Ego may lack restraint, and the Superego may fail to develop. if the weak Superego cannot adequately balance irrational Id impulses, the individual becomes what Freud called a "moral invalid," or, in contemporary terms, a psychopath or sociopath. Increasing levels of Thanatotic energy that are free from socially desirable constraint, or that become too great for a weak Superego to suppress, are finally expressed in cathartic eruptions of self-destructive or aggressive behavior.

Other individuals, called *overcontrolled aggressors*, have extreme inhibitions against acting aggressively, and fail to vent Thanatotic energy with sufficient frequency. The energy builds to extreme levels; hence, cathartic energy release for overcontrolled aggressors is often quite brutal.

Thus, according to psychodynamic theory, either lack of or excess constraint of the Id could predispose an individual to severe aggressive outbursts which, for the serial killer, might take the form of murder. After these cathartic explosions of aggression, cyclic processes of energy accumulation and discharge would continue, giving rise to the serial nature of such murderers' aggressive activities.

Although the libidinal energy of Eros is usually expressed independently of Thanatotic energy, sometimes these energies coexist, as *ambivalence,* or fuse, as *sadism.* From a psychodynamic perspective, the sexual nature of the serial killer's motivations would derive from the blending or fusion of Erotic and Thanatotic energies. Support for this theoretical perspective is exemplified in the statements of serial killers such as Joseph Kallinger and Edmund Kemper, who describe mutilation and murder as titillating and climactic components of their aberrant behavior.

Furthermore, past researchers have alluded to the prevalence of contact weapons utilized in serial murder. This physical aspect of the offenses has been attributed to the greater intimacy of contact weapons, exemplifying the sexual component of the killer's motives. Psychodynamic theorists note the sexual symbolism of certain weapons, such as knives, comparing these to phalluses in physical dimension and penetrative ability. Joe Kallinger's descriptions of murder are particularly concordant with these interpretations. "I had only one thing in mind," Kallinger recalled, "...the pleasure of soft spots...the hand thrust the knife into the left side of her neck, once, twice, three times. I had an orgasm."

Freud believed that this blend of sexual and aggressive energies begins as an *unbound* force, but is then invested, or *cathected,* in the instinctual object, that consists of the material or procedural elements requisite for need satisfaction. In *identification,* symbolic objects are substituted for the actual instinctual objects. Such identification would, theoretically, be the source of some serial killers' victim choice. According to Freud, individuals harbor intense hostility toward parental figures. The child, who wishes to destroy the parent, may displace this hostility. The potential killer would then stalk those who were irrationally identified with the hated parental figure. Kemper, for instance, admitted that the individual whom he *really* desired to murder was his mother, and for a long while, Edmund stalked and killed the coeds at a university where his mother taught. After finally mustering the courage to actually murder the ultimate victim—his mother—Kemper promptly turned himself in to authorities.

According to psychodynamic theory, compulsive behaviors such as serial murder arise from childhood psychosexual fixations. Because psychodynamic theorists believe that personality is established early in life and is unchanging, it is suggested that there is no cure for the serial murderer's erratic pattern; the only treatment for such killers is isolation.

Development and learning-theory approaches: Conditioned fusion of sex and aggression—
Another motivational model of sexual homicide emphasizes the principles of conditioning, through which a cognitive fusion of sexuality and aggression may result from traumatic sexual experiences. The individual learns to anticipate sexuality as an accompaniment to violence, and the two types of experiences may be viewed as inseparable. Former police officer and "Sex Beast" Girard Schaefer, who may have been responsible for more than twenty Florida murders, claimed that his sister used to beat him in order to ensure secrecy after forcing him to engage in sexual activity with her. This trauma, although extreme, provides a lucid example for the case of violent sexuality as a conditioned response.

The potential serial killer's association between sexuality and aggression is cultivated and reinforced as violent fantasies result in intense sexual excitement. As Holmes and DeBurger have noted, there usually exists, before and after the murder, a "homicidal fantasy that rewards, reinforces, and restimulates to further homicide."

Presumably, the conditioned response can be reversed either by counter-conditioning or by constructing a "conscience" for the serial killer via the judicious application of avoidant conditioning to violent stimuli. Author Anthony Burgess provides an account of such conditioning in the popular novel *A Clockwork Orange.* Burgess' young thrill killer Alex is apprehended by authorities and subjected to the experimental "Ludovico Technique" in order to dampen Alex's taste for violence. After the conditioning, Alex, a helpless pawn and model patient, is set "free," into society. Like the fictional Ludovico model, the present conditioning model suggests that any deviant pattern of behavior, including serial murder, can be reversed. Thus, the serial killer can be "cured," and, in theory, can be returned to society.

Developmental and learning-theory approaches: A social learning model—One of the most controversial theoretical models of serial murder is based upon the work of Bandura, who has argued that observing violence leads to violent actions on the part of the observer. Subsequently, this theory has provoked a barrage of public concern about media portrayals of aggression, especially that of sexual violence. Several researchers who have exposed males to violent rape scenarios which depict victims as aroused suggest that viewing such material may create less negative attitudes about rape, more of a proclivity to personally commit rape, and more aggression toward females. Whether media portrayals actually teach violent behaviors to "normal" individuals has not been definitively established, but displays of aggression might serve as social prompts for a person's existing urges to commit violence, or may weaken that person's inhibitions against acting on such feelings.

Thus, from a modeling approach, the availability of information about murder may provide potential killers with insight regarding the crime and procedures to avoid detection. Additionally, media attention might provide impetus for "copycat" killings, and depictions of violent sexuality and aggression may increase viewer proclivity to commit such acts due to disinhibition, violence-myth propagation, and perceived reinforcement.

Developmental and learning-theory approaches: Conditioned conscience—Behaviorists have explained aggression as a conditioned response, either as a result of direct or vicarious reinforcement. Such theorists have also explained aggression as a function of *deficient* conditioning, with "normal" behavior being viewed as a result of conditioned conscience. Through consistent social application of punishment, individuals are postulated to eventually anticipate the negative ramifications of deviant behavior. The resultant anxiety response, perceived as "conscience," inhibits aggressive behavior. According to such theories, the serial killer fails to internalize social mores, and hence, lacks inhibitions against aggression.

Learning cultural norms must supersede exposure to those norms, hence, failure to demonstrate ordinary social conditioning may result from the killer's personal alienation. Accordingly, there are indications that serial murderers may be profoundly isolated individuals, who often display symptomatic manifestations of alienation, such as normlessness, meaninglessness, powerlessness, isolation, and self-estrangement.

SOCIOLOGICAL APPROACHES

Containment Theory

A sociological approach which is similar to conditioning models is that of containment theory. Social control theorists argue that various cultural institutions serve to keep individual behavior constrained by social norms. These institutions also cultivate within the individual a buffer against aggressive impulses.

As noted, the serial murderer's isolation may inhibit socialization, and therefore prevent the development of internal buffers. External buffers may not be sufficient sources of social control, as Norris explains, citing the potential serial murderer's apparently improved and "normal" adjustment patterns in correctional facilities. Norris states that because the institution provides the individual with an imposed rigid structure for existence, the lack of that person's internal control is not problematic. This external structure allows the individual to function within the culture's desired constraints and to appear superficially suitable for release into the larger society. When the individual achieves freedom from such external control, however, his or her internal framework fails to suffice, thus, isolation and alienation once again lead to the potential killer's preoccupation with a self-focused mindset.

Ritualization—Fromm noted that two major strategies exist for addressing alienation: an individual may withdraw completely and have minimal interaction with others, or that individual may ritualize behavior. Ritualization is a way in which individuals can react to social forces at a personal level by allowing ritual to become the substitute for social interaction. Such ritualization may provide a framework of predictability for the individual's existence.

Fromm and Maccoby have noted an association between ritualization and a necrophilous tendency to eliminate distinctions between the living and the nonliving. Accordingly, some theorists point to a disregard for the distinction between the living and the inanimate as the source of the serial killer's deviant activity. Such a cognitive deficiency may combine with newfound hedonic and individualistic emphases of Western societies to cultivate the serial killer.

Conflict Theory

Leyton views serial murder as a consequence of social class conflict and frustration. From a conflict theory perspective, the murderer perceives the outcomes of his or her social interaction to be below desired levels. Consequently, the potential killer searchers for alternatives. The individual may choose to isolate himself or herself from the disturbing environment, to attempt to resolve the conflict in some way, or to rebel against the perceived source(s) of conflict.

Some theorists posit that the serial killer simply withdraws into isolation, and that antisocial activity stems from the negative ramifications of this isolation. Leyton, however, contends that the serial murderer chooses the path of revolution. Class oppression, says Leyton, results in the killer's rebellion—a social statement in the form of murder—through which the killer is able to terrorize the community as a whole, and to achieve identity and celebrity. Rebellion is often based upon the killer's inferences of *collective liability,* in which the killer holds an entire class of people responsible for perceived injustices perpetrated by a fraction of class members. From a conflict-theory perspective, the aggressor acts in order to redress a perceived grievance and to maintain social control despite the "unjust" actions of this societal class.

Though Leyton refers to conflict as the serial murderer's *motive,* Ressler, Burgess, and Douglas contend that conflict acts only as an aspect of victim selection—a *justification* for killing. Justifications differ from motives in that justifications are typically attributions made after the action, whereas motives are inferred as existing before the action. The issue of whether victim selection is a result of the killer's motives or of the killer's need to justify murder is difficult to resolve. Research concerning other types of sex criminals, for example, has indicated that many rapists describe "punishment rapes" as apparent justification—yet, that the victim was often being "punished" for an action that took place *after* the rapist's decision to commit rape. Justifications, in which the murderer accepts responsibility for the act but denies that the crime was wrong, may arise from a murderer's *cognitive dissonance* over aggressive impulses. Alternatively, the killer can *excuse* the behavior by acknowledging the reprehensible nature of aggression but denying full responsibility for his or her actions. Justifications and excuses may serve to ease the killer's own dissonance, or may be fabricated in order to appease other individuals. The latter case is termed *aligning action,* by which the deviant attempts to avoid stigma via an account stated in culturally-appropriate terms. One way in which criminals do so is by *denying the victim.* Victims are described as "dirty" women, "sluts," or "whores," thereby pseudo-legitimizing the deviance and somehow rendering the murder more "acceptable."

URBANIZATION AND SERIAL MURDER

There are some indications that urbanization may play a contributing role in the cultivation of sociopathic behavior. Calhoun for instance, demonstrated that sheer population density can induce aberrant behaviors in rodents, noting that densely-populated environments increase the number of social adjustments that the individual must make each day. Calhoun concluded that the resultant stress from social interaction in these environments leads to an increase in pregnancy disorders, disruption of maternal behavior, and higher infant mortality rates. In Calhoun's study, the normal behavior of lab rats was replaced by cannibalism, sexual deviation, pathological social withdrawal and disorientation, and exaggerated sexual and social aggression. According to some theorists, however, apparently "dysfunctional" behaviors would actually lead to restoration of optimal population density via the elimination of some individuals from the overcrowded environment.

Milgram also addresses asocial manifestations of "adaptive" responses to over-crowding. He contends that the profusion and diversity of inputs experienced in dense environments may induce a sense of stimulus overload. The individual may be unable to process all inputs fully, and must cope by establishing a cognitive filtration of inputs. In such environments, low priority inputs may be disregarded, social relationships may become more superficial, and the individual may respond selectively to the needs of others. This might result in impaired cognitive functioning, inattentiveness to social norms, reduction of social responsibility, and indifference to the discomfort of other persons. This hypothesis of social apathy and empathic deficiency is consistent with Fromm's characterization of mechanized society as the "ultimate death and decay." Thus, from these sociological perspectives, a recent increase in serial murder may have been impelled by cognitive and social dysfunction which derives from the negative characteristics of urbanized culture.

Although institutions might develop to compensate for some social functions that become neglected in an impersonal society, some individuals may continue to experience alienation and isolation. Increased mobility and division of labor allow for exposure to a plethora of divergent and contradictory value systems, thereby rendering internalization of a single normative system less likely and exaggerating the potential killer's sense of failed integration into society.

Another way in which urbanization and technology may contribute to the problem of serial murder is through facilitation of the serial killer's elusive abilities. Social dysfunction may proliferate due to a lack of cohesion and intimacy in urbanized environments, that would, presumably, hinder external monitoring of deviant behavior. In addition, serial killers now benefit from increased geographic mobility, and the dense depersonalization of urban contexts intensifies anonymity. The serial killer, then, may stalk and murder a victim and escape unscathed in this "society of strangers." Ironically, technological advances that possibly facilitate the serial killer's random victimology are also responsible for the increasingly rapid detection of serial murder provided by breakthroughs such as the Violent Criminal Apprehension Program "VICAP," a nationwide computer network which helps to link police forces exploring similar cases of violent crime.

INTEGRATIONAL MODELS

The BSU's Motivational Model

Researchers from VICAP's Behavioral Science Unit (BSU) have developed a motivational model of sexual homicide which integrates psychosocial forces and physiological factors that might lead to serial murder. According to the model, the source of the serial killer's deviance is an ineffective social environment, in which the child is not provided with adequate social bonding or guidance. The formative events of the child may be riddled with unresolved trauma, causing sustained emotional or physiological arousal in the child in the absence of appropriate structure. The child may develop a diminished emotional response, from which Fromm's ritualization and necrophilia may emerge. Alternatively, if the trauma ceases, the child may develop behavioral responses in order to maintain the level of arousal to which he or she has become accustomed. This process would then result in a need for arousal analogous to that of the sensation seeker.

Children who experience such trauma may then develop antisocial or asocial personality traits and distorted cognitive processing as coping mechanisms. According to BSU researchers, the behavioral manifestations of these coping responses could intensify alienation by distancing social contacts. Additionally, the individual may create defensive responses within other persons, thereby eliciting antagonistic feedback which would propagate the negative development of the potential killer. Eventually, the individual's development would be so distorted that escalating aggressive and violent responses would evolve.

Norris' "Disease" Model

Another motivational model of serial murder which integrates biological factors with environmental influences has been described by Norris. In addition to innate genetic or neurological anomalies, Norris notes a number of environmental factors that may contribute to the phenomenon of serial murder. Child abuse and negative parenting, Norris states, may lead to the individual's loss of sense of self; initial antisocial or asocial personality characteristics may arise from this deficiency. Further damage to the individual's functioning may result from chemical imbalances induced by alcohol and drug use, prolonged malnutrition, and poisoning from environmental toxins. Norris posits that head injuries, which, like malnutrition, may result from sustained abuse, could cause damage to aggression-related neural regions, thereby intensifying the potential killer's dysfunctional behavior. Norris explains that the serial murderer suffers from a painful "disease" that is generationally-transmitted, either genetically or socially. The physical discomfort is beyond the killer's own control, and the serial murderer actually wishes for death in order to end his or her own suffering.

Norris presents some provocative case studies in support of this argument for biological and environmental interaction in the origins of serial murder. He states that most serial killers who are given PET or CAT scans show damage to the limbic region of the brain, and that evidence of cobalt or lead toxicity are regular features in chemical analyses performed on serial killers. Furthermore, the familial relationships of serial killers such as Joseph and Michael Kallinger (father and son), Angelo Buono and Kenneth Bianchi (cousins), and Henry Lee Lucas and Bobby Joe Long (alleged distant cousins) would support Norris' contention that serial murder is a chromosomally-related disorder. However, Norris' does not provide rigorous explanations of the research from which his conclusions are derived. Hence, theorists should exercise caution in embracing Norris' conclusions. Nevertheless, he has offered a provocative hypothesis that deserves further exploration.

CONCLUSIONS

One of the more disturbing aspects of serial murder is that virtually everyone is at some risk. Even cautious and circumspect persons are not safe from a serial killer; the victims need not provoke or even be acquainted with the killer. Such physical and emotional threats imposed by serial killers increase the urgency of coherent theoretical and empirical analyses. BSU researchers have noted that understanding the psychosocial nature of serial murderers may aid in identification and apprehension. A number of motivational theories are relevant to exploration of serial murder, but readers are cautioned not to place excessive explanatory potential on any one theory. Individuals differ, and the motivational dynamics of these killers are, in all likelihood, diverse. Integrational approaches, such as those of Norris and of the BSU team, seem to be the most theoretically fecund. These frameworks allow for a number of contributing motivational factors and allow flexibility for individual differences, yet are relatively comprehensive, delineated, and articulate. Continued empirical and theoretical investigation of serial murder would benefit from interdisciplinary approaches which allow for consideration of genetic, neurological, psychological, and social influences upon the serial killer.

Antisocial Personality Disorder, Sexual Sadism, Malignant Narcissism, and Serial Murder

VERNON J. GEBERTH & RONALD N. TURCO

PSYCHOLOGICAL AND PSYCHOSEXUAL PATHOLOGIES

There is frequent reference in the media to the apparent "craziness" of serial murderers. This cannot, however, be taken to imply that the offender is psychotically disordered; cases such as Joseph Kallinger, a diagnosed schizophrenic, as described by Schrieber is an exception. There are researchers who suggest that serial murders are not the product of major mental illness but more a matter of free will and conscious choice. Ritter analyzed 27 well-known serial murder cases, drawing upon information from secondary sources. Ritter held that high dominance needs and psychopathy were the most important traits toward an explanation for serial murder behavior. She decries major mental illness as an adequate explanation for this behavior, and suggests that serial murderers choose their avocation.

Levin and Fox focus on the concept of psychopathy as integral to the personality structure of the serial murderer. Psychopathy does not provide an adequate explanation of serial murder. Without doubt, not all those with antisocial personality disorder will kill; nor are all serial murderers psychopaths.

Brown refers to several diagnostic categories that may be considered in addition to antisocial personality disorder. He states that most serial murderers are diagnosed as either personality disorders (antisocial and sadistic personality disorders) or suffering from some form of sexual disorder, a small percentage are diagnosed with a psychotic illness and that some, both psychotic and not, have been found to have an organic disorder. Brown contends that "most serial killers display obsessive-compulsive features in the commission of their crimes and that probably the only uninvestigated DSM-III-R category which applies to these persons is multiple personality disorder."

Leibman states that serial murderers are ego disharmonious, dissociating themselves from their actions. Another way of describing this behavior could be that it is ego-syntonic.

According to the research of Ressler and Burgess, 81% of the 36 sex murderers consumed pornographic materials; 72% demonstrated fetishistic behavior such as stealing, wearing, or masturbating with women's undergarments; 71% engaged in voyeurism. Other activities included sadomasochistic bondage, bestiality, making obscene phone calls, frotteurism, and coprophilia. Because the majority of these subjects were serial killers, these results suggest a variety of sexual deviations existing among serial murderers. The degree to which sadism was present as an element in the behavioral repertoire of the subjects is not clear. Sadistic behavior was noted in the childhood histories of these offenders. The authors report that the early aggressive behaviors of the subjects were first acted out against animals. The sadistic behavior then extended beyond animals to other objects and included peers. The sexual aggression becomes established in the child's mind and is reinforced in ritualistic play with other children. The patterns of aggressive arousal first acted out in play are later directed towards people. In his recently published book on serial murder, Ressler went into more detail about the childhood and adolescence of the serial murderers in his 1986 study. All had come from dysfunctional families and experienced a "childhood of violence." Half of the sample had a history of mental illness in the family and half had parents that were participants in criminal behavior. Nearly three fourths (70%) came from alcohol or drug-abusing family environments. Emotional abuse was common to all of the murderers and some were also physically abused. As adolescents, violent sexual fantasies were the precursor to later violent behavior. As adults, all were sexually dysfunctional and unable to sustain consensual adult relationships. Ressler felt that the combination of inadequate socialization, violent fantasies, and the precipitating incident served to push these men "over the line" of acceptable behavior.

ANTISOCIAL PERSONALITY DISORDER

The concept of a disorder whereby an individual persists in antisocial behaviors throughout his/her lifetime, although seemingly having no guilt about it, has a formal documented evolution that spans nearly two centuries. Pinel first observed and documented a group of patients who behaved in impulsive and self-destructive ways yet evidenced no defects in reasoning ability. Another among the early denotations for this cluster of socially objectionable behaviors was Prichard's notion of "moral insanity." The idea of a diseased "moral faculty" to explain criminal behavior formed the central position in much of the debate of the nineteenth century. The German psychiatric community spoke of "psychopathic inferiority," leaning toward a physical basis for the disorder. Kraepelin, in successive editions of his psychiatric text, from 1887 to 1915, developed the theory of psychopathy in terms of degenerative moral structure, biogenic in its origin. Similarly, Lombroso ascribed moral insanity to the "born criminal" whom, he believed, suffered from a variant of epilepsy.

Meloy attributes Birnbaum with introducing the term sociopathy to the literature to describe the disorder as the product of social learning in a deficient formative environment, thus emphasizing a psychogenic basis. Freud noted that "among adult criminals we must no doubt except those who commit crimes without any sense of guilt, who have either developed no moral inhibitions or who, in their conflict with society, consider themselves justified in their actions."

Cleckley describes 16 traits symptomatic of the psychopathic personality. In this clinical picture is included evidence of poor judgment, irresponsibility, and lack of remorse or shame, as well as the recognition that the psychopath can be charming and successful. Reich speaks of the psychopathic character type as one who is self-assured, sometimes arrogant, elastic, energetic, and often impressive in his bearing. Notable to Reich was an absence of reaction formation on the part of the psychopath to his openly aggressive and sadistic behaviors. McCord and McCord focus on impulsivity and aggression in an emotionally isolated individual who seeks to fulfil his craving for excitement without being inhibited by social norms or personal conscience.

Kernberg refers to malignant narcissism, a form of antisocial personal disorder. In this syndrome, ego pathology is characterized by four factors: Narcissistic personality structure (disorder), overt antisocial behavior (passive or aggressive), manifested by sadistic cruelty (with murder as its most extreme form), egosyntonic aggression, or sadism (a source of pleasure—accepted and rationalized against the normal prohibition that most persons have against sadism, and a reprojection of primitive persecutory superego features in the form of paranoid tendencies). The sadism is characterologically integrated and justified by a chronic sadistic arrogance. The reprojection of the primitive persecutory superego features may be characterized by classifying others as suckers, fools, or dangerous enemies.

Meissner has enlarged our concept of paranoid projection to encompass this facet. According to Meissner, "The theory of the paranoid process is an extension of the theory of internalization, particularly concerning itself with those forms of internalization that have pathogenic potential."

With serial murderers, we find the pathological self-love, the lack of object love, the superego pathology, and especially the general sense of emptiness and dissatisfaction. These people are nonaffiliates. There is an impoverishment of internal life in these nonaffiliates as the result of their having devalued what they have not received from others. In other words, there has been a failure of early object integration. The internal world of object relations is destroyed. Psychological development does not occur using normal methods of identification and empathy. There is a sense of aloneness, emptiness, and meaninglessness in life without the pleasure of learning or empathic bonding. One finds a stimulus hunger, the need to be entertained, and stimulated to replace the missing world of object relations. The perpetrator of serial murder expects the victim to perform and initiate certain behaviors to "entertain" him. A sadistic perversion of the learning experience may occur when the murderer dissects or otherwise mutilates the victim.

According to Markman, the primary ingredient missing from the sociopath's psyche is conscience. Psychopathy, sociopathy, and antisocial personality disorder are not generally classified as a mental illness per se, but rather as a disorder of character. McCord notes that psychopathy has been defined either as a discrete category whereby one is considered either psychopathic or not, or as representing a point along a continuum in which some individuals occupy an extreme position relative to specific traits and behaviors.

Hare presented the emotional and interpersonal traits of psychopathy in "Without Conscience—The Disturbing World of The Psychopaths Among Us." Hare described what he referred to as the "Key Symptoms of Psychopathy," which he divided into two groupings: The emotional/interpersonal consisting of glib and superficial egocentric and grandiose, lack of remorse or guilt, lack of empathy, deceitful and manipulative, shallow emotions; and social deviance consisting of impulsive, poor behavior controls, need for excitement, lack of responsibility, early behavior problems, and adult antisocial behavior. According to Hare, psychopaths have "...a deeply disturbing inability to care about the pain and suffering experienced by others..." We find this perspective consistent with observable data and applicable to investigation. Hare's work best represents our point of view.

In an examination of psychopathy as a concept, Blackburn notes the interchangeability of the terms sociopath and psychopath, particularly in the American literature. He notes the particular influence of Robin's work in its explicit equating of "sociopathic personality" with violation of social rules, on the determination of DSM-III-R criteria for antisocial personality disorder.

According to the DSM-IV, the essential feature of the disorder is to be found in patterns of irresponsible and antisocial behaviors beginning in childhood or early adolescence and continuing into adulthood. Lying, stealing, truancy, vandalism, initiating fights, running away from home, and physical cruelty are typical childhood signs. In adulthood, the antisocial pattern continues and may include failure to honor financial obligations, maintain consistent employment, or plan ahead. These individuals fail to conform to social norms and repeatedly engage in antisocial behaviors that are grounds for arrest, such as destroying property, harassing others, and stealing. Often these antisocial acts are committed with no seeming necessity. People with antisocial personality disorder tend toward irritability and aggressivity, and often become involved in physical fights and assaults, including spouse and child beating. Reckless behavior without regard for personal safety is common, as indicated by driving while intoxicated or getting numerous speeding tickets. Frequently, these individuals are promiscuous, failing to sustain a monogamous relationship for more than one year. They do not learn from past experiences and tend to resume the same kinds of antisocial behaviors they were punished for. They lack feelings of remorse about the effects of their behavior on others and may feel justified in having violated others.

SEXUAL SADISM

Money defines a paraphilia as a "condition occurring in men and women of being compulsively responsive to and obligatively dependent upon an unusual and personally or socially unacceptable stimulus, perceived or in the imagery of fantasy, for optimal initiation and maintenance of erotosexual arousal and the facilitation or attainment of orgasm." Paraphilias are thus sexual deviations marked by persistent sexual arousal patterns in which unusual objects, rituals, or situations are required for sexual gratification. They are understood to reflect psychosexual disorder in which the preferred or exclusive means of sexual gratification is deviant. Unusual or bizarre imagery or acts are necessary for sexual excitement. According to the DSM-IV, such imagery or acts tend to be insistently and involuntarily repetitive and generally involve either a preference for use of a nonhuman object for sexual arousal, repetitive sexual activity with humans involving real or simulated suffering or humiliation, or repetitive sexual activity with nonconsenting partners. Nine paraphilias are currently recognized in the DSM-IV. These are fetishism, transvestic fetishism, voyeurism, exhibitionism, sexual sadism, sexual masochism, pedophilia, zoophilia, and frotteurism. Meloy defines sexual sadism as "the conscious experience of pleasurable sexual arousal through the infliction of physical or emotional pain on the actual object."

The object of our research is to examine the extent to which criteria for antisocial personality disorder and sexual sadism appear to be met in a sample of serial murderers, and to examine the validity of frequent references in the serial murder literature that put forth serial killers as "psychopathic sexual sadists."

METHODOLOGY

Persisting variations in definition provide problems for researchers who must be mindful that specific cases may or may not qualify as serial murder depending upon the particular definition used. Although there has been a number of scholarly works on the broader subject of multiple murder, the initial challenge for this study was to isolate a specific population—serial murderers who violated their victims sexually—from a literature based upon research using different operational definitions of serial murder.

For the purposes of this research, the authors will focus on only male offenders and will use the operational definition of serial murder as follows: *A serial murderer is an individual who, either alone or with a partner is suspected of killing at least three people, over a period of time with time breaks between the murders.*

Sample of Cases

The authors compiled a list of serial murderers within the United States on the basis of a computer search of newswire services through the Nexis system specifying the key term "serial murder." This search revealed the names of all serial murderers reported by the AP and UPI newswire services from the earliest available data until December 1993. Records of the F.B.I.'s National Center for the Analysis of Violent Crime (NCAVC) were also examined for additional serial murder cases.

Finally, the authors supplemented this list with other known cases from personal records derived from information given one author in his capacities as homicide consultant, crime scene photographs, official police reports, and police files as well as from files related to our previous research on the subject of serial homicide from 1988 to 1993. This includes psychiatric as well as law enforcement data.

Those cases that met the operational definition of serial murder in this study provided the authors with a base population of 387 serial murderers with various motivations.

The authors then examined those 387 cases for evidence that the serial murderer violated his victim sexually. For the purposes of this study, the authors used the following definition "sexual homicide describes murders with evidence or observations that indicate that the motive for murder was sexual in nature. These include the condition of the victim's body, sexual positioning of the victim's body, insertion of foreign objects into the victim's body cavities, evidence of sexual intercourse (oral, anal, vaginal), and evidence of substitute sexual activity, interest, or sadistic fantasy."

The primary sample of this research is 248 of the 387 serial murderers who violated their victims sexually. These offenders were both male and female and also included serial killers who were not apprehended such as The Bound Torture Killer, The Baltimore Murders, Ft. Worth Murders, Green River Killer, New Bedford Killings, and the like.

This current research, however, concentrates on male offenders who were suspected of killing three or more persons over a period of time in a manner that included sexual violation. The primary sample of 248 included four female offenders and 12 unapprehended serial killers.

The authors eliminated the four female offenders and the 12 unknown unapprehended serial killers from the primary sample of 248 resulting in a total population of 232 identified, male serial killers who had violated their victims sexually.

Application of *DSM*-IV Criteria

This research focused on an identified sample of serial murderers whose behaviors were available for review. The authors used a case history evaluation protocol, based upon the DSM-IV criteria of antisocial personality disorder and sexual sadism to examine the population of 232 serial killers, who had violated their victims sexually. Examination of data sources for those 232 killers revealed information for only 68 of them to complete the protocols for this study. The data sources used by the authors consisted of crime scene photographs, police files, and confidential police reports provided to the primary author in his capacity of consultant, as well as psychiatric and related psychological reports and published biographical materials on the subjects of this study. Sixty-eight cases met the rigorous definition of antisocial personality disorder and sexual sadism. Tables 1 and 2 summarize the application of DSM-IV criteria of antisocial personality disorder to the 68 subjects of this study.

CONCLUSION

The 68 offenders in this study displayed aggressive and antisocial behaviors during their childhood which escalated and took on elements of sexual sadism in adulthood.

There was also a style and pattern to their killings that involved domination, control, humiliation, and sadistic sexual violence. The murders were committed

Table 1
Application of DSM-IV criteria of antisocial personality disorder:
A. Current age at least 18, B. Conduct disorder before age 15

Behavior/Conduct	N=68	
	Number	Percent
Lied	66	97%
Stole	58	85%
Cruel to others	41	60%
Forced sex on others	24	35%
Truant	23	34%
Fought	13	19%
Vandalism	11	16%
Ran away	10	15%
Cruel to animals	10	15%
Used weapons	7	10%
Robbery	5	07%
Set fires	5	07%

with the least sense of guilt or shame, and the killers displayed a total lack of remorse.

Jerry Brudos, dubbed "The Lust Killer," murdered four young women during 1968 and 1969 in a series of lust murders that were predicated on a sadistic and bizarre plan to kidnap and kill women, whom he would force to dress and pose in various sexually provocative positions. In some instances, he would continue his sexual fantasies by dressing the bodies after death. His perversions included necrophilia and sexual mutilation of the corpses.

Ted Bundy, who represents the epitome of the serial killer, brutally murdered and sexually violated over 30 young women. Bundy's attacks on women centered around control and total domination. Bundy wanted his victims to be totally submissive to him. His plans involved sadistic fantasies with a combination of sex and violence featuring a dominant male and a submissive female. Most of his

Table 2
Application of DSM-IV criteria of antisocial personality disorder:
C. Antisocial behavior since age 15

Behavior/Conduct	N=68		
	Number		Percent
Repeated criminal acts	66		97%
Lack of remorse	65		96%
Impulsive	64		94%
Lied	63		93%
Reckless in behavior	59		87%
Irritable and aggressive	35		51%
Poor employment	25		37%
No monogamous relationships	14		21%
Irresponsible parenting	11		16%
Poor financial records	3		04%

victims were raped, traumatized, and then killed. Bundy performed necrophilia shortly after killing them.

Lawrence Bittaker and Roy Norris met in prison. They shared a mutual interest in female domination, rape, torture, and murder. They murdered five young women using a combination of methods that included stabbing them through the ears with an ice pick and strangling them manually, and with wire coat hangers, which were tightened around the victim's necks with pliers. They tape-recorded two of their torture sessions while they repeatedly raped, sodomized, and tortured the young women. The victims were chosen at random and the murders carried out in an almost obsessive manner.

The behaviors of these subjects are appropriately described as psychopathic sexual sadism. There were no "dual" diagnoses or comorbidity in this study. Such people abandon all ambitions and dedicate themselves to immediate enjoyment which Kernberg termed "unambitious hedonism" and social isolation, a primitive ego organization is part of all severe personality disorders that also have identity diffusion. This represents a lack of integration and a lack of the concept of the self and significant others. Instead, a grandiose self integrates with the resultant ego-syntonic sadism. The more evident the antisocial features and the more disintegrated the internal object relations, the worse the pathology.

Sex and aggression (as we understand them in psychoanalytic terms), and the perversion of a destructive and hostile libido, are at the core of the narcissistic personality that perpetrates these acts. The severe ego splitting may or may not be a manifestation of psychosis. Most of these perpetrators were not grossly psychotic or insane in the legal sense because they were not judged insane at time of trial.

The presentation of these killers is different depending on the defense structure and the degree of grandiosity. Scientific and psychological investigation has not led investigators to the conclusion that the majority of sexual murderers are emotionally ill, in either the medical sense or by legal definition. Few have been known to have been driven by either delusions or hallucinations.

The term "psychopath" developed from the concept of "psychopathic inferiority." Cleckley's review of "psychopathic states" is both comprehensive and basic. Kraepelin further subdivided psychopaths and discussed "early inhibition" in the origin of the disorder. Other authors have used the term "psychopathic" to encompass a wide variety of individuals who lack a sense of responsibility, do not profit from experience, fail to alter their behavior after punishment, and exhibit a lack of guilt. In the *Diagnostic and Statistical Manual* of the American Psychiatric Association, the term "sociopathic personality disturbance," was listed under "personality disorders" and later discarded by the APA in 1968 when specific diagnostic entities such as antisocial personality were used. The *Diagnostic and Statistical Manual IV* lists antisocial personality in individuals where there was a pervasive pattern of disregard for and violation of the rights of others since age 15 years and indicated by at least three or more of seven specific characteristics. This category is now used to encompass a wide spectrum of individuals who commit criminal behavior.

Thus the term "sociopath" or "psychopath" can be subsumed under the diagnostic entity of Antisocial Personality Disorder, the former being much more general descriptions of individuals who evidence various behavioral disorders characterized by criminal activity (chronic antisocial behavior). For the most part, the most common observation is that psychopaths are unreliable and irresponsible; and, secondarily, untruthful and insincere.

The authors believe that "psychopathy" represents a failure of the development of the individual's personality and conscience. Psychopaths are not out of contact with reality, do not suffer from a thought disorder, and have no other evidence of

Lack of guilt is the Hallmark of antisocial personality disorder.

psychotic disturbance. "Psychopathic" behavior represents a failure of the development of the conscience and sense of self.

The subjects of this study were extremely violent and fit the criteria of antisocial personality and sexual sadism. These 68 cases were the ones with sufficient data to draw conclusions and apply the criteria of antisocial personality disorder and sexual sadism. The behaviors of these subjects indicated that psychopathic sexual sadists killed because they liked to kill.

Technically, this meant that they satisfied psychological desires. That is to say, they sought sensual gratification. These desires were aggressive libidinal wishes that were not expressed in their daily lives and were a product of their developmental arrests and unresolved needs. Following the outburst of lust murder, behavior returned to "normal" until the next outburst of murder. The victim, in the majority of cases, a woman, became the target of the "badness" displaced from the mother. This fusion of the destructive impulses resulted from disorganized developmental experiences and faulty object relations along with the incapacity for empathic bonding both typically found in the antisocial personality disorder individual. This dynamic was consistent with their superficial adaptation and noninvolvement in any socially integrative manner.

In the homosexual serial murderers, the mechanism of projection was utilized to displace the "badness" to the same sexed victim. The perpetrator unconsciously identified with the victim, yet destroyed him, and thus preserved himself.

They have conscious detailed plans, which involve sadistic fantasies. According to Cartel, " . . . they apparently achieved euphoria through torturing and killing people without experiencing guilt or compassion for the victims or their families." This lack of guilt is the hallmark of antisocial personality disorder.

With serial murderers, aggressive and destructive elements are externalized, allowing a temporary reestablishment of psychological equilibrium. Object relations theorists discuss these individuals with regard to "unmetabolized" elements and this is useful in understanding the targets of such aggression. These researchers point to the failure of adaptive responses in the separation-individuation phase of development.

Somehow, the act of murder allowed the lust murderer to deal with internal frustrations that are related to early developmental conflicts. According to Liebert, "In absorbing the elements of badness through projection and displacement, female targets become objects of psychotic disorganization with a lack of realistic perception and true identification of the potential victim."

In the homosexual serial killings, the mechanism is the same. The perpetrator, however, has identified with the mother and projected his rage to the same sex victim and thus preserved himself. The destructive elements of the early mother-child relationship were "introjected" and "split," and then projected with a recycling of this badness through projection and displacement. The female victim became dehumanized and, from the point of view of the killer, possessed the "badness." The same is true for the homosexual murderer utilizing the mechanisms of identification (with the mother) and then projection. The role of the father as a passive "object" in the lives of the homosexual perpetrator also played a role in the displacement of the aggression to another male. The victim became the "object" of the "badness" the perpetrator perceives about himself and can "act out" without destroying himself.

The results of this study may have implications for health practitioners for the assessment, treatment, and management of persons with the identifiable criteria of antisocial personality disorder and sexual sadism. An example of this application may be the clinical assessment of the future dangerousness of incarcerated offenders diagnosed as having antisocial personality disorder and the paraphilia of sexual sadism.

With what we know about science, the empirical world is in constant change. A good classification system allows the integration of new material and the opportunity for consistent study of changes, thereby allowing for the advance of scientific understanding.

Sexual Murder

DON GRUBIN

The incidence of sexual murder of women is unknown. Evidence of a sexual element in a killing is often difficult to discover, particularly when offender and victim are known to each other. In England and Wales, for instance, about a third of female homicide victims are killed by their spouses or co-habitees, but it is not clear how many of these are of a sexual nature. Statistics are difficult to obtain in both the UK and North America because, even for those murders that are discovered, the offence is classified as homicide and not as a sexual crime.

There are a number of ways in which homicide and a sexual offence may become associated. An offender may murder his victim in order to silence his potential accuser, he may become angry and kill in response to her resistance, he may simply panic, death may be accidental, or homicide may be the result of pathological group behaviour, such as may occur when an army goes on the rampage in an occupied territory.

The killing may also be closely bound to the sexual element of an attack. In these cases the offender's control of his victim, and her pain and humiliation, become linked to his sexual arousal. Murderers of this last type, often referred to as sadistic, have attracted much of the little research in the area, partly because of the possible presence of psychopathology, and partly because it is in this group of men that serial offenders, that is, men who attack and kill numerous victims, are thought most likely to be found.

Perhaps the classic picture of the sadistic murderer was drawn by Brittain, who, based on clinical anecdote and experience rather than formal research, described an introverted, timid, overcontrolled and socially isolated man, overdependent on a mother with whom he had an ambivalent relationship. Brittain said that these men were sexually prudish, reserved, and inexperienced, but sexually deviant (being for instance voyeurs, fetishists or transvestites), with rich and sadistic fantasy lives and interests in violent pursuits. Other characteristics of the sadistic killer noted by Brittain were his hypochondriasis, the absence of drug or alcohol addictions, and low self-esteem in spite of great vanity and egocentricism; Brittain suggested that the sadistic killer most commonly offended after a blow to his self-esteem.

Like Brittain, most researchers writing about sadistic offenders and sexual homicide have followed a descriptive approach. However, MacCulloch et al., in a study of 13 sadistic offenders in a British special hospital (only some of whom had killed), went beyond mere description by providing evidence for the importance of fantasy in the motivation of sadistic crime. They argued, contrary to Brittain, that offending by these men was driven by fantasy and occurred in the absence of external stimuli, a concept that has been explored more fully in a series of American studies based on data collected by the FBI.

That fantasy may be a key motivational factor in sadistic killings was further demonstrated by Prentky et al., who compared serial with single sexual killers, and found that fantasy was related to offending in significantly more of the former group: a higher proportion admitted to rape fantasies, were paraphilic, and left "organised" crime scenes aimed at avoiding detection, which suggested some forethought and planning.

The emphasis on sadistic and serial offenders has meant that little research has taken place in relation to sexual murder in general; indeed, other than the study by Prentky et al. there has been little attempt to compare putative sadistic murderers with other types of sexual murderer, or even with other sex offenders. In addition, the literature is often less than specific about the type of victim killed, even though in sex offending generally both the sex and age of victims are important discriminators between offenders. The lack of a comparative framework limits the confidence with which aetiological models can be put forward, and handicaps the search for factors which may help identify those individuals who are most at risk of committing sexual murder, or of killing again.

In order to better understand the phenomenon of sexual murder, this study describes a group of men who killed in the course of a sexual attack, and compares them with men convicted of rape, using Brittain's description of the sadistic murderer as a starting point.

METHOD

In a study of rapists, funded by the Home Office, 142 men were interviewed in six English prisons. Prisons were not chosen randomly, but were selected to provide a cross-section of security categories, and included one young-offenders' institution. Men were eligible for inclusion if they had been convicted of the rape of a woman over the age of 15, or, in the case of offenders under 21, of a woman or girl over the age of 12; incest offenders were excluded from the study. Men were also eligible for inclusion if they had been convicted of the murder of a woman in which a sexual assault was likely to have occurred, although this need not have involved penetration.

In each prison, every second man who met these criteria was asked to take part in the study. Each subject was guaranteed confidentiality and anonymity. Of the 152 men approached, only 10 refused to be interviewed. Information was gathered from prison files, and victim statements were obtained in 103 cases (73%); where these were not available, as in cases of murder, police and prosecution summaries provided a description of the offence.

A semi-structured interview lasting about 90 minutes was used. Subjects were also asked to complete a number of questionnaires, including the Eysenck I–7 as a measure of impulsivity and the Schonell reading test as an estimate of educational attainment.

Of the 142 men interviewed, 21 had murdered in the course of a sexual attack; one of these sexual murderers had murdered twice, and five others had committed additional rapes or other serious sexual offences. Of the remaining 121 men, 90 had been convicted of a single rape, 26 of two or more rapes, and 5 of one rape together with another serious sexual offence against a second victim.

RESULTS

At the time of their offences, the mean age of the 21 men who had murdered was 30.0 (s.d. 8.7, range 18–50), significantly older than the mean of 25.9 (s.d. 6.9, range 15–53) for the rest of the sample (t = 2.05, d.f. = 140, $P < 0.01$); 8 (38%) of the murderers were over 30 when they offended compared with 23 (19%) of the non-murderers (χ^2 = 3.82, d.f. = 1, P = 0.05). All of the murderers were white, in marked contrast with the remainder of the sample where whites represented just 60% of the total population (χ^2 = 10.87, d.f. = 1, $P < 0.001$). Intelligence was not formally tested, but mean scores for the two groups on the Schonell reading test were similar: 12.1 (s.d. 0.9) for the murderers compared with 11.8 (s.d. 1.4) for the non-murderers.

Table 1

Main features distinguishing sexual murderers from men who had raped but not killed

	Rapists (n=121)	Murderers (n=21)	χ^2	P<
Not part of childhood peer group	23 (19%)	9 (43%)	5.83	
Lives alone	26 (22%)	9 (43%)	4.40	
Socially isolated	6 (5%)	6 (29%)		
Few sexual relationships	23 (19%)	13 (62%)	17.40	0.0001
No sex partner in year of offence	18 (15%)	8 (38%)	6.45	
"Bottles" temper	21 (18%)	8 (38%)		
Past convictions for rape	9 (7%)	6 (29%)	8.46	0.01

All but one of the victims was white. Excluding prostitutes, just under half (45%) of those who were killed knew their attackers, a similar proportion to the 47% of victims who were not murdered.

Some of the characteristics suggested by Brittain as typical of the sadistic murderer were found in this group of sexual killers; those which distinguished them from the men who had raped but not killed are listed in Table 1. Most of these features related to the increased likelihood of social isolation among the murderers, many of whom had infrequent social contacts and lived alone. Even as children, the murderers as a group tended to be more isolated, with over 40% interacting poorly with their peer groups compared with under 20% of those who had not murdered. A majority were judged to have had little heterosexual interaction throughout their lives. Moreover, 18 (86%) of the murderers had at least one of these features suggestive of social isolation, compared with 54 (45%) of the non-murderers (χ^2 = 12.09, d.f. = 1, $P < 0.001$).

In Table 1 it can also be seen that more of the murderers said that they tended to keep their anger "bottled up" before exploding, perhaps reflecting a tendency for overcontrol; impulsivity scores on the I–7, however, were not significantly different between the groups, with a mean of 9.0 (s.d. 5.4) for the murderers compared with a mean of 9.5 (s.d. 5.1) for the non-murderers.

Other elements of Brittain's description were also observed in the sexual murderers, but these did not distinguish them from the men who had raped but not killed. About half the men in each group had past convictions for violence and an interest in aggressive pastimes such as martial arts or hunting, while 5 (24%) of the murderers and 39 (32%) of the non-murderers owned weapons. Paraphilic behaviour was noted for 9 (43%) of the murderers and 31 (26%) of the non-murderers (actual paraphilias were diagnosed in just four of the murderers), and about 15% of each group admitted to some form of sexual dysfunction in the year of the offence. Offending in general was similar between the two groups, as were past convictions for sexual offences, with the exception of previous convictions for rape (see Table 1).

Other components of Brittain's description did not fit this population of sexual murderers at all. Contrary to his expectation that alcohol abuse would not be common, alcohol dependence was diagnosed in 9 (43%) of the men who had killed. Eight (38%) of the murderers had previous contact with psychiatric services, while just 2 (10%) had evidence of symptoms of anxiety or depression either within or outside prison, again contrary to Brittain's account.

Fantasies

Most of the men were reluctant to divulge sexual fantasies at interview, with just one of the murderers and eight of the non-murderers admitting to more than occasional sexual fantasies, and two of the former and eight of the latter admitting to having had rape fantasies some time in their lives. Other indicators of an active sexual fantasy life were therefore sought.

Frequent use of pornography, any paraphilic behaviour (ever), frequent fantasies or rape fantasies, or regular use of prostitutes was more common, but not significantly so, among men who had killed (8; 38%) than among non-murderers (33; 27%). Another possible indicator of a rich fantasy life, evidence of a ritual component in the offence, also failed to distinguish the two groups, with 3 (14%) of the murderers and 24 (20%) of the non-murderers appearing to have followed a predetermined mental script in their offences.

Childhood

Brittain did not comment in detail about the childhood characteristics of sadistic murderers. In this study, other than having less interaction with their peers as children, the killers and non-killers did not differ over a range of characteristics such as the incidence of conduct disorder, possible neurotic traits such as bedwetting or somatic symptoms, or their reports of childhood victimisation, including sexual abuse.

The family structure of those who had killed appeared to be relatively more stable, at least superficially. They were less likely to have experienced a change in primary care, this having occurred in 9 (43%) of the murderers compared with 80 (66%) of the non-murderers (χ^2 = 4.14, d.f. = 1, P < 0.05), and when this did happen it occurred less frequently, with just 2 (10%) of the murderers experiencing three or more such changes compared with 43 (36%) of the non-murderers (χ^2 = 5.59, d.f. = 1, P < 0.05); 19 (91%) of the murderers spent the first ten years of their lives with their own families compared with 95 (79%) of the non-murderers (χ^2 = 1.76, d.f. = 1, NS). Fathers were more likely to be present throughout the early lives (up to age 10) of those who had killed, being present for 16 (76%) of the murderers compared with 63 (52%) of the non-murderers (χ^2 = 4.21, d.f. = 1, P < 0.05). On a rating of paternal stability during these early years (based on paternal absence, criminality, unemployment, alcoholism, or chronic ill health), 12 (57%) of the fathers of the murderers were rated as "stable" compared with 42 (35%) of the non-murderers' fathers (χ^2 = 3.82, d.f. = 1, P = 0.05). Similar proportions of the mothers of the murderers and non-murderers were present throughout their first ten years, and the mothers of 15 (71%) of the murderers and 78 (65%) of the non-murderers were rated as "stable." The proportions who were single children were also similar, as were the proportions who were eldest children.

The murder offences

Forensic evidence suggested that seven of the murderers had intercourse with unconscious or dead victims. It might be expected that these men would differ from the remainder of the murderers, but as a group they did not seem to be any more sexually or psychologically disturbed. Just one had a past sex offence, none were serial offenders, none admitted to heavy pornography use, none to rape fantasies, and in just one was there a history of paraphilic behaviour. Although four of these men were not in an established relationship at the time of their offences and three lived alone, just one was considered to be socially isolated. One had evidence of neurotic symptoms as a child and one of conduct disorder, while none admitted to childhood sexual or physical abuse. Two were diagnosed as alcohol dependent, but 6 of the 7 (86%) had used alcohol in the hours before the offence compared with just 5 (36%) of the other murderers.

The average age of the murder victims was 38.3 (s.d. 24.8) compared with 28.2 (s.d. 14.4) for victims who were not killed (t = 1.87, d.f. = 140, P = 0.06), but five of the murdered women were over 60 years of age—excluding women over 60 in both groups, mean victim ages were 25.8 (s.d. 10.2) and 26.1 (s.d. 10.2) respectively. Even excluding victims over 60, however, and counting only the first victims of men with multiple offences, only 7 of 16 murder victims (44%) were within 10 years of age of their attackers, compared with 84 of 117 (72%) of the victims who were not killed (χ^2 = 5.12, d.f. = 1, P < 0.05).

In the majority of murder-rapes, access was gained to the victim either by breaking into her home (29%), usually in the course of a burglary, or by stalking her on the street (29%). In about a third of the murders the sex attack, although not necessarily the murder, appeared to have been planned in advance. Weapons, usually knives, were present in 8 (38%) of the attacks, but 14 (67%) of the victims were strangled and just 2 (10%) stabbed. A gun was involved in only one offence, the attacker shooting the male companion of his victim before raping her and then beating her to death with the barrel of the gun. In five cases the offender said that his victim had shown no physical resistance, but the violence used in all but one of the murder-rapes was extreme. For example, in one case the cord used to strangle a woman had been pulled so tight that the ambulance crew were unable to untie it, and in another an elderly woman was beaten so badly that she had 16 broken ribs, a torn liver, and a ruptured heart.

Six of the murderers gave an account of some form of sexual dysfunction during the offence: four described premature ejaculation and two said that they had been unable to ejaculate; in at least three of these cases the sexual dysfunction was related to the murder. One man, for instance, said that his inability to ejaculate made him increasingly angry, which led him to strangle his victim. He told the police at the time that he discovered, "a sense of power in depriving a body of life." Semen was found in the victim's anus and vagina, and presumably it was this sense of power that finally enabled him to ejaculate.

Brittain's observation that murderous attacks were precipitated by a recent loss of self-esteem was clearly found in just 7 (34%) cases. Anger, either because of the victim's lack of cooperation or of a more general nature, was the most common precipitant of the murderous assault, judged to be present in 9 (50%) of the 18 cases for which a motive could be discerned. In only three cases was the process of causing death itself clearly sexually arousing for the offender, while silencing a potential accuser appeared to be the motive in four cases and panic in two.

DISCUSSION

This study is the first in the UK to look in detail at the sexual murder of women. There is no way of knowing how representative this particular group of men is, however, as the numbers of men who kill in a sexual context is unknown and data about them limited, and inferences drawn from this population must be made cautiously. This caveat applies to all studies of sexual offenders, which by their nature depend on the small proportion of perpetrators who can be identified, usually only after the filters of accusation, arrest, conviction and sentencing have been negotiated.

The description of the sadistic killer articulated by Brittain has been generally accepted, but it has never been validated and his use of the term "sadistic" never defined. Many of the features put forward by him as characteristic of sadistic killers were not found in this sample of sexual killers. Others, such as an interest in aggressive pursuits, sexual deviation, and rich, if not sadistic fantasy lives, were observed here, but they were also found in a comparison group of men who had raped but not killed; if relevant, these features are more likely to relate to sexual offending in general rather than sexual murder in particular.

Many of the American studies of sexual murder also suffer from a lack of a comparative framework. For instance, childhood histories of family instability, victimisation and behavioural problems were common in the backgrounds of the sexual killers described by the FBI, and are postulated to be of important aetiological significance, but in the present study these features were if anything less prominent in the murderers than in the rapists who had not killed.

The lack of evidence of frequent or preoccupying sadistic fantasies, or of sadism in general, in the sexual killers described here is in marked contrast to the FBI studies. Twenty-nine of the 36 men in the American studies, however, were serial killers, and 25 had killed three or more times. It is in this group of repeated offenders that fantasy is postulated as being an important "drive mechanism." While serial murder was not a feature of the men in the present study, a small number of men had committed other sexual offences in addition to murder, and in this group frequent fantasies, paraphilic behaviour, convictions for sexual offences, and ritualised offending were more often found. In contrast, other factors, in particular anger, sometimes related to a recent specific incident, sometimes of a more general and pervasive nature, appeared more relevant in men who were not repeated offenders. Anger has been found to be a useful typological discriminator in some rapist typologies.

Social isolation

The most robust finding in the present study was the theme of isolation in the sexual killers. Many of the murderers lived alone, and many had little in the way of social contacts or social interaction; even as children many were not part of their peer groups. In addition, most of the murderers had few if any intimate relationships with women, and the relationships they did form tended to be emotionally limited, with little sharing or confiding. Social and emotional isolation, although not emphasised, are also characteristics that appear consistently in the published work on sexual murderers.

isolation w/ sexual killers

The isolation experienced by sexual killers may be causally relevant to their crimes in two ways. First, this isolation may be an indicator of underlying personality abnormalities which both cause the isolation and allow an individual to cross the boundary between sexual attack and murder. In particular, it may signal an abnormality of affect whereby these men are unable to empathise normally with other people, either being unable to experience the pain and suffering of their victims, or if they do they experience it as pleasurable and arousing. Alternatively, the isolation may itself be an important contributing factor that allows the killing to take place. Lack of personal contact, and perhaps an increased dependence on an internal fantasy life, may weaken the restraints that inhibit excessive violence even in the course of a sexual attack. In a sense, these men may lack practice in controlling their aggression when their desires are frustrated; some will be habitually aggressive, others will match the description of overcontrolled personalities who explode in infrequent but seriously violent aggression. Men of this second type will be those whose killing is driven by anger (either in general or specifically towards women) rather than by sadism.

While fantasy and behavioural rehearsal are an important prognostic sign in some offenders, it appears to be present in only a small proportion of men who kill in a sexual context. The current study suggests that a less specific but perhaps more sensitive sign is a history of social and personal isolation, particularly when combined with sexual deviance, sexual offending, or sadistic fantasies. Such isolation may have many causes, ranging from biological to developmental to environmental, and it is unlikely that a common aetiological factor underlies all cases. Social and personal isolation, whether perceived by the individual or not, is a common thread running through many sexual killers, whether the killing is the result of escalation within an offence or was planned from the outset. A better understanding of what causes an individual to become isolated in this way may shed light on why only some men with sadistic fantasies become sexual offenders, and why some sexual offenders go on to kill.

Adolescents Who Kill

KENNETH G. BUSCH, ROBERT ZAGAR, JOHN R. HUGHES,
JACK ARBIT, & ROBERT E. RUSSELL

Over the past 50 years, some juveniles who committed homicide had physical problems: psychomotor epilepsy, EEG abnormalities, limbic and reticular activating system disorders, and neonatal deficits. Among homicidal juveniles, psychiatric and social factors of psychopathology, violent families, gang participation, parental psychiatric illness, and low socioeconomic status have been found.

Three theorists have described homicidal adolescents: Freud, Bender, and Lewis. Freud thought that child murderers, who had death wishes toward parents: (a) had inconsistent parenting; (b) witnessed violence; (c) experienced physical abuse; and (d) suffered rejection. To explain children and adolescents who kill, Bender (1959) presented five situations: (1) severe family rivalry; (2) inability of a guardian to curb aggressiveness; (3) organic inferiority and deprivation; (4) insurmountable educational difficulties; and (5) severe familial aggressiveness. Lewis et al. demonstrated four symptoms of teenage killers: (a) violent fathers; (b) seizures; (c) suicidal tendencies; and (d) psychiatrically hospitalized mothers.

The goal of this study was to compare the homicidal adolescents with nonviolent delinquents who were matched by age, race, sex, and SES on psychological and educational tests. Second, the purpose of this investigation was to describe and to contrast both groups on the following physical, psychological, psychiatric, and social characteristics: (a) neurological and neonatal causal factors (frequency of

CNS and neonatal disorders and epilepsy); (b) severe educational difficulties (retardation, perceptual handicaps, and underachievement); and (c) psychiatric and social characteristics (home situations, gang participation, weekly substance abuse, psychiatric hospitalizations, hallucinations, and overdose).

Past research often has been anecdotal in nature and has compared case studies and small groups (range, N = 3 to 33) of homicidal with nonhomicidal children and adolescents. With 71 homicidal adolescents and 71 matched nonviolent delinquents, this sample size allowed for sensitive statistical analysis of data derived from a broad array of diagnostic and evaluative procedures. From a large sample size, one was able to ascertain those characteristics that differentiated homicidal adolescents from nonhomicidal, nonviolent, but otherwise delinquent adolescents on physical, psychological, psychiatric, educational, and social characteristics.

METHOD

Subjects

There were 71 adjudicated (judged within a court) juveniles (4 females and 67 males), aged 10 to 17 years, all of whom committed and were convicted of homicide. The homicides were familial, random, friend, drug- or gang-related. The control group included 71 children and adolescents who were matched by age, race, sex, and SES and was composed of nonviolent delinquents adjudicated for the offenses of criminal property damage; theft; truancy; or violating court order, curfew, or probation.

Most of the two groups of homicidal juveniles and matched nonviolent delinquents were lower class (less than $8,000/year/family), much as were most of the sample of 1,956 delinquents from whom they were selected and much as were most of the population of 27,595 delinquents. SES was determined by family income, parental occupation, and area of residence. This group of 71 homicidal juveniles represented every delinquent charged with homicide from the sample of 1,956, but not from the larger population of 27,595. This sample of 1,956 consisted of all adjudicated delinquents who were referred for physical, psychological, psychiatric, educational, and social examination and for whom there were complete records. Children and adolescents who had not received physical examinations, or one or more of the tests in the psychological and the educational test battery, or psychiatric examinations were excluded from this sample. The sample of 1,956 delinquents were from a larger population of children and adolescents adjudicated before the court from 1981 through 1986 who totalled 27,595 or approximately 7% of the population of adjudicated delinquents.

The age, race, sex, and family compositions of *the population, the sample* and *the groups of* homicidal and matched nonviolent *delinquents combined* were similar.

Procedure

Medical histories and physical examinations were performed by pediatricians to discover central nervous system (CNS) conditions, neonatal problems, psychological disturbances, and substance abuse, which were coded using the International Classification of Disease (ICD-9). Medical histories were obtained at the time of referral and included hospital and neonatal records and a thorough pediatric examination of neurological, respiratory, musculoskeletal, circulatory, gastrointestinal, hepatic, renal, genito-urinary, endocrine, and skin systems.

Intellectual and perceptual testing consisted of the Wechsler Intelligence Scale for Children–Revised and the Bender Visual-Motor Gestalt Test.

Educational assessments measures employed were : (1) the Gates MacGinitie Reading Tests, which measured reading speed and accuracy, vocabulary, and reading comprehension of paragraphs; and (2) the Standford Achievement Tests, which evaluated addition, subtraction, multiplication, and division. The raw scores of the intellectual, perceptual, and achievement tests were the ordinal data for this study. To facilitate understanding, scaled scores and grade levels were presented.

Developmental and disruptive behavioral disorders were classified by two psychologists who worked independently and who used data from physical, psychological, psychiatric, educational, and social examinations within Diagnostic Statistical Manual III-Revised (DSM-III-R) criteria. The major DSM-II-R categories were: (a) mental retardation; (b) attention deficit-hyperactivity disorder (ADHD); (c) attention deficit disorder (ADD) undifferentiated; and (d) developmental delays in reading, language, and arithmetic.

The psychiatric examination of the child, the adolescent, the parent(s), the relative(s), or the guardian(s) were unstandardized, but included any mention of hallucinations, prior hospitalizations, overdoses, mental status examination, and medical and family hostility. These diagnostic examinations were conducted by 12 different psychiatrists and totalled approximately 1 hour or longer. The social investigation reports compiled by probation officers and supplemented by social workers included descriptions of: type of offense, family composition, school history, and demographic data.

The nominal data for both groups were: (a) a criminally violent (homicide, assault, batter, rape, robbery, stabbing, shooting) family member (parent, sibling, aunt, uncle, grandparent) as established from court records; (b) physical abuse (documented bruises, lacerations, contusions, or other injury as determined by evaluation of physicians, the State of Illinois Department of Children and Family Services, investigators, and police officer reports); (c) active gang participation; (d) substance abuse (at least weekly use of any amount alcohol or drugs); and (e) diagnostic category (CNS conditions, mental retardation, ADHD, ADD).

Analysis

The stepwise discriminant analysis was used to determine which of the variables contributed to the significant differences. The assumption of normality and homogeneity of variance was met for most variables. Criminal characteristics of juveniles for inclusion within each group were independent, an assumption necessary for discriminant analysis. Discriminant analysis was chosen because of the inevitable correlations among independent variables as discovered by correlational and chi-square analysis. Ordinal variables (violent family, physical abuse, gang participation, substance abuse, retardation, ADHD, ADD, and CNS conditions) were dummy coded. No significant differences in the interpretation of the results were found when stepwise discriminant analyses were performed with or without dummy coding.

In the discriminant analysis, the two groups of 142 were randomly split in half. Next discriminant analysis was performed on one half of the two groups of 142. Then, the second half the two groups of 142 was classified using the discriminant analysis functions developed on first split half of these two groups.

RESULTS

Adolescents who were convicted of homicide differed from matched nonviolent delinquents as presented in Table 1.

In Table 1, four symptoms differentiated teenage killers from matched nonviolent delinquents: (1) criminally violent family members, 58% vs. 20%; (2) gang participation, 41% vs. 14%; (3)(alcohol abuse, 38% vs. 24%; and (4) severe educational difficulties (including retardation, 21% vs. 10%, lower perceptual IQ scores, 86 vs. 90 and lower full IQ scores, 80 vs. 84).

Killers and delinquents also differed on : epilepsy, 7% vs. 1%; CNS conditions, 7% vs. 1%; hallucinations, 1% vs. 0%; overdoses, 0% vs. 1%; and physical abuse, 25% vs. 20%. Both groups were similar in terms of neonatal problems (8%) and psychiatric hospitalization (7%).

The most important and consistent findings across all of the samples were the large proportion of criminally violent family members and gang participation among homicidal juveniles. Alcohol abuse and severe educational difficulties also appeared to be significant.

Table 1

Characteristics that best differentiated adolescents who kill from matched nonviolent delinquents (compared with sample of all delinquents)

		Group		
Characteristic		Killers (n = 71)	Matched nonviolent	Total delinquent sample (n = 1956)
1. Criminally violent family member		41/71 (58%)	14/71 (20%)	446/1956 (23%)
2. Gang membership		29/71 (41%)	10/71 (14%)	373/1956 (19%)
3. Alcohol abuse		27/71 (38%)	17/71 (24%)	568/1956 (29%)
4. Severe educational difficulties				
Mental retardation		14/71 (21%)	7/71 (10%)	290/1956 (15%)
Verbal IQ	(100.4 ± 12.6)	77.9 ± 12.8	80.5 ± 12.9	81.3 ± 16.2
Perceptual IQ	(98.1 ± 10.7)	86.0 ± 14.4	90.5 ± 14.0	88.7 ± 15.9
Full IQ	(99.9 ± 21.6)	80.4 ± 13.3	84.2 ± 12.1	83.6 ± 15.6

DISCUSSION

Homicidal juveniles had four symptoms that differentiated them from matched nonviolent delinquents: (a) criminally violent family members; (b) gang participation; (c) alcohol abuse; and (d) severe educational difficulties that included mental retardation; perceptual deficits; and lowered intellectual, perceptual, and achievement test performance.

Previous reports of juvenile murderers used case studies, small samples (range 3 to 33), mixtures of adults and children, or did not include all the components of a complete evaluation. This study presented a combination of physical, psychological, psychiatric, educational, and social characteristics that differentiated homicidal teenagers from matched nonviolent delinquents.

Adolescents who killed had more parents, siblings, aunts, uncles, and grandparents who committed homicide, assault, battery, rape, armed robbery, stabbing, and shooting. They often participated in gang activity. Alcohol abuse and severe educational difficulties were also significant in characterizing these adolescent killers.

Children who murder are not exotic individuals, but, rather, persons with violent, abusive, inconsistent, and aggressive environments. Juvenile murderers drank more alcohol and had severe educational difficulties. Not all of these adolescent murderers had these four symptoms, but a majority did. Knowledge of these symptoms could alert the judge, the clinician, or the educator who must deal with these homicidal adolescents.

Current thinking more often has considered adolescent murderers as the victims of an unloving family in which revenge was often a motive. Popular opinion traditionally has associated the behavior of adolescent killers with a milieu of violence and disorganization.

In summary, adolescents who killed came from violent, aggressive families, lived in a peer environment with gang participation, had severe educational difficulties, and alcohol abuse.

JUVENILE MURDER

Profile of a Predator:
Child Abduction Murder by a Stranger

JOSEPH G. WEIS, ROBERT D. KEPPEL, & KENNETH A. HANFLAND

INTRODUCTION

Every parent has felt their heart pound, their pulse quicken, their mind
race, and their instinctual fear of losing their child, all strike them at the
very instant it is recognized that their child is missing—whether it is
when he is late coming home from school, she disappears from sight in a
department store, or he does not return home on time from a weekend party.
Some parents feel the more powerful sense of loss when they receive a phone call
from a kidnapper with a ransom demand, or they answer an unexpected knock
on the door from police who have discovered the body of a young child.
Fortunately, parents' greatest fear is not realized very often.

Most children who are not where parents expect them to be, are "missing"
for a very short period of time and reappear on their own, with no evidence of
foul play. However, some children are missing against their will—they have not
simply loitered on their way home from school, but rather, may have been taken
or abducted by someone. Fortunately, the great majority of those children, even
though they have undergone a traumatic experience, are not harmed physically
and are returned home alive. Many of them are taken by estranged parents or
other family members. A smaller group is victimized by more predatory abductors,
who want to make money by ransoming the child, to fulfill their sexual fantasies
by molesting the victim, or . . . to kill the child.

The list of children who are abducted and killed each year by someone who is not a family member is relatively small, compared to the vast number of missing children or to other types of child murder. The best estimates range from only 50 to 150 per year. However, the names of many of those victims, due primarily to the national media coverage, are well-known. Etan Patz. Adam Walsh. Polly Klaas. Jimmy Ryce. Because of their rarity, even among criminal homicides, and their complex, emotion-laden, high profiles, they are extremely difficult to investigate. *This research was undertaken in an effort to better understand these types of murders, and to identify investigative techniques and strategies that will improve the efficiency and effectiveness of the criminal investigations of the murders of abducted children.* The focus is on cases of child murder in which the victims were abducted or, at the time of the initial report to the police, were suspected to have been abducted, typically by a stranger or nonfamily member.

This paper discusses some of the findings of a three-year research project that examined the investigations of murders of more than 600 abducted children. It focuses on the characteristics, motivations, and behavior of the *killers*.

METHODOLOGY
Identifying Potential Cases
In order to identify the murder cases to be used in the research, every municipal police department and county sheriff's office in the United States that had a service population of 100,000 or more, or that had fifteen or more murders reported to the Federal Bureau of Investigation's (FBI) Uniform Crime Report (UCR) in 1987, was identified (227 agencies). Depending on the size of the agency, either the Office of the Department Head, the Detective Division Commander, the Homicide Squad Supervisor, or a detective was contacted by telephone and the research project was explained in brief. The purpose of this call was to identify someone within that agency to whom correspondence could be directed regarding a formal request for preliminary case information. In most cases, the person contacted on the telephone was the person to whom a formal letter of request was made.

This letter was an explanation of the research project and a request for each agency to provide some basic information about child murder cases that might meet the criteria established in the letter. The rate of response to these letters requesting case information was 75%.

In addition, a teletype message that was a variation of the letter was sent to all police agencies in the United States. This teletype was sent out three times, on different days of the week, at different times of the day, to increase the chances of response. This teletype message requested the agencies with child murder cases meeting our stated criteria to contact us.

Other avenues were also pursued to identify cases. State and federal agencies that collect murder information were contacted and requests for case information were made. Also, homicide detectives across the country who were known to project team members were contacted for information.

In all, information was received on 1,025 "nominated" cases. These responses came from large police agencies like the New York City Police Department and from agencies as small as three-officer departments. The responding agencies were from all regions of the country.

Case Criteria

Cases were selected for study based on the following criteria:

1. the victim was a child murder victim, *younger than* 18 years of age (except as described in 3, below), whose body had been recovered, or the killer was identified, tried, and convicted; and
2. the police agency receiving the initial contact about the case, whether as a missing, abducted, runaway, or dead body case, acted on the premise that an abduction was a possibility; or
3. the case was part of a series in which at least one victim in the series met the above stated criteria.

The word "abduction" means different things to different people. For this research, a legal operational definition is used. For example, included in this sample of cases are:

- Murders in which the victim was abducted in a righteous kidnap
- Murders in which the victim was detained and his/her freedom of movement was restricted
- Murders in which the victim was the victim of domestic violence, but the family (or someone else) reported the incident as an abduction or as a missing child
- Murders in which the police were initially of the opinion that the case was an abduction, whether or not that turned out to be the case in the end

The *major criterion* for case selection was whether the agency believed that an abduction homicide was a possibility and began investigating the case as such. A secondary factor for keeping a nominated case was whether the detective who worked the case was available for interview.

Detective Interviews

The data collected came directly from two sources: interviews with the detectives who investigated the cases being reviewed, and thorough reviews and coding of case investigation files. To make the interview process consistent, training was given to the Washington Attorney General Office HITS investigators who conducted the interviews. In the beginning, these HITS investigators each conducted detective interviews in Washington state to familiarize themselves with the instrument and the interview process.

Selected volunteers from law enforcement agencies in different parts of the U.S. also agreed to assist in the data collection process. These volunteers, experienced homicide investigators, were teamed up with HITS investigators for on-site training, and detective interviews were conducted at various locations.

Detective interviews across the nation were then scheduled over a two year period and assigned to interviewers. These interviews were conducted at the original investigating police agency.

The Data

It was clear to the research team that the information being sought was to be found in both *solved* and *unsolved* cases. It was necessary to collect unsolved cases to use as a control. To illustrate the need for collecting unsolved cases, consider the question, "Is a condition that typically exists in solved cases typically absent in unsolved cases?"

It was felt that what was necessary was to have enough unsolved cases in the data base to facilitate important and meaningful comparisons. *Thirty-five percent* of the cases of child murder in this study were unsolved at the time the data were collected.

The data represent cases from 46 states. There are 577 case investigations with a total of 621 victims (some cases had multiple victims) and 419 killers; 562 of the victims are under the age of 18 years. Those who are adult victims are typically in "mixed" juvenile and adult victim mass or serial murder cases. In series cases, as many of the victims as possible were included in the data for comparative analyses. Reported findings refer to only cases in which the victim is less than 18 years of age, unless stated otherwise.

THE KILLERS

As the victims of non-family child abduction murders are unique among murder victims, so too are their killers. They share many characteristics with other types of murderers, but are unique in other important ways that suggest a different etiology to their predatory behavior and different investigative strategies. The discussion will focus on three features of these types of child abduction killers: 1) their personal and social *attributes;* 2) the typical *M.O.s;* and 3) their *post-offense behavior.*

Killer Attributes

Killers of children whom they abduct can be characterized as *social marginals:* They are not active, successful participants in mainstream, conventional social life, but, rather occupy a position in society that is, indeed, on the "edge, brink, border, precipice, or margin." They are not integrated, personally or socially, into the kinds of relationships or activities that produce and sustain effective self, or social, controls. Their personal and social attributes establish and define their social marginality.

In terms of their *sociodemographic attributes,* these killers can be typified as white males who are, on average, about 27 years old. In general, this picture is not much different than for murderers in general. However, within these primary sociodemographic attributes, there are some interesting and meaningful variations. First, there are no important differences in race between child abduction killers and other types of killers—about two-thirds are white, 20 percent are black, and the remainder are other racial/ethnic groups. Second, we know that murder is a predominantly male phenomenon—the great majority of killers and victims are males. However, the killing of children during an abduction is almost a totally-male domain of behavior. 98.5 percent of these killers are males, compared to 87 percent of all murderers. Female killers in these kinds of child murders are almost non-existent (1.5%), whereas among general child murder, they are much more likely to be involved as a killer (13%). In fact, women are more likely to kill their own young children than are the fathers. The clear overrepresentation of male killers is related to the predatory nature of the murders and the sexual motivation of most child abduction killers, whether they are killing boys or girls.

Contrary to popular belief, child abduction killers are not aged perverts—if anything, they are dirty young men. The age distribution of killers, for child abduction murder and all murders, is very similar: There are not many juvenile (under 18) killers (and most of them are 15–17 years old), and the great majority are under 30 years old. A more apparent and significant difference emerges at around age 40, where only 9 percent of the child abduction killers are over 40, compared to 19 percent of all murderers. The former are younger than the latter, and the most marked differences between the two are at the older ages. Seven percent of the child abduction killers are between 41-49 years old, and only 2 percent are 50 years old or older, with the oldest murderer in the study being 57 years old. In short, these child abduction killers are even more male and younger than the average killer.

There are a number of indicators of the pronounced *social marginality* of child abduction killers. A number of features of their personal and social lives suggest that they are not integrated into mainstream, conventional social relationships, contexts, and activities, as compared to the general population, as well as to other types of killers.

Marital Status

First, only 15 percent of these killers are married at the time of the murder—73 percent are single and 13 percent are divorced. This is very different than for young adult males in the general population, as well as among murderers in general, where the pattern is almost the opposite, with the great majority of them being married. This means that a very large 85 percent of these child abduction killers are not intimately attached or bonded to a "significant other," partner, or spouse at the time of the abduction and murder of the child.

Employment

A primary indicator of social marginality for adults is their employment status. Those with histories of unemployment or disemployment are more likely to occupy a position of economic marginality, which affects a variety of other aspects of their personal and social lives, usually in a negative way. Incredibly, 50 percent of the child abduction killers were unemployed at the time they committed the murder. This rate of unemployment is more than five times greater than the national unemployment rate for the general population.

Occupations

When they are working, they are primarily employed in "unskilled" and "semiskilled" labor occupations. The typical job, listed on an open-ended question, for these killers is *construction worker*—this occupation appeared more than three-to-five times as often (28 %) as the next five most popular jobs. Of course, this is a somewhat generic category, which includes skilled, stable workers, such as carpenters, as well as less skilled, itinerant laborers. The other most frequently listed occupations include truck driver, food industry worker, student, service industry, and auto maintenance. "Skilled" labor and "professional" occupations are dramatically underrepresented among the typical jobs of child abduction killers.

Rather, they tend to work in what economists refer to as "secondary sector" occupations, which require little formal education, produce low wages, are characteristically unstable, indicate lower status, do not lend themselves to career commitments, and so on. In short, workers in these types of occupations are less integrated into the economic and social lives of the community.

Residential Status

With their unusually high rate of unemployment, and typical occupations that are unstable and low-paying, their living arrangements might make more sense than at first glance. Contrary to another popular belief child abduction killers are not "loners" in the strictest sense—only 17 percent of them live alone, while 83 percent are living with someone else. However, who they are living with may be more unusual. The small number who are married are living with their spouses (15%), some are living with girlfriends (or boyfriends) (16%), and others are living with roommates (12%). But, oddly enough, 34 percent of these male killers who average 27 years old, are still living with their parents, which in a broader sense, could qualify them as loners—or social isolates from other young adult males or females with whom they might be intimate and share a residence. So, this group who lives with parents and those who do live alone, together comprise more than 50 percent of the child abduction killers in this study. They may not truly be loners, but they are more likely to often be "social isolates," particularly from their peers, both male and female.

They are also quite mobile—they change their residences quite often, more than most people. Seventy-nine percent of these killers moved at least once within the past five years. This may not be that unusual, but 43 percent of them changed residences three or more times, and 21 percent moved five or more times during the five years preceding the murder. They do not seem to stay anywhere very long, where they could (or would) connect themselves to others or to a place. Or, vice versa, because they are less attached to significant others, they are more free and, therefore, more likely to move more often. It is also likely that for many of them, their criminal activity makes it more necessary to move around, either seeking out more fertile grounds for victims and/or avoiding apprehension.

Killers' Lifestyles

The lifestyles—and, therefore, public identities—of these killers are quite often described by those who know them as being nonconforming, deviant, or "marginal." For example, compared to the victims' parents (45%), only 4 percent of child abduction killers are perceived as "model citizens." Rather, they are most commonly described by others as "strange" (40%). Since the killers could be described with more than one term, a number of other "deviant" lifestyle characteristics are often apparent. For example, 32 percent are identified as alcohol abusers, 27 percent as drug abusers, and 19 percent as sexually promiscuous. There are a few other characteristics that are also among the seven most common attributions, but they do not focus on ostensibly deviant behavior. For example, 21 percent of the killers are seen as being friendly to children, 20 percent as reclusive, and 16 percent as transient.

Taken together, many of the killers were not perceived or described by others as ordinary, conventional people, but rather, as leading the kinds of lives that are already deviant or have the potential to lead to trouble, particularly with children. In short, whereas the typical victim might be described as "the kid next door," the killers were not (before they became identified as a murderer) and are not the kind of guy you would want living in your neighborhood.

Killers' Past Behavior

In accord with their perceived lifestyles and identities, most child abduction killers—*three-fourths* of them—have a history of at least one serious "personal behavioral problem" of some sort.

Many of them had more than one of these problems. What is most striking is the distribution of prior "sexual problems": of the possible behavior problems, sexual problems are the most prevalent (42%) among the child abduction killers, but the least prevalent (3%) problem among all murderers. This difference is substantial and dramatic. The most common problem among all murderers is alcohol (27%), followed by drugs (14%), and mental problems (13%). The prevalence of prior alcohol problems (30%) is similar among child abduction killers, but a higher percent of them have drug (27%) or mental problems (23%). Overall, the child abduction killers have a higher rate of past behavior problems than murderers in general, and a much higher rate of past sexual problems (14 times higher than among all killers). This suggests, rather strongly, that their past behavior problems are related to, and predictive of, the extant murders.

Their prior criminal acts, against adults and juveniles, also indicate a predisposition to violence, including murder and sexual assaults. Based on a search of their criminal records, it was discovered that the majority of child abduction killers have histories of violence. Sixty percent of them had prior arrests for violent crimes. And, alarmingly, their crimes of violence are being perpetrated at a high rate against child victims. The majority (53%) of the killers committed crimes against children, and the most frequent of those crimes are *assaults* and/or *sexual assaults.* Rapes (or attempted rapes) comprise 31 percent of the prior crimes against children, and 45 percent of them are other sexual assaults. There is a definite sexual component to the crimes committed against children by those offenders who have also killed a child during an abduction. Incredibly, 28 percent of the priors are for murders (or attempted murders) of children. And, 15 percent of the prior crimes are for other kinds of assaults. A significant group (19%) of these offenders also have histories of kidnapping children. Taken together, it is clear that among many child abduction killers there is a predisposition to predatory violence, sexual and otherwise, against children.

Not surprisingly, the typical killer in these types of child abduction murders— a stranger—is most likely to have this kind of violent, sexual criminal history, compared to killers who are not strangers to their victims. Almost two-thirds (64%) of the killers who are total strangers to their victims have committed prior crimes against children, which is twice as likely as a killer who is a family member or intimate (32%). However, it is somewhat surprising that almost one-third of those offenders who are closest personally and emotionally to the victims have priors against children, because it suggests that their own children, perhaps as well as others, were targets of violence before. In between, 41 percent of the child abduction killers who are friends or acquaintances of the victims have committed crimes against children.

Killers' Custody Status

Even though these child abduction killers have sordid, troubled histories, including substantial evidence of prior crimes of violence against children, most of them (61%), like murderers in general (66%), are not in any "official custody status" at the time of the extant murder. That is, the majority of them are ostensibly free of legal controls when they commit the murder. At the same time, a meaningful proportion of them (27%) are either on parole or probation when they kill, compared to 17 percent of all murderers. So, on the on hand, most child abduction killers may not be immediately accessible in the custodial system, but compared to other murderers, they are more likely to be found in the active files of the correctional or judicial systems.

Overall, child abduction killers possess a number of important and meaningful indicators of social marginality and of a concurrent predisposition to commit crimes of violence against child victims. Most of them exhibit the weak social bonds to conventional others, contexts, relationships, and activities that criminologists propose are among the strongest predictors of involvement in crime. In the language of control theory, these types of individuals are more "free to deviate"—that is, they are on the verge of committing a crime, given an appropriate motivation and opportunity.

The M.O. (Modus Operandi) and Motivation

Surprisingly, two-thirds (67%) of the prior crimes committed against children had an M.O. that was similar to that *in the murder* that was committed by the same offender. For example, a child abduction killer is very likely to commit a rape against a child in a way that is quite similar to the way he kills another child. The similarities in M.O.s produced other surprises: They were most alike, by a large margin, in the "commission of the offense," or the way the crimes were committed. In 70 percent of the cases that had similar M.O.s, the priors were committed in similar ways—for example, the choice of weapon (say a knife) was the same across different crimes committed by a killer. Contrary to what the literature on murder suggests, these child abduction killers were much less likely to select certain types of victims based on their personal characteristics: Only 28 percent of prior crimes were committed against victims with similar personal attributes—for example, the killer had a prior for an assault on a victim with long blonde hair and the murder victim also had long blonde hair. The crimes were even less likely (21%) to be similar in their approach to the victim—for example, using deception to gain control over an eventual molestation victim and, later, the murder victim. Last, 17 percent of the prior crimes against children were similar to the extant murder in the kinds of specific acts that were performed during the commission of the crimes—for example, the killer used duct tape to subdue and control a kidnap victim, as well as the subsequent murder victim.

These findings regarding the similarity of M.O.s across the great majority of crimes committed by child abduction killers show that there is more consistency in the M.O.s of these types of killers than expected and as compared to other types of murderers. The data also suggest that there may be a greater predisposition to serial offending among child abduction killers.

Sexual Motivation

Another characteristic that most of them share with serial murderers is a sexual component to their motivation to kill. In the case of child abduction murders, the overwhelming majority—69 percent—of the cases are classified as sexual murders, therefore, implying a sexual motivation, compared to only 7 percent of all murders, and 14 percent of child murders. These are extremely big differences in what is likely to be the primary motivation to commit these murders. Almost one-half (48%) of the child abduction murders are classified as rapes, and 21 percent as other sexual assaults. And as one would expect in these types of murders, a large group (30%) are righteous kidnappings, which is *15 times greater* than in all child murders, and *30 times greater* than in murders in general—it is one of the defining characteristics of child abduction murders. Some of the kidnappings may also include a secondary sexual component, because there is physical evidence that almost two-thirds (64%) of the child abduction murder victims had been sexually assaulted, compared to only 7 percent of all murder victims and 15 percent of child murder victims. Again, these are dramatic differences in the role of sexual motivation and behavior across the different types of murder.

Pornography

There is a common belief that pornography plays an important role in the process of motivating sex offenders and lust killers. The evidence simply does *not* support that conclusion regarding these child abduction killers. The role of pornography in the sexual motivation of these murders is insignificant. In only 4 percent of child abduction murders is there any evidence or indication that pornography was used as a "trigger" to motivate or initiate the murder. We suspect that for these types of killers, their predisposition to engage in violent and sexual acts with children is a deep-seated element of their flawed characters, making the exposure to pornographic materials unnecessary in the process of "getting motivated" to commit the murder. They do not need an external source to get ready to kill— *being* ready is part of who they are.

Crises and Stressors

Some observers of murder have proposed that certain kinds of personal problems—usually revolving around employment or marriage—may serve as "precipitating crises" that contribute to the motivation of the killer. In the case of child abduction murders, there is evidence of at least one precipitating crisis (or stressor) in the life of the killer in 38 percent of the cases. What is striking is that of these cases, the usual crises or stressors emphasized in the literature do not seem to be as important as others that seem to resonate with the character of the killers and with their choice of predominantly female victims. For example, only 12 percent involved marital problems, 14 percent involved employment problems, and 17 percent involved financial problems. The prevalence of these archetypal precipitating crises pales in comparison to two types of personal problems that are apparently more characteristic of child abduction killers. These murderers are much more likely to have had a "conflict with a female"(45% of the cases with crises) or "criminal/ legal problems" (36%). We know that the majority of these killers have extensive criminal histories, so it is not surprising that their related criminal/legal problems might be implicated somehow in the motivation to commit murder. We also know that there is a dramatic, disproportionate preponderance (76%) of young, vulnerable female victims—should it surprise us that conflicts with females (including marital problems) is the most common problem or stressor implicated as a precipitating crisis in child abduction murders? There seems to be some degree of psychological symmetry—albeit distorted—in the nature of the crises and the choice of victims.

Choosing and Controlling the Victim

A theoretical perspective in criminology—"lifestyle" or "routine activities" theory—proposes that there are three basic elements in a crime: a motivated offender, the opportunity to commit the crime, and ineffective guardians. In keeping with the prior observation that most of these child abduction killers seem to be predisposed or "ready" to kill, if they are given the opportunity, and the risk of identification or apprehension is minimized because the potential victim is not being monitored, the probability of an abduction and murder increases. Absent any one of the elements, the chances of murder decline. However, given this kind of group of motivated offenders, it should not be surprising that 57 percent of the murder victims are simply "victims of opportunity"—they were killed because of the opportunity to act on a general predisposition to commit violence against children (only 13% had a "specific motivation" to kill a particular victim). It is clear that most of these killers are not searching for and selecting a specific type of victim. Only 14 percent of them chose their victim based on distinguishable physical characteristics, such as hair color, body type, or race/ethnicity. And in keeping with these types of murders, only 15 percent of the killers chose their victim because they had any kind of prior relationship with the victim—remember, most of these killers are total strangers or acquaintances. These types of child abduction killers are not typically targeting specific victims for specific reasons (or motives) but, rather, they seem to be more like "killers-in-waiting"—given the right opportunity coupled with a vulnerable child, they are more likely to spring into action, changing from a chronic hunter to an occasional predator to an episodic killer.

When they do spring into action, the great majority of them are not subtle or clever predators. Almost two-thirds of them simply assault the victim and subdue her: 62 percent engage in a direct physical assault and another 3 percent threaten an assault. Therefore, control over the victim is usually the result of a "blitz" confrontation with the victim at the point of approach and abduction. It is a "snatch and grab." With most children, this is relatively easy to accomplish because of their small physical stature.

They are also more vulnerable in a psychological sense—they are immature and more easily duped or deceived by a predatory abductor. Of course, victim vulnerability (16% of the cases) and the use of deception (19%) by the offender go hand-in-hand. Child abduction killers prey upon the innocence of the youngest victims (the "little kids" and "children"), upon whom deception is used much more often than on older victims. The killer knows that the lure of "seeing my puppies" may be sufficient to get a young child into his car and, therefore, under his control. A direct assault to gain control over the victim is unnecessary, at least at the point of initial victim-killer contact.

There is evidence that child abduction killers are 6 to 12 times more likely than other murderers to "bind" their victims. In one-fourth of the cases the killers bound their victims, compared to only 2 percent in child murders and 4 percent in all murders. The much more frequent binding of child abduction murder victims reflects both *control* and *sexual* elements. Binding a victim makes control easier, and for uncooperative, strong victims it may be absolutely necessary. For child victims, this control function of binding is less critical. But in these types of murders, with their strong sexual component, the binding (or "bondage") is likely to serve more primary sexual functions. These victims are being bound less to physically control them than to fulfill the sexual fantasies and needs of the killers. There is evidence that many of these killers are sexual sadists.

Cause of Death

Whereas firearms are the most common cause of death among murders in general (43% in Washington state and over 50% in most states), they are the least common cause of death among child abduction murders (only 11%). Strangulation is the least common cause of death in all murders (only 9%), but it is the most common cause among children who are abducted (33%). To the contrary, the most common cause of death among all child victims of murder is blunt force (37%)—they are beaten to death, typically by one of their parents.

Comparing the causes of death of the victims of child abduction killers versus all child murderers: The former are more likely to strangle (33% versus 13%) and stab/cut (24% versus 9%) their victims than the latter, and less likely to beat or bludgeon (21% versus 37%) and shoot (11% versus 16%) them. Direct, *"hands on"* ways of killing the victim are the clear preference of child abduction killers—strangulation and stabbing/cutting account for 57 percent of the deaths, compared to 22 percent for all child murderers.

There are also differences in the cause of death by the age of the victim. As one might expect, since it is physically easier to kill younger and, therefore, smaller and weaker victims with one's hands, killers are more likely to use firearms on older victims, especially boys, and strangulation on younger victims. So, some of the ways of killing (e.g., strangulation) have psychological or symbolic meaning for the murderer, while others (e.g., firearms) reflect more expedient choices.

Unusual Acts

There is a common belief that killers who commit murders that are out of the ordinary are involved in a variety of unusual acts during the murder incident, ranging from cult rituals to "posing" victims to grotesque mutilation. In general, the data suggest that child abduction murders are *not* characterized by unusual, bizarre, or weird acts or rituals. There is almost no evidence (less than 1% of the cases) that would indicate that unusual ceremonies or acts had been performed at the crime scene (e.g., burnt candles, dead animals, satanic symbols). The extreme rarity of these kinds of acts in child abduction murders is consistent with what is found in all murder cases.

Likewise, once the murder has been committed, child abduction killers are much more likely (52%) to *conceal* the victim's body when they dispose of it than murderers in general (14%). Therefore, they are also much less likely to be unconcerned about body disposal (39% versus 69%), as well as to place the body in the open (to leave it where it drops) for anyone to see who might come upon it (9% versus 17%). In short, they do not want the body to be seen or discovered, at least easily and quickly, but at the same time, they do not go out of their way to intentionally display or pose the body. In only 3 percent of the cases did the killer intentionally "pose" the victim's body in an unusual—and typically symbolic—position. This rate of public display of the body is comparable to that found for all murders, as is the removal of body parts from the victim's body (5% of the cases) before it is disposed of.

In summary, child abduction murders are part of a general pattern of violence against children, typically with a strong sexual component.

Post-Offense Behavior

After the murder is committed and the body disposed of, the killer apparently engages in a variety of behaviors that are related to the murder, which for many of them constitute a prelude to apprehension and arrest.

The killers do a number of things after the murder, but six behaviors are most common and, at the same time, most telling. Approximately one-out-of-five of these child abduction killers left town right after the murder, confided in someone about their involvement in the murder, and/or followed the case in the media. About one-in-ten contacted the victim's family, revisited the crime scene, and/or actually interjected himself into the murder investigation in some way. Of course, skipping town or moving after the murder, or maintaining ties to the murder and its investigation, all may provide leads for investigators to pursue.

In 15 percent of the cases, the killer kept the body longer than necessary to dispose of it, and he kept it in convenient and accessible places where it could be concealed, moved quickly, and/or "played" with. In 50 percent of these cases, the killer kept the body in his residence, in 28 percent in his car, and in 22 percent of the murders, a variety of other places within easy reach. However, contrary to beliefs about murderers, especially serial killers, who prolong their relationship with the victim, these child abduction killers only held onto the bodies for very short periods of time. Of the bodies that were kept by the killer, 31 percent were in his possession for less than three hours and 69 percent for less than 24 hours. So, it is likely that most of the bodies were being kept only until they could be disposed of safely. Only 6 percent of the bodies that were kept by the killer were in his possession for more than a week; it is more likely that in these cases there was a reason other than delayed disposal—for example, to play out sexual fantasies with the corpse or to treat it like a trophy—for keeping the body.

More striking is the number of child abduction killers who returned to the body disposal site. Almost one-fourth (22%) of the killers return to the body after they have not only killed the victim but have also disposed of the victim and left the crime scene for some meaningful period of time. Of these killers who return, an incredible *81 percent* do so *prior* to the discovery of the body, and *56 percent* do so within *three days* after the murder. Clearly, a significant proportion of child abduction killers return to the body disposal site, particularly soon after the murder has occurred. As one would expect, very few return after the body has been discovered and reported in the media. But an opportunity exists—albeit for a short period of time—for investigators to observe potential suspects between the time the body is reported to the police and, then, made public by the media.

This potential for contact with anyone who may physically be around some aspect of the murder, crime scene, or body disposal site is critical to investigations. The evidence shows that the police had "contact" with *the killer* about some aspect of the case—*before* he became the prime suspect—in more than one-third (34%) of the cases. The police usually do not realize or know that they have come this close to the killer, and probably early in the investigation, when many names are being recorded, interviews are being done, canvassing is taking place, records are being searched, tips are being received, and so on. Police need to know and recognize this in conducting the investigation of a child abduction murder—the killer's name may be in the possession of investigators in a substantial proportion of cases, and early in the investigation.

Surprisingly, the data show that the killer's name became known—in any way, not necessarily even as the "suspect"—very early in the course of most of the investigations of child abduction murder. In almost one-third (30%) of the cases, the killer's name came up *immediately*. In a majority (51%) of the cases it appeared within *24 hours*. In three-fourths (74%) of the cases it emerged within a *week*. This might be cause for alarm, but there is other evidence that the police are on the tail of the killer relatively early in the investigation as well.

In 25 percent of the cases, investigators "focused" on the killer as a suspect or person of interest almost "immediately," meaning at the beginning of the investigation. In more than 50 percent of the cases, police moved on the murderer within one and one-half days. But then there is a dramatic drop-off—after a month from the beginning of the murder investigation, there is still no primary suspect in more than 20 percent of the cases. Fortunately, this also means that by a month's end, in 78 percent of the cases investigators have focused on the eventual identified killer.

DOMESTIC MURDER

Patterns of Marital Homicide: A Comparison of Husbands and Wives

ANN GOETTING

M ost Americans view the family as a center for warmth, affection, acceptance and happiness that serves as a refuge from the more competitive, stressful and violent outside world. This image remains intact in spite of the fact that for over a decade now, research and the media have demonstrated the "underside" of domestic life. It has become clear that the home is a dangerous place; more violence occurs there than outside its doors. Perhaps we cling to notions of the idealized family with good reason. Maybe the image of wise and devoted husbands and wives lovingly nurturing one another and their attractive, courteous, obedient and charming children through the typical stages of the life cycle provides us with an important source of comfort. Or perhaps, as is suggested by Steinmetz and Straus, this myth of domestic tranquility plays a critical role in the maintenance of the social institution of the family by encouraging individuals to marry, to stay married and to have children. Whatever causes the persistence of this ideology, we should recognize that it may not occur without cost, for it likely has served to limit the objective analysis of family violence. It is only through such analysis that we may become freed to understand and perhaps ultimately prevent such violence.

The purpose of this study is to contribute to the very limited data base on one form of family violence in the United States, that is marital homicide, which involves the killing of a person by his or her spouse. In 1984 marital homicide accounted for nearly half of intrafamily homicide, making it the most frequent type of intrafamily victim-offender relationship. This research is intended to update sociological knowledge on the subject, and to extend current information by introducing additional variables. What remains the most important sociological inquiry into marital homicide, Wolfgang's Philadelphia study, is now dated by over three decades. More recent efforts focus exclusively on homicidal wives. The concerns addressed by this study relate to the general contextual nexus of marital homicide as well as to specific gender-based comparisons. What kinds of people kill their spouses? When, where and under what circumstance do they act: What weapons do they select?; What motivational forces come into play?; Is the fatal act typically offensive or defensive?; Is alcohol involved?; Are there witnesses?; Does the offender flee the scene?; What legal dispositions are associated with this behavior? Finally, do husbands and wives differ from one another on these factors? Wolfgang discovered gender to be a critical determinant of weapon selection, room of offense, victim precipitation and legal disposition. Do these correlates hold true in the 1980s in a different Midwestern city?

RESEARCH METHODS

The subjects selected for this study include the total population of eighty-four arrestees, twenty-eight male and fifty-six female, accused of having killed their spouses (both legal and common-law) in the city of Detroit, Michigan during 1982 and 1983 (except those attributed to the negligent use of a vehicle). An important limitation of the study lies in its lack of generalizability; its subjects are drawn from an urban, predominantly Black population with an inordinately high homicide rate. In fact, in 1987, its third consecutive year for ranking highest in the nation, Detroit reported 54.6 homicides per 100,000 inhabitants. The eighty-four cases constituting this study population account for 11.2 percent of all closed homicide cases in that city during those two years. Data collection took place in June of 1986 in the offices of the Homicide Section of the Detroit Police Department. Police-recorded information regarding each case, including the Investigator's Report, Interrogation Record, and Witness Statements was electronically copied for subsequent perusal.

The data were tabulated and, when feasible, comparisons are made with the total population of Detroit arrestees for homicides committed during 1982 and 1983, and with previous homicide studies employing general populations and offenders. Since the proportion of homicide arrestees who are accused of having killed spouses remains between 8 and 9 percent (U.S. Department of Justice, 1982–85), this means that the comparisons employed should have, according to the laws of probability, utilized populations and samples constituting approximately 91 percent members who are not offenders against spouses. Clearly the comparisons applied for this study are less than ideal on two counts: (1) the comparison groups are not totally mutually exclusive (i.e., the other-than-offender-against-spouse groups actually contain some offenders against spouses) and (2) except when 1982 and 1983 Detroit data are available, the comparison groups are not geographically and temporally comparable. Throughout the analyses, notable differences between male and female subjects are acknowledged. Population characteristics and gender differences are summarized in Table 1.

ANALYSES
Demographic and Social Characteristics of Offenders and Victims

Race

Research repeatedly has verified that homicide offenders and their victims in the United States are disproportionately Black. Detroit provides no exception to this generalization, and neither do the men and women who kill their spouses in that city. In 1980, 63 percent of the Detroit population was Black. Of all arrestees for homicides committed in Detroit during 1982 and 1983, 89.1 percent were Black, and 81.9 percent of victims were Black. Information on the offenders against spouses in that population indicated that 90.5 percent (76) of them and 91.7 percent (77) of their victims were of that racial category. Three of the offenses under observation here were interracial: In two cases a White woman killed her Black husband, and in the remaining case a Black woman killed her White husband.

Age

The study population of offenders ranged in age between eighteen and eighty-two years, with a mean of 35.5. Their victims showed approximately the same age range, with a mean of 37.9 years of age. As might be expected, the victims of the women generally were older than they, while the victims of the men generally were younger than their slayers. The killers and victims under observation here were slightly older than the general population of arrested killers and slain victims in Detroit during 1982 and 1983. Those mean arrestee and victim ages were 31.5 and 35 years, respectively.

Residential Mode and Parental Status of Offender

Nearly all (95 percent or 76) of the eighty killers who reported residential mode were living in a family setting; all except eleven (86.9 percent) of the total population were residing with their victimized spouses at the time of the offense. Nearly 81 percent (59) of the seventy-three offenders for whom data were available acknowledged at least one living child.

Chapter 4: *Types of Murder*

Table 1

Summary of population and subpopulation (by gender) characteristics

Characteristics	(Sub) Population Size[a]	Number	Percent	Mean
Demographic and Social Characteristics				
Offender: Black	84	76	90.5	
Women	56	54	96.4	
Men	28	22	78.6	
Victim: Black	84	77	91.7	
Women	28	22	78.6	
Men	56	55	98.2	
Offender: Age	84			35.5 years
Women	56			34.1 years
Men	28			38.3 years
Victim: Age	84			37.9 years
Women	28			34.8 years
Men	56			39.4 years
Offender: Lived in Family Setting	80	76	95.0	
Women	54	52	96.3	
Men	26	24	92.3	
Offender: Residing with Spouse	84	73	86.9	
Women	56	51	91.1	
Men	28	22	78.6	
Offender: Child(ren)	73	59	80.8	
Women	53	43	81.1	
Men	20	16	80.0	
Offender: Completed 12 Years School	63	33	52.4	
Women	45	22	48.9	
Men	18	11	61.1	
Offender: Unemployed	72	53	73.6	
Women	50	39	78.0	
Men	22	14	63.6	
Offender: Welfare Recipient	33	22	66.7	
Women	28	20	71.4	
Men	5	2	40.0	
Offender: No Residential Telephone	74	18	24.3	
Women	52	14	26.9	
Men	22	4	18.2	
Offender: Arrest Record	53	30	56.6	
Women	35	18	51.4	
Men	18	12	66.7	
Circumstances of Offense				
Motive: Domestic Discord	84	79	94.0	
Women (O)[b]	56	53	94.6	
Men (O)	28	26	92.9	
Method: Gunshot	84	49	58.3	
Women (V)[b]	28	18	64.3	
Men (V)	56	31	55.4	

236

Characteristics	(Sub) Population Size[a]	Number	Percent	Mean
Method: Stabbing	84	27	32.1	
Women (V)	28	4	14.3	
Men (V)	56	23	41.1	
Single-Victim/Single-Offender	84	81	96.4	
Women (O)	56	55	98.2	
Men (O)	28	26	92.9	
Victim Precipitation	55	33	60.0	
Women (O)	45	32	71.1	
Men (O)	10	1	10.0	
Location: Residence	84	75	89.3	
Women (O)	56	51	91.1	
Men (O)	28	24	85.7	
Location: Bedroom	69	27	39.1	
Women (O)	49	15	30.6	
Men (O)	20	12	60.0	
Time: Weekend	82	49	59.7	
Women (O)	56	34	60.7	
Men (O)	26	15	57.7	
Time: 8 PM–1:59 AM	81	34	42.0	
Women (O)	55	25	45.5	
Men (O)	26	9	34.6	
Offender: Alcohol	31	27	87.1	
Women (O)	21	18	85.7	
Men (O)	10	9	90.0	
Victim: Alcohol	33	31	93.9	
Women (O)	24	25	96.2	
Men (O)	7	6	85.7	
Audience	82	32	39.0	
Women (O)	55	23	41.8	
Men (O)	27	9	33.3	
Fled Scene	77	21	27.3	
Women	51	8	15.7	
Men	26	13	50.0	
Arrest Disposition				
Denied Warrant	78[c]	23	29.5	
Women	54[c]	20	37.0	
Men	24[c]	3	12.5	
Convicted of Murder or Manslaughter	53[d]	33	62.3	
Women	34[d]	16	47.1	
Men	19[d]	17	89.4	
Prison Sentences	38[e]	27	71.1	
Women	21[e]	12	57.1	
Men	17[e]	15	88.2	

[a]Number of subjects for which information was available
[b]O = offenders; V = victims
[c]Number of subjects at risk of prosecution
[d]Number of subjects processed by Court
[e]Number of subjects convicted

Social Class Indicators of Offender

Just over half of the sixty-three offenders for whom information on formal education Was available had completed at least twelve years of school. Over 20 percent (13) were educated beyond that level. These data reflect a relatively low level of formal education when compared with the general United States population at the same point in time. Employment information was available for seventy-two of the arrestees; nearly three quarters (73.6 percent or 53) of whom were unemployed, one of them having retired and another currently collecting disability compensation.

These data on education and unemployment, in conjunction with the facts that two-thirds (22) of the thirty-three subjects for whom information was available were welfare recipients, and 24.3 percent (18) of the seventy-four for whom data were recorded reported having no residential telephone, are congruent with other studies suggesting that homicide offenders are concentrated in the lower social classes.

Arrest Record of Offender

Homicide records indicate that 56.6 percent (30) of the fifty-three offenders for whom data were available had been arrested at least once prior to the offenses that precipitated them into the study population. While this is a crude measure of criminal history, since it fails to delineate the particular charges and dispositions associated with arrests, it does suggest that a high proportion of the spouse killers under observation here are likely to have had criminal backgrounds. Available research indicates a basic consistency when comparing this particular category of offender with general populations of homicide offenders on this dimension. Wolfgang reports 64 percent and Swigert and Farrell report 56 percent of their homicide offender populations as having had previous arrests.

CIRCUMSTANCES OF OFFENSE

Homicidal Motive

Most marital homicides occur in the context of domestic discord. The typical scenario involves an argument or a physical or verbal confrontation, perhaps over sexual indiscretion, money, or the threat of terminating the relationship. In such cases, the death blow usually is the culminating event in a long history of interpersonal tensions entrenched in violence. It is struck in the urgency of passionate anger; the fatal outcome commonly is realized with shock and disbelief. Often the offender had not intended to go so far. Homicidal marriages appear to be strongly ambivalent in nature, and the deadly act seems to dissipate hateful sentiments on the part of the offender, leaving a sense of despair at the loss of a loved one.

Homicidal Method

Firearms are the most common means of inflicting death in this country. Between 1968 and 1978 the proportion of homicides committed with firearms varied between 63 and 65.7 percent. In Detroit during 1982 and 1983, 65.8 percent of the 1138 reported homicides were shootings. Another 17.8 percent were stabbings, 11.4 percent were beatings, .7 percent were burnings and 4.2 percent were conducted by some other means. The distribution of homicidal methods associated with the victims of marital homicide in Detroit during those years differs from that associated with the general population of victims primarily in that a somewhat lower proportion of the spouses (58.3 percent or 49) died of gunshot wounds, and a much higher proportion (32.1 percent or 27) were stabbed. Five victims (5.6 percent) were beaten to death, three (3.6 percent) with blunt instruments, and two (2.4 percent) through use of hands and or feet as weapons; and another three (3.6 percent) were strangled or suffocated. Distributions of methods vary distinctly by gender. A somewhat lower proportion of husbands than wives died of gunshot wounds, and a much higher proportion (nearly triple) were stabbed This is consistent with Wolfgang's observation that wives were more than twice as likely as husbands to use cutting instruments, attributing that difference to "cultural tradition." Because of their domestic role (i.e., involving food preparation), women are more accustomed to using knives than are men. Additionally, all beatings using hands and/or feet and all strangulations or suffocations were inflicted on wives.

Number of Victims and Offenders

Almost all homicides are one-on-one incidents, with a higher concentration among domestic killings. Detroit provides no exception to this generalization, and neither do the men and women who kill their spouses in that city. In Detroit during 1982 and 1983, 87.9 percent of the 578 homicides for which information is available involved a single victim and a single offender. Another 10.6 percent of those offenses were single victim/multiple-offender; 1.4 percent were multiple-victim/ single-offender; and the remaining .2 percent were multiple-victim/ multiple-offender. All except three (96.4 percent) of the homicides against spouses occurring in that city during those years were one-on-one. Two of the exceptional incidents, both perpetrated by men, involved a single offender, one with two victims (a wife and their eighteen-year-old daughter), and the other with three (a common-law wife, her ten-year-old son and their eight-year-old son). The third case involved the woman and her boyfriend who conspired to kill her husband for insurance benefits.

Victim Precipitation

The concept of victim precipitation originated with von Hentig in the 1940s, who observed that "the victim shapes and molds the criminal" and that "the victim assumes the role of a determinant." The actual term "victim precipitation" was later coined by Wolfgang, and is applied to those offenses in which the victim is the first in the homicide drama to use physical force directed against his subsequent slayer. Information on victim precipitation could be gleaned from 1982 and 1983 Detroit police records for fifty-five homicides perpetrated against spouses. Sixty percent (33) of these cases were victim precipitated. This proportion is high when compared with data from studies of general homicide populations, which report victim-precipitation to characterize between 22 and 37.9 percent of deadly encounters. This discrepancy can be explained by the predominance of homicidal wives in the study population (45 of the 55 subjects for whom information was available were wives). It has been established that a relatively high proportion of spousal homicides perpetrated by women are victim precipitated (Wolfgang reports 59.6 percent), and the wives under observation here conform to that generalization (71.1 percent of their offenses were of that nature).

Spatial Considerations

A survey of homicide research suggests that between 42 and 53 percent of homicides occur at a private residence. Consistent with Wolfgang's study, the present Detroit data suggest, as might be expected, that marital homicides are far more likely to occur in that setting than are the general population of homicides. Over 89 percent (75) of the killings in this study were accomplished in a home: 78.6 percent (66) occurred at the common residence of the offender and victim, 8.3 percent (7) at the residence of the offender, 1.2 percent (1) at the residence of the victim, and another 1.2 percent (1) at the residence of a friend. Additionally. eight offenses (9.5 percent) took place on public streets. and one (1.2 percent) at the place of business of the victim.

Over 39 percent (27) of the sixty-nine offenses committed at a private residence for which information was available occurred in a bedroom; again, this closely approximates the 35 percent reported by Wolfgang. Another 21.7 percent (15) took place in the living room. Approximately 10 percent (7) occurred each outside the actual residence (usually on the porch or in the yard) and in the kitchen, 7.2 percent (5) in the dining room, 4.3 percent (3) in a hallway, 2.9 percent (2) in each a bathroom and an "other" room, and 1.4 percent (1) in the basement. Like the husbands observed in the Wolfgang study, those under observation here were twice as likely to kill in a bedroom as were the wives. Only one of the six offenses occurring in the kitchen was perpetrated by a husband, and all seven of the outdoor incidents were perpetrated by wives.

Temporal Considerations

Clearly there is a temporal order inherent in violent behavior. While the tempo of homicide varies slightly according to season, it varies markedly by days of week and hours of day. Homicide is a leisure-related activity, and is closely associated with periods typically devoted to recreation.

For 1982 and 1983 combined, the frequency distribution of all Detroit homicides over the twelve months indicates a general overall stability except for slight increases during August-September (the hot season) and December-January (the Holiday Season), and a discernable dip in April (the introduction to Spring). Except for a moderate increase during January and February, the marital homicides in that city during those years displayed no apparent seasonal fluctuations. Their frequencies over the ten or perhaps twelve months appear to be randomly distributed, with a high of 13.1 percent in January to a low of 4.8 percent in May and October.

Relative to days of week, the research population of marital homicides conformed closely to the norm. Data are consistent in indicating that homicide is concentrated during weekends, peaking on Saturdays, and these husbands and wives provide no exception to that generalization. Nearly 60 percent (49) of the eighty-two killings in this study for which information was available occurred on Fridays, Saturdays and Sundays (the days of the three highest single frequencies), which clearly is in line with the range extending between 56.6 and 84 percent reported by studies using general populations of offenders.

The subjects conformed less closely to hourly norms. Wolfgang and Pokorney provide the only two sources of information on homicide that effectively can be compared with data describing the Detroit killers on the subject of time of offense. The two studies are consistent with one another in indicating that approximately half of homicides occur between 8:00 P.M. and 1:59 A.M., and another quarter occur between 2:00 P.M. and 7:59 P.M. Basically congruous with these general homicide populations, the spouses under observation here executed 42 percent (34) of the eighty-one homicides for which information Was available between 8:00 p.m. and 1:59 A.M., and 28.4 percent (23) between 2:00 P.M. and 7:59 P.M. The remaining 29.6 percent (24) of the cases apparently were evenly distributed throughout. the remaining hours of the day.

Alcohol Consumption

Available information suggests that alcohol consumption makes a critical contribution to the homicide drama and to marital violence. The information gleaned from Witness Statements for this study of homicidal spouses is limited in that data were available for just over a third of the subjects. But these data suggest that alcohol may have played a vital role in many of the incidents. At least 32.1 percent (27) of the total population of offenders had been drinking prior to the homicide, as had at least 36.9 percent (31) of their victims.

Audience and Offender's Response

Thirty-nine percent (32) of the eighty-two victims for whom data were recorded received their fatal blows before witnesses. Most (67.5 percent of 52) of the seventy-seven offenders for whom information was available remained at the homicide scene until investigators arrived; only 27.3 percent (21) fled to avoid detection. Another four (5.2 percent), all men, committed suicide at the scene. It is interesting to note that more than three times the proportion of men than women fled the scene.

ARREST DISPOSITION

Prosecuting Attorney

Prosecuting attorneys are recognized as yielding weighty influence in the determination of criminal processing outcomes. They are allowed much discretion in their decisions as to what criminal charges, if any, will be filed against arrestees in Court. Of the seventy-eight spouse killers for whom information was available who were at risk of prosecution (excluding the four suicides), 29.5 percent (23) were denied warrant for criminal charge by the Prosecutor. This proportion is congruent with the estimated 30.4 percent of the general population of homicide arrestees for that city during 1983 who enjoyed similar denial, suggesting an absence of prosecutorial bias toward this category of offender. Nearly three times the proportion of women as men who were at risk were denied warrant, which is not surprising in light of the fact that such a high proportion of incidents perpetrated by women were victim precipitated. Additionally, the notion of chivalry may enter in here; most studies of felony defendants have found that women are more likely to be released prior to trial than are their male counterparts.

Court

Court dispositions associated with the fifty-three arrestees who were processed by the Court (excluding the subject never taken into custody, the four suicides, and one subject who skipped bond) indicate that 62.3 percent (33) were convicted of Murder or Manslaughter; 9.4 percent (5) were convicted of a Misdemeanor including Careless Discharge, Intentionally Point a Firearm Without Malice, and Careless and Reckless use of a Firearm: Death Resulting (High Misdemeanor); and 28.3 percent (15) were acquitted. Of the thirty-eight convicted arrestees, 71.1 percent (27) received prison sentences: three for life, and the rest for a mean minimum of 7.7 years. A total of twenty-six of the thirty-three convicted of Murder or Manslaughter (78.8 percent) were sentenced to incarceration. One woman convicted of a misdemeanor received a prison sentence of fifteen days. Again, with Court disposition, leniency toward women is suggested. Consistent with the observations of Wolfgang, a much lower proportion of women than men who were processed by the Court were convicted of Murder or Manslaughter. Also, a much lower proportion of convicted women Were sentenced to incarceration. This apparent leniency directed toward Women by the Court system is incongruent with the discrimination applied to them as described by Browne.

DISCUSSION

The construction of a statistical profile describing the population of eighty-four men and women arrested for killing their spouses in the predominantly Black city of Detroit, Michigan during 1982 and 1983 yields the image of a Black man or woman in his or her middle thirties who lives in a family setting. He or she is an undereducated, unemployed parent with an arrest record, whose final in a series of heated arguments or confrontations with his or her spouse culminated in a defensive fatal gunshot in a bedroom or the living room of their residence on a weekend.

The findings reported herein are totally consistent With those derived from Wolfgang's Philadelphia study conducted over thirty years ago. This fact suggests that a robust and predictable pattern of circumstances surrounds marital homicide. It also verifies that the marital homicide experience differs significantly by gender: For the homicidal husband the act is nearly always offensive; for the wife it is usually defensive. This supports the popular contention that marital homicide, regardless of who inflicts the fatal blow, typically is a reflection of wife abuse. In the words of Russel: "The statistics on the murder of husbands, along with the statistics On the murder of wives, are both indicators of the desperate plight of some wives, not a sign that in this one area, males and females are equally violent." Previous research indicates that homicides do not occur without warning—nonlethal violence precedes domestic homicide. Abused women have been warned, yet they remain in a violent situation hoping for improvement. Consistent with other studies, the wives involved here along with witnesses to the incidents, usually children and other family members, seemingly accepted the situation as normal or at least tolerable. Even more disheartening is the suggestion that such violence inflicted in the context of a romantic relationship is in some cases perceived as a sign of love, and therefore perhaps even encouraged of the participants by one another.

Domestic Violence and Homicide Antecedents

MURRAY A. STRAUS

This paper is divided into three sections. The first section describes the nature and extent of homicides between family members, including some information on trends since 1966. The second section describes the extent of nonlethal violence within the family and its connection to homicide. The final section views intrafamily violence from a public health perspective, and discusses the implications for primary prevention.

INTRAFAMILY HOMICIDE IN THE UNITED STATES

The public image of homicide tends to focus on the type of wanton killing featured by the press and television—someone shot in the course of a robbery or a sadistic killer who attacks a stranger with no apparent motive. In fact, such killings are only a relatively small proportion of homicides. In about 80% of the cases, the victims and assailants were known to each other before the murder, and in a substantial proportion of the cases they are members of the same family. For the United States in 1984, 24% of all murder victims were related to their assailant. This percentage has fluctuated within a relatively narrow range (from 22.4 to 28.8%) since the FBI first started reporting data on intrafamily homicide in 1962, even though the total number of homicides has changed drastically in this period.

Overall intrafamily homicide rates. Although the intrafamily homicide percentage is an interesting and important statistic, there are at least three other statistics which need to be considered: the homicide rate, the number of deaths and the relative distribution of homicides among various family relationships such as wives killed by husbands, children killed by parents, etc. None of these other statistics are reported in the annual Uniform Crime Reports. However, it was possible to use Uniform Crime Reports to estimate these statistics, and the results are described and interpreted below.

These calculations produce an estimate of 4,408 intrafamily homicides in the United States in 1984. These 4,408 cases produce an intrafamily homicide rate of 1.86 per 100,000 population. Although this is a much lower rate than that for murders of unrelated persons (6.04 in 1984), it is high by comparison with other countries. In fact, just the family fraction of the United States intrafamily homicide rate is greater than the rate for all homicides which occurred in many countries with a low homicide rate. Denmark, for example, had a rate of 0.64 per 100,000 in 1969, England and Wales had a combined murder and manslaughter rate of 0.93 in 1972 and Germany a rate of 1.26 in 1972.

Specific family relationships. Intrafamily homicide covers a great many different types of relationships, and it is important to know if these differ from each other. For example, is the rate of children killed by parents higher than of parents killed by children? Table 1 allows us to compare the number of deaths and the homicide rate for several different family relationships for 1984.

Spouse murders. The first row of Table 1 shows that more than two thousand murders of a spouse occurred in 1984, and that spouse-murders were almost half (48%) of the intrafamily homicides which occurred in 1984, making them the most frequent type of intrafamily victim-offender relationship.

The second and third rows of Table 1 show that many more wives were killed by husbands than husbands killed by wives—roughly one third to two thirds, as shown by the figures in parenthesis on the second column. The fact that wives kill husbands at only one third the rate that husbands kill wives is consistent with the lower level of violence by women in all spheres of life. At the same time, the fact that women commit 38% of the spouse murders, compared to only 14% of the nonfamily homicides, and only 13% of the aggravated assaults, shows that within the family women are much more violent than they are outside the family. The violence of women within the family (as contrasted to their relative nonviolence outside the family) will also be shown later in this paper for assaults which do not end in death. A previous paper analyzes the reasons why women are much more violent within the family. Time available only permits me to say that one reason is self-defense or retaliation: women are rarely assaulted outside the family, whereas this is a common occurrence within the family.

Table 1

Number and rate of homicide by relationship of victim to offender, 1984[a]

Assailant	Victim	Number	Percent	Rate per 100,000 pop.
Spouse	Spouse	2116	48.0	0.89
Husband	Wife	1310	(62.0)	0.55
Wife	Husband	806	(38.0)	0.34
Parent	Daughter or son	730	16.6	0.31
Parent	Daughter	327	(45.0)	0.14
Parent	Son	403	(55.0)	0.17
Child	Parent	504	11.4	0.21
Child	Mother	202	(40.0)	0.09
Child	Father	302	(60.0)	0.13
Child	Sibling	403	9.1	0.17
Child	Brother	327	(81.0)	0.14
Child	Sister	76	(19.0)	0.03
Other family relationships		655	14.9	0.28

[a]Computed from data from Federal Bureau of Investigation.

Child murders. The term "child," as used in this paper, refers to a family relationship, not an age group, because Uniform Crime Reports data combines homicides of minor children and adult children. To remind readers of this, "child" will be put in quotation marks from time to time.

Murder of a son or daughter by a parent was the second most frequent type of intrafamily homicide. The 730 murders of sons and daughters which occurred in 1984 were 16.6% of the intrafamily murders that year.

The figures in parenthesis in the second column of Table 1 show that there was no important difference in the proportion of male and female "children" killed. However, an important question that cannot be answered with published data is whether there are important differences between fathers and mothers. On the one hand, women have the overwhelming (often the exclusive) responsibility for child care. The combination of the stress involved in this responsibility and the greater "time at risk" probably accounts for the higher rates of child abuse by mothers than fathers. On the other hand, many of the "children" killed were adults and the greater child care responsibilities of women do not place them at greater risk of killing adult children. Moreover, since male rates of every type of violence are much higher than rates for women, more of these "children" might have been killed by fathers than mothers. A study of 51 fatal child abuse cases in Georgia is consistent with this because it found a much higher rate of fatal child abuse committed by fathers.

Parent murders. Just over 500 parents were murdered by a son or daughter (who could be either a minor or an adult) in 1984, and this was 11.4% of the intrafamily homicides. As in the case of murders of children, the Uniform Crime Reports do not indicate the sex of the "child" who carried out the murder. We only know that fathers are somewhat more likely to be killed by a child than mothers. However, for the reasons just given, we suspect that sons committed many more of these homicides than daughters.

Sibling murders. About 400 persons were murdered by a sibling in 1984. In sharp contrast to children murdered by parents—who were about equally divided between sons and daughters—those killed by a sibling were overwhelmingly males (81 %). Again, the sex of the murderer is not available from published data, but because of their generally higher rates for all types of violence, we suspect that those who killed a sibling were most often males.

Other intrafamily homicides. All other family relationships together account for 655 (or 15% of intrafamily) homicides. Our data do not provide information on subdivisions within this category of intrafamily homicide.

Trends in the Number and Rate of Intrafamily Homicide

Trend in deaths and death rate. Perhaps the most fundamental statistic of all is the number of people who die at the hands of other family members. Figure 1a shows the trend in intrafamily homicide since 1966. There was an almost continual increase from 1966 through 1980. However, after reaching a peak of 5,778 deaths in 1980, there has been an almost equally consistent decrease over the past four years. My estimate for 1984 is that about 4,408 people were killed by another member of their own family. Although this represents a substantial and important reduction from the peak figure, it still constitutes a large number of presumably avoidable deaths. The increase to 1980 and subsequent decline shown in Figure 1a for the absolute number of homicide deaths is also shown in Figure 1b for the homicide rate. It is not possible to include in this paper an adequate analysis of the factors that may account for the increase in family homicides during the 1960s and 70s and the decrease since about 1980. All that can be said at this point is that the decrease in intrafamily homicides is part of a broader trend. Actually, in a certain sense, it is leading the trend. The overall homicide rate in the United

Figure 1a
Estimated *number* of intrafamily homicides, 1966–1984

Figure 1b
Estimated *rate* of intrafamily homicides, 1966–1984

States has declined from a rate of 10.2 per 100,000 in 1980 to a rate of 7.9 per 100,000 in 1984—a 22.5% decrease since 1980. The rate for nonfamily homicides decreased from 7.6 to 6.0 per 100,000—a 20.4% decrease. The decrease in the family homicide rate was greater than either of these—a 26.6% reduction.

Whatever the reasons, the decrease in family homicides since 1980 is an important development. The decrease has continued each year since 1980, it applies to the homicide rate as well as to the absolute number of deaths and the decrease in both the number and the rate is substantial.

Trends in the Distribution and Rate of Intrafamily Homicide

Murder of spouses. We have seen that in 1984 murder of a spouse was by far the largest category of intrafamily homicide. Presumably, this represents typical situations. To see if that is the case, the percentage of spouse murders was plotted in Figure 2a. This shows that spousal murders hovered around half of all intrafamily homicides during this 19-year period, but with a tendency for the percentage to have decreased.

Percentages such as those in Figure 2a can be misleading because they ignore, as they are intended to, changes in the absolute number and rate. Figure 2b therefore presents the trend in the spouse homicide *rate* from 1966 to 1984, which shows that the spousal part of the intrafamily homicide rate follows a pattern very similar to the trend for the overall intrafamily homicide rate (shown earlier in Figure 1b).

Other family relationships. Was there an equally large decrease in the homicide rate for other victim-offender relationships within the family? Since the overall decline in rates begins with 1980, we examined the plots for the five-year period from 1980 through 1984 for such a trend. Rather than burden the paper with additional plots, the information can be summarized by means of time series correlations. For example, the decrease in spousal homicides since 1980 shown in Figure 2b can be expressed as a correlation between year and spousal homicide rate of -0.94. Similar sharp declines occurred for murders of a brother or sister by a sibling (-0.79) and for "other family relationships" homicides (-0.96). However, during this five-year period of dramatic decrease in most categories of intrafamily homicide, there was no decrease in murders of "children" by parents or in murders of parents by "children" (as shown by their respective correlation with year of 0.02 and -0.04).

Summary on intrafamily homicide. This analysis has presented a series of statistics on different aspects of intrafamily homicide which have not been available previously. The main findings revealed by these new statistics can be summarized as follows:

A total of 4,408 intrafamily homicides occurred in 1984, of which about half were murders of spouses. Of the spouses killed, two thirds were wives. Sizeable

Figure 2a
Percent that spouse murders are of all intrafamily homicides

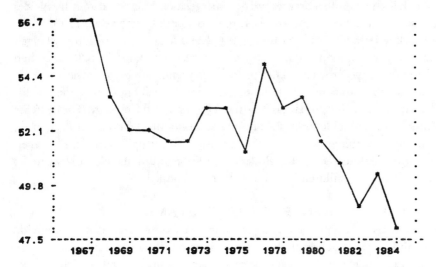

Figure 2b
Spouse-murders per 100,000 population

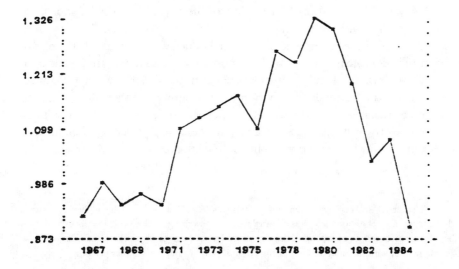

numbers of murders occurred between other family members, including 730 sons and daughters killed by parents in 1984, 505 parents killed by a son or daughter, 433 persons killed by a brother or sister and 655 other relationships. Intrafamily homicides increased from just over 3,000 cases in 1966 to a peak of 5,777 cases in 1980, and then declined steadily to 4,408 cases in 1984. The intrafamily homicide rate ranged from 1.62 per 100,000 in 1962 to a peak of 2.54 per 100,000 in 1980, and then declined year by year to a rate of 1.86 per 100,000 population in 1984. The homicide rate for just the intrafamily fraction of homicides is much higher than the rate for all homicides in such countries as England, Denmark and Germany. The decrease in intrafamily homicides from 1980 to 1984 is pronounced for murder of spouses, for murders of siblings and for "other family relationship" murders. However, murders of "children" (which includes both minor and adult children) by parents and of parents by "children" remain at their 1980 peak.

NONLETHAL VIOLENCE WITHIN THE FAMILY*

The statistics just presented on the nature and extent of intrafamily homicide clearly indicate that, at least in the extreme, intrafamily violence is a major source of premature mortality. However, for a variety of reasons, it is one which we have come to accept, even though it accounts for more years of potential life lost than many other avoidable deaths. In 1980 for example, cancer was responsible for a loss of 39,500 years of potential life among men aged 25 to 44, and in 1984 AIDS was responsible for a loss of 32,300 years. But homicides resulted in a loss of 174,600 years of potential life, including 43,700 years lost due to intrafamily homicides.

A key issue is whether this large loss of life is really avoidable, and, if so, whether public health workers can make a contribution to that end. In this section of the paper I shall present evidence from several studies which indicate that nonlethal intrafamily violence is a major source of morbidity and an important precursor of mortality. Thus, intrafamily homicides are not unpredictable events. Of course, inexplicable killings by previously non-violent family members do occur, and they make headlines. But it is partly because they are so rare that they make headlines. The day-to-day reality is that most family murders are prefaced by a long history of assaults. In short, there is time for life-saving intervention, and the final section

---

*The term "violence" (and even more, "family violence") is used in such widely varying ways that, except in cases of homicide, it is essential for anyone writing on this topic to inform readers of how the term is used. For purposes of this paper, "violence" refers to physical violence, defined as an act carried out with the intention of causing physical pain or injury to another person.

of this paper will present some of the research evidence on which such interventions can be based.

High incidence and prevalence rates. The study of a nationally representative sample of 2,143 families conducted 10 years ago is the only source of epidemiological data for a large and representative sample of American families. We are now in the process of replicating and extending that study. My guess is that the new study, like the original study, will show extremely high incidence rates for child abuse and spouse abuse. The original study revealed a minimum annual incidence rate for spouse abuse of 16 per 100 couples (not per 100,000) and for child abuse a minimum of 14 per 100 children. That translates to about 8.6 million spouses and 8.8 million children assaulted each year. The details are in Table 2.

Many resulting injuries. Despite the publicity given to domestic violence during the past few years, few people, including few physicians, realize that family violence is a public health problem of major importance. Let us look at some of the evidence, starting with a survey by Stark et al. of patients at a large metropolitan hospital: 21 % of all women who use the emergency surgical service were battered, and almost half of all injuries presented by women to the emergency surgical service occurred in the context of abuse. One in four women who attempt suicide were battered (for black women the figure is one out of two).

More recent work by Stark and Flitcraft suggests that the figures are even greater for pregnant women: not one out of five, but two out of three pregnant emergency room trauma patients are victims of family violence. This is consistent with the data first reported by Gelles which suggests that violence against women may actually increase during pregnancy. Not surprisingly, Stark et al. found that abused women have had more miscarriages than other women.

Findings from a representative sample of 1,793 women in Kentucky indicate that injuries inflicted by a male partner resulted in 4.41 physician visits per year per 100 women, of which 66% were emergency room or other hospital visits. A survey of 1,210 women in Texas found a 1 % per annum rate of injuries which required medical treatment. Extrapolating the mean of the Kentucky and Texas rates to the United States, I estimate that about a million and a half women each year receive medical attention because of an assault by a male partner, of which almost a million were hospital visits.

A mental health problem. Evidence suggests that intrafamily violence has major adverse effects on mental health. Carmen, Rieker and Mills, for example, report that almost half of a sample of 188 female psychiatric patients had histories of physical or sexual abuse at the hands of another member of their family. However, this study, and all other studies so far located of mental health consequences, lacks a

Table 2
Annual incidence rates for violence in a nationally representative sample of 2,143 families, and United States estimates based on these rates[a]

Type of intrafamily violence	Rate per 100 couples or children	Number assaulted each year[b]
A. Violence between husband and wife		
Any violence during the year (slap, push, etc.)	16	8,600,000
Severe violence[b] (kick, punch, stab, etc.)	6	3,200,000
Any violence by the husband	12	6,500,000
Severe violence by the husband	4	2,200,000
Any violence by the wife	12	6,500,000
Severe violence by the wife	5	2,700,000
B. Violence by parents		
Any hitting of child during the year	Near 100% for young child	
Severe violence ("child abuse")	14	8,800,000
Very severe violence	3.5	2,200,000
Any violence against 15–17 year olds	34	3,800,000
Severe violence against 15–17 year olds	6	700,000
Very severe violence against 15–17 year olds	3.4	400,000
C. Violence by children		
Any violence against a brother or sister	80	50,200,000
Severe violence against a brother or sister	53	33,300,000
Any violence against a parent	18	9,700,000
Severe violence against a parent	9	4,800,000
D. Violence by children age 15–17		
Any violence against a brother or sister	64	7,200,000
Severe violence against a brother or sister	36	4,000,000
Any violence against a parent	10	1,100,000
Severe violence against a parent	3.5	400,000

[a]The data are from Straus, Gelles and Steinmetz. Violence is defined as an act carried out the intention of causing physical pain or injury to another person.
[b]Severe violence refers to assaultive acts included in the *Conflict Tactics Scales* which go beyond pushing, slapping and throwing things, and which therefore carry a high risk of causing an injury serious enough to require medical attention. This includes kicking, punching, beating up, stabbing, shooting.

case-control comparison group. Comparison groups are needed because more than half of all married women have probably been hit by their husbands at least once during the course of their marriage. Therefore, the 50% rate found for psychiatric patients might not differ from the general public.

Nonlethal violence frequently precedes homicide. A tabulation of homicide cases in Kansas city found that the police "...had responded to disturbance calls at the address of homicide victims or suspects at least once in the 2 years before the homicide in 90 percent of the cases, and five or more times in the 2 years before the homicide in 50 percent of the cases." Browne's study of 42 battered women who had killed their husbands found a long history of serious assaults and many injuries, including threats of being killed by the husband. These studies indicate that intrafamily homicide is typically just one episode in a long standing syndrome of violence.

INTRAFAMILY VIOLENCE FROM A PUBLIC HEALTH PERSPECTIVE

The importance of a preventative approach is all too obvious in the case of homicide, but the need is just as great in the case of nonlethal violence. There are two reasons for this: Nonlethal violence is a frequent antecedent of homicide, and no mailer how extensive the treatment services for battered children and battered wives, the underlying conditions will continue to generate new cases. Our epidemiological survey shows that child protective services and shelters for battered women treat only a small fraction of the cases: there are at least eight times more abused children than come to public attention, and many times more abused spouses than are aided by shelters. There is little chance of increasing treatment services to deal with anywhere near the full population suffering from intrafamily violence. Even if such services were to become available, it would be an endless process because of the constant production of new cases.

Primary Prevention of Domestic Violence and Homicide

Granted the importance of prevention, is there anything that can be done within a medical context? Physicians, in their role as physicians, can do little about such causal factors as racial discrimination and unemployment. However, a wide range of risk factors have been identified, and a substantial number of them have been confirmed across two or more studies. Thus, there is a knowledge base which meets minimal scientific standards to serve on which to build public health prevention work. Possibilities are illustrated by the Straus et al. national survey, which identified 25 risk factors for spouse abuse. Figure 3 shows that with each additional risk factor, the probability of spouse abuse increased at an accelerating rate. Couples with none, one or two of these risk factors have a near zero probability of violence during a one-year period. From there, the chance of a violent incident occurring gradually increases with each additional risk factor up to eight risk factors. Couples with six to eight of the risk factors have about a one in 10 chance of violence. The probability of violence then climbs precipitously with each additional risk factor until those with 12 or more have about a two out of three chance of violence during the year.

These findings are based on a large and nationally representative sample of American families, but they are retrospective rather than prospective. A prospective study is needed to see whether the risk factors have temporal predictive validity. However, in my opinion, public health programs aimed at prevention of violence do not have to wait the many years before the results of a prospective study becomes available. This is because a number of the risk factors represent aspects of the family and society-such as early marriage, unwanted children, lack of skills in child management and social isolation-which need remedial action even if they have no impact on intrafamily violence.

Dangers in a Public Health Approach to Intrafamily Violence

I also need to point out that there are at least two reasons to be cautious about involving medical agencies and professionals in primary prevention of family violence, despite the fact that it is a major contributor to morbidity and mortality.

Exceeding public expectations. The first danger arises because many of the basic underlying causes of family violence are not characteristics which the public recognizes as health-related. For example, one of the most important risk factors summarized in Figure 3 is "male dominance in family decisions." However, the public thinks of equality between husband and wife as a religious or moral problem, not a health problem. So the down-side of making prevention of intrafamily violence a health issue is the possibility of alienating and antagonizing the public and therefore of undercutting support for public health work in general.

In view of the problem just mentioned, I suggest that only a limited subset of risk factors should be put on the public health agenda, and that these be risk factors most likely to be accepted by the public as health related. Fortunately, even this limited subset constitutes a large and important agenda. Here are some of the risk factors for which I see at least a reasonable chance of public acceptance as appropriate domains of the health professions: early marriage and/or child bearing, unwanted or large numbers of children, premature and handicapped children, use of physical punishment in child rearing and marital conflict.

256

Figure 3
Couple violence rate by checklist score

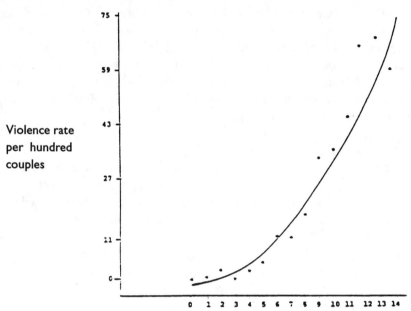

Violence rate per hundred couples

Of course, even this agenda may encounter public support and public relations problems. Some of the problems grow out of conflicting attitudes and behavior in respect to sex, as indicated by the sexualization of advertisements for almost everything, coexisting with the fact that television networks will not accept public service announcements about contraception. Contraceptive programs for sexually active teenagers encounter great opposition although this is the age group whose life chances are most adversely affected by an unintended pregnancy.

Medicalization of a social problem. A number of sociologists have also identified problems connected with "medicalizing" deviant behavior. Conrad defines medicalization as "…defining behavior as a medical problem or illness and mandating or licensing the medical profession to provide some type of treatment for it. Examples include alcoholism, drug addiction, and treating violence as a genetic or brain disorder." The negative aspects of medicalizing behavior problems include harm to individuals through stigmatizing labels, such as labeling a child as hyperkinetic; usurpation of social control functions by a particular profession (and one which,

257

furthermore, is untrained to deal with social issues); and diversion of attention and remedial action from the social conditions which produce the deviant behavior.

The position taken in this paper, however, is the reverse. It advocates the sociologicalization of a medical problem, not the medicalization of a social problem. Although a small percentage of violent behavior (perhaps 0.1%) is traceable to a genetic or brain disorder, violence is primarily a behavior which reflects a certain set of social conditions and behavioral patterns learned under those conditions. Public health programs to reduce morbidity and mortality can and should be directed to altering some of those social conditions.

Secondary Prevention

In addition to the primary prevention role just outlined, the medical professions can also make an important contribution to secondary prevention. By secondary prevention I mean steps to prevent reccurrence of family violence. Here the medical professions are in a particularly advantageous position because of two factors: case identification and public trust.

Case identification. Although fewer than 5% of physically abused children and spouses suffer injuries serious enough to require medical attention, in absolute terms the numbers are very large. The evidence cited earlier suggests that about a million and a half battered women require medical care each year. At least an equal number of cases can be assumed for children who require medical attention because of injuries inflicted by a parent. Almost all of these injuries are presented to the attending physician or nurse as having some origin other than intrafamily assault. However, it would not be difficult to develop a brief and practical (in the sense of accepted by patients) set of diagnostic criteria to identify a large percentage of the cases caused by intrafamily assault.

It may take no more than embedding the crucial questions in a diagnostic interview. For example, the National Health Interview Survey questions on accident or injury start by identifying the nature of the injury. Subsequent questions ask where the accident happened and whether a vehicle was involved. Our experience with the Conflict Tactics Scale indicates that by starting with nonthreatening questions of this type one can gradually address the key issue of whether the injury was caused by another person and who that person was. If this is correct, medical facilities offer an exceptional opportunity to identify cases in need of immediate help and also cases for secondary prevention.

Public trust. Despite growing complaints about the medical profession, the level of public confidence remains high. I am convinced that if the health professions were to take the initiative, they could make a tremendous contribution to the reduction of child abuse and spouse abuse-perhaps more than any other profession. The basic problem is that, rather than taking an active role, the health professions have tended to ignore or deliberately to avoid family violence. Like the public, the medical profession has tended to treat family violence as a private family matter, just as smoking was once viewed only as a matter of individual taste. But by recognizing and reconceptualizing intrafamily violence as the enormous threat to health that it actually is, the public will accept it as a legitimate sphere of the health professions. It is instructive to remember that only 20 years ago health professionals took little or no interest in smoking. But these issues have been reconceptualized from their previous status as a matter of individual taste to matters of direct health relevance. And the public has responded. I think they would also respond to a medical approach to family violence, and that this could make a major contribution to the reduction of homicide mortality.

Stranger Homicides in Nine American Cities

MARGARET A. ZAHN & PHILIP C. SAGI

P ast studies of homicide have focused either on the general demographic characteristics of homicide or on causal factors or processes descriptive of selected types, such as homicides within the family or those associated with felonies. Few studies have examined homicide comparatively by describing ways in which various types of homicide differ from each other. Even fewer studies describe the interactions between demographic variables such as age, sex, and race between and within types of homicide. For example, while numerous studies have established a greater volume of homicide victimization for young black males, these studies seldom determine whether such victimization exists in all contexts, such as within the family, between friends, and in robbery situations. This Article will first describe different types of homicide in terms of characteristics of victims, offenders, location, method of attack, and presence of witnesses.

This Article will next explore the types of homicide in terms of interactions among the variables of age, sex, and race.

TYPES OF HOMICIDE

While numerous typologies of homicide have been suggested, a typology used in homicide research is generally based on differences in victim–offender relationships. Classification schemes for such studies are diverse and inconsistent across studies.

Wolfgang has classified victim-offender relationships into thirteen categories; Boudouris has used twelve categories; and Curtis has used four primary categories. In Curtis' study of seventeen American cities in 1967, 24.7% of homicides were found to be within the family; 9% were within other primary relationships, which include lovers and close friends; 45.4% were within non-primary relationships, which include prostitutes, acquaintances, neighbors, and strangers (15.6% of the combined group were strangers); and 20.9% were unknown.

More recent studies, such as Straus, Gelles, and Steinmetz in 1980, Loftin in 1986, and Cook in 1985, have focused on violence or homicide within specific relationships, such as family homicide versus robbery homicide. These studies have added immensely to our understanding of family and robbery murders. Gelles, for example, found that the families which have the most violence within them are those families which are isolated and lack social supports. Unlike family homicides, robbery-motivated homicides are relatively more likely to occur in urban environments. High rates of robbery-murder are likely to be found in urban areas which have concentrated poor populations and which have young males who possess guns and are ready to use them to secure material goods. Smith and Parker in 1980 and Parker in 1984, however, studied felony types of homicide and discovered important differences in causal factors for intimate versus felony-related homicides. In their work, Smith and Parker examined predictors of four types of homicide: robbery murders; other felony murders; homicides occurring between friends and acquaintances; and homicides occurring among family intimates. Some predictors were type-specific. For example, racial composition is a factor in the robbery and the friends and acquaintances homicide types, but not in the other types.

Theoretically, as Parker has shown, the search for the causes of homicide can only be effectively completed with a refined set of appropriate categories of types of killings. Pragmatically, strategies for intervention should be quite different if there are clearly different types of homicide with different populations involved. For example, if stranger murders involve young male felons and family homicides involve middle-aged adult females, the causes and strategies of intervention and prevention will most likely differ.

Four types of homicide will be examined in this Article. The first two categories are homicide within the family and homicide among friends and acquaintances. The third and fourth categories emerge as a result of the distinction between two types of stranger murders: those associated with felonies and those not associated with felonies. To date, the research literature has for the most part associated robbery or felony-related murders with stranger killings as though the two were synonymous. Statistical evidence from a national study suggests, however, that stranger felony and stranger non-felony homicides may be distinct. These data show that stranger homicides are associated with felonies in 57.3% of the cases and are not so associated in 42.7% of the cases, although the ratio between felony-related and non-felony-related stranger murders is as low as 1:1 in some cities. Given these data and the importance of this issue, this Article stresses the importance of the investigation of factors affecting the two types of stranger murder and how such murders differ from murders in more intimate circles.

METHODS

Data for this report were drawn from a nation-wide study of the nature and patterns of homicide in the United States. The nine cities selected for study were: Philadelphia and Newark, New Jersey in the Northeast; Chicago and St. Louis in the Midwest; Memphis and Dallas in the South; and Oakland, San jose, and "Ashton" in the West. In these cities, with the exception of Chicago, data on all cases of homicide occurring in 1978 were collected. In Chicago, because of the large number of homicide cases (over 800), a 50% sample was used.

In each of the nine cities, police and medical examiner departments were asked to supply records for all homicide cases which had occurred in their jurisdictions in 1978. This particular year was selected because the departments have closed active investigations on most of the cases occurring in 1978, yet the data were sufficiently recent to have relevance for current policy and understanding of current homicide patterns. Once permission was secured, coders, persons familiar with the extensive data form used, went to each site and coded information on various aspects of each case, including: characteristics of the offender, such as age, sex, race, and past criminal history; characteristics of the victim; the relationship between the victim and the offender; and a variety of elements surrounding the homicide event, such as the number of witnesses present and the type of weapon used.

Data on a total of 1,748 homicide cases in the nine cities were collected. The original data collection included seventy killings by police in which a police officer was the "offender" and a number of cases in which data were either missing from the files or in which the relationship between the victim and the offender remained unknown (N = 260). For the most part, police killings and those homicides in which offender-victim relationship remained unknown have been eliminated from this analysis. After eliminating police killings and those killings in which the relationship was unknown, 1,373 homicide cases with known victim-offender relationships remained.

Victim-offender relationships were classified into four types. The first type, homicides within the family, includes immediate family members, unmarried couples living together, and separated or divorced couples. The within family type does not include heterosexual partners who have had some sexual relationship but have not lived together or had some other more extended relationship. These types of cases were classified as the friends and acquaintances homicide type. This second type, friends and acquaintances, includes people who have known each other in some way, ranging from neighbors and business associates to close personal friends. Stranger killings are those in which there is no evidence of prior acquaintance between the victim and the offender. The stranger type is further subdivided into those situations in which a felony is involved and those in which a felony is not involved. Most stranger felonies are robbery-connected, while stranger non-felonies represent a variety of situations.

General descriptive data for the four types of homicide will be presented. The types of homicide will be described by the age, race, and sex of both the victims and offenders, as well as by method of assault, the location of the killing, and whether or not witnesses were present. Following the discussion of general characteristics, the types of homicides will be examined, with race, age, and sex held constant in the statistical analysis. White, black and Hispanic groups will be examined. Homicides among "other" races were too sparsely represented in the data set to justify inclusion in the analysis and, therefore, were eliminated.

RESULTS

Types of Homicide in Nine Cities

As shown in Table 2, of the 1,373 cases with known victim–offender relationships, 18% occurred within the family, 54% occurred between friends and acquaintances, 16% were stranger felonies and 12% were stranger non-felonies. Clearly, the largest percentage of murders were those in which the killer and victim were acquainted. Twenty-eight percent of those with known relationships, however, were stranger killings, and stranger killings surpassed the percentage of people killed by family members. These data indicate that, among murder victims in the nine cities, the most likely offender was a friend or an acquaintance, and the second most likely offender was a stranger.

Characteristics of Types of Homicides

Gender and Type of Homicide

The majority of victims and offenders in all four types of homicide were males. In terms of victimization, both a percentage and a rate analysis show males to be at a greater risk than females. In situations which the victim-offender relationship is known, 82% of the victims were male and 18% were female. Both male and female victims were more likely to be killed by someone that they knew (70% for males and 81% for females). The victims of stranger killings were predominately male; 85% of the victims involved in stranger felony killings and 92% of the victims involved in stranger non-felony killings were male. Although males were killed in many relationships, females were primarily killed within the friends and acquaintance, and family categories.

Furthermore, males were more frequently the offenders in each of the four homicide types, with this dominance increasing as the relationship between the victim and the offender became more distant. Males were almost exclusively the offenders in stranger murders, with 96% of stranger felonies having male offenders and 93% of stranger non-felonies having male offenders.

Race and Type of Homicide

This Article makes contrasts only among the race categories of white, black and Hispanic. The victimization rates are dramatically higher for black males than for any other group, with 84.4 per 100,000 black males killed as compared to 46.8 per 100,00 for Hispanic males and 16.2 per 100,000 for white males. In addition, black females have higher victimization rates than white or Hispanic females, although these rates are not as high as the rates for any male victims. The highest rates of victimization for black males were in the friends and acquaintances, and family types of homicide. The highest rates for white males were in the friends and acquaintances, and stranger felony types. The highest rates for Hispanic males were in the friends and acquaintances, and stranger non-felony contexts. Women in all three racial groups were more frequently killed within intimate circles and had very low rates of victimization in stranger contexts.

Rates for offenders follow the same pattern, with black males having much higher rates than any other population group. Rates of offenders by race and sex, from highest to lowest, are: black males, Hispanic males, black females, white males, Hispanic females, and white females. Seventy-one percent of the offenders were black, 16% were white, and 12% were Hispanic. Black males were more likely to be, in both rate and percentage, offenders in all type of killings.

In terms of offending, the general pattern is the same for black and white males. While black males killed more frequently in all contexts, these contexts were the same for blacks and whites. The major difference by race seems to be the decreased relative frequency of killing within the family by Hispanic males and

Hispanic females and the higher relative frequency of Hispanic male offending and victimization in stranger non-felony killing within the family by Hispanic males and Hispanic females and the higher relative frequency of Hispanic male offending and victimization in stranger non-felony killings.

Racial Homogeneity and Type of Homicide

Among all types of homicide in which the victim-offender relationship is known, 14% of the victims were whites killed by whites, 68% were blacks killed by blacks, and 3.7% were Hispanics killed by Hispanics. Thus, approximately 86% of these types of homicides were intraracial, and 14% of the homicides occurred between racial groups. These percentages, however, change dramatically within types.

As would be expected, 95% of the homicides in the family category and 92% of the homicides in the friends and acquaintances category were intraracial. The highest percentage of interracial killing occurred in the stranger felony category. Forty percent of the stranger felonies were interracial. In stranger felony killings with a white offender, 34.4% were interracial homicides. In stranger felony killings with a black offender, 38.8% were interracial homicides. While the numbers are small for stranger felonies involving a Hispanic offender (n = 17), 41 % of the homicides involving a Hispanic offender were interracial.

Although 89% of the black victims were victimized by blacks, 74% of the white victims in stranger felony homicides were victims of interracial homicides. Among Hispanic victims, 41 % were interethnically assaulted.

Stranger non-felonies displayed a lower percentage of interracial killings than did stranger felonies. Twenty-one percent of the stranger non-felonies were interracial homicides. White offenders seldom crossed racial lines in a non-felony stranger homicide. Thus, race appears to determine the rate of homicide and, to a limited extent, the type of homicide.

Age and Type of Homicide

Victims were older than offenders in all four types of homicide. The difference in mean age between victim and offender is small in all types except stranger felonies. In stranger felonies, the mean age of the victim was forty years, while the mean age of the offender was twenty-six years. Clearly, the stranger felony murder is distinct from the other three types by virtue of the greater age difference between victim and offender. The offenders in family killings were also somewhat older than the offenders in the other three homicide types.

Location, Witnesses, and Type of Homicide

The homicides occurred in a variety of locations. Locations were divided into public space, such as a street, subway, bar or other commercial establishment, and private space, such as the victim's residence or other residence. The largest single group of victims (641 out of 1323, or 46%) were murdered on the street. The second largest group of homicides occurred in the victim's residence (521 out of 1373, or 38%). Fifty-five percent of the homicides took place in public spaces, as compared to 42% in private spaces.

Not unexpectedly, the percentage of family killings occurring at home was higher (78%) than with other types of killings. The percentage of killings occurring in public settings increased as the relationship between the victim and the offender became more distant. The stranger non-felony homicide is clearly the most public homicide type, with 85% of these killings occurring in a public space. The public nature of the stranger non-felony homicide is also revealed by analyzing the number of witnesses to the event.

Most killings outside of the family were witnessed. While family killings were the most private (53.7%), stranger non-felony homicides were the most public. Eighty-nine percent of stranger non-felony homicides were witnessed by at least one other person. It appears, therefore, that there is an absence of caution in stranger non-felony homicides.

Method of Assault and Type of Homicide

Methods of assault included guns, knives, beatings and strangulation, and other methods. Guns predominated as the means of killing in all types of homicide; 65% of all homicides involved firearms. This percentage was somewhat lower for family killings and was somewhat higher for the other three types. Stabbing accounts for 21 % of the homicides, with a higher percentage in the family homicides and a lower percentage in stranger felonies. Beatings and strangulation occurred in only 11 % of the cases, with a higher percentage in family killing only.

Important differences emerge in a comparison of the mean age differences between offender and victim by method of assault. In family homicides and in both types of stranger killings, offender mean age was older when a gun was used and younger when stabbing or beating and strangulation was the method of assault. The average age of an offender who used a gun was older (mean age = 32) than the offender who used a knife (mean age = 27). The youngest offenders used their hands, feet, or other means of beating (mean age = 25).

Victim mean age also varies by weapon type, especially in family and stranger killings. In family type homicide, the mean age of those killed by a gun or a knife was decidedly older (35 and 33 years respectively) than in those situations in which the victim was killed by beating and strangulation. In homicides in which the offender beat and strangled the victim, the mean age of the victim was eighteen years old. Stranger felony killings, when divided by method, show pronounced mean age differences between victims, according to method. A victim of a stranger felony killed with a gun averaged thirty-six years of age; a victim killed by a knife averaged forty-six years of age; and a victim killed by beating and strangulation averaged fifty-nine years of age. The mean ages for victims in friend and acquaintances homicides and in stranger non-felony killings do not show dramatic differences, although, in stranger non-felony homicides, victims of beating and strangulation were older (mean age = 38) than victims of other methods.

This analysis suggests that it is the age of the victim, not the relationship between victim and offender, which determines the method of assault used. Specifically, those victims who are young and those victims who are old were more likely to be killed by beatings and strangulation than by any other method. Such victims were also killed by more youthful offenders. It could be argued that youthful offenders choose victims who they perceive as being defenseless because these offenders are less likely to possess a weapon.

OVERVIEW OF HOMICIDE TYPES

This Article has discussed the interactions of methods of assault, victims' and offenders' ages, and types of homicide. There is considerable variation in the mean age of victims and offenders by type of homicide, race, and sex. This pattern of variation is an indication of main and interaction effects among the variables of race, sex, and homicide type in the determination of the mean ages of offenders and victims. Each variable affects the mean age of the victim and the offender, and particular combinations of variables also affect mean age.

The analyses support the following general picture of homicide types. The features that distinguish family homicides from other homicide types are the lack of witnesses and the proportion of homicides involving a female offender. While males were the predominant offenders in this homicide type, a much higher proportion of family homicides involved a female offender than any other type. Males were almost equally likely to offend against males and females in the family. Women offenders, conversely, had victims who were almost exclusively male. The one exception to this general pattern of female offenders was Hispanic women, who seldom offended within the family group at all. The interaction between race, age, and sex categories, therefore, is quite important within the family homicide type.

The friends and acquaintances homicides are distinguishable from other homicide types by their relative frequency of occurrence. Fifty-four percent of homicides with known victim-offender relationships occurred between friends and acquaintances. The friend and acquaintance killing involved predominately a male with an average age of thirty years killing a somewhat older male in the same racial group. Black males had much higher offender and victimization rates than other racial groups of this type of homicide.

The striking features that distinguish stranger felony homicides from other homicide types are the proportion of intraracial homicides and the difference in mean ages between victims and offenders. The age disparities and the victim-offender age ratios become accentuated for white victims, both male and female. The average age of white male victims is twice that of their offenders (ages 46 and 23, respectively). The average age for white females victims is nearly three times that of their offenders (ages 59 and 21, respectively). With black and Hispanic victims, mean age differences persist, but the differences are smaller, thus making the victim-offender ratio smaller. The average age of black male victims is 1.4 times that of their offenders (ages 35 and 25, respectively). The average ages for Hispanic male victims is about 1.6 times that of their offenders (ages 35 and 22, respectively). Although most victims of homicide were victims of offenders of the same race, stranger felony homicide is characterized by the highest interracial rate. Young black and Hispanic male offenders appear more likely to victimize older whites. Finally, there were very few women offenders in stranger felony homicides (n = 7). All of the women were black and had an average age of twenty-one.

The stranger non-felony homicides category had the lowest rate of occurrence of the four homicide types. Both victims and offenders were overwhelmingly males and were of similar ages. The average age of the victim was thirty, and the average age of the offender was twenty-nine. The victim and offender mean ages did not vary dramatically by race or sex, although Hispanic male victims and offenders were younger than their black and white counterparts. The stranger non-felony homicides were similar to the friends and acquaintances homicides in characteristics of victims and offenders. Stranger non-felony homicides are distinguished from other types, however, by their public character. A high percentage of stranger non-felonies occurred in public, and a high percentage were witnessed.

CONCLUSION

The preceding analysis shows that there are clear differences between types of homicide. The importance of age, sex, and race specific studies on both victims and offenders of types of homicide also has been established. The finding that white victims and offenders were older in most types of homicide and that Hispanic victims and offenders were younger deserves closer scrutiny. This phenomenon, as in the disparity between the victim-offender ages in stranger felony homicides, may reflect differences among age-race structures in American cities. In the data base of the nine cities, it is quite possible that whites in central areas of the cities were older than the blacks and Hispanics in the area, because in the past, white families with young children have tended to leave central cities for the suburbs, while older whites remained. Blacks and Hispanics have migrated to cities, have higher birth rates than whites, and, therefore, constitute younger populations. The age-race findings in homicide victimization and offending, especially in family and stranger murders, may reflect these demographic-ecological city realities.

This Article has also demonstrated that the general category of stranger homicide, frequently used in homicide research, is too heterogeneous and needs to be subdivided. The stranger felony type is one subdivision which seems distinct and useful for analysis. The stranger non-felony category, however, needs additional exploration. The stranger non-felony homicide type is similar to the friends and acquaintances homicide type along most dimensions examined. The major exceptions are the locations and the percentage of cases with witnesses. The stranger non-felony homicide was often a very public act; this quality suggests that subsequent research should focus on the role of the public as witnesses to murder. Witnesses may facilitate such killings either by becoming actively involved in the disputes or by providing a climate which facilitates a lethal conclusion. In other types of homicide, such as killings within the family, witnesses may inhibit aggressive responses. This inhibition by the presence of witnesses does not appear to be the case in the stranger non-felony type. Perhaps society's notions of social control should be re-examined to better understand how and when audiences inhibit rather than facilitate homicide. Subsequent research should also examine the perpetrator's view of witnesses and the public.

Because most people 80-85%
know each other - kill each other
   55% ALL MURDER:
show prior conflict
   80-85% DOMESTIC HOMICIDE
show prior conflict
-Conflict can explain most
murders-

Theories:
seperate theories to explain
violent crime vs property crime.
Property Crime:
material gain - low % victim/offender relationships
easy to explain
Violent Crime: "crimes of passion" Hard to explain
high % victim/offender relationships

PERSPECTIVE THEORIES OF MURDER

Motives:	Theories	Circumstance
$political	Age	Gang involvement
lust	Poverty	situations
passion	Personality	context
religion	Gender	opportunity
pity	Race	
fear		
abuse	**Conflict**	**Types of Person Theories**
fun/desire	Dispute	mental disorder
gratification	Argument	brain leision
jealosy		neuroproblem
anger	**Facilitators**	chemical imbalance
control	drugs	cannibalism
occupational	alcohol	lack of impulse
no witness	availability	control
	of weapon	hormonal imbalance
	(CATALYSTS)	

WHAT IS IT ABOUT MEN THAT MAKES
THEM MORE LIKELY TO MURDER?
ASS HOLE THEORY

CHAPTER 5

Perspectives &
Theories of
Murder

Theories attempt to help us understand and explain the causes of murder. They are simply "educated guesses," based on what we know (or think we know) about murder. Unfortunately, the quantity and quality of empirical research on murder has lagged far behind research on other types of crime. We think it is fair to say that we know less about the crime of murder, particularly at the individual level, than most other crimes. Likewise, theories of murder are not highly evolved and empirically supported explanations, nor do the more general theories of crime (whether differential association, social control, labeling, etc.) seem to explain murder very well. For many years, psychiatric and psychological theories based on small clinical case studies of unusual murderers (for example, sexual sadists), and which proposed that killers are mentally disordered in some way (as psychotics, psychopaths, abnormal personality types), were predominant. They offer rich insight into the minds of those types of killers, but are difficult to test and are limited in their generalizability to the great majority of murder cases that clearly involve psychologically "normal" offenders. There are a number of papers that represent this perspective in Chapter 4, "Types of Murder."

SOCIAL STRUCTURAL

Among the most influential sociological theories of homicide are social structural theories, which propose, in general, that differences in *rates* of homicide across

Messner : role of SES on homicide rates.
racial and economic inequality = ↑ homicide rates
racial segragation = ↑ black homicide rates.

Chapter 5: Perspectives & Theories of Murder

groups (whether cultures, races, social classes, communities, etc.) reflect structurally-produced *inequalities* that affect economic opportunities, neighborhood characteristics, residential patterns, effectiveness of social control institutions, social relationships, and individual-level motivation to commit crime (e.g., frustration). The "anomie" theory of deviance proposed by Merton set the stage for social structural theories of more specific types of deviant behavior, including homicide. For example, the work of Blau on the relationship between economic inequality and homicide has been followed by a number of studies of the impact of a variety of inequalities on involvement in violence.

Messner examines the impact of economic class on murder rates by analyzing data on the role of poverty and income inequality in homicide in urban areas, and shows that the relationship between being poor and committing murder is not simple and direct, but is mediated by social structural arrangements based on economic inequality. In a similar vein, Peterson and Krivo assess the role of racial segregation, and its concomitant social isolation, in the production of a higher than average black homicide rate. They show that the social structure institutionalizes social inequality, based on race, that creates the conditions in neighborhoods and among individuals for heightened involvement in crimes of violence.

SOCIAL PSYCHOLOGICAL

More recent theories of murder tend to focus on broader social factors in murder, ranging from micro-situational to macro-structural kinds of analyses and explanations. Luckenbill describes the individual social psychological processes that are part of murder events anchored in volatile social situations. Murder is conceptualized as an outcome of certain kinds of interactions between potential victims and offenders.

Lukenbill = murder is an outcome of interaction between victim & offender.

Daly and Wilson propose a provocative theory of murder—they characterize it as social psychology—between family members, which draws heavily from evolutionary social biology. It attempts to explain the observation that a substantial percent of murder occurs between family members, but that some members of a family are more likely to be killers and others more likely to be victims, depending on their genetic distance from each other.

CULTURAL

A variety of cultural theories of murder have been proposed, the most famous being the subculture of violence theory of Wolfgang and Ferracuti. In general, cultural theories propose that some cultural contexts are more criminogenic than others, and if an individual is socialized in that kind of learning environment, the

SUBCULTURE OF VIOLENCE
WOLFGANG

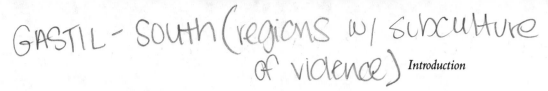

chances of committing crime, including murder, are enhanced. Erlanger tests the subculture of violence theory, which proposes that there is a violent subculture anchored in urban black communities that not only supports but almost demands violent behavior from young males. He suggests that there are conceptual and logical problems with the theory, and offers empirical evidence that does not confirm the theory.

Another version of this perspective, proposed by Gastil, is a regional subcultural theory. He attempts to explain the historically higher rates of violence and murder in the South as products of a relatively unique southern culture, with its emphasis on masculinity, guns, physical prowess, and so on. Another variation of the cultural theory of murder focuses on the impact of one of the major cultural forces in our society, the mass media. Do the mass media cause or contribute to the high murder rate in the United States? Phillips analyzes the relationship between the media coverage of high profile violent events (e.g., championship boxing matches, football games) and subsequent acts of murder, and reports that there is a significant correlation between the two— murder goes up shortly after those kinds of events are covered by the media. There are problems with this research, and other studies have suggested that the media reflect what's going on in society, rather than causing it to happen. It may, in fact, be a little bit of both.

ROUTINE ACTIVITIES

With few exceptions, a murder can only occur if a potential killer and victim come into contact at the same time in the same place. There must be the opportunity for a potential offender to act on his predispositions. As Messner and Tardiff point out, some victims and offenders lead the kinds of lifestyles, or are engaged in the types of "routine activities," that increase the likelihood that they will either kill someone or end up dead themselves. People who engage in occupations and social lives that take them to certain places at those times when violent confrontations are more likely (for example, a late Friday night party after a major sporting event where alcohol and drugs are being served), increase their odds of getting hurt, perhaps killed. There is a definite connection between what we do routinely and legitimately, and what may happen of an illegal nature, including murder.

Murder can only occur if victim & murderer are in same place @ same time.

273

SOCIAL STRUCTURAL

Poverty, Inequality, and the Urban Homicide Rate

STEVEN F. MESSNER

An important development in the study of social stratification over the past decade or so has been the call for a reconceptualization of the phenomenon of poverty. Historically, the notion of poverty has been associated with subsistence levels of economic resources. People are poor, according to the subsistence approach, when their incomes are so low that they are unable to purchase the necessities for a healthy life. Poverty from this perspective represents deprivation relative to a fixed standard of physiological well-being.

An alternative conceptualization of poverty has been proposed in recent years by Townsend and by Miller and Roby. These authors argue that the essence of poverty is *relative* deprivation. People are poor when they cannot live in ways which are ordinary for their own communities. People are poor, in other words, when they are unequal. For the relativists, "lagging incomes rather than low incomes are the issue."

The call for a reconceptualization of poverty has quite naturally been accompanied by a call for different measurement techniques. Traditionally, poverty has been conceptualized in terms of a "poverty line" which is designed to reflect the minimum cost of securing satisfactory health. One way that poverty can then be measured is by means of the proportion of the population falling below this standard. Such a poverty measure might be called "absolute" in the sense that the poverty line is determined with reference to a fixed set of human needs rather than with reference to the incomes of others.

The "relative deprivation" conceptualization entails a different mode of operationalization. Since the concern is with lagging incomes rather than low incomes, the measurement of poverty essentially involves the measurement of the dispersion of the overall income distribution. Poverty measures thus become identical to measures of economic inequality.

In short, theorists have long suspected that poverty in one form or another would give rise to high levels of criminal activity. Recent theoretical discussions seem to imply that relative poverty is more important than absolute poverty for explaining behavior, including crime. The interesting empirical question which has not been confronted is whether the crime rate is better predicted by measures of poverty corresponding to the relative approach or by measures reflecting the subsistence approach. The purpose of this article is to report findings which bear on this question as it pertains to the particular offense of criminal homicide.

PREVIOUS LITERATURE

There is some available evidence to support the claim by relativists that income inequality and not simply low income is related to the rate of criminal activity. For example, a previous cross-national study reveals a significant effect of income inequality on the societal murder rate. Nations with high levels of income inequality also tend to exhibit high levels of homicide. Most importantly for present purposes, the effects of the inequality variable do not disappear when a measure of the overall affluence or poverty of the population (Gross Domestic Product per capita) is entered into the regression equation.

Research on income distribution and crime rates within the United States also suggests that income inequality might be a significant determinant of serious criminality. Ehrlich has examined the effects of inequality, among other variables, on several measures of crime, including murder. He operationalizes income inequality in terms of proportion of the population below one-half of the median income and examines its relationship to state homicide rates in 1950 and 1960. His results are mixed.

Danziger and Wheeler also consider the effects of income inequality on crime rates within the United States. They conclude that crime rates respond to the interpersonal welfare comparisons which are likely to be associated with varying levels of income inequality. More specifically, they maintain that high levels of inequality entail "malevolent interdependence." This promotes, they speculate, high rates of criminality. Furthermore, their data indicate that these effects are not limited to property crime, but that they also apply to the personal crime of assault. Danziger and Wheeler do not investigate the patterns for the offense of primary interest here, i.e., criminal homicide.

The previous research most relevant to the present study is that of Loftin and Hill, who analyzed average state homicide rates for the years 1959–1961. Their study includes measures of both income inequality and "structural poverty" and their findings indicate that "structural poverty" is by far the more important determinant of homicide. There are, however, two limitations associated with Loftin and Hill's study. First, this study uses states as units of analysis. States are rather arbitrary statistical aggregations, a point which the authors candidly acknowledge. I would argue that the boundaries for SMSAs are more likely to coincide with those for genuine social communities, and that as a consequence SMSAs are more meaningful aggregations than are states.

Second, Loftin and Hill's measure of "structural poverty" is not really a clear indicator of poverty per se. The authors calculate an index which combines a measure of low income population (percentage of families with incomes less than $1000) with indicators of family structure, educational attainment, and general health conditions. The structural poverty index thus combines a measure of poverty in the usual sense of the term with the empirical correlates of poverty. This procedure might be justified for purposes of assessing the overall effect of structural variables on the homicide rate, but it is not well suited for identifying the unique effects of poverty in the sense of a low income population. In short, Loftin and Hill's research does not fully resolve the issue at the core of the present study, namely, the importance for explaining the homicide rate of absolute versus relative measures of poverty.

Data and Variables

The sample for the study consists of the 204 SMSAs for which crime figures are reported in the FBI's Uniform Crime Reports, 1970. The FBI provides a breakdown of crime rates by geographical area, including SMSA.

The dependent variable for the analysis is the rate of "murder and non-negligent homicide" per 100,000 population. The figures refer to the number of offenses known to the police.

The two key independent variables are the relative and absolute measures of poverty. For the relative measure, the Gini coefficient of family income concentration (GINI) has been selected. This is a common measure of dispersion and it can be understood as the ratio of the average income difference between pairs of recipients in an SMSA to the average income. The absolute measure of poverty is the percentage of the population below the U.S. Social Security Administration's poverty line (PCTPOOR).

Although the primary focus of the analysis will be on the economic measures, it is necessary to consider other possible determinants of the homicide rate to avoid specification error. Six control variables have consequently been selected because previous research has indicated their theoretical and/or empirical importance. More specifically, controls for racial composition and regional location have been selected on the basis of the "subculture of violence" literature. Blacks, it has been argued, are more likely than whites to adhere to a violent subcultural orientation. This argument implies that the size of the black population will be positively related to the homicide rate, a prediction which has in fact been substantiated in some previous analyses.

Subcultural factors have also been linked to regional differentiation, with the basic hypothesis being that there is a subculture of lethal violence in the South which leads to relatively high homicide rates. A measure of regional location has consequently been included in the analysis as well. Finally, three population measures have been selected because of their frequent appearance in earlier studies. The specific control variables and their respective sources are as follows:

> BLACKPOP—the proportion of the population black;
> SOUTH—Southern region—a dummy variable scored "1" if the SMSA is located in the South and "0" otherwise;
> POP15–29—the proportion of the population age 15–29;
> LNPOP—total population;
> LNPOPDEN—population per square mile.

The last two population measures are highly skewed. Hence, natural log transformations have been performed to improve the linear fit in the correlational analysis.

Since the independent variables are intercorrelated, it is important to consider the partial effects. Table I reports the results of a regression analysis with the complete list of independent variables. Controlling for these other variables does indeed affect the observed relationships for the economic measures. The estimate for the Gini coefficient is positive, but it is not statistically significant. More surprisingly, the estimate for the absolute measure is significant but the sign is negative. Poverty conceptualized in absolute terms appears to be *inversely* related to the homicide rate once the other independent variables have been taken into account.

Evidently, "lagging incomes" are relatively unimportant for the homicide rate and low incomes have an effect opposite to that to be expected. This inverse relationship for the absolute measure of poverty is really quite perplexing and

Table 1
Regression of the 1970 homicide rate for 204 SMSAs

Independent Variable	Standardized Coefficient	F-Ratio
BLACKPOP	.527*	70.630
SOUTH	.340*	21.376
LNPOP	.269*	19.738
LNPOPDEN	−.186*	9.142
PCTPOOR	−.217*	6.609
POP15–19	−.057	1.384
GINI	.116	1.775
R^2 = .621		

*Signifies that the coefficient is statistically significant at the .05 level.

requires further consideration. Research on homicidal offenders indicates that the relationship between socioeconomic status and homicide is not linear. Homicides tend to be concentrated at the extreme depths of the socioeconomic hierarchy, with the likelihood of homicide dropping very quickly as social status rises.

For this reason, I have selected an alternative measure of poverty which is focused on the very low income population. This measure refers to the proportion of families with incomes below $1000. The regression results reveal that substituting a poverty measure which focuses on the very poor has little effect on the relationship with homicide. Once again, the size of the poverty population has a statistically significant negative effect on the homicide rate.

The finding of significant net effects for racial composition and regional location in my sample of SMSAs is thus contrary to that observed in previous studies using states as units of analysis. I have not attempted a strict replication of these earlier state studies here, but if these results are sustained in future studies with fully comparable variables lists, the credibility of the subcultural explanations of homicide outlined above will be greatly enhanced. Recall that these explanations maintain that the high homicide rate in Southern regions and in areas with large minority populations is not entirely a reflection of socioeconomic factors but reflects distinctively violent subcultural orientations. If the subcultural explanations are correct, there should be an effect of racial composition and region on the homicide

ABSOLUTE POVERTY = inversely related to homicide rate [handwritten annotation]

rate which is independent of socioeconomic and demographic factors. Such an effect appears unmistakably in the regression analyses reported above.

SUMMARY AND CONCLUSIONS

This study has examined the relationship between two types of poverty measures and the homicide rate for a sample of 204 SMSAs. The relative measure, a Gini coefficient of family income inequality, exhibits a moderate zero order correlation with the homicide rate. This association becomes insignificant, however, once various demographic controls are introduced.

The absolute measure of poverty, the proportion of the population below the U.S. Social Security Administration's poverty line, also exhibits a moderate positive zero order correlation with the homicide rate. But, in contrast to the findings for the relative measure, the partial effect for the absolute measure is significant in the regression analysis, and it has a surprisingly negative sign. In other words, the absolute measure of poverty is *inversely* related to the homicide rate. SMSAs with large numbers of families below the poverty line tend to have low rates of criminal homicide after controlling for various demographic variables.

Similar results are obtained when another absolute measure of poverty focusing on the very poor is employed (namely, the proportion of families with incomes less than $1000).

These findings raise some perplexing questions. Given the extensive theoretical work linking crime and relative deprivation, why does the level of inequality have such a trivial effect on the homicide rate? I can offer three possible explanations. First, the range of inequality across the sample may be too restricted to permit a reliable assessment of the effects of inequality. There is not much variation, therefore, in measured inequality, which may account for the limited explanatory power of this particular variable.

A second possibility is that the measure of inequality is not a very accurate indicator of the level of relative deprivation actually experienced in a given locality. An implicit assumption underlying the use of any statistical measure of dispersion as an indicator of relative deprivation is that the units upon which the statistical computations are based are also relevant units for social comparisons. If in the present case SMSAs do not serve as relevant frames of reference in the assessment of economic well-being, then the statistical inequality of income will not necessarily reflect relative deprivation, and the empirical results will not be able to determine any criminogenic effects of relative deprivation.

A third possibility is that relative economic deprivation simply is not an important determinant of criminal homicide. Disparities in income may have little bearing

279

on the everyday disputes and quarrels which ultimately affect the homicide rate. If this interpretation is correct, it implies that Americans are much less concerned with the incomes of others than many social scientists tend to believe.

Even more puzzling than the absence of a significant effect for the inequality measure is the negative effect for measures of the size of the poverty population. This finding, in conjunction with research on the characteristics of homicidal offenders, creates a paradox: Homicidal offenders are recruited disproportionately from the ranks of the poor, yet a large poverty population appears to be associated with a low homicide rate. Perhaps widespread poverty somehow reduces the probability that any given poor person will commit homicidal acts. Such an effect of poverty could reflect psychological factors—the experience of being poor might be more psychologically disturbing when poverty is rare than when poverty is pervasive. Alternatively, widespread poverty might actually entail less objective deprivation insofar as such poverty increases the likelihood that poor people will voluntarily share the limited economic resources that they do have. In any case, the findings reported in this note would seem to call for serious reconsideration of the linkages between poverty, inequality, and the homicide rate.

Little correlation between relative poverty & crime.
- people less interested in what their neighbours make than scientists believe.
WEAK LINKS BETWEEN: poverty, inequality & homicide rate

SOCIAL STRUCTURAL

Racial Segregation
and Black Urban Homicide

RUTH D. PETERSON & LAUREN J. KRIVO

Lethal violence among African Americans is a serious problem in the United States. For example, a 1986 report based on national health statistics revealed that over a 14-year period between 1970 and 1983 the black homicide rate ranged from five to nine times that for whites. Similarly, O'Carroll and Mercy's analysis of Federal Bureau of Investigation (FBI) statistics indicates that over the period from 1977 and 1984 the risk of homicide victimization was six times greater for blacks than for whites. Clearly then, in the aggregate, African Americans are victims of lethal violence at a far greater rate than whites. This substantial racial difference in homicide is a major cause of the lower life expectancy of blacks in the U.S.

While the seriousness of the black homicide problem is well recognized, its determinants are not well understood. Among contemporary scholars, a major perspective on black violence focuses upon the criminogenic consequences of the social and economic inequality that African Americans experience in the U.S. This explanation has its roots in Merton's social structure and anomie thesis and Coser's analysis of deprivation, discrimination, and diffuse aggression. In general, such perspectives link criminal and deviant behavior to the deprivation that certain segments of the population experience when there is a disjuncture between cultural goals (economic success) and structural arrangements (socioeconomic resources). This disjuncture results in feelings of frustration and alienation that are reflected in criminal and deviant patterns.

Blau and Blau argue that the expression of frustration in the form of violent crime is particularly pronounced when economic inequality is based upon ascriptive characteristics like race. Criminal violence occurs because in democratic societies such as the U.S., access to resources should not be based on ascribed criteria. Ascriptive inequality reinforces ethnic and class differences and engenders pervasive conflict. Due to the weak political power of "have-nots," which accompanies ascriptive inequality, racially and ethnically disadvantaged groups are unable to organize successful collective action (e.g., strikes, boycotts). Instead, the conflict and hostilities engendered by ascriptive inequality find expression in diffuse aggression, including criminal violence.

A relatively large body of recent empirical research has evaluated this argument by examining the relationship between a variety of measures of socioeconomic deprivation and rates of violent crime including homicide. Many analyses demonstrate that one or more measures of general and/or racial socioeconomic inequality are associated with higher homicide rates for the general population. Studies have also demonstrated that absolute deprivation (low income or poverty) is linked to higher levels of homicide.

While these studies are instructive about the determinants of overall homicides, they do not inform us fully about the structural causes of variation in black killings for three primary reasons. First, they do not examine that variation directly. Instead, scholars tend to analyze homicides for the total population rather than for the black population. In so doing, they fail to take into account the contribution of black killings to overall homicide rates, and they disregard the considerable variation in black homicide rates across jurisdictions. For example, Supplementary Homicide Reports (SHR) data show that for the period from 1979 to 81 average homicide victimization rates ranged from a low of 6.6 to a high of 62.7 per 100,000 blacks for the sample of 125 large U.S. central cities analyzed below. A better understanding of black homicide requires that we examine this variation directly.

Second, many homicide researchers have used general population rather than race-specific measures of social and economic deprivation as explanatory variables. Similar to black homicides, there is substantial variation in the social, economic, and demographic conditions of blacks across communities in the U.S. For example, 1980 census figures for the sample of cities examined in the current study indicate that the percent of black families living in poverty ranged from a low of 8.0% to a high of 36.1% with a mean rate of 26.0%. Also, on average about 15% of employed blacks held professional or managerial positions in 1980, but the range was from a low of 9% to a high of 31%. As a final example, on average for 1980 the median family income of whites exceeded that of blacks by a factor of 1.63. However in some cities, the average income of whites and blacks was almost identical, and in others white income was more than twice that of blacks. By no means then are African Americans similarly situated in terms of their socioeconomic status in U.S. cities. The question is whether the variation in black homicides is connected systematically to the variation in the social and economic conditions of blacks across communities in this society. Few studies have attempted to answer this question.

A third reason why past studies have not fully examined structural causes of variation in black killings is that scholars have tended to conceptualize social deprivation in terms of a limited number of economic factors (e.g., poverty, general income inequality & racial income inequality). In so doing, they have ignored potentially important noneconomic aspects of inequality that may influence lethal violence. A critical analysis of the structural determinants of African-American violence requires that such killings be linked directly to measures of the socioeconomic status of African Americans, including important noneconomic aspects of social inequality.

One of the most central and enduring dimensions of racial inequality in the U.S. is the high level of black-white residential segregation found in most urban areas. Residence in segregated black neighborhoods is a fact of life for a large portion of African Americans. Segregation appears to be associated with a number of negative social conditions for blacks, including greater poverty, more physical deterioration, poorer schools, and higher crime rates. Despite these possible consequences, studies have been more concerned with describing levels of residential segregation and analyzing its determinants than with studying its impact on other social conditions. In the present study, we attempt to extend our understanding of both the consequences of black-white segregation in the U.S., and the structural determinants of African-American killings. We do so by analyzing the impact of racial residential segregation on the incidence of black homicide victimization in large U.S. central cities.

CONCEPTUAL ARGUMENT

Residential segregation between blacks and whites is a pervasive aspect of racial inequality in the U.S. Numerous studies report high levels of racial residential segregation in U.S. cities and suburbs that cannot be explained by black-white income differentials. Rather, prejudice and discrimination in the housing market produce residential environments that are separated largely along racial lines. A growing body of research suggests that these separate black and white communities provide markedly different social environments for their residents. Higher levels of unemployment, welfare dependency, dilapidated housing, mortality, unwed motherhood, and crime pervade segregated African-American neighborhoods. Similarly, poorer schools and higher taxes plague predominantly black areas—the types of areas where a large portion of blacks reside. Thus, black-white residential segregation means not only that African Americans live in separate communities, but that they live in areas that are inferior to neighborhoods more heavily populated by whites.

Despite indirect evidence that residential segregation is linked closely with inferior community outcomes, few studies have examined directly the influence of this dimension of social stratification on social conditions for the African-American population. It is particularly unfortunate that residential segregation has seldom been considered in studying such important social problems as lethal violence among blacks. If, as Blau and Blau maintain, ascriptive inequality has a particularly strong impact on violent crime, then the results of most previous analyses of homicide may be biased since they do not include one of the most central components of ascriptive inequality—racial residential segregation.

Logan and Messner argue that high levels of racial segregation should result in feelings of greater resentment, frustration, hopelessness, and alienation among African Americans, which in turn would be reflected in diffuse forms of aggression, including high rates of criminal violence.

Wilson suggests another mechanism by which residential segregation may be linked to violent crime. Given high rates of black poverty in most central cities (higher than the highest white poverty rates in most cities), black-white residential segregation is inextricably linked with concentrated black poverty. Thus, residential segregation implies isolation from mainstream society, an isolation that ties blacks into a local setting of multiple disadvantages. These disadvantages are reinforced by the impact of racial residential segregation on types and levels of community social control. At a formal level, individuals in more heavily poor and predominantly black neighborhoods may be unable to obtain adequate police protection. At an informal level, segregated black communities may lack the internal resources to organize neighborhood structures to help prevent crime (e.g., crime-tip hot lines and other reporting projects, home security surveys, volunteer patrol organizations, and neighbor-hood crime watches). These communities simply lack the monetary, social, and institutional resources to combat crime. At the same time, the condition of anomie implies that the legitimacy, and therefore the effectiveness, of social norms are undermined, which in turn increases the likelihood of deviant behavior.

There are very few studies of the effects of racial residential segregation on violent crime. Among these, Logan and Messner, Rosenfeld, and Sampson have found that higher residential segregation is associated with higher levels of murder. However, these effects are not always statistically significant. Logan and Messner found a significant relationship between segregation and criminal homicide in the suburban rings of 54 metropolitan areas for 1980 but not 1970. In contrast, Rosenfeld found that residential segregation had a significant positive effect on murder rates in standard metropolitan statistical areas (SMSAs) for 1970. Using race-specific homicide arrest rates for cities, Sampson also showed that residential segregation significantly influenced white but not black homicides for 1970. In a related vein, Potter found that residential isolation had a sizable significant effect on the difference in homicide between blacks and whites in 27 metropolitan areas for 1980.

Messner and South and South and Felson considered the effect of residential segregation on violent crimes in evaluating Blau's macrostructural theory of intergroup contact. According to this perspective, residential segregation should be associated negatively with interracial victimization and positively with intraracial victimization. This pattern of association would occur because segregation reduces the opportunity for interracial contacts and increases the opportunity for intraracial contacts. Both studies found the expected pattern for robbery and rape.

Although these investigations indicate the importance of residential segregation for violent crime, they fall short of fully illuminating the influence of segregation on *black* homicide. In general, the studies are few; their results are inconsistent; and rarely are they concerned with race-specific crime rates. Also, individual studies have some specific limitations. For example, Logan and Messner analyze suburban crime patterns for the total population although the majority of African Americans reside in central cities where most street crime occurs. Potter examines the black-white homicide gap rather than the levels of race-specific homicide and does so for a small sample of metropolitan areas (27 places). Sampson provides a direct test of the effect of segregation on black homicide. However, his analysis is based upon arrest data which raises questions about his conclusions. Reported crimes do not always result in arrests, and all arrested persons are not associated unequivocally with crimes.

In brief, there are important theoretical reasons to expect that racial residential segregation should contribute to higher homicide rates among disadvantaged minorities. Nonetheless, the role of this factor has not been given due attention in the empirical literature. As a result, we have little understanding of the merits of theoretical arguments regarding segregation and violent crime for African Americans. The analyses that follow address this important question, and thereby contribute to our understanding of the consequences of segregation and the structural determinants of the killings of blacks.

DATA AND METHODS

Our analysis examines the influence of black-white residential segregation and other dimensions of African Americans' socioeconomic status on rates of black homicide victimization in large cities for 1980. The sample includes the central cities of SMSAs where there was a 1980 central city population of at least 100,000 and a black population of at least 5,000 (N = 125).

Dependent Measures

Average black homicide (murder and non-negligent manslaughter) victimization rates per 100,000 blacks are computed for the period from 1979 to 1981 for each city. In addition to examining the overall black homicide rate, we disaggregate killings and compute rates for different types of killing based upon the relationship between the victim and the offender: family, acquaintance, or stranger. All homicide rates are based on data from the FBI's Supplementary Homicide Reports (SHR). These data include homicides known to the police in jurisdictions participating in the SHR Program. SHR data are slightly less complete than the FBI's Uniform Crime Reports (UCR) data, the most common source used for this type of analysis. However, general homicide rates based upon the two sources are correlated very highly for the 125 cities considered here (r > .90). SHR data are used because the UCR do not report the race of either the victims or offenders in homicide incidents. We use victimization rates rather than offending rates because reporting of the race of homicide victims is nearly complete in the SHR files, while the race of the offender is missing for a large number of SHR homicide incidents.

In calculating rates, we restrict our analysis to homicide incidents in which there was a single victim and single offender. Williams and Flewelling note several reasons why such a restriction is necessary. First, they point out that the "situational circumstances of events involving multiple offenders and/or victims tend to be different from one-on-one event[s]." Therefore, the determinants of multiple-offender/multiple-victim homicides may be different from those involving a single victim and a single offender. Until we have improved knowledge of the similarities and differences between the two kinds of killing, Williams and Flewelling recommend that we keep analyses of them separate. Second, they note that multiple offender or victim killings are relatively rare (approximately 16% of incidents in which there was a known offender during 1979 to 1981) and that an understanding of homicides (African-American homicides in this context) should begin with the most common type, that is, one-on-one killings. Third, and of particular relevance for our analysis, Williams and Flewelling note that certain practical considerations preclude examining multiple-offender/multiple-victim homicides when researchers are interested in the determinants of different types of killing, Below we will examine rates for family, acquaintance, and stranger homicides. Unfortunately, in multiple victim situations, the SHR provide information only on the relationship between the first victim and each offender. Therefore, the victim-offender relationship cannot be determined for second and subsequent victims. Moreover, considerable ambiguity would result from attempts to classify victim-offender relationships when events involved multiple kinds of relationships.

Independent Variables

The explanatory variables, their operationalizations, and the predicted directions of effect on homicides are presented in Table 1. Two measures of segregation are examined: (1) the index of dissimilarity (D), and (2) the correlation ratio (η^2). The index of dissimilarity is a widely used indicator of evenness in the distribution of two groups (in our case blacks and whites) across census tracts within an urban area. Values of D range from a minimum of 0 when blacks and whites are distributed evenly across tracts to a maximum of 100 when blacks and whites are segregated completely. Index values between 0 and 100 indicate the percent of blacks (or whites) that would have to change their tract of residence to achieve perfect integration (i.e., a D-value of 0).

The correlation ratio (η^2) is a measure of racial concentration. It is included in this analysis to capture better our theoretical interest in segregation as an indicator of the concentration of blacks in neighborhoods that are socially isolated from more heavily white communities. That η^2 indicates this exact aspect of segregation is illustrated by Stearns and Logan's statement that η^2 is "an aggregate measure of the polarization of neighborhoods toward all-black and all-white." The correlation ratio (η^2) ranges from 0 to 1. For a given city, it approaches the maximum of 1 when most tracts are nearly all black or nearly all white.

Measures of the remaining independent variables indicating blacks' socioeconomic status and demographic composition are straightforward. These variables are similar to those used in many studies of crime and inequality except that most are based upon characteristics for the African American population rather than for the general population. Economic inequality is measured by the gini index of income inequality among blacks, and the black-white income ratio. The gini index uses other blacks as the reference in considering the role of income inequality, while the income ratio compares blacks with whites. Although some

Table 1
Predictor variables of black homicides:
operationalizations and expected directions of effect

Variables	Operationalization	Expected Direction of Effect
Segregation		
Dissimilarity (*D*)	Index of dissimilarity of black-white residential segregation across census tracts	+
Racial concentration (η^2)	The correlation ratio of black-white residential segregation across census tracts	+
Black Socioeconomic status		
Black income inequality	Gini index of family income inequality among blacks	+
Black-white income inequality	Ratio of white to black median family income	+
Poverty	Percent of black families below the federal poverty line	+
Education	Percent of black population older than 24 that graduated high school	–
Professionals	Percent of employed blacks in professional and managerial occupations	–
Demographic factors		
Percent black	Percent of the total population that is black	+
Percent of black males, aged 15–34	Percent of black males aged 15–34	+
Divorce rate	Percent of black population older than 15 that is currently divorced or separated	+
Population	Natural log of the total city population	+
Region	South = 1, Non-South = 0	+

studies use the black-white income gap as a measure of interracial inequality, we use the income ratio to control for differences across cities in average income. The black family poverty rate, percent high school graduates, and percent of employed blacks in professional and managerial occupations are included as measures of the level of socio-economic status within the black population. Several demographic factors are considered as control variables because they have been found in previous research to influence general homicide rates: percent black population, percent of black males aged 15–34, percent of blacks divorced, log of population size, and region (South/non-South).

Statistical Analysis

The total black homicide victimization rate is regressed on black-white residential segregation and the other independent and control variables using ordinary least squares (OLS) techniques. However, as Williams and Flewelling note, use of an aggregate rate "can mask or imprecisely reveal empirical relationships indicative of a differential causal process operating in the social production of criminal homicide." Hence, to further understand the causal processes at work in black homicide, we disaggregate killings and compute rates for three subtypes based upon the relationship between the offender and the victim: family, acquaintance, and stranger.

Family, acquaintance, and stranger homicides differ from one another in important ways. Williams and Flewelling note that family and acquaintance homicides occur between people with existing relationships during their routine everyday interactions. In contrast, homicides involving strangers take place in more impersonal situations among individuals with no prior contact or relationship. They include such felony homicides as robbery killings. Structural conditions might have varying effects by homicide type because of the differing relationships and situations under which these homicides occur. For example, we might anticipate increasingly weaker effects of our structural variables on homicides as we move from stranger to acquaintance to family killings. This would occur because homicides involving individuals in more primary relationships may be more responsive to a variety of interpersonal and situational factors. This possibility was illustrated in Williams and Flewelling's analysis of 1980 general homicide rates disaggregated by the victim-offender relationship and the precipitating incident (conflict or other). The researchers found that the strength of the effects of percent poor (and divorce rate) are generally weaker for homicides involving family members than for those involving acquaintances or strangers. By contrast, Smith and Parker found that their resource measure (the structural-poverty index) had a significant influence on primary (e.g., killings of family members and lovers) but not nonprimary (e.g., gangland slayings and felony murders) homicides for 1970. Methodological differences between the two studies may account for the differential patterns of influence of the resource deprivation measures. For our purposes what is important is the differential effect of these measures across different types of homicide. The variable effects of structural conditions on different types of general homicide also have been demonstrated in other empirical work.

Analyses that disaggregate black homicides by the type of relationship between the victim and the offender (i.e., family, acquaintance, or stranger) are estimated using generalized least squares (GLS) techniques. This makes it possible to perform significance tests of differences in coefficients for the explanatory variables.

BLACK HOMICIDE AND RESIDENTIAL DISSIMILARITY

Total Black Homicide Rates

Table 2 presents the results of the OLS model examining the effects of black-white residential segregation, as measured by the index of dissimilarity, and the socioeconomic status measures on total black homicide rates controlling for other structural characteristics of central cities. Beginning with the demographic variables, the results show that only one of these factors is a significant predictor of black homicide. In line with considerable past research on total homicide rates, percent black has a significant effect on black killings. However, in contrast to the results of studies of general homicides, a larger black population is associated with a lower black homicide rate. This finding directly contradicts the common subcultural interpretation that suggests a larger black population strengthens a black violent subculture and thereby increases the rate of killing. In fact, just the opposite occurs for blacks in central cities. Previous studies of race-specific homicide rates also contradict the subcultural argument by demonstrating either a negative or nonsignificant influence of percent black (or nonwhite) on black killings. The other control factors in our model do not play a role in explaining black homicides. Apparently, the social disorganization implied by higher marital dissolution and the cultural effects often imputed to region do not operate among African Americans.

Turning to the variables of theoretical interest, only one indicator of socio-economic status (occupational composition) is an important determinant of African-American killings. Of particular note when the analysis is performed for black homicides using race-specific explanatory variables, neither black income inequality nor black-white income inequality is a significant predictor of black

Table 2
OLS regression of black homicide rates on segregation (*D*), black socioeconomic status, and demographic factors: Central Cities, 1980

	Unstandardized Coefficient	Standard Error	Standardized Coefficient
Independent variable			
Segregation (*D*)	.224**	.112	.702
Black income inequality[a]	–.001	.069	–.002
Black-white income inequality	6.457	4.654	.149
Poverty	–.085	.369	–.044
Education	–.023	.201	–.021
Professionals	–.843*	.370	–.279
Percent black	–.123*	.064	–.194
Percent of black males, aged 15–34	.531	.435	.161
Divorce rate	.973	.618	.187
Population (logged)	.780	1.324	.060
Region	3.720	2.537	.180
Constant	–18.596		
R^2	.257		
(N = 125)			

[a]The coefficients and standard errors of the gini index of black income inequality are multiplied by 1,000 because the gini index varies only from 0 to 1 and hence produces extremely small parameters.
*p < .05   **p < .01

killings. As noted, occupational composition is related significantly to homicide, but neither education nor poverty is significant. Further, occupational composition is the most important contributor to black killings. This finding suggests that increased access to professional, managerial, and other supervisory positions has a particularly salient effect on reducing homicide rates for the African-American population.

Most central to the argument of this article is the finding that racial residential segregation (D) has a strong significant positive effect on black homicide rates. More specifically, a 10-point increase in the index of dissimilarity (about a one standard deviation increase in this segregation index) is associated with a 2.4-person increase in the number of homicides per 100,000 blacks. Further, black-white residential dissimilarity has a relative effect on black homicides that is nearly identical to that for occupational composition. It is particularly striking that segregation has more influence than measures (the gini index, the white/black income ratio) of some of the most central theoretical constructs (anomie, relative economic deprivation) in discussions of crime. Therefore, omission of this important dimension of racial inequality from past research may have undermined our ability to understand how inequality influences violent crime.

A Disaggregated Analysis

To explore how structural conditions may vary in their effects on different types of homicide, we estimated models distinguishing among killings of family members, acquaintances, and strangers.

These analyses show that each type of homicide is influenced significantly by one or more of the structural factors. Family homicides are higher in central cities in the South, and in central cities where there are relatively fewer black professionals and more black high school graduates. Acquaintance killings are more likely in communities where segregation (D) is higher, where fewer blacks have a high school education, where the percent black is relatively smaller and in the South. Homicides involving strangers are influenced by segregation (D), percent of black professionals, percent of black males aged 15 to 34, and population size.

The set of structural variables provides a better fit moving from family homicides to acquaintance and stranger homicides. This pattern is consistent with some previous research showing that structural factors are less influential in killings involving family members. Beyond this however, there are few clear patterns in the relationships across the three types of killing. None of the individual explanatory factors is significant for all three types. Nor does the strength of the association for significant variables increase (or decrease) monotonically when moving from one type of homicide to another. Moreover, different types of homicide cannot be explained in terms of distinct types of structural factors, i.e., segregation, black socioeconomic status, or demographic characteristics. Rather, the three types of killing simply are affected by discrete individual variables. In sum, the analysis of aggregate homicide rates obscures the varying influence of structural conditions on black homicides; but the results do not reveal a pattern that leads to clear theoretical conclusions.

Yet, we gain insight by examining the significance of the coefficients for the structural variables *within* types of homicide, and the significance of the difference in effects *between* homicide types. First, the disaggregated analysis shows that more of the demographic factors influence the specific types of homicide than was apparent in the analysis of the total rate. Location in the South positively influences killings involving family members. Size of the black population and region affect killings involving acquaintances, and percent of young black males and size of the central city population influence killings involving strangers. A larger black population significantly reduces the level of acquaintance homicide; and this effect is significantly different from the negligible influence of this variable on family and stranger killings. Moreover, as is the case for the total homicide rate, the negative effect for percent black directly contradicts the common subcultural interpretation attributed to this variable. This finding is particularly noteworthy since a violent black subculture should have very pronounced effects on killings involving acquaintances. By contrast, the coefficients for region suggest that there may be a southern cultural effect for family and acquaintance killings.

An additional difference across homicide types is that a greater percent of young black males is related to more stranger and acquaintance homicides but not family homicides. The impact of age reaches statistical significance only for stranger killings although the age effect for both stranger and acquaintance homicides is significantly greater than that for family killings. This finding makes sense in that the circumstances leading to family killings may be less age restricted (e.g., lover's triangles and arguments over money). In contrast, young males likely comprise proportionately more of the people in contexts in which acquaintance and stranger homicides occur (e.g., bars and street corners).

The only other noteworthy differences are those for the variable of primary theoretical interest here—segregation (*D*). First, the disaggregated analysis makes clear that residential dissimilarity has a significant effect only for acquaintance and stranger killings. Family homicides are not affected by this variable. Further, the influence of segregation is relatively strong—the second strongest predictor of acquaintance killings and the fifth most important factor (of 11) in homicides involving strangers. Of note, there is very little differentiation among the standardized coefficients for segregation, black income inequality, black-white inequality, and education in the model for stranger killings. The magnitude of the unstandardized coefficients illustrates the importance of segregation's effect. A 10-unit increase in the index of dissimilarity (approximately a one-standard deviation increase) is related to an increase of 1.5 and .6 homicides per 100,000 blacks for killings involving acquaintances and strangers, respectively. Such increases are relatively large given mean rates of 16.5 for acquaintance homicides and 3.0 for stranger killings.

One possible explanation for a segregation effect on homicides involving acquaintances and strangers, but not family members, is that segregation is more indicative of social isolation than of relative socioeconomic deprivation. To the extent that the most segregated black areas are subject to social isolation and weak social control, this would have an effect largely on acquaintance and stranger killings which tend to occur in more public settings (e.g., bars, street corners, and businesses). Slow or inadequate response by police and emergency medical services, absence of neighborhood crime prevention structures, and unwillingness of bystanders to intervene in conflicts (personally or by calling formal authorities) all would increase the likelihood that conflicts in public places would have a lethal outcome.

However, indicators of social isolation should have much less influence on violence between family members. Such violence more commonly occurs in the home or another private setting where violent encounters are particularly sheltered from, and therefore not constrained or encouraged by, levels of intervention by police, emergency medical authorities, or other third parties. That is, family killings may be determined more by interpersonal and situational precipitants than by external agents of control.

While the influence of residential dissimilarity is greater for killings involving less intimate parties, the effect of this variable is especially pronounced for acquaintance homicides. The reason for segregation having a greater influence on acquaintance than on stranger killings is not clear. Perhaps, even in highly segregated contexts in which many aspects of social control are weak, formal mechanisms may decrease stranger violence but not limit violent encounters among individuals that know one another. Thus, police may perceive encounters between strangers as more serious and hence respond more quickly, offer greater assistance, and be less likely to discount such violence than when these encounters involve acquaintances. In other words, variation in segregation may be a better indicator of variation in social control for acquaintance encounters and hence this factor has a stronger effect on this type of killing,

CONCLUSION

A sizable body of past research on homicide has examined the impact of *economic* inequality on general homicide rates. The premise of this study is that the tendency to focus on economic deprivation and total homicides limits our understanding of the relationship between inequality and lethal violence in two ways. First, it ignores a central theme regarding how inequality influences homicide. Anomie and social isolation perspectives imply that the criminal consequences of inequality are most likely for oppressed minorities and other ascriptively disadvantaged groups. But most prior research has analyzed total rather than group-specific crime rates, and examined general rather than group-specific social and demographic predictors.

Second, prior research has overlooked the empirical consequences of excluding a major component of inequality in examining crime. It is unlikely that the effect of deprivation on homicide is limited to economic factors. Thus, the exclusion of important noneconomic dimensions of inequality, particularly residential segregation, has limited our understanding of the effect of inequality on crime, and may have resulted in biased conclusions about the criminogenic consequences of economic deprivation. Our analyses sought to address these limitations of past research.

Indeed, our findings underscore that to better understand black lethal violence it is important to: (1) analyze racially disaggregated homicide rates, (2) differentiate types of killing by the victim-offender relationship, and (3) include segregation in models of homicide.

First, our analysis confirms that, like general homicides, African-American killings are associated with a number of structural characteristics. However, black homicides do not have the same structural precipitants as general rates of killing. In models of black homicide that include segregation and measures of blacks' socioeconomic status, many of the structural factors examined in studies of general homicide do not influence black killings, or do so in a manner that is inconsistent with prior research for the total population. Specifically, with the exception of region (South), the demographic factors considered here have weak effects on black homicide. This indicates that the social disorganization, cultural or other crime-producing effects implied by the age composition, divorce rate, size of the city population, and percent black do not operate (or operate differently) within the black population. While in sharp contrast with the consistent effect of demographic factors found in the large body of research on general homicide rates, this negligible role for demographic characteristics is not uncommon in research that considers disaggregated or race-specific homicide rates.

Our analysis also demonstrates that poverty and income inequality (intraracial and interracial) do not influence black killings. These findings are especially noteworthy in light of prominent arguments concerning the relationship between resource deprivation and crime. Perhaps income inequality is not critical for African Americans in assessing their economic well-being given that absolute economic deprivation is generally very high in the black population. The high level of absolute deprivation for African Americans may also explain why the poverty rate has no effect; it may be that poverty is so widespread among blacks that variation across communities is not especially meaningful for predicting homicide rates. Although these interpretations are speculative, our findings make it clear that the underlying structural determinants of black killings are not identical to those for general homicides.

Second, our analyses of homicides disaggregated by type of victim-offender relationship illustrate that examining aggregate patterns of homicide indeed "mask... empirical relationships indicative of a differential causal process operating in the social production of [black] homicide." The same structural factors do not underlie all types of black killing. Rather, a different combination of characteristics appears to influence each of the three types of homicide. Further, these characteristics explain less of the variance in family killings than in killings involving either acquaintances or strangers. This suggests that structural factors are more important for explaining acquaintance and stranger killings, and that interpersonal and situational conditions likely play a greater role in family victimizations.

Finally, of central concern here, the analysis confirms our view that racial residential segregation is an important aspect of inequality that should be considered in studies of lethal violence. Consistent with our premise, the analysis of total black homicides demonstrates that racial residential segregation (particularly when measured as residential dissimilarity) has a sizable positive impact on black homicide rates. This finding is consistent with resource deprivation perspectives derived from Merton's anomie thesis, and with Wilson's recent arguments regarding the consequences of social isolation for minority communities. However, this result does not permit us to determine whether resource deprivation or social isolation is more salient for explaining the effect of segregation on homicide.

The analysis of different types of homicide contributes to a better understanding of how segregation influences black lethal violence. Specifically, the disaggregated analyses make clear that the effect of segregation exists only for killings involving strangers and acquaintances, particularly the latter. This is true whether segregation is measured as dissimilarity or racial concentration. This pattern suggests that social isolation and the related lack of social control is the mechanism by which segregation leads to more homicides.

We draw this conclusion for two reasons. First, if the influence of segregation reflects resource deprivation, then we would expect the pattern of influence of this variable to be similar to that of the other inequality measures (the gini index, white/black income ratio). We do not find this to be the case. Second, acquaintance and stranger homicides can be distinguished from family killings in that they often occur in more public settings. Homicides that are more public may be escalated because of inadequate protection i.e., "benign neglect" by law enforcement and other agencies, and the inability of neighborhoods to develop peacekeeping activities (e.g., neighborhood watches). In contrast, family homicides tend to occur in more private contexts. As such, the presence or absence of more public social control mechanisms should have little effect on these more private killings.

These findings suggest that efforts to reduce black lethal violence should include attempts to alter important structural conditions underlying such violence. In particular, racial residential segregation and the accompanying social isolation are important targets for policymakers seeking to reduce African-American homicide in U.S. cities. Doing so will not be easily or quickly accomplished. Black-white residential segregation is entrenched in the U.S., especially in some of the large metropolitan areas where a very sizable portion of African Americans reside. Recent evidence indicates that various types of housing discrimination, which can reinforce patterns of residential segregation, are still widespread. Thus, one step that might be taken to reduce segregation would be to monitor more closely real estate and banking practices. However, segregation is also associated with inequality in economic resources (income and wealth) and with differences between blacks and whites in their preferences for neighborhood racial composition. These factors are less subject to intervention.

A more direct route to reducing black lethal violence might be achieved through programs aimed at reducing social isolation and increasing formal and informal control in segregated African-American communities. This might include strategies to improve the response time of police and emergency medical services, and to strengthen or re-establish important social institutions (e.g., local churches, banks, schools, stores, recreational facilities) within such neighborhoods. Also, where plausible, efforts might be made to establish a variety of community crime prevention programs within black localities.

In conclusion, the above analysis has helped to refine our understanding of the role of inequality in lethal violence, and particularly, the role of segregation in black homicides. The study makes it clear that consideration of racial residential segregation is important for understanding the alarmingly high rates of black homicide in U.S. cities. More generally, it appears that one important consequence of the "American Apartheid of residence" is a higher level of lethal violence for African Americans.

Criminal Homicide as a Situated Transaction

DAVID F. LUCKENBILL

By definition, criminal homicide is a collective transaction. An offender, victim, and possibly an audience engage in an interchange which leaves the victim dead. Furthermore. these transactions are typically situated, for participants interact in a common physical territory. As with other situated transactions, it is expected that the participants develop particular roles, each shaped by the others and instrumental in some way to the fatal outcome. However, research, with few exceptions, has failed critically to examine the situated transaction eventuating in murder. At most, studies have shown that many victims either directly precipitate their destruction, by throwing the first punch or firing the first shot, or contribute to the escalation of some conflict which concludes in their demise. But how transactions of murder are organized and how they develop remain puzzles. What are the typical roles developed by the offender, victim, and possible bystanders? In what ways do these roles intersect to produce the fatal outcome? Are there certain regularities of interaction which characterize all transactions of murder, or do patterns of interaction vary among transactions in a haphazard fashion? Making the situated transaction the unit of investigation, this paper will address these questions by examining the character of the transaction in full.

METHOD

Criminal homicide is presently defined as the unlawful taking of a person's life, with the expressed intention of killing or rendering bodily injury resulting in death, and not in the course of some other criminal activity. This conceptualization excludes such forms of unnatural death as negligent homicide and vehicular manslaughter. This investigation will examine all forms of criminal homicide but felony murder. where death occurs in the commission of other felony crimes, and contract murder, where the offender conspires with another to kill in his behalf for payment.

The present data were drawn from all cases of criminal homicide over a ten-year period. 1963–1972, in one medium sized (350,000) California county. Sampling was of a multi-stage nature. Because criminal homicide may be mitigated through charging or plea negotiation to various types of manslaughter, it was necessary to gather all cases, for the years 1963–1972, found in the four charge categories of first and second degree murder, voluntary and involuntary manslaughter. In this way, ninety-four cases were gathered. Taking all cases of unnatural death except suicide documented in coroner's reports, those twenty-three cases not fitting the present conception of criminal homicide were eliminated. These consisted of fourteen vehicular manslaughters, eight felony murders, and one negligent homicide. The remainder, seventy-one deaths or seventy transactions (one double murder), were examined.

All official documents pertaining to these cases were secured. The character of the larger occasion as well as the organization and development of the fateful transaction were reconstructed from the content analysis of police, probation, psychiatric. and witness reports, offender interviews. victim statements, and grand jury and court testimony. These materials included information on the major and minor participants; who said and did what to whom; the chronology of dialogue and action; and the physical comportment of the participants. Material relating to matters of law and legal processing were not examined.

In reconstructing the transaction, I first scrutinized each individual document for material relating only to the step-by-step development of the transaction. I then used the information to prepare separate accounts of the transaction. When all the individual documents for each case were exhausted, one summary account was constructed, using the individual accounts as resources. In the process of case reconstruction, I found that the various parties to the transaction often related somewhat different accounts of the event. Discrepancies centered, in large part, in their accounts of the specific dialogue of the participants. Their accounts were usually consistent with respect to the basic structure and development of the event. In managing discrepancies, I relied on interparticipant consistency in accounts.

This methodological strategy should provide a fairly strong measure of reliability in case reconstruction. By using several independent resources bearing on the same focal point, particular biases could be reasonably controlled. In other words, possible biases in singular archival documents could be corrected by relying on a multitude of independently produced reports bearing on the transaction. For example, the offender's account could be compared with witnesses' accounts and with reports on physical evidence.

The Social Occasion of Criminal Homicide

Criminal homicide is the culmination of an intense interchange between an offender and victim. Transactions resulting in murder involved the joint contribution of the offender and victim to the escalation of a "character contest," a confrontation in which at least one, but usually both, attempt to establish or save face at the other's expense by standing steady in the face of adversity. Such transactions additionally involved a consensus among participants that violence was a suitable if not required means for settling the contest.

Before examining the dynamics of these transactions, it is useful to consider the larger context in which they were imbedded. A "situated transaction" refers to a chain of interaction between two or more individuals that lasts the time they find themselves in one another's immediate physical presence. A "social occasion," in contrast, refers to a wider social affair within which many situated transactions may form, dissolve, and re-form (Goffman). And, as Goffman aptly demonstrates, social occasions carry boundaries of sorts which establish what kinds of transactions are appropriate and inappropriate.

Social occasions which encompassed transactions ending in murder shared several features. First, all such transactions occurred in occasions of non-work or leisure time. The majority of murders occurred between the leisure hours of six P.M. and two A.M. and especially on weekends. More important, they were always found in leisure settings: almost half the cases occurred while members engaged in leisure activities at home; fifteen percent occurred while members frequented a favorite tavern; another fifteen percent occurred while members habituated a street corner or "turf;" little over twelve percent occurred while the offender and victim drove or "cruised" about the city, highway, or country roads; the few remaining cases occurred while members engaged in activities in some other public place such as a hotel room.

Second, occasions of murder were "loose," informal affairs permitting a wide range of activities definable by members as appropriate. In contrast to work and such tighter occasions of leisure as weddings and funerals, where members are bound by rather strict sets of expectations, occasions of murder were permissive environs allowing the performance of various respectable and non-respectable activities. An "evening at home," the most prominent occasion in the cases, finds people engaging in many activities deemed suitable under the aegis of the private residence yet judged inappropriate for more formal affairs. Similarly, "an evening at the corner tavern," "hanging on street corner," or "cruising about town" have long been recognized as permissive settings providing access and opportunity to drink, take drugs, sell and purchase sex, or gamble without fear of censure by colleagues.

In the sample, members engaged in a variety of activities within such loosely structured occasions. In about seventy-five percent of the cases, the offender and victim were engaged in pleasurable pursuits. They sought to drop serious or work roles and pursue such enjoyable activities as drinking alcoholic beverages, dancing, partying, watching television, or cruising main street. In the remainder of the cases, members were engaged in reasonably serious concerns. Here, conversations of marital or relational futures, sexual prowess, beauty, trust-worthiness, and integrity were central themes about which members organized.

A third feature of such occasions was their population by intimates. In over sixty percent of the cases, the offender and victim were related by marriage, kinship, or friendship. In the remaining cases, while the offender and victim were enemies, mere acquaintances, or complete strangers, at least one, but often both were in the company of their family, friends, lovers, or co-workers.

Dynamics of the Situated Performance

These are the occasions in which situated transactions resulted in violent death. But examination of the development of these situated interchanges is not to argue that such transactions have no historical roots. In almost half the cases there had previously occurred what might be termed rehearsals between the offender and victim. These involved transactions which included the escalation of hostilities and, sometimes, physical violence. In twenty-six percent of these cases, the offender and, sometimes, victim entered the present occasion on the assumption that another hostile confrontation would transpire.

Whether or not murderous episodes had such rehearsals, an examination of all cases brings to light a conception of the transaction resembling what Lyman and Scott term a "face game." The offender and victim, at times with the assistance of bystanders, make "moves" on the basis of the other's moves and the position of their audience. While these moves are not always of the same precise content or degree, it was possible to derive a set of time-ordered stages of which each shares certain basic properties. Let me first say that the "offender" and "victim" are heuristic labels for the statuses that either emerge in the transaction or are an artifact of the battle. In seventy-one percent of the cases, the statuses of offender and victim are determined by one's statement of intent to kill or injure the other. Hence, in sixty-three percent of the cases, the victim initiates the transaction, the offender states his intention to kill or injure the victim, and the offender follows through by killing him. In eight percent of the cases, the offender initiates the transaction, later states his intention to kill or injure the victim, and follows through by killing him. But in twenty-nine percent of the cases, the statuses of offender and victim are determined by the results of the battle. Here, the initially cast victim initiates the transaction while the initially cast offender states his intention to kill or injure the victim. Due to strength or resources, the initially cast victim kills the initially cast offender in the course of battle. In discussing the first five stages, the labels of offender and victim will be used to refer to the statuses that emerge in the course of interaction and not the statuses resulting from the battle. Furthermore, the labels will be employed in a manner consistent with the pattern characteristic of the majority of the cases. Consequently, in thirty-six percent of the cases (those where the initially cast victim kills the initially cast offender and those where the offender initiates the transaction, later states his intention to kill or injure, and follows through), the adversary labeled "victim" kills while the adversary labeled "offender" is killed. In the discussion of the sixth stage the labels of offender and victim will be used to refer to the statuses resulting from the battle.

Stage I. The opening move in the transaction was an event performed by the victim and subsequently defined by the offender as an offense to "face," that image of self a person claims during a particular occasion or social contact. What constitutes the real or actual beginning of this or any other type of transaction is often quite problematic for the researcher. The victim's activity, however, appeared as a pivotal event which separated the previous occasioned activity of the offender and victim from their subsequent violent confrontation. Such a disparaging and interactionally disrupting event constitutes the initial move.

While the form and content of the victim's move varied, three basic types of events cover all cases. In the first, found in over forty-one percent of the cases, the victim made some direct, verbal expression which the offender subsequently interpreted as offensive. This class of events was obviously quite broad. Included were everything from insults levied at some particular attribute of the offender's self, family, or friends to verbal tirades which disparaged the overall character of the offender:

> *Case 34* The offender, victim, and two friends were driving toward the country where they could consume their wine. En route, the victim turned

to the offender, both of whom were located in the back seat, and stated: "You know, you really got some good parents. You know, you're really a son-of-a-bitch. You're a leech. The whole time you were out of a job, you were living with them, and weren't even paying. The car you have should be your father's. He's the one who made the payments. Any time your dad goes to the store, you're the first in line to sponge off him. Why don't you grow up and stop being a leech?" The offender swore at him, and told him to shut up. But the victim continued, "Someone ought to come along and really fuck you up."

A second type, found in thirty-four percent of the cases, involved the victim's refusal to cooperate or comply with the requests of the offender. The offender subsequently interpreted the victim's action as a denial of his ability or right to command obedience. This was illustrated in transactions where parents murdered their children. When the parent's request that the child eat dinner, stop screaming, or take a bath went unheeded, the parent subsequently interpreted the child's activity as a challenge to rightful authority. In other cases, the violent escalation came about after the victim refused to conciliate a failing or dead relationship. In yet other cases, the victim failed to heed the offender's demand that he not enter some "off limits" territory, such as the "turf" of a juvenile gang.

The third type of event, found in twenty-five percent of the cases, involved some physical or nonverbal gesture which the offender subsequently defined as personally offensive. Often this gesture entailed an insult to the offender's sexual prowess, and took the form of affairs or flirtation:

> *Case 10* When the victim finally came home, the offender told her to sit down; they had to talk. He asked her if she was "fooling around" with other men. She stated that she had, and her boyfriends pleased her more than the offender. The offender later stated that "this was like a hot iron in my gut." He ripped her clothes off and examined her body, finding scars and bruises. She said that her boyfriends liked to beat her. His anger magnified.

Of course, the victim's activity was not always performed on the murderous occasion. In fifteen percent of the cases, the event was performed on some previous occasion when the offender was not present. Nevertheless, it was on the murderous occasion that the event was made known to the offender by the victim or bystanders and so was symbolically re-enacted.

Although the content and the initial production of these events varied, each served to disrupt the social order of the occasion. Each marked the opening of a transformation process in which pre-homicide transactions of pleasurable, or serious yet tranquil, order came to be transactions involving an argumentative "character contest."

Stage II. In all cases ending in murder the offender interpreted the victim's previous move as personally offensive. In some cases the victim was intentionally offensive. But it is plausible that in other cases the victim was unwitting. In Case 43, for instance, the victim, a five-week old boy, started crying early in the morning. The offender, the boy's father, ordered the victim to stop crying. The victim's crying, however, only heightened in intensity. The victim was too young to understand the offender's verbal order, and persistent crying may have been oriented not toward challenging his father's authority, but toward acquiring food or a change of diapers. Whatever the motive for crying, the child's father defined it as purposive and offensive. What the victim intends may be inconsequential. What the offender interprets as intentional, however, may have consequences for the organization of subsequent activity.

In sixty percent of the cases, the offender learned the meaning of the victim's move from inquiries made of victim or audience. In reply, the offender received statements suggesting the victim's action was insulting and intentional. In thirty-nine percent of the cases, the offender ascertained the meaning of the impropriety directly from the victim:

> *Case 28* As the offender entered the back door of the house his wife said to her lover, the victim, "There's _____ ." The victim jumped to his feet and started dressing hurriedly. The offender, having called to his wife without avail, entered the bedroom. He found his wife nude and the victim clad in underwear. The startled offender asked the victim, "Why?" The victim replied, "Haven't you ever been in love? We love each other." The offender later stated, "If they were drunk or something, I could see it. I mean, I've done it myself. But when he said they loved each other, well that did it."

In another twenty-one percent of the cases, however, the offender made his assessment from statements of interested bystanders:

> *Case 20* The offender and his friend were sitting in a booth at a tavern drinking beer. The offender's friend told him that the offender's girlfriend

was "playing" with another man (victim) at the other end of the bar. The offender looked at them and asked his friend if he thought something was going on. The friend responded, "I wouldn't let that guy fool around with [her] if she was mine." The offender agreed, and suggested to his friend that his girlfriend and the victim be shot for their actions. His friend said that only the victim should be shot, not the girlfriend.

In the remaining forty percent of the cases the offender imputed meaning to the event on the basis of rehearsals in which the victim had engaged a similar role. The incessant screaming of the infant, the unremitting aggressions of a drunken spouse, and the never-ending flirtation by the lover or spouse were activities which offenders had previously encountered and assessed as pointed and deliberate aspersions:

> *Case 35* During a family quarrel the victim had broken the stereo and several other household goods. At one point, the victim cut her husband, the offender, on the arm. He demanded that she sit down and watch television so that he could attend to his wound in peace. On returning from the bathroom he sat down and watched television. Shortly after, the victim rose from her chair, grabbed an ashtray, and shouted, "You bastard, I'm going to kill you." As she came toward him, the offender reached into the drawer of the end table, secured a pistol, and shot her. On arrest, the offender told police officers, "You know how she gets when she's drunk? I had to stop her, or she would have killed me. She's tried it before, that's how I got all these scars," pointing to several areas on his back.

Such previous activities and their consequences served the offender as an interpretive scheme for immediately making sense of the present event.

Stage III. The apparent affront could have evoked different responses. The offender could have excused the violation because the victim was judged to be drunk, crazy, or joking. He could have fled the scene and avoided further interaction with the victim by moving into interaction with other occasioned participants or dealt with the impropriety through a retaliatory move aimed at restoring face and demonstrating strong character. The latter move was utilized in all cases.

In countering the impropriety, the offender attempted to restore the occasioned order and reaffirm face by standing his or her ground. To have used another alternative was to confirm questions of face and self raised by the victim. The offender's plight, then, was "problematic" and "consequential." He could have chosen from several options, each of which had important consequences both to the face he situationally claimed and to his general reputation. Thus, the offender was faced with a dilemma: either deal with the impropriety by demonstrating strength of character, or verify questions of face by demonstrating weakness.

In retaliating, the offender issued an expression of anger and contempt which signified his opinion of the victim as an unworthy person. Two basic patterns of retaliation were found. In eighty-six percent of the cases, the offender issued a verbal or physical challenge to the victim. In the remaining cases, the offender physically retaliated, killing the victim.

For the latter pattern, this third move marked the battle ending the victim's life:

> *Case 12* The offender, victim, and group of bystanders were observing a fight between a barroom bouncer and a drunk patron on the street outside the tavern. The offender was cheering for the bouncer, and the victim was cheering for the patron, who was losing the battle. The victim, angered by the offender's disposition toward the fight, turned to the offender and said, "You'd really like to see the little guy have the shit kicked out of him, wouldn't you big man?" The offender turned toward the victim and asked, "What did you say? You want the same thing, punk?" The victim moved toward the offender and reared back. The offender responded, "OK buddy." He struck the victim with a single right cross. The victim crashed to the pavement, and died a week later.

Such cases seem to suggest that the event is a one-sided affair, with the unwitting victim engaging a passive, non-contributory role. But in these cases the third stage was preceded by the victim's impropriety, the offender's inquiry of the victim or audience, and a response affirming the victim's intent to be censorious. On assessing the event as one of insult and challenge, the offender elicited a statement indicating to participants, including himself. his intended line of action, secured a weapon, positioned it, and dropped the victim in a single motion.

While ten cases witness the victim's demise during this stage, the typical case consists of various verbal and physically nonlethal moves. The most common type of retaliation was a verbal challenge, occurring in forty-three percent of the cases. These took the form of an ultimatum: either apologize, flee the situation, or discontinue the inappropriate conduct, or face physical harm or death:

> *Case 54* The offender, victim, and two neighbors were sitting in the living room drinking wine. The victim started calling the offender, his wife,

abusive names. The offender told him to "shut up." Nevertheless, he continued. Finally, she shouted, "I said shut up. If you don't shut up and stop it, I'm going to kill you and I mean it."

In about twenty-two percent of the cases, the offender's retaliation took the form of physical violence short of real damage or incapacitation:

> *Case 4* The offender, victim, and three friends were driving in the country drinking beer and wine. At one point, the victim started laughing at the offender's car which he, the victim, scratched a week earlier. The offender asked the victim why he was laughing. The victim responded that the offender's car looked like junk. The offender stopped the car and all got out. The offender asked the victim to repeat his statement. When the victim reiterated his characterization of the car, the offender struck the victim, knocking him to the ground.

In another ten percent, retaliation came by way of countering the victim's impropriety with similar insults or degrading gestures. This response entailed a name-calling, action-matching set of expressions resembling that which would be found between boys in the midst of a playground argument or "playing the dozens."

The remaining cases, some eleven percent of the sample, were evenly divided. On the one hand, offenders issued specific commands, tinged with hostility and backed with an aggressive posture, calling for their victims to back down. On the other hand, offenders "called out" or invited their victims to fight physically.

This third stage is the offender's opening move in salvaging face and honor. In retaliating by verbal and physically nonlethal means, the offender appeared to suggest to the victim a definition of the situation as one in which violence was suitable in settling questions of face and reputation.

Stage IV. Except for cases in which the victim has been eliminated, the offender's preceding move placed the victim in a problematic and consequential position: either stand up to the challenge and demonstrate strength of character, or apologize, discontinue the inappropriate conduct, or flee the situation and thus withdraw questions of the offender's face while placing one's own in jeopardy. Just as the offender could have dismissed the impropriety, fled the scene, or avoided further contact with the victim, so too did the victim have similar alternatives. Rather than break the escalation in a manner demonstrating weakness, all victims in the remaining sample came into a "working" agreement with the proffered definition of the situation as one suited for violence. In the majority of cases, the victim's move appeared as an agreement that violence was suitable to the transaction. In some cases, though, the offender interpreted, sometimes incorrectly, the victim's move as implicit agreement to violence. A working agreement was struck in several ways.

The most prominent response, found in forty-one percent of the cases, involved noncompliance with the offender's challenge or command, and the continued performance of activities deemed offensive:

> *Case 54* The victim continued ridiculing the offender before friends. The offender finally shouted, "I said shut up. If you don't shut up and stop it, I'm going to kill you and I mean it." The victim continued his abusive line of conduct. The offender proceeded to the kitchen, secured a knife, and returned to the living room. She repeated her warning. The victim rose from his chair, swore at the offender's stupidity, and continued laughing at her. She thrust the knife deep into his chest.

Similarly, a spouse or lover's refusal, under threat of violence, to conciliate a failing marriage or relationship served as tacit acceptance that violence was suitable to the present transaction.

Whether the victim's noncompliance was intentional or not, the offender interpreted the move as intentional. Take, for example, the killing of children at the hands of parents. In an earlier illustration, the first move found the parent demanding obedience and backed by a hostile, combative stance. In several of these cases, the child was too young to understand what the parent demanded and the specific consequences for noncompliance. Nevertheless, the child's failure to eat dinner or stop screaming was interpreted by the parent as a voluntary protest, an intentional challenge to authority. Consequently, the unwitting activities of victims may contribute to what offenders define as very real character contests demanding very real lines of opposition.

A second response, occurring in thirty percent of the cases, found victims physically retaliating against their offenders by hitting, kicking, and pushing-responses short of mortal injury:

> *Case 42* The offender and a friend were passing by a local tavern and noticed the victim, a co-worker at a food-processing plant, sitting at the bar. The offender entered the tavern and asked the victim to repay a loan. The victim was angered by the request and refused to pay. The offender then

pushed the victim from his stool. Before the victim could react, the bartender asked them to take their fight outside. The victim followed the offender out the door and, from behind, hit the offender with a brick he grabbed from a trash can immediately outside the door. The offender turned and warned the victim that he would beat the victim if he wouldn't pay up and continued his aggressions. The victim then struck the offender in the mouth, knocking out a tooth.

In the remaining cases victims issued counter-challenges, moves made when offenders' previous moves involved threats and challenges. In some cases, this move came in the form of calling the offender's bluff. In other cases, the counter came in the form of a direct challenge or threat to the offender, a move no different from the ultimatum given victims by offenders.

Unlike simple noncompliance, physical retaliation against offenders and issuance of counter-challenges signify an explicit acceptance of violence as a suitable means for demonstrating character and maintaining or salvaging face.

Just as the victim contributed to the escalation toward violence, so too did the audience to the transaction. Seventy percent of all cases were performed before an audience. In these cases. onlookers generally engaged one or two roles. In fifty-seven percent of these cases, interested members of the audience intervened in the transaction, and actively encouraged the use of violence by means of indicating to opponents the initial improprieties, cheering them toward violent action, blocking the encounter from outside interference, or providing lethal weapons:

> *Case 23* The offender's wife moved toward the victim, and hit him in the back of the head with an empty beer bottle stating, 'That'll teach you to [molest] my boy. I ought to cut your balls off, you motherfucker." She went over to the bar to get another bottle. The victim pushed himself from the table and rose. He then reached into his pocket to secure something which some bystanders thought was a weapon. One of the bystanders gave the offender an axe handle and suggested that he stop the victim before the victim attacked his wife. The offender moved toward the victim.

In the remaining cases onlookers were neutral. They were neither encouraging nor discouraging. While neutrality may have been due to fear, civil inattention, or whatever reason. the point is that inaction within a strategic interchange can be interpreted by the opponents as a move favoring the use of violence. Consider the statement of the offender in the following case:

Case 48 Police officer: Don't you think it was wrong to beat [your daughter] when her hands were tied behind her back? [Her hands and feet were bound to keep her from scratching.]

Offender: Well, I guess so. But I really didn't think so then, or [my wife] would have said something to stop me.

Stage V. On forging a working agreement. the offender and, in many cases, victim appeared committed to battle. They contributed to and invested in the development of a fateful transaction, one which was problematic and consequential to their face and wider reputation. They placed their character on the line, and alternative methods for assessing character focused on a working agreement that violence was appropriate. Because opponents appeared to fear displaying weakness in character and consequent loss of face, and because resolution of the contest was situationally bound, demanding an immediacy of response, they appeared committed to following through with expressed or implied intentions.

Commitment to battle was additionally enhanced by the availability of weapons to support verbal threats and challenges. Prior to victory, the offender often sought out and secured weapons capable of overcoming the victim. In about thirty-six percent of the cases, offenders carried hand guns or knives into the setting. In only thirteen percent of these cases did offenders bring hand guns or knives into the situation on the assumption that they might be needed if the victims were confronted. In the remainder of these cases such weapons were brought in as a matter of everyday routine. In either event, to inflict the fatal blow required the mere mobilization of the weapon for action. In sixty-four percent of the cases, the offender either left the situation temporarily to secure a hand gun, rifle, or knife, or transformed the status of some existing situational prop, such as a pillow, telephone cord, kitchen knife, beer mug, or baseball bat, into a lethal weapon. The possession of weapons makes battle possible, and, in situations defined as calling for violence, probable.

The particular dynamics of the physical interchange are quite varied. In many cases. the battle was brief and precise. In approximately fifty-four percent of the cases, the offender secured the weapon and dropped the victim in a single shot, stab, or rally of blows. In the remaining cases, the battle was two-sided. One or both secured a weapon and exchanged a series of blows, with one falling in defeat.

Stage VI. Once the victim had fallen, the offender made one of three moves which marked the termination of the transaction. In over fifty-eight percent of the cases, the offender fled the scene. In about thirty-two percent of the cases, the offender voluntarily remained on the scene for the police. In the remaining cases, the offender was involuntarily held for the police by members of the audience.

These alternatives seemed prompted by two lines of influence; the relationship of the offender and victim and the position of the audience vis-à-vis the offense. When there is no audience, the offender appeared to act on the basis of his relationship to the victim. When the offender and victim were intimately related, the offender typically remained on the scene and notified the police. Sometimes these offenders waited for minutes or hours before reporting the event, stating they needed time to think, check the victim's condition, and make arrangements on financial matters, the children, and work before arrest. In contrast, when victims were acquaintances or enemies, offenders typically fled the scene. Moreover, these offenders often attempted to dispose of their victims and incriminating evidence.

Seventy percent of the cases, however, occurred before an audience, and offenders' moves seemed related to audience reactions to the offense. Bystanders seemed to replace the victim as the primary interactant, serving the offender as the pivotal reference for his exiting orientations. The audience assumed one of three roles: hostile, neutral, or supportive. In the hostile role, accounting for nearly thirty-five percent of the cases, bystanders moved to apprehend the offender, assist the victim, and immediately notify police. Such audiences were generally comprised of persons who either supported the victim or were neutral during the pre-battle escalation. In several of these cases, bystanders suggested, without use of force, that the offender assist the victim, call the police, and so forth. These audiences were comprised of the offender's intimates, and he followed their advice without question. In either case, hostile bystanders forced or suggested the offender's compliance in remaining at the scene for police.

In almost seventeen percent of the cases, the audience was neutral. These people appeared as shocked bystanders. Having witnessed the killing, they stood numb as the offender escaped and the victim expired.

In the remainder of the cases, the audience was supportive of the offender. These audiences were usually comprised of persons who encouraged the offender during the pre-battle stages. Supportive bystanders rendered assistance to the offender in his escape. destroyed incriminating evidence, and maintained ignorance of the event 'when questioned by the police. breaking down only in later stages of interrogation. Thus, while a hostile audience directs the offender to remain at the scene, the supportive audience permits or directs his flight.

CONCLUSION

On the basis of this research, criminal homicide does not appear as a one-sided event with an unwitting victim assuming a passive, non-contributory role. Rather, murder is the outcome of a dynamic interchange between an offender, victim, and, in many cases, bystanders. The offender and victim develop lines of action shaped in part by the actions of the other and focused toward saving or maintaining face and reputation and demonstrating character. Participants develop a working agreement, sometimes implicit. often explicit, that violence is a useful tool for resolving questions of face and character. In some settings, where very small children are murdered, the extent of their participation cannot be great. But generally these patterns characterized all cases irrespective of such variables as age, sex, race, time and place, use of alcohol, and proffered motive.

Evolutionary Social Psychology and Family Homicide

Martin Daly & Margo Wilson

Homicide within the family is a theme of great psychological significance. In many mythologies, the primordial murder was a fratricide or patricide. Freud's "Oedipal theory" made the urge to kill one's father a normal element of the male psyche; Bloch maintains that the "central preoccupation of childhood" is the fear of parental filicide. Moreover, these murderous impulses are apparently manifest not just in imagination, but in action. Two prominent experts on domestic violence in the United States have written:

> With the exception of the police and the military, the family is perhaps the most violent social group, and the home the most violent social setting, in our society. A person is more likely to be hit or killed in his or her home by another family member than anywhere else or by anyone else.

These allegations present a puzzle from the perspective of contemporary evolutionary theories of social motives and behavior. The species-typical appetites, aversions, motives, emotions, and cognitive structures of all creatures, including *Homo sapiens*, have been shaped by selection to produce social action that is effectively "nepotistic": action that promotes the proliferation of the actor's genetic elements in future generations, by contributing to the survival and reproductive success of the actor's genetic relatives. Apprehensions of self-interest—such as the absence of pain and hunger, or the positive satisfactions derived from social and sexual successes and from the well-being of one's children—evolve as tokens of expected genetic posterity ("expected" in the statistical sense of that which would be anticipated from past evidence). It follows that individual self-interests conflict because of rivalry for representation in future gene pools. Genetic relatedness is a predictor of reduced conflict and enhanced cooperation because the genetic posterities of blood relatives co-vary (are promoted by common exigencies) in direct proportion to their degree of relatedness. The heuristic value and essential soundness of this theoretical framework have been abundantly confirmed by recent research on nonhuman animals, and there is a growing body of empirical studies indicating its applicability to human sociality, too.

What, then, of family violence? We propose (i) that genetic relationship is associated with the mitigation of conflict and violence in people, as in other creatures; and (ii) that evolutionary models predict and explain patterns of differential risk of family violence.

We shall focus on an extreme form of interpersonal violence: homicide. One may protest that homicides are too infrequent and extreme to illuminate conflict generally, but there is advantage in focusing on acts so dire. The issues over which people are prepared to kill are surely those about which they care most profoundly. Moreover, because homicide is viewed so seriously, there is less reporting bias in homicide archives than in the records of any lesser manifestation of conflict. Homicides thus provide an exceptionally valid "assay" of interpersonal conflict.

GENETIC RELATIONSHIP AND MITIGATION
OF HOMICIDE RISK WITHIN FAMILIES

Criminological studies of homicide in the United States have generally used a limited categorization of victim-killer relationships. In a classic study of homicides in Philadelphia, for example, "relatives" constituted almost one-fourth of all victims, and most of these were spouses; blood relatives and in-laws were not distinguished, together constituting just 6.5% of solved cases. These results are apparently typical: "Relatives" have never been found to exceed one-third of any substantial sample of U.S. homicides, and, wherever spouses have been distinguished, they outnumber all other relatives combined. In two studies, genealogical and marital relatives were distinguished: 19% of Detroit homicide victims in 1972 were related to their killers by marriage compared to 6% by blood; 10% of Miami victims in 1980 were marital relatives of their killers compared to 1.8% blood relatives.

These data suggest that blood kin may be relatively immune from lethal violence in the United States, given the high frequency and intensity of interactions among relatives. However, in order to decide whether this is really so, one needs some sort of denominator representing "opportunity": the number and availability of potential victims in different categories of relationship to potential killers. One approach to this problem is to confine attention to cases involving members of the same household, so that the universe of accessible potential victims can be specified. Given the prevailing household compositions in Detroit in 1972, for example, coresidents unrelated to the killer by blood, whether spouses or not, were more than 11 times more likely to be slain than coresiding genetic relatives. Comparable analyses have not been conducted in other U.S. cities (nor can they be with information in typical data sets, since coresidence has not ordinarily been recorded); however, the fact that the distribution of victim-killer relationships in Detroit was unexceptional suggests that similar results would obtain.

Another approach to the issue of whether kinship mitigates conflict when opportunity is controlled entails comparing the distribution of relationships between killers and their victims with the distribution of relationships between collaborators in homicide. The logic is this: If conflict and cooperation were to arise merely in proportion to the frequency and intensity of interactions, relatively intimate types of relationships would provide more opportunities for both. Those intimate links that are prevalent among victim-killer relationships should thus prove to be similarly prevalent among co-offenders. But such is not the case. Among coaccused pairs of killers in Miami, for example, 29.6% were blood relatives as compared to just 1.8% of victims and killers. In fact, the average degree of relatedness between collaborative killers is far higher than the corresponding value for victim and killer in every society for which a relevant sample of cases is available, including tribal horticulturalists, medieval Englishmen, Mayan villagers, and urban Americans.

STEP-RELATIONSHIPS

A particularly apt comparison for assessing effects of (perceived) relationship on conflict is that between the parent-offspring relationship and surrogates thereof. Parental solicitude has evolved to expend animals' resources (and even their lives) in enhancing the reproductive prospects of their descendants. It is therefore not surprising that parental solicitude evolves to be discriminative with respect to predictors of the offspring's probable contribution to the parent's genetic posterity. One implication is that substitute parents will often care less profoundly for "their" children than will genetic parents.

"Cruel stepparent" stories are cross-culturally ubiquitous and reflect a recurring dilemma. Mothers and fathers have been widowed or abandoned with dependent children throughout human history, whereupon the fate of the children became problematic. A worldwide solution to the problem of single parents unable or unwilling to raise their children is fosterage to close relatives such as maternal grandparents. In some societies, widows are customarily married to their dead husbands' brothers (the levirate); in others, widows with dependent children may spurn remarriage and reside with siblings or other close relatives. In the absence of such arrangements, children come under the care of stepparents who may have no benevolent interest in their welfare. In a study of the foraging Ache Indians of Paraguay, for example, Hill and Kaplan traced the careers of 67 children raised by mother and stepfather after the natural father's death: 43% had died, of various causes, before their 15th birthdays, as compared to just 19% of those raised by two surviving parents.

Children in stepparent families are disproportionately often injured in industrial nations, too. The specific kinds of injuries involved suggest that such children are not at risk merely by virtue of decreased parental vigilance and supervision, but are also more often assaulted. When injuries are attributed to "child abuse," the difference between stepparent and genetic parent homes is large and is independent of risk attributable to low socioeconomic status, maternal youth, family size, or personality characteristics of the abusers. Abusive stepparents are discriminative, sparing their own children within the same household. Presently available data do not reveal whether stepmother or stepfather households entail greater risks.

Overrepresentation of stepfamilies in child abuse samples might be dismissed as a product of reporting biases but for the fact that stepparents are even more strongly overrepresented in cases of child homicide, where biases of detection and reporting are presumably minimal. An English sample of "fatal battered baby cases" included 15 killed by stepfathers and 14 by genetic fathers, although fewer than 1% of same-age English babies dwelt with stepfathers. Similarly, an Australian sample of fatally battered babies included 18 slain by substitute fathers compared to 11 by genetic fathers. A child living with one or more substitute parents in the United States in 1976 was approximately 100 times more likely to be fatally abused than a same-age child living with genetic parents.

In view of the costs of prolonged "parental" investment in nonrelatives, it may seem remarkable that step-relationships are ever peaceful, let alone genuinely affectionate. However, violent hostility is rarer than friendly relations even among nonrelatives; people thrive by the maintenance of networks of social reciprocity and by establishing reputations for fairness and generosity that will make them attractive exchange partners. The kindly deportment of most stepparents may prove to be explicable mainly in the context of reciprocity with the genetic parent; moreover, insofar as indulgence toward unrelated children is a general attribute of men (or other male animals), it may be attributable to sexual selection as a result of female mate choice. The fact remains, however, that step-relationships lack the deep commonality of interest of the natural parent-offspring relationship, and feelings of affection and commitment are correspondingly shallower. Differential rates of violence are one result.

SPOUSAL CONFLICTS

The customary extension of the category "relative" to encompass spouses and in-laws is metaphorical, but not arbitrary. By cooperative rearing of joint offspring, mates in a species with biparental care forge a powerful commonality of interest analogous to that existing between blood relatives. Indeed, the genetic interests of an exclusively monogamous pair coincide even more closely than those of blood relatives. However, two considerations act against the evolution of perfect harmony in mated pairs: (i) the possibility of extra-pair reproduction and (ii) the partners' nepotistic interests in the welfare of distinct sets of collateral kin.

Mutual progeny contribute to spousal harmony, whereas children of former unions contribute to spousal conflict. U.S. divorce statistics reflect these effects of children: For a given duration of marriage, children of former unions elevate divorce rates, whereas children of the present union reduce them. We predict parallel influences of children on spousal homicide rates. There is some evidence that the presence of stepchildren is associated with spousal homicide, but available data do not permit quantitative assessment of the risks in households of various compositions.

In many animals (including people in their environments of evolutionary adaptation), female reproduction is resource-limited whereas the reproductive capacities of females are themselves the limiting "resource" for males. Male reproductive output in such species has a higher ceiling and greater variance than that of females, with the result that reproductive competition is more intense and dangerous among males. One tactic in such competition is sequestering and guarding mates, which increases in utility (relative to alternative tactics like maximizing copulatory contacts) in species with biparental care, since parentally investing males can be fooled about paternity.

Human marriage is a cross-culturally general institutionalization of reproductive alliance, entailing mutual obligations between the spouses during child-rearing, rights of sexual access (often but not necessarily exclusive and usually controlled by the husband), and legitimization of the status of progeny. Men take a proprietary view of women and their reproductive capacity, as witness the widespread practices of bridewealth and claustration and infibulation of reproductively valuable women, and the near universality of sexually asymmetrical adultery laws that treat poaching by rival males as a property violation.

Male sexual proprietariness is the dominant issue in marital violence. In studies of "motives" of spousal homicide, the leading identified substantive issue is invariably "jealousy." Interview studies of North American spouse killers indicate that the husband's proprietary concern with his wife's fidelity or her intention to quit the marriage led him to initiate the violence in an overwhelming majority of cases, regardless of whether it was the husband or wife who ended up dead. Similarly, in other cultures, wherever motives in a sample of spousal homicides have been characterized in detail, male sexual proprietariness has proven relevant to more than half of those homicides. Sexual proprietariness evidently lies behind most nonlethal wife beating, too, suggesting that spousal homicides are not primarily cold-blooded "disposals," but are the tip of the iceberg of coercive violence. Men strive to control women by various means and with variable success, while women strive to resist coercion and maintain their choices. There is brinkmanship in any such contest, and homicides by spouses of either sex may be considered the slips in this dangerous game.

This view of spousal violence as the coercive tactic of proprietary men suggests that women will be extremely at risk when perceived as likely to end the relationship. Indeed, there is a remarkable prevalence of recently estranged wives among homicide victims. In an Australian study, 98 of 217 women slain by their husbands (45%) were separated or in the process thereof, compared to just 3 of 79 men slain by their wives (4%). Estrangement has also been implicated in spousal homicides in Canada. A correct apprehension of the lethal risk in deserting a proprietary husband is surely one factor in the reluctance of many abused wives to leave.

The above considerations suggest, moreover, that young wives may be especially at risk, for two reasons: Youth per se makes the woman more attractive to rival men, and the short duration of the marriage means that deep commonalities of interest have yet to be forged, making the marriage potentially unstable. In Canada, young wives are indeed likeliest to be spousal homicide victims. One might attribute this differential risk to the fact that young women are married to young men, the most homicidal demographic category, but the woman's age is apparently more relevant to spousal homicide risk than the man's; the wife's declining risk as a function of age is apparent within each age class of husbands (although risk rises again for wives much older than their husbands). To date, no analysis has fully unconfounded the variables of the two parties' ages and marital and reproductive histories in order to assess their separate relevances to spousal homicide risk.

PARENT-OFFSPRING CONFLICT AND VIOLENCE

Parents and children engage in frequent battles of wills, major and minor. Traditional social scientific views of these conflicts attribute them to imperfect adaptation in one or the other party, for example, "immature" egoism in the child or poor parenting skills.

Trivers proposed a radically different perspective on parenting and socialization: Even though offspring are the parents' means to genetic posterity, parent-offspring conflict is an endemic feature of sexually reproducing organisms, because the allocation of resources and efforts that would maximize a parent's genetic posterity seldom matches that which would maximize a particular offspring's. Selection favors inclinations in both parties to achieve one's own optimum against the wishes and efforts of the other. This theory accounts for the seemingly maladaptive phenomenon of weaning conflict, as well as for disparate parental and offspring attitudes to collateral kin, "regression" to earlier stages of development on the birth of a sibling, and adolescent identity crises. In some circumstances, an offspring's reproductive prospects (according to cues that were predictive in the species environment of evolutionary adaptation) may be insufficient to offset that offspring's detrimental effect on the parent's capacity to pursue other adaptive action, in which case parental solicitude may be expected to fail.

People everywhere recognize that parents may sometimes be disinclined to raise a child, and anthropologists have collected much information about the circumstances in which infanticide is alleged to be common, acceptable, or even obligatory. If parental inclinations have been shaped by selection, there are at least three classes of circumstances in which we might anticipate some reluctance to invest in a newborn: (i) doubt that the offspring is the putative parent's own, (ii) indications of poor offspring quality, and (iii) all those extrinsic circumstances, such as food scarcity, lack of social support, and overburdening from the demands of older offspring, that would have made a child unlikely to survive during human evolutionary history. The great majority of ethnographic accounts of infanticide in nonindustrial societies reflect one or another of these three categories of strategic allocation of lifetime parental effort.

Moreover, we may expect maternal psychology to exhibit sensitivity to the mother's own residual reproductive value: A newborn's compromising effects on the mother's future diminish with maternal age, and hence maternal willingness to jettison an infant may also be expected to decrease. This prediction is upheld. This maternal age effect is not an artifact of marital status; it is observed in both married and unmarried women.

Evolutionary considerations suggest several predictions about filicide in relation to the child's age, too. In ancestral environments. the child's probability of attaining adulthood and contributing to its own and its parents' genetic posterity increased with age, especially during infancy, as the child passed through a stage of high mortality risk. The predicted consequence is that parental psychology should have evolved to cherish the child increasingly over a prolonged period, as the child's reproductive value increased. Hence:

1) Parents are expected to be more willing to incur costs on behalf of offspring nearer to maturity and to be more inhibited in the use of dangerous tactics when in conflict with such offspring. Filicide rates are thus predicted to decline with the child's age, whereas no such effect is predicted in the case of child homicides by nonrelatives, whose valuation of the child is not expected to parallel that of the parents.

2) This decline is predicted to be negatively accelerated and concentrated in the first year postpartum, because (i) in the environments of human evolutionary adaptation, the lion's share of the prepubertal increase in reproductive value occurred within the first year, and (ii) insofar as parental disinclination reflects a "strategic" assessment of the reproductive episode, an evolved assessment mechanism should be such as to terminate hopeless ventures as early as possible.

3) Filicides perpetrated by the mother are predicted to be a more steeply declining function of the child's age than those perpetrated by the father, because (i) women's reproductive life spans end before those of men, so the utility of alternative reproductive efforts declines more steeply for women than for men; (ii) the extent to which children impose greater opportunity costs on mothers than on fathers is probably maximal in infancy; and (iii) phenotypic and other evidence of paternity may surface after infancy and is expected to be relevant to paternal but not maternal solicitude.

Offspring kill parents, too. Because violence toward parents, like violence toward children, is associated with economic and other stressors, and because parricides often follow a history of parental mistreatment of the eventual killer, one might expect factors related to the risk of filicide to affect the risk of parricide in a directionally similar fashion. An evolutionary theoretical perspective, however, suggests one likely exception to this generalization. Just as a parent's valuation of an offspring is predictably related to the ages (reproductive values) of both parties, so too is the offspring's valuation of the parent. An offspring of a given age may be expected to disvalue an elderly parent more than a younger one. These considerations suggest that parental age at the child's birth will have opposite effects on the rates of violence perpetrated by parent and offspring against each other.

An alternative to Trivers's evolutionary analysis of parent-offspring conflict is Freud's "Oedipal theory": It is allegedly a normal phase of infant male psychosocial development to lust after mother and wish father dead. An evolutionary perspective suggests that Freud apprehended two distinct parent-offspring conflicts and conflated them. There is indeed a conflict between father and infant son over the wife-mother, but it is not sexual rivalry. The optimal birth interval from the child's perspective exceeds that from the father's, and it is not implausible that toddlers have evolved specific adaptive strategies to delay the conception of a sibling, including tactics to diminish mother's sexual interest and thwart father's access to her. In many societies, there is a later conflict between father and son over the timing of the son's accession to reproductive status, often subsidized by the father at a cost to his own continuing reproductive ambitions; this later conflict is "sexual," but it is not over the mother.

If Trivers's evolutionary model is correct, then conflict between parents and young children exists irrespective of the child's sex. According to Freud, children are in conflict primarily with the parent of the same sex, at least in the "Oedipal phase" (ages 2 to 5 years) if not from birth; such a same-sex contingency in parent-offspring antagonisms is allegedly endemic to the human condition. Trivers's account predicts no such infantile same-sex contingency, although elements of sexual rivalry could arise later. Canadian data on parent-offspring homicide cases support Trivers's view, as do British and U.S. data.

CONCLUDING REMARKS

Analyses of "family violence" have hitherto ignored crucial distinctions among relationships. Elucidation of the nature of relationship-specific confluences and conflicts of interest requires a conception of the fundamental nature of self-interests. Evolutionary theory provides such a conception by considering perceived self-interests to be evolved tokens of expected genetic posterity. From this perspective, the spousal relationship is unique in its potential for generating shared interests and betrayals thereof, and the commonalities and conflicts of interest even among blood relatives are relationship-specific.

The application of such an evolutionary model to the study of violence (or other social behavior) is neither simple nor direct. In particular, an evolutionary model need not imply that the behavior in question effectively promotes the reproductive success of the actors or their relatives. Homicide is a rare, extreme product of motivational mechanisms whose outputs are only expected to be adaptive on average, and in environments not crucially different from those in which we evolved. Murder-suicides forcefully illustrate why adaptation is most usefully sought at a psychological level of abstraction rather than in each category of overt behavior. Men are far more likely than women to commit suicide after killing a spouse and are especially likely to do so when the couple are estranged. A frequently expressed rationale is "If I can't have her, no one can." In such a case, the killer has apparently fallen into futile spite, but the counterproductiveness of sexual proprietariness in these extreme cases hardly gainsays its candidate status as a masculine psychological adaptation. The more typical consequences of fierce proprietariness have surely been effective deterrence of rivals and coercive control of wives. Similarly, the proposition that discriminative parental affection has been favored by selection is not undermined by the consideration that fatal child abuse may land a stepfather in jail. Although specific acts may be maladaptive (especially in evolutionarily novel environments), selection has shaped the social motives, emotions, and cognitive processes underlying them. Evolutionary psychological constructs like "discriminative parental solicitude" or "male sexual proprietariness" are domain-specific, but they influence a range of actions both conflictual and cooperative. The evolutionary psychological hypotheses that we have tested against homicide data should be further assessed with less extreme behavioral measures of conflict and with positive measures of harmony and solicitude.

Evolutionary models have enabled us to predict and discover patterned variations in the risk of lethal violence, as a function of the parties' ages, circumstances, and specific relationships to one another. As predicted, genetic relationship is associated with a softening of conflict, and people's evident valuations of themselves and of others are systematically related to the parties' reproductive values. Evolutionary theory can provide a valuable conceptual framework for the analysis of social psychologies.

~Men commit suicide
~Non blood relative, most likely to be killed b/c blood relative interferes w/ evolutionary aspects (soften the argument w/ blood relative)

CULTURAL

The Empirical Status of the Subculture of Violence Thesis

HOWARD S. ERLANGER

In the study of adult interpersonal violence (which may be defined as acts of physical aggression directed at persons, excluding acts under the aegis of, or directed against, political, parental, or other authority), one of the most important and most often cited theoretical statements has been the "subculture of violence" thesis. According to Wolfgang and Ferracuti, violence results from adherence to a set of values which supports and encourages its expression. These values are seen as being in conflict with but not totally in opposition to those of the dominant culture. It is said that within the subculture, various stimuli such as a jostle, a slightly derogatory remark, or the appearance of a weapon in the hands of an adversary are perceived differently than in the dominant culture; in the subculture they evoke a combative reaction.

Although violence obviously is not and cannot be used continuously, Wolfgang and Ferractuti see the requirement to be violent as a norm governing a wide variety of situations. They judge the subcultural theme to be "penetrating and diffuse" and argue that violations of the subcultural norm are punished within the subculture. Adherence to the norm is not necessarily viewed as illicit conduct, and "a carrier and user of violence will [generally] not be burdened by conscious guilt...[and] even law-abiding members of the local subcultural area may not view various expressions of violence as menacing or immoral."

When preparing the 1967 volume, Wolfgang and Ferracuti could locate no data on the distribution of values regarding violence, so they were forced to rely on inferences from available data on criminal acts of interpersonal violence. Since criminal statistics indicate that the groups with the highest rates of homicide are males, nonwhites. lower- and working-class whites. and young adults, it is, therefore, among these groups that "we should find in most intense degree a subculture of violence." They acknowledge that their reasoning here is circular, and they agree that individual data on values are necessary for an adequate test of the theory.

In the years since the subculture of violence thesis was first introduced, there have been a variety of studies which directly or indirectly bring data to bear on the thesis. In the study of juvenile delinquency, for example, there has been a related controversy over the value system of adolescent gangs. W. Miller has argued that these gangs reflect the "focal concerns" of lower-class culture, which he sees as including "toughness" and "excitement." However, the analysis of gang values by Short and Strodtbeck failed to confirm the existence of these focal concerns, and a study by Lerman has questioned the existence of a distinctive lower-class culture reflected in gangs. In addition, various studies have concluded that gang activity is related more to group processes than to a violence oriented subculture, and later work by Miller and his colleagues does not indicate that physical aggression ms an important part of lower-class gang life.

Some studies, such as those of Kobrin et al. and Yablonsky have found that status within the gang is at least in part based on the criteria outlined by Wolfgang and Ferracuti, but Yablonsky has also emphasized the fluid nature of group membership and the limited ability of leaders to sanction members who do not conform. Moreover, it is important to remember that the existence of violence as a criterion of status in gangs in low-income neighborhoods is insufficient to establish the existence of such norms among nongang juveniles in those neighborhoods, especially since it is generally the most extreme gangs that have been studied. When the whole juvenile population is studied, the patterns can be quite different.

In the study of adult interpersonal violence, research has been much more limited. Various studies and texts in sociology and social psychology have stressed the subcultural view, but they have not used individual data to support their arguments. The idea of a subculture of violence is conspicuous by its *absence* in various well known ethnographic studies of adult lower-class communities. Since these writers are not explicitly concerned with the issue, the absence of discussion is not definitive evidence against the thesis. It does, however, suggest that violence is not a major theme in the groups studied.

Few systematic studies of class differences in values or attitudes among adults have been reported in the literature, and some of the most often cited are quite dated. Most studies that do exist do not specifically deal with low-income groups; the lower class is either omitted or combined with the working class for analysis. Insofar as the present author can determine, until the late 1960s no survey data on the values or attitudes of adults toward violence were available.

In a recent paper, Ball-Rokeach analyzes responses to the Rokeach Value Survey given by males with various degrees of participation in violence. She finds no important differences in the ranking of 18 "terminal values" or of 18 "instrumental values" by men classified as having no, a 'moderate," or a "high" degree of participation in violence at any time in their life. She reports that controls for education and income, which are crucial for the examination of a subculture which is said to be class-based, do not affect the findings. A comparison of prisoners convicted of violent crimes and persons convicted of non-violent crimes also found no important differences in the ranking of values. Although there are some difficulties with the data used in these studies, they are the only recent materials which attempt to measure directly value hierarchies; and they yield findings incompatible with the subculture of violence thesis.

Attitudinal data collected for the President's Commission on the Causes and Prevention of Violence in 1968 also call the subcultural thesis into question. In a national survey, for which questionnaire construction was supervised by Ball-Rokeach, respondents were asked about their general approval of the use of physical aggression in certain kinds of interpersonal interactions; those who gave this general approval were then asked about four or five more specific situations. The general approval questions asked whether there were "any situations that you can imagine" in which the respondent would approve of such acts as a husband slapping his wife's face; a husband shooting his wife; a man punching (or choking) an adult male stranger; one teenage boy punching (or knifing) another. Because these items and their follow-ups are so general, acceptance of them does not imply membership in a subculture of violence. But conversely, it seems reasonable to assume that persons who are in such a subculture would find it quite easy to support many of the items, especially those dealing with relatively minor forms of violence. If levels of support in low-status groups are relatively low, then the finding can be taken as suggestive evidence contrary to the thesis.

Preliminary analysis of these data has been reported elsewhere. The present author has undertaken a detailed analysis of these data, using cross tabulation and multiple regression. My analysis does not alter the basic preliminary findings, which showed an absence of major differences by race or class in approval of

325

interpersonal violence, and in general a low rate of approval. For example, marital fighting is often thought to be a characteristic of the "subculture of violence," but when approval of a husband slapping his wife's face is examined, only 25 percent of white and 37 percent of black married men aged 18–60 say that they can imagine any situation in which they would approve, with no systematic variation by income or education. (There is an age effect, with men over 40 being sharply lower in approval, but it is independent of race, education, or income.) Moreover, both the level of support and the variation by race decrease markedly when follow-up items are examined. A similar pattern is found for items relating to approval of a man choking an adult male stranger; while on items relating to punching an adult male stranger, approval by whites is higher than that by blacks.

Attitudes toward machismo can be gauged by an index made up of items relating to approval of teenage fighting. The items on this index seem to be very easy to support—"Are there any situations you can imagine in which you would approve of a teenage boy punching another teenage boy?" if yes, or not sure, "would you approve if he didn't like the other boy?"…"if he had been ridiculed and picked on by the other boy?"…"if he had been challenged by the other boy to a fist fight?"…"if he had been hit by the other boy?" The index was constructed by scoring a yes response to each of the five items as 2, a not sure as 1, and a no as 0. The range is thus 0–10.

Whites tend to score higher than blacks on this index; and when parents with at least one teenage child are analyzed separately, only 12 percent of black parents, compared to 38 percent of white parents, score above six on the ten point index. Among whites, parents with low-income score lower than those with high-income.

If a subculture of violence existed among low-status adults, or if low-status adults valued the expression of violence among their children, the general trend on this index would be expected to be the reverse of that found, and the rate of support at the high end of the index would have been much higher. The data and conclusions say nothing about the extent of fighting among lower-class or black teenagers; and the questions of unintentional socialization through the latent effects of parental behavior, or of socialization to violence by teenage peers, remain open. It may well be that lower-class or black teenagers are involved in a disproportionate number of fights, and the lower rate of approval by their parents could be a result of the frequency or seriousness of these fights. But such a situation would only support the conclusion that lower-class parents in general, and black parents in particular, do not especially like the idea of their children fighting and that teenage fighting is probably not a product of an adult value system emphasizing violence.

Some New Data: Peer Esteem and
Psychological Correlates of Fighting

In addition to the investigation of verbal support for a "subculture of violence," support and sanction in peer interactions can be examined. Wolfgang and Ferracuti argue that nonviolent members of a subcultural group are subject to great pressure to conform, that sanction is an integral part of the existence of a norm, and that "alienation of some kind...seems to be a form of punitive action most feasible to this subculture." It seems to follow that, conversely, persons who adhere to the values would be more likely than those who do not to be liked, respected, and accorded high status in the group. Data from a 1969 survey of black and white males aged 21–64 in Milwaukee, Wisconsin, give some evidence on this point. Physical aggression is indicated by the item "How often do you get in angry fist fights with other men?" (never, almost never, sometimes, often); perceived esteem accorded by others is indicated by two items, "How do you compare with most men you know on being respected and listened to by other people?" (five point code from much worse to much better) and "How do you compare with most men you know on being well liked by other people and having lots of friends?" (same code). Since the esteem items are double-barreled, they are less precise than desirable. However they are useful for exploratory purposes.

Because the subcultural hypothesis posits statistical interaction, separate analyses were made for the "lower class" (income less than $5,000) and "nonpoor" (income over $5,000), and for blacks and whites. As a result, low-income whites have a small sample size and detailed analysis cannot be carried out for this subsample.

The bottom row of Table 1 shows that the pattern of fighting by race and income group is consistent with the subcultural thesis; blacks are more likely to fight than whites, and the poor are more likely to fight than the nonpoor. (Contrary to expectations, poor whites are more likely to fight than poor blacks, but the percentage for whites is unreliable because of the low N.) However, this pattern is also consistent with several other non-subcultural theories, such as those of Henry and Short, Coser, Gold, or Cloward and Ohlin. The important question here is whether men who fight are accorded (or at least see themselves as being accorded) more esteem by others.

Although the subculture of violence thesis does not make a prediction about the overall association between race or economic status and peer respect or high status among peers, it predicts that the basis of the respect of status will be different in different groups. Subcultural theory would seem to predict a relatively strong positive correlation between the peer esteem item and fighting for low-income blacks, a somewhat smaller (but at least statistically significant) positive correlation for low-income whites and nonpoor blacks, and a relatively strong negative correlation for nonpoor whites.

Table 1 shows the relationship between fighting and perceiving "respect by others," in terms of zero order correlations and as the net effect (beta) of fighting on perceived esteem by others, controlling first for social desirability bias and then for social desirability bias, occupation, and age. The findings are inconsistent with the predictions outlined, with the betas and zero order correlations being either very close to zero or having a sign opposite that predicted. Table 2 shows the relationship between fighting and perceptions of being "liked by others," in terms of zero order correlations and the net effect of fighting on perceived esteem. Here the findings are somewhat as predicted by subcultural theory, with low-income blacks and low-income whites showing a positive net effect of fighting on perceived esteem. But the former beta is rather small; and although the latter is larger, neither of them is statistically significant. Moreover, for nonpoor white men, the predicted strong negative correlation does not appear.

Although the findings here do not refute the subculture of violence thesis, taken as a whole they cast doubt on it. To the extent that violence is important to low-income or black men, and to the extent that a subcultural norm is being enforced through ostracism or peer rebuke, we would expect to find a relatively strong positive relationship between fighting and perceived general esteem. Similarly, if a counternorm of nonviolence is important in the white middle class, a strong negative relationship should have been found. Overall the data here are not consistent with this predicted pattern; and if we take statistical significance as a minimal criteria of support, none of the predictions of subcultural theory is supported. It is possible, of course, that the available indicators mask the relationships predicted. For example, perhaps responses to fighting draw approval or rebuke as predicted, but these responses do not affect the overall evaluation perceived by the violent person. In this case, how ever, we would have to conclude that violence is not as important to the subculture as hypothesized, for as the sanction gets stronger— e.g. ostracism—consequences for general esteem should follow.

As a corollary to the analysis of violence and esteem, the relationship between violence and feeling of well being can be examined. The subcultural thesis holds that violence is normal behavior and is the product of normal group processes. Similarly, it posits that violent people do not feel guilty about their actions. An empirical inquiry could examine psychiatric records or administer various personality tests; alternatively, various measures of psychological adjustment can be included in an interview schedule or questionnaire. One such measure is an index of happiness which can be constructed from items in the Milwaukee survey. It would seem that outside the subculture men

Table 1

Effect of fighting on feeling "respected and listened to by others"
By race and income, with controls
Milwaukee men, aged 21-64, 1969

	White			Black		
	<$5,000	≥$5,000	Total	<$5,000	≥$5,000	Total
Hypothesized Relation	Positive	Strong Neg.		Strong Pos.	Positive	
Zero order r	−.15	.02		−.25	−.18[a]	
Beta, net of social desirability index (SDI)	−.05	.02		−.22	−.18[a]	
Beta, net of SDI, occupation and age		.08		.02	−.14	
(N)	(15)	(207)	(222)	(51)	(184)	(235)
% who fight	47%	19%	21%	39%	29%	31%

NB: Indicates beta significant at .05 or better.

Table 2

Effect of fighting on feeling "well-liked by other people and having lots of friends"
By race and income, with controls
Milwaukee men, aged 21-64, 1969

	White		Black	
	<$5,000	≥$5,000	<$5,000	≥$5,000
Hypothesized Relation	Positive	Strong Neg.	Strong Pos.	Positive
Zero order r	.22	−.01	−.12	−.01
Beta, net of social desirability index (SDI)	.21	−.01	−.09	−.01
Beta, net of SDI, occupation and age		−.03	.16	−.04
(N)	(15)	(207)	(51)	(184)

NB: None of the coefficients in the table are significant at .05 or better.

Table 3

Relationship between fighting and happiness
By race and income, with controls
Milwaukee men, aged 21–64, 1969

	White		Black	
	<$5,000	≥$5,000	<$5,000	≥$5,000
Hypothesized Relation	Positive	Strong Neg.	Strong Pos.	Positive
Zero order r	−.09	−.07	−.36[a]	−.19[a]
Partial r, net of social desirability index (SDI)	.08	−.07	−.33[a]	−.19[a]
Partial r, net of SDI, occupation and age		−.09	−.30[a]	−.18[a]
(N)	(15)	(207)	(51)	(184)

[a]Indicates partial r significant at .05 or better.

who are violent would be less likely to be happy than would non-violent men, both because they were receiving negative sanctions for their violence and because in this group it would be the more marginal men who would be violent. By contrast, within the subculture, happiness would be positively correlated with violence, since violence is posited as not being a pathological condition and since non-violent men are hypothesized to be negatively sanctioned. Table 3 shows that fighting is negatively correlated with happiness for all four subgroups, and (statistically) significantly so for blacks. Except for nonpoor whites, these findings run directly counter to the predictions of the subcultural thesis. And even for nonpoor whites, the finding of a correlation even less negative than for blacks can also be considered evidence contrary to the thesis.

DISCUSSION

Although much suggestive evidence on the subculture of violence exists, there is a clear need for further research in this area. Methodologically, this research should be designed so that there is adequate representation of minorities and of poor whites for analysis; and it should make some attempt to cover both "streetcorner men" and more traditional householders. A major limitation of existing survey data is that they are based only on persons in households. Another is that the surveys do not have concentrated samples in a given neighborhood. These difficulties are alleviated, but not erased, by the data from the field studies.

Substantively, work needs to be done on establishing the pervasiveness of a subculture. At least three quite different degrees of pervasiveness may exist. In the most extreme case, a large majority of the demographic group presumed to have the subcultural trait would exhibit it in some way, as opposed to a minority of members of other demographic groups. In this case, one could characterize the demographic group as subcultural. A more limited pervasiveness exists when the trait is exhibited by a minority of a particular demographic group, as compared to a virtual absence in other groups; this would constitute a subculture *within* a demographic group. Finally, some analysts would consider a small but statistically significant difference between demographic groups as evidence of a subculture. However, it seems incorrect to characterize such a subculture as being located in the demographic group with greater support for the value, or to characterize that demographic group as a subculture. Rather, the subculture would have to be defined as the group of people who hold the value, irrespective of their demographic group.

These differences in the pervasiveness of subcultures have important implications for the public imagery of social groups. In the case of the subculture of violence, if class or racial groups can in fact be characterized as being different (or if findings are presented as though they could), popular conceptions of widespread pathology among nonwhites and low-income whites would be supported. By contrast the existence of a subculture within a class or racial group, or of value difference that are statistically significant but not large, would be more consonant with the view that there is wide variation in the values, needs, and problems of the poor and of nonwhites.

Future research should also focus more closely on the precise content of supposed subcultural differences. It is possible, for example, that rather than a "subculture of violence," something like a "subculture of masculinity" exists, with violence being only one of many possible outlets, and not necessarily the preferred one. In this case, violence may result from the blocking of alternative opportunities to exhibit "machismo." Another possibility is that the use of liquor may be part of a broader social configuration which generates situations conducive to violence. A value system which sanctions or even encourages either drunken brawls or wild behavior on certain special occasions would not necessarily be the same as one which requires "quick resort to physical combat as a measure of daring, courage, or defense of status" in everyday interaction.

Finally, the origins, permanence, and relationship to social structure must also be given careful consideration in future research. These considerations are especially important in the formation of social policy.

CONCLUSION

Although the subculture of violence thesis has received a certain measure of acceptance in the field, a wide variety of evidence suggests that it is questionable. All of the data available have limitations of various sorts, and the thesis cannot be said to have been definitively tested. On balance, however, more of available evidence is inconsistent with the thesis than consistent with it.

At this time we do not know how important a deviant value system is in explaining violence in the United States; and, if it exists, we do not know whether such a value system can be said to be found predominantly within the black or low-income white communities or whether it can be said to be relatively independent of social structure. But there is enough evidence to conclude that these groups are not *characteristically* different from the dominant society in their rate of approval of the use of physical aggression. This conclusion, along with a growing empirical literature on other aspects of the lives of poor and black (and other minority) persons in the United States, is compatible with the view that the social and economic deprivations experienced by members of these groups are primarily the result of social structural factors, rather than the product of group pathology.

Poor whites more fighting than poor blacks.
blacks > white
rich < poor.
Subculture of violence.
social & economic deprivation in minority groups result of social structure rather than pathology.

—➤◆◄—

Homicide and a Regional Culture of Violence

Raymond D. Gastil

In this paper I will develop an argument and present statistical evidence that suggests more conclusively than previously studies that it is a predisposition to lethal violence in Southern regional culture that accounts for the greater part of the relative height of the American homicide rate. This regional culture was already developed before 1850. Popularly mentioned causes of violence such as poverty or inequality or ignorance seem of relatively less importance, at least as far as the historic homicide rates are concerned. It is hoped that these findings will help to define the problem for later research in homicide and certain other aspects of American violence.

Although there have been few studies of homicide, reference to a broad spectrum of research may be found in Wolfgang and Ferracuti, *The Subculture of Violence* (1967). In a less theoretical manner Wolfgang's *Patterns in Criminal Homicide* (1958) summarized what was known up to that time and presented a detailed study of a series of homicides in Philadelphia. Perhaps his most controversial finding was that murderers are generally people who have been involved in crime previously, as are a large proportion of their victims. He confirmed the general impression that most murders are intraracial, which is related to the evidence that they are among those known to one another. It is generally established that in the United States murder is more often committed by blacks than whites, by lower class than middle class, by men than women, by Southerners than Northerners.

There have been a number of studies of the differential between Northern and Southern behavior in homicide statistics. Hoffman was particularly concerned by the high American rates compared to the rest of the world, going back at least to 1910, and not at all a rural phenomenon. He especially noted the city of Memphis which led the nation for a number of years with rates up to 88 per 100,000. Brearley, a Southern scholar, seriously explored the reasons for differences between Northern and Southern states, developing figures for the 1920's comparable to those found today He also was qualitatively interested in the traditions and quality of life that might be responsible. The later studies did not make the point as sharply because of their concern with other issues such as general crime rates or the relation of homicide and suicide.

In a recent review of the problem of Southern violence, Hackney questioned several noncultural explanations He pointed out that many theories of differences in child training practices, frustration-aggression etc., do not hold up under examination. For example, it is the less competitive, less commercially minded rural South that has historically been the source of high homicide rates. European countries with relatively rigid child-training practices have much lower rates. In this country economic and status positions in the community cannot be shown to account for differences between whites and Negroes or between Southerners and Northerners. While the possession of firearms does contribute to actual murder statistics, laws against firearms often seem ineffective in the South, and differences in aggravated assault rates reflect the murder differentials in any case.

This suggests that a cultural explanation be given particular emphasis in explaining American homicide rates, and that this explanation must be primarily based on an understanding of the influence of Southern regional culture. Psychological, societal and cultural explanations have been advanced in a number of forms, and each "explains" part of the evidence. For example, Henry and Short tried to tie the first two together by viewing murders as aggressive reactions to frustration, with differences in rates stemming from variations in the social situation of groups or classes. Cultural explanation can be related to general theory in criminology by pointing out that cultural differences both produce and result from "differential association." This is particularly true if "culture" refers to all group-related differences in learning. In groups with high murder rates, individuals have on the average (or a few regularly have) a different set of learning experiences than those in groups with lower rates. There is a different balance of culturally defined rewards and punishments, and these are determined by differences in the subcultures of the respective groups.

The following material will support the case that persistent differences in homicide rates seem best explained by differences in regional culture. Qualitatively a number of elements in Southern life and very early references to a Southern tendency to lethal violence lend support to the cultural explanation. With the mingling of the American population through internal migration, the Southern tendency to violence has diffused broadly, but the differences between sections of the country in homicide rates can still be related to an inferred degree of Southerness based on migration patterns. This paper is concerned primarily with the transmission of Southern culture from generation to generation within families and the movements of successive generations among states. The exchange, both horizontally and vertically, of cultural patterns of violence or nonviolence among peoples with differing backgrounds is considered when we speak of the influence of elites on the general populace, but this type of transmission should be examined in more detail elsewhere.

The theory of a subculture of violence advanced by Wolfgang and Ferracuti is similar to that of a "regional culture of violence" advanced here. There are, however, several differences. The concept of a subculture of violence is explicitly based on a view of culture that stresses norms and values while the regional concept does not. Violent people do not necessarily develop a culture that condones violence. A violent tradition may be one that in a wide range of situations condones lethal violence, *or* it may be a tradition that more indirectly raises the murder rate. For example, the culture may put a high value on the ready availability of guns, or it may legitimize actions that lead to hostile relations within families or between classes, and these in turn may frequently lead to lethal violence. The regional concept also suggests more persistence over time and intergenerational reinforcement than does the subcultural concept. As an additional note, in this paper "violence" means "lethal violence"; Wolfgang and Ferracuti seem at times to have a broader definition. In any event, differences in the lethality of violence among groups should not be obscured. If "subculture of violence" were given a broader significance and limited to lethal violence, then the concept would be fully complementary to what is being advanced here. In these terms a society characterized by a regional culture of violence would be likely to be characterized also by: (1) more extreme subcultures of violence and/or a larger percentage of the population involved in violence (with less limitation by class, age, race etc.); (2) lethal violence, a more important subtheme in the general culture of the region; and (3) weapons and knowledge of their use as an important part of culture. The concept of a regional culture of violence will help to explain why subcultures of violence do not develop equally everywhere under apparently similar conditions and go only part of the way toward explaining the particularly lethal subculture among black Americans.

After establishing the theoretical context, let us return to a more detailed examination of the evidence for a regional culture of violence. If Southern culture is primarily responsible for the high murder rates in the United States, then at what time and in what way did Southern culture come to support such a noticeable tendency? John Hope Franklin has diligently explored the Southern tendency to violence in the period before the Civil War. Franklin's evidence for a violent Southern culture in the antebellum era ranges from the continued institutionalization of the duel long after it had been given up in the North to the love of violence on much lower levels of society. The rulers of the South were seldom any longer the more aristocratic Southerners of Virginia that ruled during the golden age of the republic. Other than carrying the Southern-Northern difference back to 1800, Franklin also documents the relation of Southern violence to an expansive foreign policy and to the deep Southern interest in everything having to do with military training and display.

More important are clues to the Southern tradition that Franklin offers. Large landholders generally came to the South for easy wealth to establish for themselves the type of feudal estates that were not available to them in England. In the 19th century their vision remained that of the exploiting, 17th-century rural aristocracy, and many reached their goal through the availability of poor indentured whites and then Negroes. Extreme class differences were expected from the beginning, and the poor white and Negro fit into this picture, as did the acknowledged fact that such societies had ultimately to be maintained by violence. It is also important to remember that more whites in the South came from a low status in England than was true in New England.

However, perhaps more important is the fact that the South remained a frontier society geographically for a much longer time than the North. Settlement in the North was to a greater extent continuous and contiguous; towns were more important and closer together and cities grew more rapidly. Until the Civil War, many parts of the "settled" South were wilderness and remained wilderness, suggesting that there might have been a decline in civilization in the South among the descendants of the immigrants, regardless of the original culture. Distances made schools harder to support or reach, and made the frontier skills with rifle and knife much more vital generation after generation than they were in the North. In the North this unsettled, dispersed, isolated type of life was only experienced by one generation in most places; the people could preserve in their memories the image of another more civilized life until it became possible for their children.

In spite of considerable work there has been relatively little attempt to see how much of the Northern-Southern differential could be attributed to factors other than a separate, identifiable homicidal trait among those of Southern background. In attempting to apply the multiple regression approach to this problem, I have included evidence relating to a number of alternative hypotheses. It has long been thought that homicide in this country was associated with factors such as low education and low income. In particular, the positive relation of "low status" to homicide suggested by Henry and Short may be checked by including these factors. Popularly it is believed that crime is related to urbanism or the large city environment, while others have pointed to its rural affinity. It is obvious that variations in the percent of a population at ages (20–34 or 18–45) with high murder rates would also be responsible for much of the difference in the reported rates. Since murder rates reflect victim survival rates, a decline in murder rates has been associated with improving medical services; it also seemed reasonable to suppose that differences in the availability of medical services might affect murder statistics. One could only discover the influence of "Southerness" while controlling for such factors. Of course, even if it appeared that the apparent influence of "Southerness" on homicide rates could be explained by those common sociological variables, such as low education and income that are also associated with Southernness, one could imagine that Southern culture "caused" them all. However, there would not be, in this case, a separate regional cultural trait for homicide, and the claim of Southern cultural influence on the rate would be much harder to make convincing.

It is difficult to define exactly where and in what proportions the influence of Southern and Northern culture are to be found today. To examine the relation of homicide to Southernness, however, we must, give a numerical value to its cultural influence in the states, or other units, we wish to examine. For this purpose an Index of Southernness was constructed on the basis of available evidence with a high score of 30 given the most purely Southern states and a low score of 5 to the least. This is at least an improvement over a simple South or Non-South dichotomy; it makes it easier to check the validity of the regional differences in homicide rates in 1960 that Redfield noted in 1880. The Index reflects the parallel expansion of our population from a core of New England culture and a core of Southern culture, with migrations generally much more out of the South than in. To this must be added the fact that immigrant groups after 1880 came almost exclusively to non-Southern areas, and Southerners have migrated very little to New England or northwest of Illinois and southern Iowa. They have had overwhelming influence in parts of the Southwest. Southerners made up a large part of the original migration to the Far West and Rocky Mountain states, and of the later migration to work in industry in the Middle States from New Jersey to Illinois. As the Index suggests, Mormon Utah is relatively uninfluenced by the South.

Applying standard techniques of multiple correlation to the murder statistics, we obtained the results. Index of Southernness explains a great deal of the variance and more than any other variable. (With all 50 states, including Alaska and Hawaii, where our approach makes the least sense, the total variance explained drops to 87.7% and that explained by Index of Southernness to 71.3%). However, it is characteristic of this form of regression that the relative influence of the first variable entered appears to be more than it is, even if there are low intercorrelations. The high correlation of Index of Southernness with percent Negro, low education, and low income must be noted (intercorrelations of .71, .52, and .47 respectively). As elsewhere, since the Index of Southernness and percent 20–34 are not closely correlated (intercorrelation of .39 is higher here than is general), they contribute quite separately to the explained variance. It is important to note that it is still highly significant in the partial correlation after all other variables have been accounted for.

If we take white homicides alone, the correlation of Southernness and homicide is somewhat reduced, although still remarkably high and significant. Percent nonwhite has significant positive correlation with homicide, although it adds little to the variance explained. However, if we look at the partial correlation of percent nonwhite after Index of Southernness is entered, it falls to .07; after both Southernness and percent 20–34 have been taken out, it becomes -.37. This indicates that having nonwhites in a state certainly does not add to tendencies to white homicide, as a theory of generalized conflict might predict. Omitting percent nonwhite entirely in an excursion did not reveal any other significant variable that had been submerged by its presence. Forcing Index of Southernness last in this case gives a considerably more decisive result than for all homicides. Here the Index adds in this last position 16% to the variance, and its partial correlation, after everything else is accounted for, is almost as high as the original correlation.

Detailed examination of results and further statistical excursions suggest that it would be possible to create an Index of Southernness that would correspond both more closely with the homicide rates and with the historical backgrounds of the people in the several states. Examination of residuals suggests that there should be a reduction in extent of ascribed "Southernness" above the North-South regional frontier; on the other hand, Texas and Florida act like extreme Southern states. We should also examine, for historical reasons, where we might make changes in the Index of Southernness although it would not help the correlations, e.g., New York should perhaps be treated as a New England state in terms of Southernness. However, I thought it more useful here to stay with the original fairly clean index, developed largely independently of knowledge of homicide rates.

CONCLUSION

It seems established that there is a significant relationship between murder rates and residence in the South. This relationship can be traced back to differences between the North and South that were already observable before the Civil War. It can be shown that outside of the centers of Southern and Northern society, state homicide rates grade into one another in rough approximation to the extent to which Southerners have moved into mixed states. While differences in standard demographic or economic variables such as age composition, median education, or median income account for a good deal of the variance among sections of the country in murder rates, there is a significant remainder that may be related to "Southernness" alone. There seems, then, on both qualitative and quantitative grounds to be evidence that the culture that developed in the Southern states in past centuries leads to high murder rates. International and state comparisons seem to indicate that this specifically Southern culture accounts for most of the difference between the murder rates of the United States and those of comparable countries such as Canada and Australia. A description of the traits accounting for violence in the several Southern subcultures, of their rise and fall, of the diffusion of these traits outside of the South, of present trends in their importance, and of the cause of alternative subcultural traits accounting for high homicide rates unrelated to Southern culture—all these are subjects for further study.

The Impact of Mass Media Violence
on U.S. Homicides

DAVID P. PHILLIPS

S tudies of media effects on homicide have been extremely rare and there is no systematic evidence to date indicating that mass media violence elicits additional murders. This paper presents what may be the first systematic evidence suggesting that some homicides are indeed triggered by a type of mass media violence. The current study builds on earlier research which showed that U.S. suicides increase after publicized suicide stories.

It would be interesting to discover whether *homicide* stories elicit additional homicides. But it is difficult to conduct such a study because, unlike suicide stories, homicide stories occur so often that it is very difficult to separate the effect of one story from the effect of the others. However, some other types of violent stories occur much less often, and it is possible to discover whether these types of stories trigger a rise in U.S. homicides.

In reviewing the literature on media effects, Comstock concluded that violent stories with the following characteristics were most likely to elicit aggression: When the violence in the story is presented as (1) rewarded, (2) exciting, (3) real, and (4) justified; when the perpetrator of the violence is (5) not criticized for his behavior and is presented as (6) intending to injure his victim.

One type of story that meets all of these criteria is the heavyweight prize fight, which is almost universally presented as highly rewarded, exciting, real, and justified. Furthermore, the participants are not criticized for their aggressive behavior and are presented as trying to injure each other.

In a well-known series of studies, Berkowitz and various associates examined the impact of a filmed prize fight in the laboratory. They found that angered laboratory subjects behaved more aggressively after seeing a filmed prize fight scene. In contrast, angered laboratory subjects exposed to a track meet film displayed a significantly lower level of aggression.

In sum, the heavyweight prize match is a promising research site because (1) it meets Comstock's criteria for stories most likely to elicit aggression, and (2) it is known to elicit aggression in the laboratory.

DATA SOURCES

An exhaustive list of championship heavyweight prize fights and their dates was obtained from *The Ring Book Boxing Encyclopedia*, which is the standard reference on the topic. The period 1973–1978 has been chosen for analysis because, for this period, daily counts of all U.S. homicides are publicly available from the National Center for Health Statistics.

METHOD OF ANALYSIS

A standard time-series regression analysis is used. Homicides are known to fluctuate significantly by day of the week, by month, and by year. In addition, as we will see, homicides rise markedly on public holidays. All these "seasonal" effects must be corrected for before one can assess the effect of prize fights on homicides.

Initially, the effect of the prize fight is examined for the ten-day period following it; later, a longer period is studied.

RESULTS

After the average championship prize fight, homicides increase markedly on the third day (by 7.47) and on the fourth day (by 4.15), for a total increase of 11.62. The rise in homicides after the prize fight is statistically significant.

The third day displays by far the largest peak in homicides. It is interesting to note that this "third-day peak" appears not only in the present study but also, repeatedly, in several earlier investigations: California auto fatalities peak on the third day after publicized suicide stories, as do Detroit auto fatalities and U.S. noncommercial airplane crashes. At present we do not know the precise psychosocial mechanisms producing the third day lag, but this phenomenon has now been replicated so often in different data sets that it seems to be a relatively stable effect which will repay future investigation.

The observed peak in homicides after a prize fight cannot be ascribed to day-of-the-week, monthly, yearly, or holiday effects, because all of these "seasonal" variables were corrected for in the regression analysis. In addition, one cannot plausibly ascribe the homicide peak to random fluctuations, because the peak is statistically significant.

SOME ALTERNATIVE EXPLANATIONS
FOR THE PEAK IN HOMICIDES

For each fight, Table 1 indicates: (1) The number of homicides observed three days after the prize fight. (2) The number of homicides expected on the third day, under the null hypothesis that prize fights have no effect on homicides. (3) The difference between the observed and expected number of homicides. (A positive difference indicates that homicides are higher than expected just after the prize fight.) (4) Whether the fight was held outside the United States. (5) Whether the fight was discussed on the network evening news.

"Personal Experience" Hypothesis

Perhaps the prize fight affects only those actually attending the fight, not those experiencing it through the mass media. If this is so, one cannot claim that *mass media* violence is triggering a rise in homicides.

If one must personally experience the prize fight in order to be affected by it, then prize fights occurring outside the U.S. should trigger few if any U.S. homicides. In contrast, prize fights held inside the U.S. should elicit much larger rises in homicides. The evidence contradicts these predictions. After the average "foreign" fight, U.S. homicides rise by 12.128, while a much *smaller* rise, 2.862, occurs after the average U.S. fight. Thus, the "personal experience" hypothesis does not seem plausible.

"Modeling" Hypothesis—First Test

Prize fights may trigger some homicides through some type of modeling of aggression. If this is so, then prize fights receiving much publicity should have a greater effect than prize fights receiving less publicity.

One way to test this hypothesis is to see whether prize fights discussed on the network evening news are followed by relatively large increases in homicides, while relatively small increases occur after the remaining, less-publicized prize fights. The evidence is consistent with this "modeling" explanation. Homicides rise by 11.127 after the average "publicized" fight, and by only 2.833 after the average unpublicized one. The difference between these two figures is statistically significant.

Table 1
Fluctuation of U.S. homicides three days
after each heavyweight prize fight, 1973–1978

Name of Fight	Observed No. of Homicides	Expected No. of Homicides	Observed Minus Expected	Fight Held Outside U.S.?	On Network Evening News?
Foreman/Frazier	55	42.10	12.90	yes	yes
Foreman/Roman	46	49.43	–3.43	yes	no
Foreman/Norton	55	54.33	.67	yes	no
Ali/Foreman	102	82.01	19.99	yes	yes
Ali/Wepner	44	46.78	–2.78	no	yes
Ali/Lyle	54	47.03	6.97	no	yes
Ali/Bugner	106	82.93	23.07	yes	no
Ali/Frazier	108	81.69	26.31	yes	yes
Ali/Coopman	54	45.02	8.98	yes	no
Ali/Young	41	43.62	–2.62	no	no
Ali/Dunn	50	41.47	8.53	yes	yes
Ali/Norton	64	52.57	11.43	no	yes
Ali/Evangelista	36	42.11	–6.11	no	no
Ali/Shavers	66	66.86	–.86	no	no
Spinks/Ali	89	78.96	10.04	no	yes
Holmes/Norton[a]	53	48.97	4.03	no	no
Ali/Spinks	59	52.25	6.75	no	yes
Holmes/Evangelista[a]	52	50.24	1.76	no	no

[a]Sponsored by World Boxing Council; all other fights sponsored by the World Boxing Association

It is perhaps worth noting that the most touted of all the prize fights in this period, the so-called "Thrilla in Manilla" between Ali and Frazier, displays the largest third-day peak in homicides.

"Modeling" Hypothesis—Second Test

The modeling hypothesis can also be tested in another way. The laboratory literature on the modeling of mass media aggression repeatedly suggests that (1) a person is more likely to imitate an aggressor on the screen if he is similar to that aggressor; (2) a person is more likely to aggress against a target victim if his target is similar to the victim on the screen. In sum, the laboratory literature suggests that there is modeling of both the *aggressor and* of the aggressor's *victim*.

If *aggressor* modeling exists after a prize fight, then after a young, black male wins a boxing match, murders by young, black males should increase (but murders by young, *white* males should not). Conversely, after a young, white male wins a boxing match, the opposite findings should occur. Unfortunately, *aggressor* modeling cannot be studied with the death certificates examined in this paper, because these certificates do not reveal the identity of the murderer, only of the victim.

However, it is possible to use these death certificates to discover whether *victim* modeling exists after a heavyweight prize fight. If such modeling occurs, then, just after a prize fight, homicide victims should be unusually similar to the losing boxer. Specifically, after a young, *white* male is beaten in a prize fight, the homicide deaths of young, white male victims should increase; no such increase should appear for young, *black* male victims. Conversely, after a young, *black* male is beaten in a prize fight, the homicide deaths of young, *black* male victims should increase, while the homicide deaths of young, white males should not.

The evidence supports the hypothesis of victim modeling. *White* loser prize fights are followed by significant increases in young, white male homicide deaths; in contrast, *black* loser prize fights do not seem to trigger young, white male homicide deaths.

White homicides increase significantly on the day of the prize fight (by 3.86 per fight), two days thereafter (by 3.14 per fight), and eight days after the fight (by 2.97 per fight). Thus young, white male homicides rise by a total of 9.97 (= 3.86 + 3.14 + 2.97) per white loser prize fight. Interestingly, the typical white loser prize fight has a larger total impact (9.97) than almost any other variable in the table. Of the 27 "seasonal" variables examined, only one (New Year's Day) has a larger impact on young, white male homicides. This suggests that the impact of a white loser prize fight is not only statistically significant, but practically significant as well. At present, it is not known why this type of prize fight seems to exert so large an effect.

Black loser prize fights are followed by significant increases in young, black male homicide deaths. In contrast, white loser prize fights do not trigger significant increases in black male homicides.

Black homicides rise significantly on the fourth and fifth days after black loser fights. The total impact of the black loser prize fight exceeds the impact of almost all seasonal variables. Only New Year's Day and Thanksgiving trigger larger increases in homicides (the coefficients for these holidays being 8.88 and 8.00, respectively). Evidently, a black loser prize fight has a significant, substantive effect on young, black male homicides.

Precipitation Hypothesis

The above evidence is consistent with the notion that prize fights sometimes serve as aggressive models and trigger some U.S. homicides. But perhaps the prize fight merely precipitates a murder that would have occurred anyway, even in the absence of the prize fight.

If a prize fight merely "moves up" a murder so that it occurs a little sooner than it otherwise would have, then the peak in homicides after a prize fight should be followed by a *dip* in homicides soon after. An examination of the three-week period following the prize fight reveals no significant dip in homicides. Hence, the precipitation hypothesis seems to be implausible.

Gambling Hypothesis

Perhaps the prize fight provokes no aggressive modeling whatsoever. It merely triggers an increase in gambling, which in turn provokes anger, fighting, and murder. If this explanation is correct, then homicides should rise not only after prize fights but also after other occasions that provoke a great deal of gambling. In the United States, the Super Bowl probably provokes more gambling than any other single event. Yet homicides do *not* rise significantly after these occasions.

There is some weak evidence that homicides actually decrease on the day of the Super Bowl and one day later, and then rise above the expected rate on the third day. Even if one considers these coefficients to be statistically significant (which they are not), it is evident that the Super Bowl is associated with a net drop in homicides rather than a rise. This is not what one would expect if the gambling hypothesis were correct. This hypothesis is also rendered implausible by some of the other evidence presented above: If the gambling hypothesis were true, then it is difficult to see why the traits of the homicide victims should be similar to the traits of the losing boxer.

In sum, we have now assessed four possible explanations for the rise in homicides after a heavyweight prize fight. At present, the best available explanation is that the prize fight provokes some imitative, aggressive behavior, which results in an increase in homicides. The size of this increase will be considered in the next section.

Size of the Increase in Homicides after Prize Fights

Whether one considers the percentage increase or the absolute increase, it appears that homicides rise by a nontrivial amount on the third day after a championship heavyweight prize fight (12 .46 percent).

This paper has presented evidence which suggests that heavyweight prize fights provoke a brief, sharp increase in homicides. Some implications of this evidence will be briefly considered in the final section of this paper.

SUMMARY

Many researchers have claimed that one cannot generalize with confidence from the impact of mass media violence *in the laboratory* to the impact of mass media violence *in the real world*. These critics point out that laboratory experiments have been set in highly artificial contexts. Typically, the sorts of aggression studied in a laboratory (like hitting plastic dolls or inflicting electric shocks) have not been representative of serious, real-life violence, such as murder or rape. In almost all studies, the laboratory subjects have been nursery school children or college students and thus not representative of the U.S. television audience. Typically, the laboratory subject is presented with a brief, violent excerpt of a television program. In contrast, the "real-life" viewer may watch several hours of television at a sitting, and the violence may be interspersed with humor, commercials, and trips to the bathroom. In contrast to the laboratory subject, who watches television alone, the real-life viewer may well be surrounded by family or friends. Their comments may distract from the television or shape the perception of its many messages. For these reasons, it is inappropriate to generalize from the laboratory to the real world.

The above argument appears to be seriously challenged by the evidence provided in this paper. The data presented in this paper indicate that mass media violence *does* provoke aggression in the real world as well as in the laboratory. In contrast to laboratory studies, the present investigation assesses the effect of mass media violence in a natural context. Unlike laboratory studies, the present study examines a type of violence which is of serious concern to policy makers. Finally, the present investigation does not focus exclusively on a mass media audience consisting of college students and nursery school children. The laboratory study, with its great potential for rigor, has always been capable of establishing the internal validity of findings. The present study has helped to establish that these findings have external validity as well.

The Social Ecology of Urban Homicide: An Application of the "Routine Activities" Approach

STEVEN F. MESSNER & KENNETH TARDIFF

The purpose of this paper is to use the routine activities approach to help interpret recent patterns of homicide in a major metropolitan area—Manhattan, New York. We will argue that the routine activities approach implies distinctive hypotheses about the relationships among sociodemographic characteristics, temporal factors, and the probability of being involved in different kinds of homicide. Detailed data on the circumstances surrounding all homicides which were detected in Manhattan in 1981 will then be presented in order to evaluate these hypotheses. Our overriding objectives are twofold: first, to describe patterns of homicidal behavior in Manhattan within the framework of the routine activities perspective and, second, in so doing, to explore the general utility of this new perspective.

THEORY AND HYPOTHESES

The routine activities approach is intended to explain "direct-contact predatory violations." These are illegal acts which involve a direct physical encounter between an offender and a victim. A key premise of the routine activities approach is that a successful "direct-contact predatory violation" requires three components: an offender motivated to commit the violation, a suitable target to be victimized by the offender, and the absence of guardians capable of preventing the violation. When each of these components is present at the same time and place, the likelihood is greatly increased that a direct-contact predatory violation will occur.

An additional premise of the routine activities approach is that the probability of the convergence in space and time of the components of a criminal incident depends upon the structure of everyday interactions. This premise follows from the notion that illegal and legal activities are interdependent.

We hypothesize that the location and type of homicides will be associated in systematic ways with basic sociodemographic characteristics (age, sex, race, marital status, and employment status) and with features of the temporal setting (time of day, day of the week, and time of year). Systematic associations are expected because sociodemographic and temporal characteristics structure routine activities and, in so doing, affect both the location of potential victims in physical space and the "pool" of personal contacts from which offenders are ultimately drawn.

Of particular importance in the structuring of routine activities is the extent to which activities are concentrated around the household and around family relationships. Persons with different sociodemographic characteristics are likely to spend differing amounts of time at home. The likelihood of being killed at or near home should be related, therefore, to these very same sociodemographic characteristics. To put it quite simply, those sociodemographic characteristics which are likely to be associated with large amounts of time spent in the home should also be associated with disproportionately high levels of homicide at or near the home in comparison with other locations.

A similar type of argument can be made with respect to features of the temporal setting. The probability that people will be at home varies during different times of the day, during different days of the week, and during different seasons of the year. It is thus expected that homicides at or near the home will be especially likely to occur at those times during which the concentration of routine activities around the household is the greatest.

Sociodemographic characteristics and features of the temporal setting should also be related to the kinds of personal contacts in which people are likely to be engaged. When activities are concentrated around the household, interactions are especially likely to involve family members or friends. Activities away from the home, in contrast, are more likely to involve strangers. We therefore predict that the probability of homicides involving different victim–perpetrator relationships (relatives, friends, or strangers) will vary along with the basic sociodemographic and temporal characteristics cited earlier.

The model stipulates that sociodemographic characteristics and features of the temporal setting affect the nature of routine activities and, in particular, the degree to which activities are concentrated around the household and family relationships. The nature of routine activities determines, in turn, the physical location of potential victims and the pool of personal contacts from which potential offenders are ultimately drawn. Finally, the location and the type of homicide are expected to vary along with the typical spatial distribution of potential victims and with the nature of the personal contacts in which these potential victims are routinely engaged.

Several specific hypotheses can be derived from the general theoretical model. With respect to the characteristic of sex, females undoubtedly spend more time than males engaged in household and family activities. Hence, female homicide victims should be more likely than male victims to be killed at or near home rather than in other locations. Using similar reasoning, females should be significantly more likely than males to be victimized by relatives than by either friends or strangers.

Age is another fundamental demographic characteristic which is associated with distinctive life-styles. The very young are dependent upon parents or guardians and are consequently more likely to spend a disproportionate amount of time at or near the family household. Those at the other extreme of the age continuum are also likely to restrict activities to the personal household. As Hindelang et al. observe in their discussion of age differences in risks of victimization, people experience dramatic shifts in daily activities as they age and approach retirement: "mobility decreases, the number of interpersonal contacts decreases, and the experiential world of the individual becomes constricted generally." We therefore predict that homicide victims in both the very young and very old age brackets will be disproportionately likely to be killed at or near the person's residence. It is further expected that, because of the concentration of activities around the household, the very young and the very old will be characterized by a relatively large proportion of "family" homicides in comparison to those in the middle-age brackets.

Race is another basic sociodemographic characteristic which is likely to be related to routine activities because of its association with income. High incomes provide flexibility for the dispersion of activities across physical and social space, while low incomes serve to constrict activities around the immediate household. Given the tendency for minority groups to receive lower incomes than members of the dominant group, we predict that blacks and Hispanics will be more likely to be killed at home and more likely to be killed by family members than will members of the dominant racial group.

A fourth characteristic which is related to the "concentration" or "dispersal" of routine activities is marital status. Married persons are expected to spend greater amounts of time at home than are single persons. Hence, the proportion of married homicide victims killed at or near home should be significantly greater than that for single persons. Likewise, the proportion of homicides involving a friend or relative should be higher for married homicide victims in comparison to homicide victims who were single at the time of the killing.

A final sociodemographic characteristic to be considered is that of employment status. Cantor and Land contend that unemployed persons spend a disproportionate amount of time at home. Our theoretical model thus implies that the unemployed should be more likely than the employed to be killed at or near the home. In addition, the unemployed should be more likely than the employed to be killed by family members or by friends and acquaintances.

Temporal characteristics are also expected to be related to routine activities and consequently to the location and type of homicide. With respect to seasons, it seems plausible to assume that activities are more likely to be concentrated around the home during the winter than during the other times of the year in Northern cities such as New York. Homicides committed during the winter should therefore be especially likely to occur at home and to involve family members as offenders. Relationships between time of day and routine activities are more difficult to specify because of the diversity of work and recreational schedules in a city such as New York. At the very least it seems reasonable to assume that activities will tend to be concentrated around the home during the late-night-to-early-morning hours (midnight to 8:00 A.M.). Homicides occurring during these hours should thus be disproportionately located at home and should involve family members. We also speculate that, on the average, more time is spent around the household on weekends than during the week. This implies correspondingly high levels of "home homicides" and "family homicides" during the weekends. Finally, it seems likely that the effect of time of day on routine activities will depend upon the day of the week. The important relationships between time, day, and types of homicide might thus be conditional rather than direct.

METHODS

The sample of subjects for the study consists of the 578 known homicide victims in the borough of Manhattan during the 1981 calendar year. Background information on these homicide victims was collected in the summer of 1982 from the autopsy records of the New York City Chief Medical Examiner's Office. The Medical Examiner's files include data on the major sociodemographic characteristics of victim—age, sex, race, marital status, and employment status—and on the time and location of the homicidal incident. The independent variables (sociodemographic and temporal factors) are thus taken directly from the Medical Examiner's records, as is one of the dependent variables, location of the homicide. Location was originally recorded as the actual street address. For purposes of the present analysis, however, location has been classified into three categories: at the residence of the victim, within 10 blocks of the victim's residence, and beyond 10 blocks of the victim's residence.

The other dependent variable—the relationship between victim and offender—has been taken from a different source. At the end of 1982, after the investigation of each homicide in the sample had been underway for at least a year, personnel at the Office of Chief Detectives of the New York City Police Department were asked to classify the circumstances surrounding the homicide and, in particular, the nature of the relationship between the victim and the perpetrator. Victim-perpetrator relationship was classified according to three categories: family members, friends or acquaintances, and strangers. The category for family members was defined broadly to include commonlaw marriages and boy friend/girl friend relationships. This broad definition of family members was employed on the grounds that, with respect to the "closeness" of the relationship, boy friend/girl friend relationships are more similar to family relationships than to other friendships or acquaintanceships. Perpetrator data were not limited to those cases in which an offender had been formally arrested, but rather included all instances in which a suspect was known to the police.

Several different types of analyses will be presented below. First, we will examine the relative frequency of the different kinds of homicide (for example, homicides taking place at home, homicides involving family members) across categories for each of the sociodemographic and temporal variables expected to be linked with routine activities. This part of the analysis will involve a comparison of percentages and an evaluation of statistical significance by means of a simple chi square.

The independent variables will all be treated as dichotomies. For some of these variables (for example, sex and employment status), a dichotomous classification occurs "naturally." For other variables, the construction of dichotomies entails "collapsing" categories. The logic for collapsing categories derives from the larger theoretical framework. More specifically, categories are combined on the basis of judgments concerning the similarity of activity patterns. For example, with respect to age, those under 15 are categorized with those 60 and over on the grounds that these individuals are more likely to confine their routine activities to the immediate household than are those in the other age category. Similar reasoning underlies the coding decisions for other independent variables. We recognize that there are dangers associated with the collapsing of multiple categories into fewer ones. However, given the relatively small number of homicide victimizations recorded, the use of the full range of categories frequently results in small base figures for percentages and in empty cells in the cross-tabulations with the dependent variables.

A second analytical strategy to be pursued will be to compute an ordinal measure of association—the gamma coefficient—to describe the strength and nature of the relationship for each factor hypothesized to be related to the location and type of homicide. The gamma coefficient measures the likelihood that the ranking of any given pair of cases on one variable will correspond to the ranking on another variable.

The sociodemographic and temporal characteristics do not possess any comparable intrinsic rank ordering of categories. Nevertheless, since these variables have been dichotomized, they can be treated as "dummy" variables. Moreover, the scoring of these dummy variables can be assigned in accordance with the theoretical arguments developed above. To be more specific, the "zero" value for each dummy can be assigned to attributes which reflect a relatively low probability that activities are dispersed away from the home.

The nature of this scoring system implies that positive associations (that is, positive values of the gamma coefficient) will be supportive of the routine activities perspective. For example, it is expected that there will be a significant, positive relationship between sex and location of homicide; that is, a high value on sex (male) should be associated with a high value on location ("beyond 10 blocks"). Negative gamma coefficients would conversely imply that the observed associations are in the opposite direction of that predicted on the basis of the routine activities model.

One final set of analyses will also be performed. The small number of homicides makes it difficult to construct multidimensional cross-tabulations. Even with the dichotomous classification of variables, the introduction of successive "control" variables quickly generates empty cells. One possible strategy for dealing with this problem is to exploit the ordinal conceptualization of variables and to apply ordinary least-squares regression techniques.

RESULTS

Simple frequency distributions are reported for the location and victim-perpetrator relationship, for the sociodemographic characteristics of victims, and for the temporal feature associated with the incident. The data reveal that, with respect to location, a slight majority of homicides (55.7%) occurred beyond 10 blocks from the victim's place of residence, while about a quarter of all homicides (24%) took place at the victim's home. With respect to the victim-perpetrator relationship, the vast majority of homicides (68.2%) fall into the category of "friends and acquaintances." Perhaps of greatest interest here is the contrast for "family" and "stranger" homicides. Homicides involving strangers were twice as prevalent in Manhattan in 1981 as were homicides involving family members (21.2% versus 10.5%), even with the rather broad definition of "family member" employed in this study. These results are almost the exact reverse of those reported by Wolfgang for an earlier period in Philadelphia, and they suggest that the widespread perception of homicide as more commonly a family matter than an encounter between strangers may no longer be appropriate for large metropolitan areas.

The frequency distributions for the sociodemographic characteristics reveal that homicide victims were considerably more likely to be males than females, to be in the middle-age bracket (where the bulk of the population is) rather than in the young-old category, and to be members of minority groups (Blacks, Hispanics) rather than members of the other racial group. Victims were also slightly more likely to have never been married and slightly more likely to have been employed than unemployed. Finally, the simple patterns for the temporal factors indicate that about a quarter of the homicide victimizations occurred on the weekends, during the winter months, and during the late-night-to-early-morning hours.

SOCIODEMOGRAPHIC CHARACTERISTICS

The results for the sex of the victim are fully consistent with theoretical explanations and with previous research. Males are significantly more likely than females to be victimized away from home and to be killed by strangers. The magnitude of the gamma coefficient for victim-perpetrator relationship (.71) is especially striking. The patterns for both of these dimensions of homicide undoubtedly reflect the greater involvement on the part of females in household and family activities.

The relationship between age and types of homicide varies across the two dimensions, location versus relationship. The hypothesis concerning age and the location of the homicide is supported by the data. Those in the very young and very old bracket are much less likely than those in the other age group to be killed beyond 10 blocks from one's residence (29.2% versus 58.5%). The positive gamma coefficient of .51 indicates a moderately strong relationship in the direction predicted by the routine activities perspective. There is virtually no ordinal association, however, between the age variable and the variable for victim-perpetrator relationship— the gamma coefficient is .01. The reason for the trivial gamma is that although those in the young-old bracket are more likely than those in the other age bracket to be killed by family members, they are also more likely to be killed by strangers.

As expected, whites and Asians are appreciably more likely to be killed by strangers than are blacks and Hispanics (gamma = .31). The hypothesis concerning race and the location of homicides, however, is not substantiated. Whites and Asians are slightly more likely to be killed beyond 10 blocks, but they are also slightly more likely to be killed at home. One possible explanation for the failure to detect an appreciable relationship between race and location of homicides may be that racial status has very little impact on the intracity mobility of persons in a place like Manhattan, where mass public transit is available at a fairly low cost.

The data thus suggest that although marital status tends to structure life-styles in the manner expected, the overall effect of this factor on the location of potential victims in physical space and the nature of contacts is rather limited. Part of the reason for such a limited effect may be the growing popularity of cohabitation as an alternative to marriage. As Hindelang et al. observe, marital status is likely to become a less accurate predictor of victimization to the extent that persons who are not formally married adopt life-styles which have traditionally been associated with married life.

The unemployed are more likely than the employed to be killed at home (28.8% versus 19.6%), and the gamma coefficient, .26, is positive and moderately strong. The hypothesis concerning the victim-perpetrator relationship, in contrast, receives only marginal support. Although the association is in the expected direction with the unemployed exhibiting a greater likelihood of being killed by family members and the employed being more likely to be killed by strangers, the differences in proportions are extremely small. These data suggest that employment status has a greater effect on the location of activities in physical space than on the nature of personal contacts to which an individual is exposed, although it is not clear why this might be so.

The final step in the analysis of sociodemographic characteristics is to examine the multivariate relationships by means of multiple regression. The results of these analyses are strikingly consistent with the bivariate, cross-tabular findings. Both the geographical distance of the offense from the household and the social distance between the participants tend to be greater for males than for females. Age and employment status are also significantly related to the location of homicide, with the employed and the middle-aged group more likely to be victimized at greater distances from the home. Lastly, the social distance between victim and perpetrator tends to be greater, as expected, for whites and Asians in comparison with blacks and Hispanics. The only noteworthy discrepancy between the bivariate findings and the multivariate patterns is that marital status appears to have a marginally significant association with victim-perpetrator relationship in the simple cross-tabulations, but it has no significant association in the regression equations.

FEATURES OF THE TEMPORAL SETTING

Contrary to expectations, there are no systematic relationships between time of day and types of homicide. The chi squares for both cross-tabulations are not significant. Also, each gamma coefficient is small, and the coefficient for location has the "wrong" sign.

The relationships for day of the week and kinds of homicide are more consistent with expectations. With respect to the location of homicides, victimizations occurring on weekends are slightly more likely to occur at home and slightly less likely to occur "beyond 10 blocks" than are those victimizations occurring on weekdays. Also consistent with expectations, the proportion of "weekend" homicides involving family members is noticeably higher than the corresponding proportion for "weekday" homicides, whereas the pattern is reversed for homicides involving strangers. These findings are consistent with the assertion that activities are more likely to be concentrated around the household on weekdays than on weekends, and that the probability of homicides involving family members varies accordingly.

The most perplexing finding concerning temporal factors is the lack of any association between time of day and the different types of homicides. Time exerts a significant impact on the conduct of routine activities and thus, given the logic of routine activities theory, time should be clearly related to the location and nature of criminal victimization. One possible explanation for the observed "null" effects is that the influence of time of day may be contingent upon day of the week. More specifically, it might be hypothesized that the tendency for activities to be concentrated around the household during the late-night-to-early morning hours will be strong only on weekdays and not during the weekends. Significant associations between time of day and kinds of homicide would then be predicted only for those victimizations during the week.

The results do not support this hypothesis of conditional effects. Once again, the associations between the time of day and both location of homicide and the victim-perpetrator relationship are generally small in magnitude and are in all cases statistically insignificant.

Another possible explanation for the unimpressive relationship observed between time of day and kinds of homicide is that the classification of time of day into dichotomous categories is too crude to detect the way in which features of the temporal setting structure routine activities and hence victimization. To get a better picture of the possible temporal patterning of homicides, frequency distributions have been prepared for each type of homicide, broken down according to two-hour intervals covering the course of the day. The percentage of all homicides of a given type (for example, the proportion of homicides occurring at home, the

355

proportion of homicides occurring within 10 blocks, and so on) which took place within a specified two-hour interval has been calculated for each of 12 intervals.

The frequency of homicides tends to be relatively low in the hours around sunrise, to increase in the late afternoon to early evening, and to peak sometime later in the night. Perhaps the most noteworthy discrepancy across types of homicide is the distinctive pattern observed for homicides at the victim's home versus those taking place elsewhere. "Home" homicides appear to peak slightly earlier in the evening than do homicides outside of the home. This probably reflects the tendency for persons to be at home during the dinner hours and then to go out in the hours immediately following.

The results do not show any marked tendency for "far away" homicides (that is, beyond 10 blocks) or for "stranger" homicides to be especially infrequent during the late-night-to-early-morning hours (the category used in the "time of day" dummy variable) in comparison with the other types of homicide. This is somewhat paradoxical given our assumption that activities will be more concentrated around the household during these hours, which implies in turn that relatively few potential victims will be located far away from home and be in situations likely to involve contacts with strangers.

A possible resolution to this paradox may lie in other aspects of routine activities which are temporally structured and related to victimization. To be more specific, the probability that "capable guardians" are present undoubtedly varies over the course of the day. Capable guardians are least likely to be present during the late-night-to-early-morning hours. Thus, even though the aggregate number of contacts with strangers is likely to be small during the late-night-to-early morning hours, each contact during these hours may carry with it a high risk of victimization. This would explain the fact that "stranger" homicides are not unusually low in comparison with other types of homicides during the late-night-to-early-morning period.

A similar argument can be formulated to explain the fact that "away from home" homicides are not especially infrequent during the late-night-to-early-morning hours even though only small numbers of potential victims are likely to be situated away from the household at these times. For those relatively few individuals who are away from home late at night, the risks of victimization are probably high, thereby resulting in levels of "away-from-home" homicides during these hours which are comparable to those observed for victimizations occurring in other locales. In short, the temporal patterning of homicides appears to be reasonably consistent with the routine activities perspective once all three of the components of a "direct contact predatory violation" are explicitly taken into account (that is, motivated offender, suitable target, and presence or absence of capable guardians).

DISCUSSION

The results of our analysis indicate that individuals with varying sociodemographic characteristics experience distinctive patterns of criminal victimization. The probable location of homicide is significantly related to the sex, age, and employment status of the victim, and the likely relationship between the victim and the offender is appreciably associated with sex and race. All of the significant associations observed in the data are compatible with the routine activities perspective. Those persons who lead lives that are centered around the home are precisely those who are most likely to be victimized at home and to be killed by family members. The consistent pattern of the findings is indeed quite striking. Although not every sociodemographic characteristic has a substantial effect on each dimension of homicide, none exhibits a significant association with either dimension in a way opposite to the predictions of routine activities theory. Moreover, with the exception of the marital status variable, the results of the simple, cross-tabular analysis are consistently replicated in the multiple regression equations.

The findings for temporal factors are less impressive but also in line with the routine activities approach. As expected, "weekday" homicides are significantly more likely to involve strangers than are those homicides taking place during the weekend. The relationship between day of the week and location of homicide is not significant, nor are the relationships between season and the two dimensions of homicide. Once again, however, the observed patterns for these factors are consistently in the direction predicted by the routine activities theory. "Time of day" exhibits no simple association with either dimension of homicide, but there does appear to be a clear temporal patterning of each kind of homicide which follows the general rhythm of daily activities.

CHAPTER 6

The Control of Murder

Theories about the control of crime have been, for the most part, derivative of social control theory. It may have greater utility in general crime prevention than in the control of murder. Large shifts in the number of murders in American cities and counties appear to be affected more by population density, heterogeneity, and mobility, the degree of social disorganization within each community, and the response of criminal justice agencies to violence that could result in homicidal events. However, not even these causal and control factors explain the apparent rise in some specific types of murder, like stranger and serial murders. When one considers the elements involved in the control of murder, the areas of police investigation, criminal profiling, deterrence, gun control, and prevention are most frequently mentioned.

POLICE INVESTIGATION

Traditionally, the characteristics of murder have been recorded on the supplemental homicide report (SHR) form of the FBI's *Uniform Crime Reports* and submitted by local police and sheriff's departments. Supplemental reports are not submitted to the FBI for other types of crime, so researchers know much more from this national data source about its commission than any other crime. It is also expected that murder would produce more case details, because it is such a serious crime and police investigators respond to it differently than to other crimes. Almost always, murder is an assigned case requiring follow-up investigation, before crimes like robbery and burglary that are usually not assigned unless there is a suspect or someone in custody. Therefore, there are higher clearance (or solution) rates for murder than any other violent crime. Since we are armed with more comprehensive data, we are able to monitor the control of murder much more accurately than other crimes.

All data gathering begins with the police response to an incident of murder. A report of a murder may start with a call of shots fired, man down, or a woman screaming. At this point, the case starts with the processing of important information received at the recovery site of the victim's body. Then, a process of investigation leads the investigator to the actual site where death-producing injuries were inflicted and, eventually, to the site where the offender initially met the victim to consummate the murder event.

This section of the chapter covers the police role in the investigation of murder. Keppel and Weis's research on "Time and Distance as Solvability Factors in Murder Investigations" was the first of its kind, since no empirical study had ever examined the factors that enhance the solution of murder cases. Previous research had only focused on robbery and burglary investigations. Without question, this research highlights the importance of discovering the major investigative components of a murder, from the initial contact between the victim and offender to the ultimate solution of the case.

The second essay is excerpted from "Identification of Serial Homicide Victims in the 'Green River Murder' Investigation." This work covers the vital role of identifying the victims and the problems related to that phase of the investigation.

CRIMINAL PROFILING

Another important police tactic in investigations is to perform a crime scene assessment, particularly if the case has an unknown suspect. This procedure is commonly called "criminal profiling," and has been done by psychiatrists, behavioral scientists, and members of the FBI. To examine the differences in the art of profiling, we have included "Criminal Personality Profiling: An Outcome and Process Study." This paper describes the routines involved in profiling criminal cases, and distinguishes the ability to profile accurately between a group of known profilers versus students.

SIGNATURE ANALYSIS

Keppel's "Signature Murders: A Report of Several Related Cases" summarizes his analyses of three female murders, all committed by the same person. The essay is particularly important because he used one of the most comprehensive data sets on murder, from Washington State's Homicide Investigation and Tracking System, to supplement his vast investigation experience to link the three murders together by analyzing the modus operandi and signature characteristics of the unknown serial killer.

DETERRENCE

In some ways, the police can prevent some types of murders by responding quickly to reports of possible violence. Other murders are prevented by having exceptional emergency room facilities that save the lives of near-death victims of violence. But the most popular question about deterrence is: What is the effect of capital punishment on committing a murder? For this discussion, we have chosen excerpts from Bowers and Pierce, "The Illusion of Deterrence in Isaac Ehrlich's Research on Capital Punishment," Parker and Smith, "Deterrence, Poverty, and Homicide," and Radelet and Akers, "Deterence and the Death Penalty: the Views of the Experts." Here, the student will be exposed to some of the arguments around capital punishment as a deterrent to criminal homicide.

GUN CONTROL

The issue of gun control as a means to control crimes of violence was one of the highlights of President Clinton's first four years in office. The passage of the Brady Bill has made the purchase of firearms much more difficult. To examine the arguments about the value of gun control, we have included a paper with very considered positions on the efficacy of gun control: Zimring's "Is Gun Control Likely to Reduce Violent Killings?"

PREVENTION

The final component of the control of murder discussed here is prevention. Whereas theories and practices of prevention seem to work for some common crimes, the prevention of murder is more difficult to accomplish. To assist the student in understanding the problems associated with the prevention of murder, we have chosen a paper, by Hawkins (a sociologist), that looks at the relationship between what we know about black homicides and the policy and strategic implications for prevention, particularly in high-rate black communities. The other paper, by Hickey, examines fatal violence committed against missing and abducted children. Runaway children represent the largest percentage of children found alive, whereas stranger abductions account for most of the missing children who are found dead. The discussion focuses on many ways of protecting potential child victims and preventing stranger abduction murders. There is a vital interdependence between scientific knowledge about murder and its practical implications for prevention and control.

[Handwritten annotations:]

① Victim Last scene
② Initial Contact
③ Initial assault
④ Murder
⑤ Dump Site
(Body Recovery)

Shorter time & dist
= ↑ solvab.

1st ↑ 5th = greatest
solvability

More that's known about time & distance
↑ solvability

POLICE INVESTIGATION

Time and Distance as Solvability Factors in Murder Cases

ROBERT D. KEPPEL & JOSEPH G. WEIS

Historically, social scientific research on murder has emphasized the ecological, demographic, social structural, and psychopathological characteristics of murder incidents, victims, or offenders. These studies typically rely on aggregate-level data or, at the other extreme, clinical case-studies, neither of which are very informative regarding the control of murder, particularly by the criminal justice system. The problem is that researchers, for whatever reasons, have neglected the criminal justice response to murder as an object of inquiry.

Consequently, there is not one rigorous, empirical study that *focuses* on the formal reaction to homicides by those agencies and agents responsible for solving the crime and apprehending the offender. Prior research has not focused on the processes, procedures, and factors that characterize the *investigation* of murder. To the authors' knowledge, there is only one study of murder investigation, but it was somewhat limited in scope and, therefore, generalizability, because it focused only on the investigation of "serial" murder, did not deal with how the murderers were caught, and depended on the veracity of information provided by 36 convicted serial-murderer interviewees. That study may illuminate the understanding of some aspects of the investigation of serial murder, but it cannot address the whole process of investigation of all types of murder.

363

There are three general sources of information on the investigation of murder: 1) case law on murder, 2) textbooks on criminal investigation, and 3) empirical research on the investigation of crimes other than murder. A somewhat remote source of information affecting the solution of murder investigations is the case law on murder convictions. The procedures used by police in murder investigations are a common source of appellate issues raised by those convicted of murder. The case law is replete with appeals that attack the quality of police investigations in murder cases. Frequently, the law points to several solvability factors: 1) The quality of police interviews of eyewitnesses; 2) the circumstances which led to the initial stop and arrest of the murderer; 3) the circumstances that established the probable cause to search and seize physical evidence from the person and/or property of the murderer; 4) the quality of the investigation at the crime scene(s); and, 5) the quality of the scientific analysis of the physical evidence seized from the murderer and/or his property and its comparison to physical evidence recovered from the victims and the murder scenes. Empirical research has not been generated from these appellate cases.

A controversial body of literature exists in textbooks on criminal investigation in the police science field. These textbooks deal with highly selective elements of murder investigation, for example, the preservation of evidence at the murder scene and various methods of analyzing and handling that evidence. The basis for these texts is limited to the practical experiences of each author, and is not the result of generalizations made from empirical research. Very little information is presented in these texts that relates to the actual steps, beyond the original crime scene investigation, that detectives should follow. The logical steps necessary to follow the clues that can be found during the formative stages of a murder investigation are not specified or analyzed in any of these texts *or* in any empirical research studies.

The empirical research on criminal investigation over the past 15 years has focused on 1) the description of the investigative process, 2) the actions of investigators and information sources used by them in solving crimes, and 3) the management of criminal investigations. Although most of this research is not directly applicable to the investigation of murder and is often flawed methodologically, it does point to a number of important research issues and questions. The early studies of criminal investigation were primarily descriptive accounts of law enforcement efforts to solve crimes. This research has been highly critical of the police role in apprehending criminals. The investigation of crime is described as a serendipitous process, wherein the actions of police have little to do with solving crimes.

A number of controversial evaluations of police productivity have reiterated the conclusion that the detective function is relatively ineffective in solving crimes.

364

But no studies have examined whether the quality of detective work is related to the apparent *declining* clearance rate for murders. Recent estimates are that, from 1960 to 1983, the solution rate for murders has declined from over 90% to approximately 76% for all types of murder. In a related study in San Diego, the major conclusion was that there had been a rapid growth of urban criminal homicide between 1970–1980, coupled with a corresponding decrease in homicide cases cleared by the police.

It is hypothesized here that there is an important relationship between solving murders and having information about a number of important locations—where the body is discovered, the place where the victim was last seen, the initial contact point between the offender and the victim, the initial assault site, and the location where the murder actually occurred. For example, if a female is found bludgeoned to death in her bedroom and the initial contact between that victim and the killer was at the same place and minutes before the murder, statistics would most likely demonstrate that, in a significant number of these types of cases, the boyfriend or husband was the perpetrator, and the investigation of the boyfriend/husband should receive the highest priority in the investigation process. The avenues of approach and the priorities of the investigative steps can be developed, both prospectively and retrospectively, from information about the various locations.

Overall, even though the empirical research on the process of investigation, the identification of solvability factors, and the effective management of investigations suffers from many of the usual methodological problems of inadequate samples, inappropriate data, weak research designs, and simplistic analyses, it points to a number of important issues in criminal investigation, particularly the critical role of *information* in solving crime. Typically, information is obtained routinely by interviewing witnesses and suspects, canvassing neighborhoods, processing crime scenes for physical evidence, examining records, and so on. One of the most prominent reasons why detectives do not solve cases is the manner in which they gather and use information. The key to solving crimes and making arrests is to understand how much and what kind of information is available and how to organize it to make it more accessible and useful. The main flaw in studies that are critical of the investigator's ability to process information is that they have focused on crimes other than murder, such as burglary and robbery. The investigative response to those crimes is different than for murder; for example, a detective is not always assigned immediately to follow-up these cases, whereas all murders are assigned for follow-up.

Murder investigations have not been the primary focus of any study but have been included as part of other research on murder. For instance, the factors of time and distance have been mentioned as factors that affect the solution of murder cases. The reference to time, however, has been expressed only in terms of its relationship to solving a case when the time of arrest is compared to the time when the murder was discovered. The research has shown that in 66% of solved murder cases, a suspect is in custody within 24 hours and, if the murder is not solved within 48 hours, the chances of it ever being solved fall markedly. The relationship of time to other factors in murder cases has not been considered in any scientific research, such as information about the time and place of death in comparison to the time and location of the body recovery site, both elements vital to any murder investigation.

Distances between certain crime scene locations in murder cases have not been included routinely as part of any research project on murder. The importance of distance was first emphasized by the National Serial Murder Advisory Group for the Federal Bureau of Investigation's Violent Criminal Apprehension Program (VICAP). The actual intervals of distance among the victim's last known location, the initial contact point between the offender and victim, the initial assault location, the death site, and the body recovery site were recorded on the VICAP Crime Report and submitted to the FBI by local law enforcement officers. Agents of the FBI's Behavioral Sciences Unit have further highlighted time and location factors as crucial to the pros of "profiling" violent offenders. They emphasize the importance of analyzing the time it takes to kill and dispose of a victim, in conjunction with the location of where the murder occurred, especially if it is different from the point of abduction and where the body was discovered.

A more recent project undertaken by the U.S. Office of Juvenile Justice and Delinquency Prevention also emphasized the importance of time and distance intervals in murder investigations. The purpose of the research was to conduct national incidence studies to estimate the parameters of the missing child problem, including the number of juvenile ""victims of abduction by strangers." The time that a child was detained and the distance that a child was transported after the abduction were major factors in this research. The research concluded, tragically, that 2% of the abduction cases where children were coerced or taken a distance of more than 20 feet, or were detained for more than one hour, ended with the murder of those children. However, this project did not consider the effect of time and distance on the solution of child murder cases.

Finally, a major concern in the literature on murder investigation is that the police are not doing their job very well. The most common indicator of their performance is the clearance rate, the barometer of successful investigation. Clearance rates for murder investigations look bad because they are declining. For example, in Illinois, clearance rates for murder have dropped from 90% to 77% since 1972. In Washington State, the 1984 murder clearance rate was 77% and has dropped to 66% in 1987. When the murder clearance rates for cities over 250,000 population are examined, the even lower clearance rate for killings is disturbing. For example, New York City reported a clearance rate of 57% in 1979. Also, the police in Denver reported a clearance rate of 46% in 1980, a figure which represents a startling decade change of 179% in unsolved criminal homicides.

It is clear that rigorous, empirical research on murder investigation is needed to clarify the issues and problems identified in the research literature and raised in case law on murder conviction appeals. This study is intended to improve the understanding of murder and its investigation, as well as the management and solution of murder cases.

A MODEL OF MURDER INVESTIGATION

The customary way that the police become involved in the investigation of a murder is in response to calls of shots fired, a missing person, a man down, or a dead body. The course of the investigation is reactive in nature in that investigators follow up the reported call after the incident has occurred.

The most frequent place for a murder investigation to begin is at the site where the victim is found. This location is commonly referred to as the "body recovery site." The finding of a dead body is the starting point and initial focus of the murder investigation. The scene of a murder is, without a doubt, the most important crime scene to which a police officer or investigator will be called upon to respond. How a murder is investigated has traditionally relied heavily upon the role of logic and very little on theories of investigation based on empirical research. To date, advances in the quality of detective work have been motivated and accomplished primarily by the ingenuity and drive of individual detectives.

For homicide investigators, there are no current models of investigation that can systematically guide their follow-up procedures in every murder case. Traditionally, detectives have relied on the facts available in a particular case and proceeded on avenues of follow-up investigation based on "gut feelings" and "common sense." This research focuses on the investigation of murder as a process. The process is called a Model for Murder Investigation (MMI). The result of using MMI in the pursuit of follow-up leads in murder investigations is that the case will be approached systematically, thus making homicide detectives more effective.

The basic premise of the model proposed here is that the crime of murder is an incident. The murder incident contains multiple components that are locations of contact between the offender and victim. MMI emphasizes the search for clues or information about the major investigative locations of a murder incident. A thorough investigator collects all the necessary information that exists around each location. The presence or absence of information that establishes the existence of each location, coupled with when and where each location is found within the incident, and the manner in which their relationships affect each other, will greatly influence the solution of the murder case. Specifically, MMI involves the gathering of information about the important locations of victim-offender contact.

Locations of a Murder Incident

1) The location where and the time when the victim was last seen, or Victim Last Seen Site, is developed from eyewitness information and records that reflect when and where the victim was last seen alive. For example, eyewitness accounts include visual sightings and telephone conversations, and records include official documents, such as traffic citations, police field interview reports, jail booking logs, long distance telephone/toll records, credit card receipts, etc.

2) The place where and the time when the offender initially contacted the victim, or Initial Contact Site, is established from evidence that the offender first met the victim at a certain time and at a specific location during the course of the murder incident. For example, if a husband killed his wife in their apartment after she returned home from work, the time and location for the initial contact within that murder incident is when the wife returned home from work and was confronted by her husband, not the date when they first met two years ago.

3) The Initial Assault Site is the location where and the time when the offender, either at the time of, or after the initial contact, kidnaps or assaults the victim in any manner during the course of the murder incident. It is not defined as the place where the actual death producing injuries occurred. For example, a male customer picks up a female prostitute at a bus stop. The customer transports the prostitute in his car to a remote location where he slaps the prostitute and handcuffs her. The slap and handcuffing is the initial assault.

4) The Murder Site is the place where and the time when the victim sustains the death producing injuries. Using the previous example, if the initial assault is followed two hours later by a shooting that causes the death of the prostitute at the customer's home, the location of the shooting is the murder site.

5) The Body Recovery Site is the location where and the time when police, medics, or witnesses find the victim, dead or alive, prior to transportation to a medical facility or morgue. For example, if a living victim is found shot outside a tavern, transported to a hospital for treatment, dies in the emergency room, the body recovery site is the tavern, not the hospital.

The MMI operates on the premise that all of the above locations occur in each incident of murder. Problems with any case's solution surface when investigators cannot obtain information about the location and its time of occurrence within the sequence of the murder incident. Fortunately, in most cases, the events occur simultaneously, and the information that is available suggests that all events are located in the same place and are not separated by intervals of distance or spans of time.

However, in many cases the locations within an incident of murder can become separated by time and distance. The separation can occur in two ways. First, the offender intentionally separates the locations. The killer believes that the separation of murder locations prolongs the investigation by delaying the discovery of various locations and contributes to the destruction of evidence. The separation also inhibits the investigation by causing problems in communication and cooperation among police agencies because the place of all locations is not within the authority of one police agency. For example, multiple murderer Theodore Bundy intentionally contacted victims in different locations than where he killed them and disposed of their bodies. He contacted a female victim at Oregon State University in Corvallis, Oregon, and then dumped her remains 265 miles away in rural King County near Seattle, Washington. Prior to his execution in Florida, Bundy made statements about his murders. He revealed that he was aware that time and distance separation among the locations of disappearance, murder, and body recovery resulted in more weathering and deterioration of human remains and physical evidence. He was also mindful of the problems in cooperation and communication among police investigators when murderers use locations in different jurisdictions when contacting victims and disposing of their bodies.

Second, the offender unintentionally separates the locations by time and distance. For example, a man picks up a woman in a tavern. He transports her to a remote location to have consensual sex in his car. Then, an argument ensues because she wants money for her efforts. The offender pulls out a gun and pushes the victim down. Her head strikes a rock, rendering her unconscious. The offender then transports the victim to a hospital where she dies. The offender has not intentionally separated the locations of the incident to deceive investigators. Additionally, the discovery of a body after the murder may be delayed more by chance than by the efforts of the offender. For instance, an elderly woman, murdered in her own home, may not have immediate family in the neighborhood to check on her welfare. The checks may only be sporadic, so the discovery of her remains might take longer than if she had someone who checked on her daily.

METHODOLOGY

This study deals with the separation of the locations of a murder incident by time and distance and their relationship to solvability. The study's general proposition is: the more time and distance information that is known about the five locations of a murder incident, the higher the percentage of investigations resulting in solution.

Five issues that flow from this general proposition were explored in this research:

1) When police investigators know the dates of initial contact, initial assault, and the murder itself, this knowledge will contribute to the solvability of the case; that is, the percentage of cases solved will be greater given this knowledge than when the dates for these locations are not known.

2) (a) When the time between a given pair of locations is less than 24 hours, such relatively close proximity in time will contribute to the solvability of the case; that is, the percentage of cases solved will be greater than when that pair of locations is separated by more than 24 hours.

(b) The time proximity of locations will contribute to the solvability of the case even if the locations are not close in time.

3) When police investigators know the distance between the sites of any pair of the five case locations, this knowledge will contribute to the solvability of the case; that is, the percentage of cases solved will be greater given this knowledge than when the distances between pairs of locations are not known.

4) When the distance between the sites of a pair of sites is less than 199 feet, the relatively close proximity of the sites will enhance the solvability of the case; that is, the percentage of cases solved will be significantly greater than when the sites are separated by more than 199 feet.

5) When the time between a given pair of locations is more than 24 hours and the distance between that same pair is more than 199 feet, such relatively distant proximity in time and distance will not contribute to the solvability of the case; that is, the rate of solvability diminishes sharply when both the time span and interval of distance are shorter for that pair of locations.

The data examined here were derived from a larger research project on murder and its investigation conducted by the Washington State Attorney General's Office, Seattle, Washington. The three objectives of the research were 1) to describe and assess the development of a model statewide homicide investigation system, 2) to determine the critical solvability factors present in homicide investigations, and 3) to identify the salient characteristics of homicides.

To determine the critical solvability factors present in homicide investigations, data were collected on all solved and unsolved murders from law enforcement agencies in the state of Washington from January 1981 through December 1986. The final sample of murders totalled 1309 victims.

Most of the information that was input to the Homicide Investigation and Tracking System was collected from each murder case file with a data collection instrument that was designed for both investigation and research purposes. The final version was used to record comprehensive detailed information on 467 items that tap the characteristics of a murder and its investigation.

The Time and Distance Variables

The dates, times, and places of the locations were recorded from data contained in various reports from each case file, including, but not limited to: 1) case reports, 2) investigator's follow-up reports, 3) crime laboratory reports, 4) crime scene diagrams, 5) autopsy reports and 6) witness statements.

Date and time were recorded as the exact date and time that each location occurred as reported in documents from the case file, or as time frame approximations. For example, a witness reported that a victim was last seen on 2-13-86, but was unsure of the time and estimated it to be between 0230 and 0630. So 2-13-86 was entered in the "exact" date area, and the time frame of 0230–0630 was entered in the "approximate" time area.

Unlike the reporting of time, which was frequently mentioned in the text of various reports, recording the distance between locations was a different matter. Some detectives' reports reflected that they had traced the travel patterns of the offender, noting the distance and the time required to drive or walk from one location to another. However, this was not a standard practice for the majority of investigations.

Since distance information was not systematically found within the case file of most murder investigations, distances between locations were calculated in the following manner. Each location was plotted on the street map for the appropriate jurisdiction. The map's legend was used to measure the shortest distance between locations as if the offender had traveled by county roads, city streets, or highways. In those cases where the locations were found on the same property or address, crime scene diagrams, drawn by investigating officers, were consulted for various measurements.

The "Solvability" Variable

The variable used to measure solvability was the status of the murder case at the time of coding. Each murder investigation was classified by Case Status into one of the five categories used in the Uniform Crime Reports of the FBI: 1) Open (active investigation), 2) Suspended (inactive investigation), 3) Open—Arrest Warrant Issued, 4) Cleared by Arrest, and 5) Exceptionally Cleared.

Unsolved murders were defined as "Open" and "Suspended" murder investigations. The former meant that the police were actively following investigative leads at the time of coding the data collection instrument; the latter, that police officers were not actively following leads at the time of coding. Solved murders were defined as "Open—Arrest Warrant Issued," "Cleared by Arrest," and "Exceptionally Cleared" (cases where the offender committed suicide, was killed by police or witnesses, or was deceased for other reasons, such as from a traffic accident or natural causes).

DATA ANALYSIS AND RESULTS

There were 1309 victims of murder in the state of Washington from January 1981 through December 1986. The case files for 38 victims were "missing" and could not be located by record's personnel from the responsible law enforcement agencies. The investigations of the available 1271 victim case files were the focus of the larger study. For purposes of this research, only single victim-single offender cases (N = 967) were used for analysis. The rate of solved, single victim-single offender murder cases was 74%, while a nearly equal percentage of solved cases was noted for all victims (77%), including multiple-victim murders.

When Any Information Is Known About Distance and Time

Since the basic model for murder investigation consists of the five locations of a murder incident, the extent to which any information was simply "known" about each location was examined before exploring the five main issues in this research. The pieces of information collected and examined on each location were 1) the date of occurrence (exact or approximate) and 2) the type of location (such as sidewalk, residence or wooded area) and/or address.

The location that was most often "known" was the Body Recovery Site, followed in order by Murder Site, Victim Last Seen Site, Initial Assault Site, and Initial Contact Site. The order of the locations makes sense, since police officers usually start the investigation of a murder at the site of body recovery and use information gathered at that time to continue the inquiry for further information or leads about the remainder of the locations. When the contribution to solvability of each location was examined, a more important order was revealed. Information on the Initial Contact Site showed the highest percentage (77%) of solved cases, but followed closely by the other locations. A dramatic finding is the drop in the percentage of solved cases (by at least 60% to 17% for the Initial Contact Site,

14% for the Initial Assault Site, and 8% for the Murder Site) when information about the locations was "unknown." Even though the Initial Contact Site and Initial Assault Site were not as frequently discovered by the police during the course of murder investigations as were the other locations, they show the strongest associations of the five locations. Clearly, the pursuit of information about these two locations should have received priority because of the higher probability of solution when information about them was known. On the other hand, the Body Recovery Site was so rarely unknown that it could not differentiate between solved and unsolved cases.

The Date of Occurrence

The data were also analyzed to determine whether solvability was enhanced when police investigators knew the dates for each of the five locations. The most notable findings are strong and significant associations between solvability and knowing dates for Initial Contact, Initial Assault, and Murder Sites.

The most efficient indicator of solvability was when the date was known for the murder site, 81% of the cases were solved. Similar percentages were found for the Initial Contact and Initial Assault Sites, 78% and 79% respectively. When the date was unknown for the location of the Murder, the cases that were solved dropped to only 41%, while Initial Contact was 44% and Initial Assault was 46%.

The remaining two locations, Victim Last Seen and Body Recovery Site, were much less strongly related to solvability. Knowledge about the dates of these two locations seems less important for the process of murder investigation. The overall findings support the first issue: When police investigators know the dates of Initial Contact, Initial Assault, and Murder Sites, this knowledge will contribute to the solvability of the case. That is, the percentage of cases solved will be greater when the dates for these locations are known.

Spans of Time Between Locations

The next analyses examined whether solvability is enhanced as pairs of locations are closer in time, given that the times for both locations were known. The time spans were examined by calculating the separation of time from one location to each of the other locations; the span, or duration of the separation of time, was measured to the nearest hour. With five locations, there were ten possible pairs of locations for which a span of time was calculated:

1. Victim Last Seen Site to Initial Contact Site,
2. Victim Last Seen Site to Initial Assault Site,

3. Victim Last Seen Site to Murder Site,
4. Victim Last Seen Site to Body Recovery Site,
5. Initial Contact Site to Initial Assault Site,
6. Initial Contact Site to Murder Site,
7. Initial Contact Site to Body Recovery Site,
8. Initial Assault Site to Murder Site,
9. Initial Assault Site to Body Recovery Site, and
10. Murder Site to Body Recovery Site.

The intervals of time ranged from zero to more than two years across the ten pairs of locations. For the solvability analysis reported here, the spans of time were collapsed into broader intervals of 0–24 hours and more than 24 hours. These intervals were chosen for two reasons: 1) the literature on solvability of murder cases emphasized that the solution rate for murders decreased appreciably after 24 hours of the discovery of the body; and 2) the interval of more than 24 hours facilitated more powerful statistical analyses since there were more cases within this category than for the intervals of more than 48 hours, 72 hours, one week, and so on.

The pair of locations with the strongest association with solvability was Victim Last Seen to Body Recovery Site. For those cases when the victim disappeared less than 24 hours prior to body recovery, 82% of the cases were solved. If the victim's body was discovered more than 24 hours after the disappearance, the rate of solved cases fell dramatically to only 42%. The results indicate that investigative problems with solvability will increase significantly when information reveals that the victim disappeared over 24 hours prior to the discovery of the victim's remains.

The findings for six of the seven location pairs support the observation that when the time between a given pair of locations is less than 24 hours, the percentage of cases solved will be greater than when that pair of locations is separated by more than 24 hours. In fact, compared to the pairs of locations when the time spans were less than 24 hours, there was an average significant decrease of 30% in solved cases for six of the location pairs when the time span was more than 24 hours between each pair.

The exceptional finding was for the elapsed time between when the murderer initially assaulted the victim and when the murder actually occurred. When the time of the assault was less than 24 hours in time from when the murder occurred, the solvability rate was 76%. But when the initial assault was more than 24 hours before the murder occurred, a surprising 89% of the cases were solved. These findings suggest that in those cases when the offender did not murder the victim within 24 hours from the time of the initial assault, the murderer kept the victim in captivity for a period of time, which increased the physical contact between the victim and offender. This longer contact probably increased the amount of incriminating evidence and, therefore, enhanced solvability.

The Distance Intervals

The next issue explored was whether solvability is enhanced when police investigators know the distances between the sites of pairs of the five locations. The same ten logical pairs of locations were used to calculate the interval distances.

In 728 investigations, the intervals of distance were known for all ten pairs of locations. Those cases had a significantly higher percentage (88%) of solved cases than in the total sample (74%). The distribution of murder cases that contained pairs of locations for which the interval of distance was known ranged from one to ten pairs of locations. In general, the percent of cases solved decreased (to a low of 4%) as the number of known-distance pairs decreased. As pairs of locations were analyzed with dichotimized distance information, for five or less pairs and more than five pairs, a strong, significant relationship was produced. When the distance interval was known for more than five pairs of locations within each investigation, 85% of cases were solved, while for five or fewer pairs of locations, only 14% were solved. These findings support the third research issue: As police investigators know the distance between the sites of more pairs of the five case locations, the rate of solvability increases.

After determining the significance of "knowing" distances between pairs of locations, the next analyses examined the actual distances between known pairs of locations. The interval of distance was measured in feet or miles for each pair of locations. Then, the actual distance was converted to one of six categories: 0 to 199 feet; 199 feet to < ¾ mile; ¾ mile to < 1½ miles; 1½ miles to < 12 miles; 12 miles to < 70 miles; 70 miles or more. These categories were based, for the most part, on natural breaks in the frequency distribution. For instance, distances for many pairs of locations were recorded as 0 feet, 100 feet, ¼ mile, 1 mile, 10 miles, and so on.

Category 1 (0–199 feet) was also based on the collective experience of several homicide detectives. The consensus of the detectives was that the maximum distance any killer was known to carry a dead body from the place where the victim was killed to the victim's final resting place was no further than 150 feet. If a killer used a vehicle to transport a dead body to another location, there were no cases in recent memory of a killer carrying the body any further than 150 feet from the vehicle. They suggested that any victim's body carried a distance of 150 feet or less be considered for investigative purposes to have been found in the same crime scene and, therefore, as if it had not been moved at all. Therefore, the distance should be considered the same as zero. Additionally, there were no geographical, psychological, or investigative differences among those cases where the victims were found within 150 feet from where they were killed.

Although the findings about distance to this point demonstrate that simply knowing information about distance for pairs of locations is important to solvability.

The most statistically significant pair of locations was, again, Victim Last Seen to Body Recovery Site. What is notable is that the distance of 0–199 feet between Victim Last Seen Site and Body Recovery Site produced an 86% solution rate, 12% higher than the average solvability rate for all single-victim murder cases. As the distance increased beyond 200 feet between Victim Last Seen Site and Body Recovery Site, the percent of solved cases dropped below 50%, to a low of 24% solved when the distance was greater than 70 miles.

These findings partially support the fourth research issue: when the distance between a pair of sites is less than 199 feet, the relatively close proximity of the sites will enhance the solvability of the case; that is, the percentage of cases solved will be significantly greater than when the sites are separated by more than 199 feet.

Time and Distance Interaction Effects for Pairs of Locations

The fifth issue explored was whether solvability was enhanced as both times and distances, together, decreased among pairs of locations. The spans of time and intervals of distance, whose relationships to solvability were previously analyzed as separate factors, were examined simultaneously to determine their joint contribution to solvability.

A statistical analysis for each of the ten pairs of locations was completed, using the time periods of 0 to 24 hours, >24 hours to less than 1 month, and more than 1 month, and the distance intervals of 0–199 feet, 200 feet to 1.49 miles, and more than 1.5 miles. Time was used as the independent variable, solvability as the dependent variable, and distance as the control variable. Once again, of the ten possible pairs of locations of a murder incident, only the pair Victim Last Seen Site to Body Recovery Site affected solvability in a significant, meaningful way. The nine other pairs either did not differentiate solved from unsolved cases or had so few cases within cells of a table that no interpretation could be drawn.

Table 6 shows the relationship between solving a case and the time and distance between the Victim Last Seen and Body Recovery Sites. The highest percent (86%) of solved cases are found in the category with the shortest period of time

(0–24 hours) and shortest distance (0–199 feet) separating the locations, while at the other extreme, an astounding 4% of cases are solved when the distance is more than 1.5 miles and the time interval is greater than one month. Therefore, in murders where both the time and distance between the Victim Last Seen Site and the Body Recovery Site are the shortest, solvability is maximized. Clearly, both short distance and time are key to enhanced solvability. Generally, for the Victim Last Seen and Body Recovery Sites, the findings regarding time and distance interactions are not markedly different than the findings when they were analyzed separately.

SUMMARY AND IMPLICATIONS

Clearly, more multivariate analyses are necessary to specify and interpret the role of time and distance as solvability factors in murder investigations. There are other variables—for example, eyewitnesses to the event, physical evidence, confessions of co-conspirators—that are likely related in important ways to the time and/or distance factors. Fortunately, the richness of the data will facilitate the explication of those kinds of interactions in subsequent analyses. To this point in our research, the analyses support the general proposition that the more information that is known about the times and distances among the locations of a murder incident, the more likely a murder case will be solved.

The research produced a number of findings that support this conclusion. First, simply having any information on the dates and locations of the five sites, particularly the Initial Contact, Assault, and Murder Sites, enhances the probability of solution. This finding challenges the efficacy of some of the curricula often included in training courses for homicide investigators, which emphasize techniques for processing the Body Recovery Site for physical evidence (for example, photography, collecting and measuring physical evidence, autopsy protocols, processing outdoor locations). Typically, little to no instruction focuses on gathering the type of information that is vital to identifying the Initial Contact, Assault, or Murder Sites, nor how important that information is to solving murder cases.

Second, knowing the dates of occurrence for the locations improves significantly an investigator's ability to identify an offender. Linking a date to the location of the murder is most important to the investigation. The Murder Site is the location where the victim and offender are typically together in time and space. Knowing the date allows an investigator to verify or refute the alibis of suspects. For example, if a murder occurred on October 3, 1991, a suspect who was in prison at the time could be eliminated as the murderer.

Third, solvability increases as the time separating pairs of locations decreases. A critical threshold is 24 hours: When the time between a given pair of locations (for example, Victim Last Seen to Body Recovery Site) is less than 24 hours, the rate of solvability is significantly higher than when it is more than 24 hours. The dramatic effect of time intervals between locations on murder investigations may reflect the influence of other factors, such as evidence deterioration or, more likely, the erosion over time of the ability of witnesses to recall accurately information about locations, dates, and events.

Fourth, as investigators know more of the distances between pairs of the five murder event locations, the rate of solvability increases dramatically. Fifth, the shorter the actual distances between locations, particularly less than 200 feet, the greater the percentage of solved cases. This relationship was strongest for the distances between where the victim was last seen to each of the other four murder incident locations. Short distances among the locations, and high solvability, reflects the fact that in a number of murder cases there is substantial overlap in the locations. For example, the victim may have last been seen at the place where the murderer made initial contact and also assaulted, killed, and left the victim for dead. On the other hand, when the distances are longer, sometimes in miles, it usually complicates the investigation because the locations will be much more difficult to discover and may even be located in different law enforcement jurisdictions. This may lead to confusion, or even competition and conflict, about which agency has primary jurisdiction and authority over the investigation. Some agencies may claim jurisdiction because the body is discovered in their domain, while others may use the location of the murder as the criterion. Of course, there are sophisticated murderers who are aware of the difficulty that police departments have in multijurisdictional investigations, and they intentionally distribute their actions, victims, and evidence across jurisdictional boundaries that, sometimes, may cover hundreds or thousands of miles.

Sixth, solvability improves as both times and distances, together, decrease among pairs of locations, especially between the Victim Last Seen and Body Recovery Sites. In murders where both the time and distance between these two locations are the longest (more than 1 month/more than 1.5 miles), an astounding 96 percent were not solved. Conversely, both the shortest time and distance maximize solvability. These results have profound implications for the efficient allocation of resources and manpower in murder investigations. Police administrators need to assess the utility of protracted investigations of murders where the last known location of the victim and the body recovery site are separated substantially in time and distance.

378

In general, this research contributes to our understanding of the process of murder investigation and should be useful to homicide investigators and police management. Some experienced investigators know that each of the five locations addressed here exist within the chronology of a murder incident. Unfortunately, detectives typically become involved in an investigation upon notification of a body discovery site. As this study has shown, information about this location is not as useful in a murder investigation as most police may believe. And less experienced detectives may have difficulty in identifying the salient characteristics of the other important locations in a murder incident.

For the experienced investigator, the findings reported here should not be surprising. One should expect that those cases about which investigating agencies have more information are more likely to be solved. However, the study shows that it is not simply any information that will enhance solvability—some information is more valuable and useful than other information in murder investigations. As the research shows, obtaining accurate information on the times and distances of the locations of a murder incident is a critical element in successful murder investigations.

[Handwritten annotations at top of page: "delay in discovery, young victims (body decomp.) (lack of dental & criminal records) lifestyle (highly mobile)" and "record retrieval — dental records, last scene info in paper, xrays, face reconstruction."]

Identification of Serial Homicide Victims in the "Green River Murder" Investigation

WILLIAM D. HAGLUND, DONALD T. REAY, & CLYDE C. SNOW

On 15 July 1982, children crossing the Peck Bridge spanning the Green River at the outskirts of the City of Kent, near Seattle, Washington, observed the body of a young woman in the water. On 12 August 1982, downstream, a meat plant employee discovered a second young woman's body floating in a quiet pool of the river. Three additional bodies of young women were found in and on the banks of the river on 15 August 1982. All five bodies had been discovered within one-half mile (0.8 km) of each other. All five had disappeared from the same general Seattle area and had connections with prostitution. Their discovery marked recognition by police of a serial homicide episode popularly termed the "Green River Murders."

At the time of this writing, 29 additional victims have been recovered in the King County, Washington, area and their deaths have been attributed to the "Green River Killer," bringing the total number of deaths under investigation from King County to 34. Two additional victims were recovered in the vicinity of Portland, Oregon, in 1985 and were identified from records on file as potential Green River victims. These two women have been added to the victim list, bringing the total number to 36. Thirty of the victims were discovered as partial to fully skeletonized remains.

In February of 1984, a multijurisdictional police investigative commitment was begun with the establishment of a task force under the direction of the King

County Police. Victim identification was assigned a high priority. Successful identifications were the result of the combined efforts of the "Green River Task Force" and the King County Medical Examiner's Office.

The main purpose of this report is to discuss difficulties encountered in the identification process and to comment on methods which proved most successful in identifying these serial murder victims. Individual case examples are analyzed, and general conclusions as to the usefulness of various methods are examined. Seventy-five percent of the victims were identified using dental X-rays, making this by far the most useful method of identity confirmation. To date, identification has been confirmed for 33 of the 36 victims, yielding an overall identification rate of 92%. In spite of this high degree of success in identification, particularly when compared with other serial homicide episodes of a similar nature, numerous problems were encountered in the identification process.

Six major sources of difficulty in the Green River victim identification process were (1) delay in discovery of bodies, (2) recovery and condition of remains, (3) age of victims, (4) lifestyle of victims, (5) their status as "missing persons," and (6) retrieval of antemortem dental and hospital records. These factors contributed to the difficulty of the identification process, increased the degree of effort needed to make an identification, and in many instances, lengthened the elapsed time from discovery to identification.

DELAY IN DISCOVERY OF BODIES

Although the initial 5 victims were found near or in the water of the Green River, the subsequent 31 victims were discovered in rural wooded areas off main highways or in urban and suburban areas on abandoned or infrequently used property with trees and dense over-growth. Most of the discoveries were made when lush ground cover was at its minimum in fall, winter, and early spring. Also contributing to seasonal discoveries were activities such as mushroom and game hunting, which brought people to isolated locations. Police found 10 victims while conducting searches of areas where bodies had previously been found. This led to certain select sites yielding clusters of victims.

In all cases, estimates of time of death were made at the scene of discovery, with time estimates given wide margins. Difficulty in establishing a time of death in cases involving skeletonized remains proved a problem to the overall identification process because these estimates set the time limits for missing persons who were treated as possible victims. Once the victim was identified, the time the victim was last known to be alive was established. Elapsed time from disappearance to body discovery in 24 identified skeletons ranged from 2 months to 32 months, with an average undiscovered time of 10.5 months. For each victim, elapsed time from date of discovery to date identified and elapsed time from date presumed to be missing to date of discovery are shown.

RECOVERY AND CONDITION OF REMAINS

Animal activity characterized by tooth marks, defleshing, skeletal disarticulation, and bone scattering was in evidence to varying degrees in many of the remains recovered. Not surprisingly, those remains in rural locations presented the greatest skeletal damage, as demonstrated by a wide degree of scattering, damage to discovered bones, and absence of many bony elements. Frequently the anthropological assessment of age and stature was jeopardized by destruction of cancellous ends of long bones and critical areas of the innominate bone such as the pubic symphysis and ischio-pubic ramus. Missing anterior teeth created difficulties in confirmation of some dental identifications.

Routine morphological methods were used to determine age and sex of victims. During the investigation the limitations of using generic skeletal features, such as age, sex, and race, in relating to the general public, became apparent. Specific information, however slight, such as hair length and color, special dental features, and fractures, greatly increased the probability of generating leads to identification. This is illustrated by one case where the press made note of medium-length, blonde hair. The reference to hair color inspired a family to report a missing person and led to identification of a previously unidentified victim. Another victim was reported missing after a description of her dental work appeared in the media.

Portions of a single victim's remains were sometimes discovered at different times and locations. For example, a skull, absent the mandible, was discovered in December of 1983 along a roadside. Other skeletal elements were located in January 1986, approximately 150 yards (137 m) from where the skull was found. In another instance, a fragment of mandible was brought to the King County Medical Examiner's Office in 1984. The mandible had been found in a residential yard comingled with animal bones a dog had brought home, approximately one-quarter mile (0.4 km) from the discovery of a partial skeleton in January of 1986. The mandible was determined to belong to this partial skeleton.

AGE OF VICTIMS

The age of identified victims ranged from 15 to 36 years with a mean age of 20 years and a median of 19 years. The majority of victims were white and between 15 and 19 years of age. The youth of the victims contributed to difficulties in identification in two major ways. First, dental records when retrieved were frequently of mixed dentition, including both deciduous and permanent teeth, while the remains of victims contained only adult dentition. Second, police records of juveniles are handled differently from those of adults. For instance, juveniles may not be fingerprinted, and juvenile records may be purged once they reach 18 years of age. Further problems in the handling of missing persons are discussed below.

VICTIM LIFESTYLES

Unstructured lifestyles of the victims complicated the identification process. A hallmark of unstructured lifestyle is mobility with frequent change of residence. Several of the Green River victims were runaways, had been placed in foster homes or detention facilities, or had lived the "street life." Prostitution, which emerged as the most common lifestyle of the victims, has associated activities, such as drug use, which hinder police tracking and inquiry on victims. Mobility also implies loss of contact with parents, acquaintances, and medical/dental facilities. With this loss of contact, disappearances go unnoticed. In addition, multiple aliases and street names were used by many of the victims. At one time, records sought on 11 missing individuals involved checking 77 names. In another instance, records collected under two aliases were treated as separate individuals, and it was not known for some time that they were the same person. It was not uncommon for several persons to use the same alias or the name of another person.

MISSING PERSONS RECORDS

Traditionally, missing persons are intensively investigated by police agencies only when a known kidnapping or other foul play is involved. For most agencies, time, funding, and manpower are not sufficient to begin to process adequately missing individuals falling outside these two categories. Acceptance, retention, followup, and purging of missing persons varies not only from agency to agency, but even within agencies. Locally, with approximately 30 separate police jurisdictions affected by the Green River investigation, 4 situations were noted:

- Some jurisdictions required missing persons to have resided within the province of their jurisdiction, while others required the missing individuals to have disappeared from their jurisdiction.
- Many jurisdictions insisted that Missing Persons Reports be made by family members, while others accepted such reports from friends or acquaintances.
- Reports on missing adults were frequently processed, retained, and followed up in a manner different from that for missing juveniles.
- Many victims were "recurrent missings."

In the case of recurrent missings police sometimes assume the person will return again and, therefore, he/she is not treated as a true missing. In one instance, a missing person mistakenly reported to be "located" and alive by a police agency in Texas was later confirmed as a Green River victim. There were also instances where files were closed on persons who had been made a ward of the court without verification of their whereabouts; hence, it was not known if they were missing. Only a thorough knowledge of how missing persons are handled by different police agencies gives some assurance of avoiding pitfalls which might prevent identification of a victim.

Missing persons files are not solely the responsibility of police. Many missing persons are not reported or their absence is not closely monitored by friends or relatives. It was not uncommon for Green River victims to be "out of touch" for long periods of time and, hence, natural for them not to be considered missing. These "missing persons" would not be reported by relatives or acquaintances during these lapses of contact. This was a consequence of their lifestyle as "street people" or having connections with prostitution or both.

Other specific problems in the Green River investigation included the public perception of Green River victims as prostitutes and the stigma attached to prostitution. Some families of unreported missing persons were reluctant to admit that their daughter might be connected with this lifestyle. Some felt that reporting a missing person was an admission that the individual was dead and implied a loss of hope. Other families were reluctant to deal with the police and found that dealing with a neutral agency such as a crisis clinic, missing persons group, or the Medical Examiner's Office was preferable. In some instances the family had lost contact and did not know the individual was truly missing. Families often waited for a magic date," such as a parent's birthday, a holiday, or some other date the victim usually contacted them, before they reported a person missing. Other families were confused because they thought that initial contact with the police had constituted a formal report. Still others assumed that another member of the family had made the report.

RECORD RETRIEVAL

Difficulties in obtaining accurate or complete dental or health records were encountered because of (1) the young age of the victims, which was associated with mixed dentition; (2) the unstructured lifestyles, resulting in lack of familiarity of families and associates with dental and other health history; and (3) incomplete or poor quality of available records. Recourse was made to family and friends, past employers, welfare agencies, and insurance providers to locate health and dental records. Once common record sources were exhausted, general inquiries were directed to local community clinics and hospitals known to provide free or low-income care. Adult and juvenile detention facilities were a fertile source of dental records.

The majority of records were obtained by Green River Task Force detectives who routinely collected them as a part of their followup on missing persons determined to be possible victims. In a few cases, this involved locating dentists who had retired and moved from the area. In only one instance were records known to have been destroyed by a health care institution. All copies of dental records of missing persons have been retained on file at the Medical Examiner's Office and continue to serve as a valuable resource to future identification.

DISCUSSION

Although the Green River investigation has had unique problems, successful identifications were aided by several factors, some of which are transferable to other investigations. These included: (1) creation of a dental/medical records file; (2) task force commitment with special emphasis on intensive police followup of missing women matching the victim profile; (3) consultation with experts in related forensic fields; (4) community, professional, and news media cooperation; and (5) cooperation between police and the Medical Examiner.

The dental/medical file and task force commitment deserve special comment. Most significant to successful identification was the creation of a dental/medical records file based on intensive screening of records from missing women. Testament to the excellent screening done by task force detectives was the fact that in many instances, records were available months before the remains were discovered. This anticipation of victims often led to immediate identification once the victim's remains were found. A continuous effort, sometimes over periods of months, was necessary to locate and gather sufficient records to insure and confirm identification of some of these victims. In addition to the 33 Green River related cases identified from these files, 6 other unidentified bodies, 5 from Washington State and 1 from Montana, were identified.

A technique most helpful for accurate record comparison was for postmortem dental films to duplicate angulation of antemortem records. This allowed accurate comparison of dental characteristics and became critical in those instances of limited or poor quality antemortem records. In those identifications dependent on fine morphological characteristics of tooth and bone morphology, the availability of original radiographic material rather than copies was critical.

Utilization of the skills of a forensic anthropologist can also be critical in generating information leading to identification. Although a physical anthropologist's skills are generally sufficient for examination of skeletal material, the observations of a forensic science specialist are sometimes invaluable.

We found institutions and individual dentists and health care providers most generous in their support of our efforts. The local dental society assisted in charting dental record files into computer forms.

Victim data were placed on computer systems including NCIC, CPIC, California Criminal Justice System, and WACIC. Unfortunately, use of such systems did not generate successful identification of any victims. The success or failure of all such computer systems is dependent upon (1) missing persons being reported, (2) timely entry into the system, and (3) removal from the system once the missing person is located. Another problem in many locations is that compliance with statutory requirements for retrieval of missing persons' dental records often cannot be enforced.

Other techniques were used to generate possible leads to identities. Among these was publishing dental charts and descriptions of remains in periodicals of state and local dental societies. Facial reconstructions were done in six instances, and facial profile sketches deduced from lateral skull X-rays were accomplished in three instances. Although these efforts proved unsuccessful in this particular investigation, they should be considered when conventional efforts fail. The main use of reconstruction was considerable media appeal, which provided a forum for drawing public attention to the identification difficulties.

CONCLUSION

The Green River Investigation is currently the longest running serial murder investigation in U.S. history. Little has been reported on methods of identification of serial murder victims. Although each serial homicide investigation has idiosyncrasies particular to that case, it is hoped that our experiences will be of value to other investigators.

Criminal Personality Profiling: An Outcome and Process Study

ANTHONY J. PINIZZOTTO & NORMAN J. FINKEL

C*riminal personality profiling*—formerly the stock-in-trade of whodunit writers, whose fictional detectives transformed crime scene facts into a portrait of the perpetrator—has itself been transformed in the last 20 years from fiction to fact. As the use of criminal personality profiling increases, empirical questions concerning its validity and reliability, and legal questions regarding its applicability, arise. Already one court has allowed partial reading of a personality profile to be introduced into testimony.

The actual origins of criminal profiling are obscure. During World War II, the Office of Strategic Services (OSS) employed William Langer, a psychiatrist, to profile the personality of Adolf Hitler; Langer described Hitler's personality, diagnosed his condition, and accurately predicted how Hitler would react to defeat. Psychological profiling was first used by the Federal Bureau of Investigation in 1971. In relatively short order, the early and isolated efforts have given way to the current era, where "professional criminal personality profilers" are trained (typically at the Behavioral Science Unit of the FBI in Quantico, Virginia) and are then called upon with increasing frequency to assist in ongoing criminal investigations.

Largely through the FBI's continued and increasing use of profiling, along with the training of profilers, the topic has become defined, its areas of applicability delimited, its procedural steps outlined, and its conceptual underpinnings articulated. A psychological profile focuses attention on individuals with personality traits that parallel traits of others who have committed similar offenses. Through close examination of the crime scene one is able to extrapolate certain relevant psychological material that leads to a profile; said another way, the forensic investigator will let the entire crime scene, including the victim, tell, in effect, what *kind* of person committed this act.

Once it is determined that a crime exhibits evidence of a mental or personality aberration and profiling is requested, a five-step procedure typically follows: (a) a comprehensive study of the nature of the criminal act and the types of persons who have committed this offense; (b) a thorough analysis of the specific crime scene involved in the case; (c) an in-depth examination of the background and activities of the victim(s) and any known suspect(s); (d) a formulation of the probable motivating factors of all parties involved; and (e) the development of a description of the perpetrator based upon the overt characteristics associated with the person's probable psychological make-up.

Once the material has been collected, referred to as the "WHAT" of the crime, the profiler attempts to determine the "WHY" of the crime: that is, the motivation for each crime scene detail and for the crime itself. A basic premise of profiling is that if the WHAT and the WHY of the crime can be determined, the WHO will follow. Thus, using behavioral, correlational, and psychodynamic principles of psychology, the profiler proceeds from the WHAT to the WHY to the WHO. Factors frequently assessed in a psychological profile of a perpetrator are: sex, age range, marital status, education level, general employment, reaction to police questioning, degree of sexual maturity, whether the individual might strike again, the possibility that this person has committed a similar offense in the past, and whether the perpetrator has a police record.

Rationale for this Study

Given the growing use of the personality profile and the fact that this growing use is largely supported by testimonials and accuracy figures that were not obtained through controlled studies, this research was undertaken to provide more precise answers to both *outcome* and *process* questions.

Regarding outcome, is the profiling of the experts accurate, and to what degree? Said another way, can the professional profilers' claim of expertise in criminal personality profiling be substantiated, when compared against control groups of experienced detectives, clinical psychologists, and college students? This outcome question will be tested using a homicide case and a sex offense case.

The second major question concerns the *process* of criminal personality profiling. That is, how do profilers and nonprofilers organize and recall knowledge related to crime scene investigations? Like the master chess player, mathematician, and physicist, experienced profilers may be able to give meaning to what might appear to the nonprofiler as random, inconsequential, or illogical. It is assumed here that because of this imposed meaning, the expert will organize and recall the details of the crime differently from the novice. In short, both qualitative and quantitative process differences should emerge between profilers and nonprofilers.

The specific research hypotheses include the following:

1. Profilers will write more detailed, informative profiles than any other group.
2. Detectives, who are trained to look at and examine every detail on a crime scene, will recall a greater number of details than any other group.
3. Profilers, who are trained to discriminate relevant from extraneous details, will recall a greater number of details that are necessary and important to writing a profile.
4. Profilers will describe more accurately the suspect in the sex offense than in the homicide offense. In the sex offense case, the profilers are supplied with a victim statement that generally gives a narrative of the crime as it occurred, but in the homicide case, no such witness statement is typically available.
5. In the professional groups (profilers, detectives, and psychologists), (a) profilers will examine each detail of a crime scene, attempting to give reason for each detail—as well as the motivation for the overall act; (b) detectives will look more to the motivation of the act (crime) itself without looking at the individual reasons for each detail on the crime scene; and (c) psychologists will examine some individual details and attempt to determine motivation, but they will remain unclear as to which details are of significance.

METHOD

Subjects

Of the 28 subjects used in this study, four (Group A, Expert/Teacher) were profiling experts who train police detectives in profiling at the FBI Academy in Quantico, Virginia. Each of these subjects is or was an agent with the Federal Bureau of Investigation. They share a combined total of 42 years of profiling, with a range of 4–17 years experience. The authors were unable to locate sufficient numbers of expert/teachers who were both actively engaged in profiling and willing to cooperate in this study. Two of the four designated expert/teachers used in the study are no longer involved in profiling.

Six subjects were police detectives from different police agencies across the country who have been specially trained in personality profiling (Group B, Profilers). The course of studies involved 1 year at the Behavioral Science Unit of the Federal Bureau of Investigation in Quantico. These six profilers have a combined total of 65 years as detectives in law enforcement (range = 7–15), and 14 years of combined experience in profiling (range = 1–6).

Six detectives (Group C, Detectives) from a large metropolitan city police department made up another subject group. Though these detectives have no training in personality profiling, they are experienced police investigators in both homicide and sex offenses. They share a combined total of 93 years in the police department and a combined total of 57 years experience in criminal investigations (range = 6–15).

Six clinical psychologists (Group D, Psychologists), naive to both criminal profiling and criminal investigations, were used. The psychologists share a combined total of 85 years as practicing clinicians (range = 7–24). For all of the subjects in Groups A, B, C, and D, participation was voluntary and no remuneration was received.

Six undergraduate students (Group E, Students) from a large metropolitan university naive to both personality profiling and criminal investigations were used. These students were drawn from several general psychology classes. The average age of the students was 19. For the students, participation in this study was voluntary, and each was given $10 for participation in this study. All of the subjects were treated in accordance with APA's Ethical Standards.

Materials

Two crime scene investigations of "closed cases" were used: these cases involve actual crimes that have been solved (an individual has been arrested, charged, and convicted of the crime). One case involved a homicide and the other involved a sex offense.

The materials in the homicide case included:

1. Fourteen black-and-white crime scene photographs.
2. Information concerning the victim of the crime (victimology report). This material was compiled from statements given by relatives and friends as found in the police reports. The victim data included race, age, education, residence, physical disabilities, drug and alcohol use, and reputation, according to friends.

3. Autopsy and toxicology reports. These reports were provided by the medical examiner's office, and included the cause, manner, and mode of death. The toxicological examination of body fluids and organs is performed in order to determine if any chemical agents were present in the victim's system that would be related to his or her death.

4. Crime scene reports. These included the report of the first uniformed officer on the scene, the detectives' reports, and the follow-up investigative reports as provided by the police department. These reports included date and time the body was discovered, and by whom, the area where the body was found, and the condition and arrangement of the body.

The materials in the sex offense case included:

1. Detailed victim statement. The victim's statement of what happened and what the offender did and said, as she relayed it to the investigative detectives, was combined with the crime scene reports. The crime scene reports included the reports of the first uniformed officer on the scene, the detectives' reports, and the follow-up investigative reports as provided by the police department. Included in the report were the date and area of the sexual offense, the race, age, and occupation of the victim, as well as the events that led up to the rape, the rape itself, and the events that followed the rape.

2. Victimology. This comprised information concerning the victim of the crime. This material was offered by the victim herself as found in the initial police report. This information included the race, age, and occupation of the victim. Her physical appearance and personality as described by her friends as well as by the detectives who interviewed her were also given. A history of the victim's alcohol and drug use was included.

For both cases, the materials were sanitized to protect the identities of both parties involved in the crime, as well as the police agencies. This unavoidable necessity meant that some material ordinarily available to profilers (e.g., maps of geographical area and neighborhood) was absent here. Prior to final selection of the cases, a search of newspaper and magazines from the areas in which the subjects resided was made. This search revealed no major news coverage of either case. As a check on "prior familiarity," all subjects were instructed (on the Information Sheet each completed) as follows: "During any part of this experiment, if you feel you are at all familiar with either of these cases, please inform the experimenter immediately."

Procedure

The study was administered in six stages.

1. All members of each group (A, B, C, D, E) were given either the homicide or the sex offense case to read. The cases were given in a balanced order. The subjects were told to read all the information concerning the particular case before them, and that after they completed the reading, they would be asked some questions concerning the materials.

2. Next, each subject was asked to cover all the material and to write down as many details of the case as the subject was able to recall.

3. At the completion of the recall of details task, the subjects were asked to follow a two-step procedure. Using the list of details that the subject recalled and wrote in Stage 2, the subject was asked to (a) write down all those details from the crime scene that you feel are *necessary and important* to be used in writing a profile concerning the characteristics and traits of the kind or type of person who would commit such an act as the one about which you just read, and (b) write down the *reason why you feel these details are important*, that is, what these details tell you about the person who committed this particular crime.

4. Each subject was then given the case jacket again and was asked to write a profile of the type of person who committed the crime they had just read and to give as much detail as possible. This step was recorded on audio tape.

5. Next, each subject was given a multiple choice question sheet which consisted of 20 questions about the suspect. These questions asked about the suspect's gender, age, race, and residence in relation to the occurrence of the crime; employment data regarding type of occupation and work habits; suspect's use of alcohol and illicit drugs; vehicle; victim-offender relationship; likelihood that the offender committed similar crimes in the past as well as the likelihood that this particular offender will commit a similar act in the future. Five of these 20 questions were not scored because there were no correct answers to these questions (e.g., level of confidence in the subject's own prediction that the offender had a police record). For the remaining 15 questions that were scorable, the gender question had only two choices, whereas the other questions had 4–8 choices, with a total of 69 possible choices for the 15 questions.

6. The last step was a lineup task. Five written descriptions of possible suspects were given to each subject. From the five descriptions, the subjects were

asked to order each of them, ranging from one to five, with number one being the suspect whom the subject thinks committed the crime, and number five being the person the subject thinks is least likely to have committed the crime. These descriptions of possible suspects varied in the number of correct and incorrect items.

Having completed Step 6 for the first case, each subject was asked to follow the same procedure—this time, analyzing the second crime.

The only procedural differences occurred with Group A, the expert/teacher profilers. Specifically, they were not asked to complete Sections 2 and 3 of the procedure, as the purpose of using these expert/teacher profilers was only to determine a base line for a comparison of the responses of the expert profilers with the other groups.

One section was performed by the expert/teacher profilers alone. At the completion of the Response Questionnaire Concerning Offender form for both the homicide and sex offense cases, the expert/teacher profilers were asked to complete the Probability Rating form in two different ways. First, these subjects were asked to rate their answers to the Response Questionnaire Concerning Offender form along an 11-point continuum. The weight given to each response was designated as: 0 = *impossible*; 5 = *uncertain*; 10 = *certain*. The subjects were informed that their responses could be placed at any point along the 11-point continuum. The expert/teacher profilers rated their answers to the questionnaire first, then they were asked to rate the remaining possible answers in that same question. In the second step, the expert/teacher profilers were supplied with the correct answer to each of the questions of the Response Questionnaire Concerning Offender form. The subjects were informed that the correct answer was to be regarded as a 10 on the same 0–10 scale, with 10 being regarded as certain. Knowing the correct answer to each of these 15 questions, the subjects were to score each of the other possible choices in its relative reasonableness as correct answers.

The Profile as an Investigative Aid

After all subjects in all groups had completed these procedures, five representative profiles, one from each of the five groups (expert/teachers, profilers, detectives, psychologists, and students), were selected in the following manner:

The longest and the shortest profiles were eliminated, and then one was randomly selected from the remaining profiles. The profiles contained no information that would link the author to a particular group (i.e., expert/teacher, profiler, detective, psychologist, student). Five detectives from a large, Eastern, metropolitan police department, who were not involved in any other part of this study, were given these representative profiles and the following instructions:

> Looking at the following five profiles, which profile might provide you with some assistance if you were investigating this homicide? Please rank order these profiles from one to five, with number one being the profile you feel might best assist you and number five being the profile which you feel would be of least assistance in your investigation.

RESULTS

Outcome Analysis

The Written Profile

If expertise differs between the profiler group and the nonprofiler groups of detectives, psychologists, and students, the written profiles, of all the outcome and process measures, should reflect such differences. It is, after all, the written profile task which is most representative of what profilers actually do in their work. It was hypothesized that the profilers would write richer (i.e., more detailed) and more accurate profiles than subjects in the nonprofiler groups. The profiles that were written by each subject in each of the four groups were analyzed for (a) the *time* spent doing the report, (b) the *length* of the report, (c) the *number of predictions* made concerning the offender, the number of those predictions that were (d) general or (e) specific in nature, the number of those predictions which were (f) confirmable and nonconfirmable (i.e., able to be determined by the police reports as a correct statement), and the number of (g) accurate predictions where the predictions were confirmable.

For both the homicide and the sex offense cases, the profiles written by the professional profilers were indeed richer than the nonprofiler groups of detectives, psychologists, and students.

For the cases variable, there were significant main effects for five of the dependent measures ($p < .05$), with only the "time spent writing the report" and the ""length of the report" variables failing to reach significance. Subjects in all groups recalled more details and made more predictions concerning the sex offense case than they did in the homicide case, with the profilers and psychologists showing the largest increases.

Looking at the detectives' rankings of which profile might best assist in an investigation, 80% of these independent detectives ranked the expert/teacher profile as the one they felt would assist their investigation the most; 80% ranked the profile written by the professional profilers as their second choice. This was followed by 80% selecting the detective's profile as their third choice, and 80% selecting the psychologist's profile as their fourth choice. There was 100% agreement that the student profile ranked fifth of the five choices.

Correct Responses

Accuracy measures for the Response Questionnaire Concerning Offender were computed on the basis of 15 possible correct answers, and all groups were significantly above chance performance in terms of the number of correct responses. A chi-square test found significant difference among the groups for the sex offense case; such difference was not found for the homicide case. Further analyses for the sex offense case showed that profilers scored significantly better than the other three groups combined; that the law enforcement groups of profilers and detectives did better than non-law-enforcement groups of psychologists and students; and that the professional groups of profilers, detectives, and psychologists did better than the nonprofessional group of students.

An analysis of the specific questions for each case shows that profilers achieved higher group scores for the sex offense case in questions dealing with the age of the offender, the education of the offender, age, and condition of the offender's automobile, and the victim-offender relationship. The profilers did not achieve higher scores than subjects in the other groups in these same categories for the homicide case, however. It was the detective group that scored higher in the homicide questions dealing with the offender's employment and the offender's residence in relation to the crime scene.

Accuracy Scores

The subjects' responses on the Response Questionnaire Concerning Offender form were analyzed in a different way by first deriving two sets of "accuracy" scores for each subject. The argument for this type of analysis is that all "incorrect" answers are not equally incorrect: Some incorrect answers are closer to the mark; others are far afield. Hence, the subjects' responses were converted into accuracy scores using weighted values for each of their 15 responses to the 15 scorable questions. Only the profiler versus student group comparison was significant.

Lineup Rankings

The question here was this: Would profilers be more apt to identify the correct offender from the lineup than would the other groups? In the sex offense case, the expert/teachers were accurate in picking out the offender 100% of the time, and the profilers were accurate 83% of the time. As for the other groups, accuracy is lower, and declines as we move from detectives (67%) to psychologists (50%) to students (16%).

Results varied between the sex offense and the homicide case in group ability to recognize the correct offender from the lineup. First, the percentages of correctly recognizing the homicide offender from a lineup were lower than the sex offense case for all the groups. And second, although the expert/teachers and profilers were more accurate than the other groups for the sex offense case lineup, these results were not reproduced for the homicide case lineup.

Process Analysis

Recall of Details

Given that the profilers scored better than the other three groups for the sex offense case, the question can be asked as to what accounts for these differences. Are the profilers processing the information given to them in ways that are different from the other three groups?

The first process area examined is the recall of details concerning the crime. From the lengthy list of details recalled by each subject, the number of correct details was tabulated for each case. In the sex offense case, there was no significant difference among the groups, although a significant difference did result for the homicide case, with profilers recalling more details than the nonprofiler groups of detectives, psychologists, and students. As to the hypothesis that detectives, of all the groups, would recall the greatest number of details, this was not confirmed. It is profilers who recall the most details.

Details as Necessary and Important

The questions that arise here are these: (a) Do profilers, as opposed to the nonprofiler groups (detectives, psychologists, students), cite more details as necessary and important, and (b) do they make different types of attributions, and come up with different kinds of correlations or implications from these details? As it turns out, profilers do cite significantly more details as necessary and important than nonprofilers for the sex offense and the homicide cases.

To answer the second question, the subjects' answers to why they thought these details were necessary and important and what types of attributions they made from these details were evaluated and placed in one of three categories: (1) *specific psychological attributions given to a specific detail of the crime scene* (specific-specific); (2) *broad, global, and general attributions given to a specific detail of the crime scene* (specific-global); (3) *broad, global, and general psychological attributes given to the general crime scene, without regard to specific details of the crime* (global-global).

To check the reliability of assigning these responses to one of the three categories, a second rater conducted an independent evaluation of these responses. The rater's results were consistent with the first author's.

Profilers, it can be argued, would attend to more specific details of the crime scene and make more specific attributions about the offender. The results do not support this hypothesis. For the sex offense case, profilers used the specific-specific category 42% of the time, whereas detectives used it 49% and psychologists 52% of the time; for the homicide case, the percentages were 61%, 57%, and 56% for the three groups, respectively. In both cases, the profilers, detectives, and psychologists most frequently used the specific-specific category. Although the profilers are not processing the data in qualitatively different ways from the nonprofilers, as the numbers show, they are doing more of it.

DISCUSSION

Concerning the outcome issue, professional profilers are more accurate (i.e., more correct answers, higher-accuracy scores, more correct lineup identifications) for the sex offense case than nonprofilers, but these accuracy differences dissipate when we look at the homicide case. There were, however, significant outcome differences between profiler and nonprofiler groups for the homicide case in all the analyses of the written profile.

While the overall outcome superiority of the profilers is most likely indicative of greater expertise, it must be kept in mind that an "investment" factor could also be invoked to explain these results. Psychologists and students may see this task as an interesting exercise, whereas profilers, and detectives, perhaps, see it as the "blood and guts" of their professions, and therefore generate lengthier profiles and spend more time on the task.

What accounts for the fact that profilers do better than nonprofilers for the sex offense case, and the fact that the outcome advantage is muted for the homicide case? One possibility that cannot be overlooked is the effect of sanitizing the crime reports. In compliance with the requests of the police agencies that offered these criminal cases, the cases had to be sanitized to the extent that no one reading them could identify the police agencies, the victims, or the offenders. Consequently, some of the very detailed information concerning the victims had to be deleted from the case file.

All of the profilers spontaneously mentioned that data were missing, whereas none of the other subjects mentioned it. Perhaps the absence of a very detailed and extensive report affected the profilers more, and particularly for the homicide case.

A second possibility is that there was more information, and more accurate information, for the profiler to work with in the sex offense case than in the homicide case. In sex offense crimes, the victim is available to offer details concerning the crime. The victim can relate what the offender did prior to the actual assault, during the assault, and following the assault. The very approach that the sex offender uses on his victim will tell the investigator a great deal about the offender. As Hazelwood states: "Through an analysis of the offender's verbal, sexual, and physical behavior, it may be possible to determine what needs were being served and to project personality characteristics of the individual having such needs." This information is lost when the victim is not able to relate to the investigator just exactly what happened, as in a homicide case. For the homicide case, the profiler must reconstruct the crime with no verbal help from the victim, and this increases the probability of inaccuracies. One area of future research might examine the possible differences among profilers' offender profiles for homicide cases that have no witness to the crime and homicide cases shere a witness to the homicide is available.

A third possibility as to why the profilers completed a more accurate profile on the sex offense case than they did on the homicide case relates to the peculiarities of this particular homicide case: That is, in a few but significant ways, the offender did not fit the base-rates. Two common base-rates that are frequently used are the victim's age and the victim's race in order to suggest the age and race of the offender. It has been found that violent crimes are generally perpetrated upon members of one's own age group and are intraracial in nature. Thus, where a white victim, approximately 25 years of age, is found murdered, the investigators might begin by narrowing the possible field of suspects to a Caucasian between the ages of 18 and 28. Because most violent crimes are committed by males, the profile might also suggest that—if there is no specific reason to think the crime was committed by a female—the offender will be a male. From these base-rates that suggest age, gender, and race, further assumptions and attributions are made. For example, if the offender is a white male between the ages of 18 and 22, some assumptions concerning his education, employment, marital status, and military record can be suggested.

What is problematic in this homicide case is that the offender did not fall within those age base-rates. Though he was a white male, his actual age was much higher than the victim's age. If the offender had been the same age as the victim, given the type of murder and defilement of the body, it would be most unlikely for this offender to have been married. Falling outside the base-rates again, this offender was, in fact, married. The errors of the expert/teacher profilers and the errors of the professional profilers were errors generally involving these base-rates. Their responses were within the distribution of the base-rates for such crimes. This same base-rate explanation might also be applied to the homicide lineup exercise. Most groups chose Profile D as their first choice (i.e., the profile that ranked fourth in correctness) because this profile fit the general and accepted base-rates in certain major categories for this kind of crime better than any of the other profiles.

It may seem surprising that the accuracy scores for the nonprofiler groups of detectives and psychologists came as close to the profilers as they did. Why were not greater differences observed between profilers and the nonprofiler groups? Two answers to this question are offered. The first is found in the very instruments used to test these differences. The use of a multiple choice questionnaire to determine measures of accuracy favors the nonprofiler groups because it gives the subjects cues as to what the possible answers are: It gives the subjects "categories" (i.e., the focal area of the question) that they might not ordinarily think about, and it gives a set number of possible choices. The correct responses of the nonprofiler groups may be artificially raised so that the true differences between profilers and the two nonprofilers groups of detectives and psychologists may be somewhat muted. This possibility seems to be borne out when a close examination of the written profile is made. It is in the written profile task—when a blank page was given to the subjects and they were required to write a profile without the assistance of cues—where significant outcome differences emerged. In the written profile, the more representative task of criminal personality profiling, the profiler group was clearly superior.

A final point on why the differences in outcome are not significantly higher for the profiler group than the nonprofiler groups: the small number of subjects. With a larger sample, the differences are more easily and more accurately measured.

Concerning the process issue, in general, profilers do not appear to process the material in qualitatively different ways from nonprofilers in their construction of profiles. There are, however, numerous quantitative process differences that favor the profiler over all nonprofiler groups for both cases.

It was hypothesized that the detectives would recall a greater number of details than any other group, given their training and orientation. A second hypothesis was that the profilers would recall more details that were necessary and important to profiling.

The first hypothesis was not confirmed: Detectives did not recall more details overall; rather, both law enforcement groups (profilers and detectives) recalled significantly more details than the non-law-enforcement groups of psychologists and students. Perhaps, as the expert/novice literature suggests, it is the law enforcement agents' familiarity with these kinds of cases and crime scenes that allows them to organize the information in ways that facilitate recall.

The second hypothesis was confirmed: As expected, the profilers did recall more details considered to be necessary and important to profiling for both cases. Combining these two findings suggests that recall per se is not the crucial factor in explaining why profilers generate more accurate predictions than detectives; rather, it is the profiler's greater ability to extract and designate more details as necessary and important than the detectives that makes the difference. Said another way, it is not a memory difference, but a higher-order extracting difference that is primarily associated with outcome accuracy.

It has been suggested that the process profilers use in deriving their profile follows a WHAT to WHY to WHO pattern. This is to say that once the details of the crime have been collected (WHAT) and the motivations for those particular details have been determined (WHY), the type of offender (WHO) can be suggested. Because we asked all the subjects to tell us their *reasons* for why a detail was important, the processes profilers and other groups used were clearly identifiable. Our analysis confirms that this motivational process is used for examining some details of the crime, but it is not the only process that is engaged. Two others have been identified in this work. Where the WHAT-WHY-WHO process is *motivational* (i.e., seeking the motivation for a crime scene detail) the second process can be described as *correlational*, a WHAT to WHO process. The third process is also correlational, but it involves a second-order correlation: It can be described as a WHAT to WHO followed by further assumptions (i.e., correlations) based on the first WHO prediction. In other words, this third process can be seen as a WHAT to WHO with a correlation/attribution loop.

The second of these processes, the WHAT to WHO, basically involves the profilers' use of correlations and crime base-rates. In knowing, for example, such a specific detail (WHAT) of a crime as the race of the victim, the profilers skip the motivational aspect (WHY) and suggest the same race for the offender (WHO). Psychological reasons or motivational causes (WHY) are not considered in this type of decision on the part of the profilers. Likewise, in the third of these processes, the WHAT to WHO loop, correlations and base-rates continue to be used. For example, given that a first-level prediction has been made based on base-rates for an offender's age, then a second-level prediction based on base-rates for marital status is made. Again, these assumptions are based not on motivational causes (WHY), but move in an "if-then, if-then" correlational sequence from specific details of the crime (WHAT) toward a more specific portrait of the offender (WHO).

From the results obtained in this work, four suggestions are offered to improve accuracy. The first is to improve the base-rates by increasing the number of details available concerning offenders. The more offenders there are that contribute to the sample population of "homicide offenders" or "sex offenders," the more detailed and specific information is available about these individuals. Perhaps when larger samples are examined, the predictions that are made on these base-rates may increase in validity and in reliability.

The second suggestion is to develop a system of matrices of specific details for crime scenes in order to create convergent and discriminative lines for certain predictors. For example, on a particular kind of crime scene, do certain details (independent lines) tend to converge on a more youthful offender—even when the age of the victim generally might lead one to predict an older offender? And, third, while the offender's motivation to commit the crime might remain a mystery— even to the offender, one area of research that would be of assistance to profiling would examine means by which offender motivation (WHY) can support or confirm the crime base-rates that are used in profiling—or, indeed, direct the profiler's line of thought about a particular offender.

A fourth suggestion derives from the observation that certain profilers were more accurate and more keenly perceptive with certain tasks than they were with others. For example, one profiler studied the medical examiner's report twice as long as any other profiler and incorporated more of this material into that particular written profile. Another profiler spent a greater amount of time studying and reviewing the crime scene photographs. Close examination with a magnifying glass revealed details others missed. A third profiler spent more time discussing the victimology report. Since individual profilers appear to enjoy certain areas of expertise within the general field of profiling, it seems plausible that more accurate and richer profiles would result from "group profiling" than from individual profiling. Empirical testing could determine whether too many cooks (profilers) spoil or enrich the broth.

From the results found here, a more elaborated conceptualization of the process of profiling needs to be developed. It has been shown in this work, as it has been theorized elsewhere, that profiling is a complex process. It involves more than a simple, one-level analysis of crime scene details (i.e., the WHAT to WHY to WHO). The WHAT to WHO and the WHAT to WHO loop are two additional levels of analysis that are used. Thus, a criminal personality profile appears to be the result of a complex, multilevel series of attributions, correlations, and predictions. In conceptualizing this process, the theory of profiling—yet to be fully developed—ought to reflect these complexities. In this regard, conceptual and theoretical development, consistent with emerging empirical results, is needed.

In a field still in its nascent stage, the population of "experts" is limited. The sample size of experts was small (i.e., there were only 6 profilers and 4 expert profilers used in this study). The small sample may have limited the significance of the results (i.e., some results failing to reach significance, or reaching only moderate significance) where larger sample sizes might reveal even greater differences. The limited sample size also raises questions of the representativeness of the sample and the generalizability of the results; cautions are thus warranted. A replication of this study, using more subjects, is another recommendation.

Though significant results were obtained for the sex offense case, not all results reached significance for the homicide case. Part of the explanation offered for this variance in results was the atypical nature of the homicide case. Specifically, many personal aspects of this particular offender in the homicide case were not consistent with existing crime base-rates. This explanation, though plausible, remains untested to date. Future research in criminal personality profiling should address this issue by using greater numbers of homicide and sex offense cases, as well as cases where profilers neither claim expertise nor typically profile. In the absence, yet, of such studies, generalizations to all sex offense or all homicide cases are not warranted.

Handwritten annotations (top margin):

Signature : ① openly displayed ② sexually degrading positions ③ insertion of foreign object

SIGNATURE ANALYSIS

Handwritten annotation:

Signature allows killer to act out fantasies.

Signature Murders:
A Report of Several Related Cases

Handwritten annotations (right margin):

Signature: Actions above & beyond the murder.

MO: modus operandi actions necessary to commit the murder.

ROBERT D. KEPPEL

For purposes of linking murder cases, police investigators traditionally have searched for certain factors that were similar from one case to another, commonly called *Modus Operandi*, method of operation, or M.O. of the killer. The way a murder is committed (the M.O.) is controlled by the actions of the killer based, to some extent, on the victim's response to the situation. For example, if the slayer in one case easily controls the victim, the killer may not change his M.O. in the next case unless he/she has trouble controlling the victim. A killer may use strangulation in the first case and, in a subsequent case, to accommodate an overcoming resistance by the victim, use a firearm because the strangling method was unsuccessful. Therefore, the M.O. of the killer includes only those actions necessary to commit the murder and can change over time as the killer discovers that some things he/she does are more effective.

There are other crime-scene indicators that link murders even when the M.O. changes. Many sexually sadistic repetitive killers, for example, go beyond the actions necessary to commit a murder. They are not satisfied with just committing the murder, but have a compulsion to demonstrate a personal expression unique only to that particular slayer. The killer's personal expression is commonly referred to as his/her "signature" or "calling card."

There is a small but growing literature in the criminal justice field that differentiates *modus operandi* and signature or trademark. Some of those works

403

deal with highly selective elements of murder investigation, for example, the sexually sadistic killer or the killer who commits necrophilic acts.

Another source of information that highlights the differences between M.O. and signature is the case law on murder convictions. Although the M.O. and signature of a killer have not been studied empirically, they are a common source of appellate issues raised by those convicted of murder. The case law is replete with appeals that attack the efficacy of the signature aspects of murders. Frequently, they illustrate that the successful linkage of murder cases to the same person is dependent upon how clearly the elements of a killer's signature are found at the murder scenes and that the killer's core, or basic, signature never changes from one murder to another.

Unlike the characteristics of an offender's M.O., the signature remains constant. However, a signature may evolve over time. A necrophilic killer, for example, may perform more and more postmortem mutilation from one murder to the next. With experience, the elements of the original personal expression become more fully developed. Unfortunately, a signature is not always recognized at the crime scene because of decomposition of the body or interruptions to the killer's routine, like the presence of unexpected witnesses.

The etiology of the signature has been described as the person's violent fantasies which are progressive in nature and contribute to thoughts of committing extremely violent behavior. As a person dreams and thinks of his/her fantasies over time, he/she develops a need to express those violent fantasies. Most serial killers have lived with their fantasies for years before they finally bubble to the surface and become translated into deeds . When the killer finally acts out, some aspect of the murder will demonstrate his/her unique personal expression that has been replayed in fantasies over and over again. It's not enough just to consummate a murder, killers must often act out fantasies in some manner over and beyond inflicting death producing injuries. For example, some lust killers have a need to bludgeon to the point of overkill, carve on the body, or leave messages written in blood. They may re-arrange the position of the victim, performing post-mortem activities which suit their own personal desires and, in essence, leave their psychopathological calling card. The following three murders exemplify the signature aspects of a serial killer.

BACKGROUND

The Bellevue and Kirkland vicinity of King County, Washington averaged only one murder per year for the ten-year period, 1981–1990. Within sixty-seven days, the locale experienced three separate atypical murders within a five mile radius of each other.

Prior to charging George W. Russell with three counts of first degree murder, deputy prosecutors from the King County Prosecutor's Office, Seattle, Washington, contacted this author and requested an analysis of the three murders. Their main question was: *were all three murders committed by the same person?* The analysis could not include any information about Mr. Russell or evidence about why he was connected to any one case. Although there was physical evidence that ultimately connected each case Russell, there was no physical evidence found, such as hairs and fibers, that connected one murder to another. The materials used for the analysis were police reports, crime scene diagrams, autopsy reports, and photographs.

VICTIM NUMBER 1

On June 23, 1990, just after 7:30 A.M., the body of a murdered female was found in a refuse area behind a restaurant, which is in a heavily-frequented area of the city. The nude body was clearly posed and placed in an open, displayed manner as though her killer intentionally left her in that particular spot so she would be discovered quickly. While she was lying on her back, her left foot was crossed over the instep of her right ankle. The victim's head was turned to the left with a snack food lid resting ominously on top of her right eye. Her arms were bent at the elbow and crossed over her abdomen with her hands gently touching, one inside the other. In her hand was a Douglas fir cone. Even though her corpse was found nude, the victim's gold metal watch was on her left wrist and her gold choker chain with a crescent shaped white pendant was around her neck. The surface of the garbage area was a cement rectangle, bordered by the asphalt pavement of the parking lot and a wooden fence. The refuge area was uncommonly clean, having just been swept by someone. A pile of debris was within 3 feet of the victim's head. In front of the trash compactor, which was located inside and in the back of the fenced area, several blood stains and chips of fingernail polish from the victim were found. One could assume from this evidence that the killer had initially taken the victim further into the garbage area, which would have been more secluded, but instead, displayed the victim prominently back toward the entrance so she could be clearly seen.

It was determined at the scene that the victim had sustained wounds indicative of strangulation, severe blows to the right eye, nose and mouth, and abrasions, postmortem in nature, to the right arm, right breast, both hips, knees, and feet. The postmortem abrasions were likely produced when the killer dragged the victim about twenty feet along the parking lot surface to inside the dumpster's fence. Her antemortem abrasions were defense wounds.

The estimated time of death determined by the medical examiner was between 2:30 A.M. and 5:20 A.M.. A late night worker of the restaurant had dumped garbage at 3:15 A.M., and the body was not there.

The autopsy examination revealed blunt impact injuries to the head resulting in a fracture to the right base of the cranium, and blunt injuries to the abdomen causing a laceration of the liver. The medical examiner found the victim's stomach empty, and her toxicological screen read a blood alcohol level of .14. Forcible rape had transpired as evidenced by the victim's anal canal being severely lacerated by a foreign object. Also, sperm were located in her vaginal vault.

Victim 1 was a white female, 27 years old, 5 feet 7 inches tall, 150 pounds, light brown shoulder-length slightly curly hair, and blue-gray eyes. She was last seen alive on Friday, June 22, 1990 at about 10 P.M. at a popular, trendy single's bar and dance spot. The bar is located about one mile northwest of the restaurant where the victim was found. In the bar's parking lot, the victim's 1984 Chevrolet Camaro was parked, undisturbed, with nothing removed from it. Her purse, which contained her car keys, was found later in the lost-and-found property at the bar.

Detectives surmised that the victim had met someone at the bar. left with that person after 10 P.M., and intended to return and retrieve her purse and car. Sometime later, she was assaulted and murdered at an unknown location and placed behind the restaurant after 3:15 A.M.. They felt that the murder began with many of, the typical characteristics of the common rape-murder, a sexual confrontation gone bad. The circumstances surrounding the victim's disappearance support the theory that the victim left the bar with a date, intending to return. Judging by the number of defense wounds and the blunt force injuries inflicted by the killer, she put up quite a struggle prior to death and left her mark on him. Undoubtedly, the killer had to wash her blood from himself.

The sexually sadistic rape-murderer, however, rarely gets sexual pleasure from the actual killing of the victim. But in this case, and atypical of rape-murderers, the slayer derived his satisfaction from postmortem sexual activities. The killer spent time after death with the victim behind the restaurant, arranging and positioning her body for her final pose, even at the risk of being seen. The victim-offender contact degenerated into a demonstration of complete possessiveness and ultimate degradation. Victim 1, therefore, was not killed by some common rape-murderer because the signature of the crime belonged to someone fitting the hypothetical profile of a necrophilic killer likely to strike again.

ANALYSIS OF VICTIM 1's CASE

Victim 1's murder was compared against the data base of the Washington State Attorney General's Homicide Investigation and Tracking System (HITS).

Her murder case contained many distinctive query features for the HITS computer to match for similar factors. The murder had three unique and significant characteristics which, when taken collectively, did not appear in any of the 2000 murders in the HITS data base up to that time. First, posing a murder victim's body was very rare. The analysis of murder victims revealed that there were only six instances of posing a victim's body or, in other words, only two-tenths of one percent of the total cases. The act of deliberate posing involves positioning the body parts, like posing a person for a photograph. In one case of posing, a deranged killer repositioned mutilated and amputated body parts back in their correct anatomical positions. Posing is not to be confused with staging, because staging refers to manipulation of the scene around the body as well a positioning of the body. For example, a convicted murderer brutally assaulted and killed his wife. To cover up her murder, he then placed her body behind the steering wheel of their motorhome and pushed it over an embankment, staging a murder to look like an accident. Both staging and posing requires that the killer spend extensive time after death re-arranging the scene and positioning the body in a certain way, going beyond the actions necessary to perpetrate the murder.

The second unique component of Victim 1's murder was the disposal of her body. In the research that formed the HITS data base, there were three notable methods found that were used by a killer to dispose of a victim's body. The *most common* method, fifty-eight percent of the time, was when the killer left the body in a position where he was unconcerned about whether the body was found. That usually occurred in domestic violence and argument murders when the body was left in its position immediately after having fallen from the death-producing injuries. A *second* method of disposal, ten percent of the time, was when the killer deliberately concealed or hid the body from discovery. That method of disposal was exemplified by burying the body, putting leaves or branches over the body in the woods, or placing the body in a crawl space of a house. leaving the body in a specific location where the body was guaranteed to be found was the *third* method of disposal, commonly referred to as open and displayed. The third method had only occurred in ten percent of the murder cases examined.

The third significant characteristic of murder in Victim l's case was sexual insertion of a foreign object. A HITS analysis revealed that there were 19 murders in which a foreign object had been inserted for sexual purposes, but the object was unknown and not found. Likewise, there were 6 sexual insertions of a foreign object, and the object was found inserted into a body cavity. Examples in the HITS data base were a zucchini was found in the anus of one victim and dildo was found in the vagina of another victim. Only one percent of 2000 murders, which occurred in the previous ten year period, had any evidence of sexual insertion of foreign objects.

The most extraordinary finding about the characteristics of posing, sexual insertion of a foreign object, and open-display of the body was that, through June 1990, there were no murder victims which had all three present simultaneously except for Victim 1.

VICTIM NUMBER 2

On August 9, 1990, a relative of Victim 2 found her body in the bedroom of her ranch-style, one-story house, forty-seven days after Victim 1's body was discovered. Her home was located in a typical middle-class suburban bedroom community and bordered on each side by neighboring houses.

Victim 2 was the single mother of two daughters, ages 9 and 13, who were asleep in their shared bedroom about 40 feet from the entrance of Victim 2's bedroom. Victim 2 was a white female, 5 feet 2 inches, 108 pounds with collar-length light blond hair. She was last seen entering her residence alone at 2:30 A.M. on August 9, 1990, by a neighbor who was out walking by himself in the warm summer night. Victim 2 had been visiting a bartender at another one of Bellevue's trendy singles' hangout, before going home. Within the city limits of Bellevue, Victim 2's residence was situated less than 2 miles from the restaurant where Victim 1 was found murdered.

Victim 2 was carefully positioned, in open display on top of her bed, a place where anyone would look that was trying to find her. Victim 2 was naked, lying on her back with her legs in the "spread-eagle" position, and wearing a pair of red high-heel shoes. She was splayed completely with her genitals facing the door of the bedroom. Inserted in her vagina was the barrel of an over and under, rifle-shotgun combination with its stock resting across her shoes. The weapon belonged to the victim. Beneath a pillow covering the victim's face, detectives found her head wrapped in a plastic dry cleaning bag. The bag was placed on the victim after she died.

Victim 2 was savagely beaten, to the point of overkill, with an unidentified blunt object that left "forked" or "Y" impressions all over her head. She had two defense wounds, one on each hand. It was determined that the foreign insertion and shoes were placed in and on the victim after death. There was no ransacking of the scene, although jewelry and cash were taken from her bedroom. The door to the victim's bedroom was closed and locked. The mode of entry and exit for her slayer was an open, sliding-glass door to her bedroom. The murder weapon was not found.

ANALYSIS OF VICTIM 2's CASE

Victim 2's murder, like Victim 1, was extremely unusual. HITS analysts found three striking consistencies between the Victim 1 and Victim 2 murders. First, the killer intentionally placed both bodies in locations where they would be readily found. Second, both had been sexually assaulted by the insertion of foreign objects into their body cavities. And third, both victims were obviously left posed by the killer in sexually degrading positions. Based on the extremely rare occurrence of those three factors in the same case and the fact that they occurred in two murders within fifty days of one another in Bellevue, Washington, the logical interpretation was that both murders were the work of the same person.

VICTIM NUMBER 3

The body of Victim 3 was discovered in her ground-level apartment in Kirkland, Washington on September 3, 1990, twenty-four days after the murder of Victim 2. Her apartment was within five miles to the north of the Bellevue restaurant where Victim 1's body was found.

Victim 3 was a white female, 24 years old, 5 feet 4 inches tall. 120 pounds, and with collar-length, dark red hair. She was last seen alive at a restaurant in Kirkland on August 30, 1990 around midnight. She was there with her friends. Like Victim 1 and Victim 2, Victim 3 was known to frequent trendy singles nightspots in the Bellevue area.

Victim 3's nude body was supine on top of her bed. A pillow covered her bloody cranium. Like Victim 1 and Victim 2, the killer clearly posed her. Her legs were spread, a dildo inserted in her mouth, and the book. *More Joy of Sex* propped in her left arm. She had been bludgeoned about the head to the point of overkill. More than 230 small postmortem cutting type wounds were present over the entire surface of her body, including the bottoms of her feet. It appeared that all knives and a ring had been removed by the killer from the residence. Her pickup truck was parked in its normal spot. Again, the murder weapon was not located. There were no signs of forced entry to the apartment. The photo-like display and postmortem mutilation of Victim 3's body signified convincingly that a sexually deviate serial killer was on the loose in the Bellevue area.

DISCUSSION

The following discussion summarizes the author's testimony in the *State of Washington v. George W. Russell*. What were the distinctive aspects of the killer's imprint? First, all three victims were intentionally left so someone would find them. They were not concealed or hidden but were placed in locations where they would be discovered quickly. The killer left them openly displayed. knowing that whoever found them would be shocked, both physically and psychologically.

Secondly, they were posed in sexually degrading positions which demonstrated their vulnerability after death. Moreover, only implements that the killer found at the scene were used. He did this consistently in all three murders. For example, he used a pine cone with Victim 1, red shoes with Victim 2, and a book about sex with Victim 3.

Thirdly, the killer used foreign objects in sexual orifices as part of his protocol. The actual object was absent in Victim 1 's case. The act of sexually inserting foreign objects and leaving them in their cavities evolved from the first murder through the third. It became more of a need for the killer to demonstrate his personal expression by leaving a rifle in Victim 2 and a dildo in Victim 3's mouth.

Fourth, the sequence of all three relatively rare characteristics in each of the three murders exemplified a very extraordinary occurrence. Notwithstanding the fact that the murders were committed in a small geographical area, the chain of interactions between those unique characteristics was the fundamental aspect of the killer's signature.

Fifth, the defense each victim was allowed to put up decreased from the first murder through the third murder. Victim 1 had multiple defense wounds, Victim 2 had two small defense wounds, and Victim 3 did not have any defense wounds.

Sixth, the killer spent an increasing amount of time with each victim after death, re-arranging their bodies in their final death poses. Remaining any amount of time behind the restaurant and at that outdoor scene of Victim 1 was very risky since someone could come upon the scene and interrupt the killer. Therefore, based upon the medical examiner's opinion, very little time was spent arranging Victim 1's body. The killer was with Victim 2 arranging her body a longer period of time than he was with Victim 1. With Victim 2's bedroom door closed, the presence of her children asleep in the house posed no immediate threat of discovery to the killer. Victim 3's apartment was conducive to taking even more time since she lived alone. Assaulting Victim 3 with those fatal strokes, carefully cutting her over 230 times, and dutifully arranging her body took a considerable amount of time, at least more than it took to pose Victim 1 and Victim 2.

Seventh, the number of injuries sustained by each victim increased from Victim l's murder through Victim 3's murder. Victim 1 sustained just enough injuries to cause her death. Victim 2 was beaten severely, more than what was necessary to kill her. Victim 3 was also beaten to the point of overkill and cut extensively The increasing number of injuries reflected the killer's need to impart more extensive harm in an effort to exercise absolute possession by creatively defiling their bodies.

The distinction between M.O. and signature is important, particularly in these cases where the M.O. varied substantially between die first and second murders. For example, the killer's approach in the case of Victim 1 was a typical tavern-date situation, and the victim was lured away from public view so the killer could privately attack. But in the cases of Victims 2 and 3, the medical examiner opined that they were murdered while in bed asleep. With that different approach, the killer changed his M.O. from the first case to the second.

Whether the killer chose to operate in an outdoor versus indoor arena was an additional characteristic of his M.O. The killer's first victim was posed outdoors and subsequent victims were left in their homes. He favored the indoor arena of Victim 2's bedroom, kept that M.O. in the third murder, and, therefore, his M.O. didn't change.

Another M.O. factor was whether or not the killer chose to transport his victims to another location. Transporting Victim 1 was not something the killer continued to do with subsequent victims. By attacking victims in their beds and leaving their bodies there, the killer avoided the uncomfortable and risky situation of transporting a victim's body to another location.

SUMMARY

In these sexually perverted murders, the killer's approach to victims and his selection of the location to leave his victims were preparatory, enabling the killer to carry out his highly personalized fantasies. Thus, evidence left as a direct result of carrying out his fantasy was far more revealing of the killer's nature than his M.O. An increasing number of injuries in each case, spending more and more time after death with each victim, and reducing the participation on the part of a live victim from the first case to the last—in conjunction with open display, posing, and sexual insertion of foreign objects—were the specific factors that identified the signature of the killer. These factors led to the conclusion that they were all killed by the same person.

Detective follow-up work and crime laboratory analyses further corroborated the opinion that the three murders were committed by the same person. First of all, George Russell's blood sample was positively linked by DNA profiles to semen found in the vagina of Victim 1. In addition, Victim 1's blood was found in a pickup truck Russell had borrowed from a friend the night of the murder. At the scene of Victim 2's murder, detectives discovered a pair of victim's panties that contained four head hairs similar in characteristics to the head hair of George

Russell. In searching Russell's apartment, detectives found his gym bag which witnesses described he always carried. Crime laboratory personnel processed the bag and found that it contained one head hair microscopically indistinguishable from the head hair of Victim 3.

Additionally, the signature analyses contributed to the recognition that some items removed by the killer, if found, could connect the killer to two of the murders. Killers frequently remove items belonging to their victims as souvenirs or for monetary gain. Both Victims 2 and 3 were missing rings that were very distinctive. Detectives pursued that information and located Victim 3's ring in Florida by tracing it through friends of Russell. Victim 2's ring was never recovered, but Russell showed what was believed to be her ring to an acquaintance shortly after her murder.

For the experienced homicide investigator, linking murder cases by distinguishing between a killer's M.O. and his/her signature or calling card should not be difficult. What is problematic is that the elements of a signature, at times, can be hidden due to decomposition of the remains and/or contamination of the crime scene. In the Russell murders, the victim's bodies were discovered soon enough after death so the killer's psychopathological imprints were present and not disturbed. Even more importantly, a highly competent forensic pathology staff in the King County Medical Examiner's Office recorded in detail and documented each and every injury to the three bodies, enabling a comprehensive signature analysis to take place. Conversely, in the cases of serial killer Theodore Robert Bundy in the Pacific Northwest, for example. investigators discovered only skeletal parts of seven of the eight suspected victims, making any signature analyses of the murders impossible, at best.

In summary, a killer's method of operation contains those actions that are necessary to commit the murder. They may change from one murder to the next as the killer gains experience and finds more beneficial method of operation from murder to murder. Whatever the killer does beyond the murder, such as mutilating, biting, posing, torturing, among other things, should be the major focus of investigators to determine if murders are committed by the same person. It is the signature that remains the same, whether it is the first offense or one committed ten years later. The ritual may evolve, but the theme persists.

DETERRENCE

The Illusion of Deterrence in Isaac Ehrlich's Research on Capital Punishment

WILLIAM J. BOWERS & GLENN L. PIERCE

In this critique of Professor Ehrlich's recent research on capital punishment, we conclude that he has failed to provide any reliable evidence that the death penalty deters murder. His data are inadequate for the purposes of his analysis and he misapplies the highly sophisticated statistical techniques he employs. We begin with an evaluation of the data he uses to measure the critical variables in his theoretical formulation and then consider flaws in his analysis which would invalidate his conclusions even if his data were adequate. We conclude by explaining how Ehrlich's analysis produces results which seem consistent with the deterrence hypothesis when in fact they are not.

INADEQUACIES IN EHRLICH'S DATA

The credibility of Ehrlich's conclusions depends on the quality of the data he has used. For measures of the variables at the core of his theoretical analysis, he relies on the Uniform Crime Reporting System (UCRS) of the FBI. The behavior he seeks to explain (the dependent variable) is the annual criminal homicide rate for the United States as reported by the UCRS, and his deterrence variables are the rates of arrest, conviction, and execution for homicide, which also come entirely or in part from the UCRS. Only if these data are sound throughout the full time period covered by Ehrlich's analysis do his findings deserve serious consideration.

413

The Dependent Variable

The FBI's national homicide statistics collected in the early years of the UCRS are unreliable. Furthermore, the President's Commission on Law Enforcement and the Administration of Justice warns that "figures prior to 1958, and particularly those prior to 1940, must be viewed as neither fully comparable with nor nearly so reliable as later figures."

Ehrlich indicates that he used "readjusted" estimates of the homicide rate supplied by the FBI. The FBI has periodically adjusted their estimates of offenses for earlier years on the basis of recent data on offenses from jurisdictions that entered the reporting program after 1958. Yet to our knowledge there are no published indications of how the readjustments are performed. In any case, the adjustment of figures for as long ago as 40 years on the basis of the current homicide levels of agencies recently added to the sample is of dubious value.

Less problematic are the willful homicide figures compiled by the Bureau of the Census. Unlike the voluntary reporting system of the FBI, Census reports of willful homicide are mandated by law in each state. The annual collection of mortality statistics including willful homicide began in 1900, 30 years before the beginning of the FBI reporting system. By 1933, all states had met the 90 percent coverage requirement for admission to the national Vital Statistics program. Thus, the Census homicide statistics for the nation have been relatively complete since the early 1930's. Furthermore, the classification of "willful homicide" has remained essentially constant over time. For these reasons, perhaps, the Census homicide figures have gained a reputation for reliability, and have been used more widely than the FBI figures in previous studies of the deterrent effects of capital punishment.

If both FBI and Census data provided accurate estimates of the homicide rate, the statistics would, of course, agree. The figures drawn from the two agencies are reasonably well correlated except during the 1930's, when the FBI's reporting system was in its inception. Notably, the FBI homicide estimates are 15 percent below the Census figures for the 1930's, whereas the difference is only about three percent lower for the period after 1940. By all indications, these discrepancies are the result of inadequate sampling, reporting, and estimating in the early years of the UCRS.

The Deterrence Variables

The FBI data on arrest and conviction rates are even less reliable. The agencies reporting arrest and conviction statistics have remained a relatively small, self-selected subsample throughout most of the period during which these statistics have been compiled. Indeed, the arrest and conviction figures are based on such small and unrepresentative samples of law enforcement agencies that the FBI has made no effort to readjust earlier arrest and conviction figures on the basis of more recent returns.

The number of agencies reporting arrest data did not reach 2,000, or about one-quarter of the total number of agencies, until the 1960's, and the number of agencies reporting convictions did not exceed 300 until the 1960's. The abrupt increase between 1960 and 1961 in agencies reporting convictions represents a major change in reporting practices for conviction statistics by the UCRS. Notably, in 1936, the first year in which conviction rates were reported, the figure Ehrlich used as a national estimate was based on only 13 jurisdictions.

The average size of jurisdictions reporting conviction data declined substantially in the late 1930's and the early 1960's. According to recent evidence, conviction rates are relatively low in the nation's largest jurisdictions. Hence the conviction data drawn from disproportionately large jurisdictions in 1936 and 1937 are apt to underestimate the national conviction levels for these years. In fact, the reported conviction levels for these two years are far below those for other years—respectively -5.94 and -4.54 standard deviations below the mean conviction level for the period 1938–1969. Because the 1936 and 1937 conviction levels figure prominently in Ehrlich's estimation of missing conviction values for the years 1933–1935, the conviction rates for the entire period 1933–1937 are apt to be grossly biased in his analysis.

Finally, the measurement of execution risk—the key explanatory (or independent) variable in Ehrlich's work—is confounded by the inadequacies in the homicide, arrest, and conviction data, because execution risk, as defined by Ehrlich, incorporates all three of these variables. Thus, like his dependent variable, all three of his deterrence variables are subject to potentially serious measurement error. While we do not contend that all of Ehrlich's data are inaccurate, we have identified substantial problems with his core variables which cast doubt on his ability to perform a meaningful regression analysis.

ERRORS IN EHRLICH'S REGRESSION ANALYSIS

We have independently applied Ehrlich's regression technique to comparable data. On the basis of this replication, we find that his evidence of deterrence emerges only under restrictive assumptions about the form of relationships among the variables and only under a narrow selection of the time period for analysis. The limitations required to obtain these results are not justified, since Ehrlich's regression model fits the data better without them. Thus, even if Ehrlich's data were free of errors, the analysis, when properly conducted, would not show that the death penalty has a deterrent effect.

Replication of Data and Regression Results

To ensure comparability in the replication of Ehrlich's regression analysis, we attempted to use exactly the same data as Ehrlich. With these data, we have reproduced Ehrlich's basic regression analysis. The results of this initial regression analysis appear to indicate that, other things being equal, as the risk of execution among convicted offenders increases, the homicide rate decreases and, conversely, as execution risk declines, the homicide rate rises. For three of the six measures of execution risk, the estimated effect is at least twice its standard error, suggesting that the effect is not likely to have occurred by chance.

These results are similar to Ehrlich's. In addition, the relative strengths of the effects of arrest, conviction and execution are the same as Ehrlich reports. Thus, by reproducing the rank order of effects among arrest, conviction, and execution rates, we have replicated an especially important aspect of his regression results.

Temporal Specification

If the results of a time series regression analysis are a faithful representation of underlying causal processes, the values of the estimated coefficients will be independent of the specific time period chosen for the analysis. Thus, if the values of the coefficients associated with the various measures of execution risk change substantially when they are estimated for alternative time intervals, the negative values reported are not a reliable basis for inferring that capital punishment has a deterrent effect on murder.

We find that all empirical support for the deterrent effect of capital punishment disappears when the five most recent years are removed from the time series that Ehrlich selected for analysis. For the period ending in 1964, there are no statistically significant negative elasticities associated with the various measures of execution risk. For the period ending in 1963, the estimated elasticities have become positive in every case. Indeed, of the 24 coefficients reflecting the effects of execution risk for periods ending in 1963 and earlier, 20 are positive and only four are negative.

Furthermore, we find that the regression results are more adequate and consistent for the periods with earlier ending dates. Hence for the periods in which the model gives evidence of being more adequately specified, the regression analysis consistently shows a slightly positive—though not statistically significant—effect of execution risk on the homicide rate.

SOURCES OF EHRLICH'S DETERRENCE EVIDENCE

We have seen that Ehrlich obtains evidence of a deterrent effect only by imposing highly restrictive conditions on his analysis. One might assume that this evidence of deterrence reflects either a strong deterrent effect operating exclusively in recent years or a more pervasive effect obscured by data inadequacies in the early years. We show instead that Ehrlich's evidence is strictly a statistical artifact, not the reflection of a deterrent effect over the entire period of analysis or the most recent subperiod.

The Recent Years

What is it about the middle and late 1960's which causes the execution variables to show negative effects on the homicide rate when they are in logarithmic but not in natural form? The answer lies in the opposing trends in the two variables and in the nature of the logarithmic transformation. The national homicide rate, as reported by the FBI, rose precipitously in the middle and late 1960's to levels well above those of the 1940's and 1950's. Indeed, between 1962 and 1969 the homicide rate rose almost 60 percent to a level exceeded only by the rate for 1933. At the same time, executions literally came to an end. Hence execution risk—the number of executions among those convicted of murder—took on extremely low values, approaching zero, in the middle and late 1960's. A property of the logarithmic transformation is to emphasize variations at the lower range of a variable. For example, if execution risk is converted into logarithms, a difference between one and two executions per 1,000 convictions will be greater than a difference between 350 and 650 executions per 1,000 convictions. Consequently, the logarithmic transformation accentuates the decline in execution risk that occurred in the 1960's.

To show the effect of the logarithmic transformation on these low values of execution risk, we present the corresponding logarithmic and natural values of one of the six measures of execution risk for the years from 1960 through 1969. The natural values of execution risk have dropped from about one percent in the years 1960–1962 to less than .05 percent for the years 1966–1969. The values for the years after 1964 are all slightly more than one standard deviation below the mean for the entire period from 1933 to 1969. Putting execution risk in logarithmic form greatly accentuates the decline. The difference between 1960 and 1969 in logarithmic values (from .229 to -3.823) is more than three times the corresponding difference in natural values (from 1.257 to .022). In fact, for the period from 1966 to 1969, the logarithmic values of execution risk are all more than two standard deviations below their mean. Thus, by using logarithmic values of execution risk, Ehrlich gives considerably more weight in his regression analysis to the extremely low values of this variable after 1964.

Ehrlich has stated that the recent behavior of arrest and conviction rates as well as that of execution risk plays an important role in his regression results. To examine the effect of using the logarithmic values of execution risk and the possibility that the logarithmic transformation of arrest and conviction rates may also influence the regression results, we present simple correlations of the arrest, conviction, and execution rates with the criminal homicide rate; these are shown for logarithmic and natural values of the variables and for time intervals with successively earlier ending dates from 1969 through 1960. The data for the recent years have an extraordinary effect on the correlation between the logarithms of execution and homicide rates; adding the last five years reduces the correlation from .836 to .123. In contrast, the recent data have much less effect on the correlation between the natural values of execution and homicide rates; adding the last five years reduces the correlation only from .729 to .553. These years have virtually no impact on the correlations, in either logarithmic or natural form, of arrest and conviction rates with the criminal homicide rates. Thus, Ehrlich's evidence of deterrence rests heavily on the relationship between the values of execution risk and homicide rates for the years after 1964.

This conclusion might suggest that the use of the death penalty at the very low levels of execution risk in the middle and late 1960's had a deterrent effect strong enough to produce a measurable effect over the entire period when these recent years are combined with earlier years.

If execution risk had a deterrent effect, states with declining numbers of executions would show a relative increase in homicide rate, and states with rising execution levels would show a relative decrease in homicide rate. There is no such pattern in the years since 1962. Among states which decreased executions, the homicide rate rose more than the national figure for two of the periods and less than the national figure for four. Among states that increased executions, the change in homicide rate was below the national change in one comparison, very nearly the same in one case, and actually above in three of the five comparisons.

The use of capital punishment during this period was restricted increasingly to a small minority of states. After 1964, no more than five states imposed executions in a single year, none of them imposed more than one execution per year, and none imposed executions two years in a row. In this situation, the national homicide rate cannot be expected to reflect possible deterrent effects presumed to occur primarily in the jurisdictions that actively use the death penalty. Thus, apart from problems of temporal specification and functional form, it would have been more appropriate, in view of the progressively restricted use of capital punishment in the nation, for Ehrlich to have shortened the effective period of analysis by removing the years after 1963, when no more than 10 percent of the states imposed executions, than to have extended the period of analysis two years beyond the end of executions in the United States.

The Early Years

We have already described the unreliability of data for the 1930's. By reproducing his regression analysis for effective periods with later beginning dates, Ehrlich may have hoped to diminish the effects of measurement error in these early years. But he has thereby given greater weight to the years after 1964, which are responsible in the first place for his evidence of a deterrent effect.

To determine the effects of measurement error in the early years, we must first remove the idiosyncratic recent years, and then successively drop years from the beginning of the time series. Accordingly, we have performed regressions for periods with 1963 as the ending date and with successively later beginning dates from 1935 through 1940.

The coefficients are again predominantly positive, and become even more so as years are successively dropped from the beginning of the time series. In fact, the effective periods beginning in 1938, 1939, and 1940 show positive effects for execution risk in all 12 cases. These positive coefficients are, of course, absurd from the viewpoint of the deterrence hypothesis, although they may not be altogether meaningless. They do, however, indicate unambiguously that data inadequacies in the early years of the time series have not obscured deterrent effects of capital punishment. Indeed, by all indications there are no deterrent effects to obscure.

CONCLUSION

We have shown that Ehrlich's findings are not a reliable basis for inferring the effects of capital punishment on the criminal homicide rate. Flaws in Ehrlich's data cast doubt on the ability to perform meaningful regression analysis. The analysis itself yields evidence of a deterrent effect only by relying on the unusual nature of the years after 1964 and on the logarithmic transformation of the data. When the analysis is performed for more appropriate periods, the hypothesis that the death penalty deters murders finds no support.

DETERRENCE

Deterrence, Poverty, and
Type of Homicide

ROBERT NASH PARKER & M. DWAYNE SMITH

Two competing models have emerged with regard to the effects of punishment on deterring homicides. Gibbs specified a general deterrence model in which state homicide rates were taken to be a function of two repressive factors—certainty of punishment (measured as the number of persons admitted to prison during 1960 on a sentence for homicide divided by the average number of homicides reported by police in 1959 and 1960), and severity of punishment (measured as median number of months served on a homicide sentence by all persons in prison on December 31, 1960).

Using elementary statistical techniques, Gibbs found that state homicide rates were negatively related to certainty and severity of punishment. Further research using more sophisticated techniques has generally supported Gibbs's findings. Given this body of evidence, the deterrent effect of punishment on crime rates has been cited frequently in criminal justice literature.

However, Gibbs acknowledged a major weakness in the specification of the model—the omission of etiological (socioeconomic and demographic) factors. Loftin argued that this omission constituted a serious deficiency. Consequently, he proposed an etiological model which included social structural factors in the form of an index of "structural poverty," as well as the repressive factors contained in the deterrence model.

The index, measured at the state level, consisted of the infant-mortality rate, percentage of persons 25 years old and over with less than five years education,

420

percentage of families with income under $1,000 per annum, percentage of the population illiterate, percentage of failures on the armed forces mental test, and percentage of children living with one parent.

Loftin found that including the structural poverty variables in an equation with homicide rates for 1960 as the dependent variable caused the effects of certainty and severity of punishment to become insignificant. While the repressive factors by themselves accounted for only 20% of the variance in the homicide rates, the inclusion of the structural poverty variables accounted for an additional 63% of the variance.

A MORE DISCRIMINATING SPECIFICATION

An assumption of both models is that homicide is a unidimensional phenomenon. However, several studies, including those by Wolfgang and Curtis, have suggested that homicide may be qualitatively distinguished on the basis of the victim/offender relationship.

Based on the nature of this relationship, criminal homicides can be broadly categorized into two general types. The first, "primary" homicide, involves family or acquaintances and is usually an act of passion. These homicides include the FBI categories of: (1) spouse kills spouse, (2) parent kills child, (3) child kills parent, (4) relation kills relation, (5) other family, (6) lovers and triangle, (7) brawl due to alcohol, (8) arguments over money or property, and (9) other arguments. The latter four categories are reported as usually occurring among friends and acquaintances. The second category, "nonprimary" homicides, are often instrumental in nature in that they generally occur in the commission of another crime. They consist of the FBI categories: (1) gangland slayings, (2) institutional homicide (occurring in criminal and mental institutions), (3) felony homicide (committed in the course of another crime), and (4) suspected felony homicide.

These two types of homicides can be thought of as having different origins: primary homicides are essentially unreasoned acts of passion, whereas nonprimary homicides seem to involve some degree of decision making or meditation. These differential origins, which are closely linked to the victim/offender relationship, should have implications for the specification of causal models of homicide. The purpose of this paper is to explore the effects of partitioning homicide by type on the estimation of the deterrence and etiological models discussed above.

DATA AND MEASUREMENT

The data analyzed in this study can be found in U.S. federal government reports, the vast majority of which are published and readily available.

Gibbs measured severity of punishment by calculating the median months served on a sentence for homicide by those who were in prison on December 31, 1960. He argued that the deterrent effect of severity can operate only over long periods of time and that severity is affected not only by the sentencing process but by the parole system as well. Tittle and Logan measure severity as the median months served on a sentence for homicide by those released in 1960. This would seem to be a more logical procedure since at least one way in which perceived severity of punishment can be influenced is through the reentry into society of those released from prison. While this measure, like Gibbs's, may contain the results of different perceptions of severity which have varied over time, it is not confounded by the most recent court commitments, that is, those who at the date of measurement have served very few months, as is Gibbs's measure. The Tittle/Logan measure also reflects the influence of the parole system, which, as Gibbs argues, is an important way in which the current perception of severity can mitigate the effects of past perceptions. Therefore, we have used the median months served on a sentence for homicide by those released from prison in 1970.

Gibbs, Tittle, and Logan all measure certainty of punishment using some form of time lag in either numbers of crimes or persons admitted to prison. While we agree that there is a certain amount of lag in the criminal justice system between discovery of a crime by law enforcement agencies and the entry into prison of an offender, we do not feel that this lag differs substantially from year to year. Therefore, we have measured certainty of punishment as the number of admissions to prison on a sentence for homicide in 1970 divided by the number of homicides reported in the Uniform Crime Reports for 1970.

The dependent variables, primary and nonprimary homicide rates for 1973, were calculated by collapsing the FBI circumstance categories discussed above. These homicide data were divided by the population of the state for 1973 and multiplied by 100,000 to obtain standardized rates. The total homicide rate was computed as the sum of the primary and nonprimary rates.

Percentage of the population nonwhite, percentage of the population living in urban areas, percentage of the population aged 20–34, all measured in 1970, and a dummy variable coded 1 for southern states and 0 for other states were all used as control variables.

Finally, we have adopted Loftin and Hill's structural poverty index with one modification: recent data on the percentage of the population illiterate are not currently available, and therefore this variable has been omitted. The other five indexes—infant mortality rate, percentage of families with less than $1,000 income, percentage of children living with one parent, percentage of the population over

25 years of age with less than five years of education, and percentage of inductees who failed the armed forces mental test—all measured for 1970, have been standardized and summed into an index. The mean interitem correlation among these five variables is .760, while Cronbach's alpha reliability coefficient is .893.

PROCEDURES AND RESULTS

Using regression analysis, the deterrence and etiological models were analyzed to determine the effects of partitioning homicide rates into categories based on the victim/offender relationship.

Three dependent variables were used: total homicide rates (to facilitate replication of the original models), nonprimary homicide rates, and primary homicide rates were regressed on identical sets of independent variables. In the deterrence model, these were certainty and severity; in the etiological model, the structural poverty index and the set of control variables discussed above were added.

Table 1 contains the zero-order correlation coefficients among the 10 variables used in this analysis. While the deterrence variables display negative relationships with the homicide variables, the relationships are relatively uniform and small in size.

In contrast, the etiological factors show relatively large positive relationships with the homicide variables. However, these relationships are not as uniform as those for the deterrence variables; the correlation of total and primary homicide with percentage nonwhite and the structural poverty index ranges from .746 to .818. But the correlation between nonprimary homicide and these same factors is approximately .4 or less in both cases.

Regression results, reported in Table 2, demonstrate a similar pattern. Certainty of punishment is found to be the only significant predictor of nonprimary homicide rates in the deterrence model. However, the inclusion of the control variables and the structural poverty index adds an additional 38.2% of explained variance. Certainty becomes an insignificant predictor of nonprimary homicide rates, leaving percentage urban as the only significant predictor.

Neither certainty nor severity of punishment are significant predictors of primary homicide rates. But the addition of the control variables and the structural poverty index enables the etiological model to explain nearly 80% of the variance in these rates.

Column 1 of Table 2 contains a replication of both models. Comparing these results with those discussed above, it is clear that partitioning homicide by type yields divergent results. The deterrence model receives no support when total homicide rates appear as the dependent variable, but certainty is a significant predictor of nonprimary rates. Loftin and Hill's structural poverty index is found to be a

Table 1
Zero-order correlation coefficients

Variables	1	2	3	4	5	6	7	8	9	10
1. Total homicide (1973)	1.000									
2. Nonprimary homicide (1973)	.779	1.000								
3. Primary homicide (1973)	.973	.615	1.000							
4. Severity of punishment (1970)	-.187	-.111	-.195	1.000						
5. Certainty of punishment (1970)	-.145	-.266	-.085	-.269	1.000					
6. Percentage nonwhite (1970)	.768	.409	.817	-.238	.008	1.000				
7. Structural poverty index (1970)	.746	.330	.818	-.182	.001	.914	1.000			
8. Percentage urban (1970)	.189	.503	.052	-.197	-.275	-.078	-.209	1.000		
9. Percentage aged 20-34 (1970)	.438	.380	.412	-.195	-.201	.268	.176	.365	1.000	
10. South[a]	.579	.146	.675	-.335	.089	.735	.772	-.281	.190	1.000
X̄	5.663	1.463	4.200	69.211	.379	10.421	.000	65.781	20.055	.333
SD	3.230	.938	2.567	16.132	.110	8.854	4.495	14.368	1.264	.476

[a]Dummy variable coded 1 - south, 0 = other for region.

424

Table 2

Regression results and comparison of models

	Total Homicide Rate		Nonprimary Homicide Rate		Primary Homicide Rate	
	Unstandardized Coefficient	Standardized Coefficient	Unstandardized Coefficient	Standardized Coefficient	Unstandardized Coefficient	Standardized Coefficient
Eq. (1)—deterrence model:						
Severity	-.049 (.030)	-.243	-.011 (.009)	-.196	-.037 (.024)	-.234
Certainty	-6.172 (4.375)	-.210	-2.772[a] (1.250)	-.319	-3.450 (3.150)	-.148
R^2	.076		.106		.058	
Overall F-test	1.845		2.681		1.387	
Significance level	N.S.		.05		N.S.	
Eq. (2)—etiological model:						
Severity	.015 (.020)	.074	.004 (.008)	.062	.011 (.015)	.071
Certainty	-.664 (2.765)	-.023	-.739 (1.098)	-.087	.075 (2.001)	.003
Percentage nonwhite	.085 (.080)	.234	.032 (.032)	.300	.054 (.058)	.185
Structural poverty index	.361[a] (.166)	.502	.049 (.066)	.237	.311[a] (.120)	.545
Percentage urban	.063[a] (.024)	.279	.033[a] (.010)	.502	.030 (.018)	.168
Percentage aged 20-34	.466 (.246)	.178	.067 (.098)	.090	.389[a] (.178)	.191
South	.614 (.994)	.091	-.207 (.395)	-.105	.821 (.719)	.152
R^2	.726		.488		.773	
Overall F-test	15.167		5.455		19.470	
Significance level	.001		.001		.001	

Note: Standard errors are in parentheses.
[a]Coefficient is approximately twice its standard error.

significant predictor of total and primary rates but is not significantly related to nonprimary rates. Further, the significant relationship between percentage urban and total homicide can be seen as the effect of the relationship between nonprimary homicide and percentage urban. Likewise, the lack of a significant relationship between total homicide and percentage aged 20–34 results from the lack of a significant relationship between nonprimary homicide and percentage aged 20–34. This same variable is found to be a significant predictor of primary homicide.

DISCUSSION AND CONCLUSIONS

In general, the results of this study show little support for the deterrence model and considerable support for the etiological model. However, even in the etiological model, the partitioning of homicide rates into primary and nonprimary types reveals certain relationships otherwise obscured.

Our analysis suggests that punishment appears to have little net effect on the majority of homicides in the United States because they tend to occur under circumstances in which laws, practices, and perceptions have little impact. Our results also show that while the variables commonly used to explain or predict homicide rates are very successful in predicting primary homicide rates, they are less successful in accounting for nonprimary homicide rates. Further study is needed to develop a greater understanding of the factors contributing to nonprimary homicide.

In a recent empirical test of a similar etiological model, Black and Orsagh add a variable which measures capital punishment as a distinct form of sanction. Although they conclude that executions have no net effect on homicide rates, they suggest that some classification of homicide in a more precise manner is necessary to adequately test a relationship between executions and homicide. Our results indicate that the net relationships between sanctions as currently measured in the literature and specific types of homicide may provide little additional predictive power.

DETERRENCE

Murder Rate is NOT affected by death penalty.

Deterrence and the Death Penalty:
The Views of the Experts

MICHAEL L. RADELET & RONALD L. AKERS

I. INTRODUCTION

The American public has long been favorably disposed toward capital punishment for convicted murderers, and that support continues to grow. In a 1981 Gallup Poll, two-thirds of Americans voiced general approval for the death penalty. That support rose to 72% in 1985, to 76% in 1991, and to 80% in 1994. Although these polls need to be interpreted with extreme caution, it is clear that there are few issues on which more Americans agree: in at least some circumstances, death is seen as a justifiable punishment.

Part of the support for capital punishment comes from the belief that the death penalty is legitimate under a theory of "just deserts." This justification suggests that murderers should be executed for retributive reasons: murderers should suffer, and the retributive effects of life imprisonment are insufficient for taking a life. While such views are worthy of debate, no empirical research can tell us if the argument is "correct" or "incorrect." Empirical studies can neither answer the question of what specific criminals (or non-criminals) "deserve," nor settle debates over other moral issues surrounding capital punishment.

On the other hand, much of the support for capital punishment rests on its presumed value as a general deterrent: we need the death penalty to encourage potential murderers to avoid engaging in criminal homicide. Politicians are often quick to use some version of the deterrence rationale in their cries for more and quicker executions when they see such appeals as a promising way to attract votes.

Whether or not the threat or use of the death penalty is, has been, or could be a deterrent to homicide is an empirical question that should not—and cannot—be answered on the basis of moral or political stands. It is an empirical question that scores of researchers, dating back to a young Edwin Sutherland, writing in the pages of this journal, have examined.

Has this long history and sizable body of research led to any general conclusions? Can any factual statement be made about the death penalty's deterrent effects, or are the scholarly studies such that no conclusions can be reached? At least two valid methods can be used to answer these questions. One is to examine individual scholarly opinions, as is done in most published research reports. Here researchers review the empirical research on deterrence and reach conclusions based on it and their own research. A second approach is to gauge the informed opinions of scholars or experts. Indeed, much research-based public policy rests on known or presumed consensus of "expert" opinions. It is the aim of this paper to address the question of the death penalty's ability to deter homicides using this second approach: by gauging the judgments of a set of America's top criminologists.

II. LITERATURE REVIEW

Measuring sentiment on the death penalty is not as easy a task as it might at first appear. When opinion polls ask respondents whether they support the death penalty, often no alternative punishments are given, and respondents are left to themselves to ponder what might happen if a particular inmate were not executed. Often respondents erroneously believe that absent execution, offenders will be released to the community after serving a short prison sentence. Even the most ardent death penalty abolitionists might support capital punishment if the alternative was to have dangerous murderers quickly released from prison. When respondents are asked how they feel about the death penalty given an alternative of life without parole, support decreases significantly. In 1991, Gallup found that 76% of Americans supported the death penalty, but that support would drop to 53% if life imprisonment without parole were available as an alternative.

While most deterrence research has found that the death penalty has virtually the same effect as long-term imprisonment on homicide rates, in the mid-1970's economist Isaac Ehrlich reported that he had uncovered a significant deterrent effect. He estimated that each execution between 1933 and 1969 had prevented eight homicides. This research gained widespread attention, in part because Solicitor General Robert Bork used it to defend the death penalty in the 1970s when the

Supreme Court was considering whether to make permanent its 1972 ban of the death penalty. Although scholars, including a panel appointed by the National Academy of Sciences, strongly criticized Ehrlich's work for methodological and conceptual shortcomings, some continue to cite it as proof that the death penalty does have a deterrent effect.

Some research has asked the general public whether the death penalty acts as a deterrent to murder. Such a question is regularly asked to national samples in Gallup Polls. In the 1991 poll, where 76% of the respondents initially indicated support for the death penalty, Gallup asked those who favored the death penalty: Suppose new evidence showed that the death penalty does *not* act as a deterrent to murder, that it does not lower the murder rate. Would you favor or oppose the death penalty?" As in the earlier poll, the respondents were less likely (76% vs. 52%) to support capital punishment if it were shown that it is not a deterrent to homicide. These findings indicate that the assumption of a deterrent effect is a major factor in public and political endorsement of the death penalty. If that assumption is undermined, even those who initially favor the death penalty tend to move away from it.

One recent survey has been conducted that examines how leading police officials, who arguably hold more expertise on criminal behavior than the general public, view the deterrence rationale for capital punishment. Telephone surveys were conducted with 386 randomly selected police chiefs and county sheriffs from throughout the U.S. Little support for the deterrence argument was found. Among six choices presented as "primary" ways to reduce violent crime, only one percent of the law enforcement respondents chose the death penalty. This choice ranked last among the options. When asked to consider the statement "The death penalty significantly reduces the number of homicides," 67% of the chiefs felt the statement was inaccurate, while only 26% said it was accurate. Reacting to the poll, former New York Police Chief Patrick V. Murphy wrote, "Like the emperor's new clothes, the flimsy notion that the death penalty is an effective law enforcement tool is being exposed as mere political puffery." For comparative purposes some of the questions we posed to our sample were taken from this survey.

III. METHODOLOGY

We operationally define "expert" as one who has been recognized by peers by being elected to the highest office in scholarly organizations. We contacted all present and former presidents of the country's top academic criminological societies. This small and elite group includes many of the country's most respected and distinguished criminologists. As such, although few of these scholars have done research on capital punishment or deterrence, they are generally well versed in central criminological issues, such as crime causation, crime prevention, and criminal justice policy issues. The presidents of three associations were surveyed: the American Society of Criminology, the Academy of Criminal Justice Sciences, and the Law and Society Association.

We began by obtaining names and addresses of current and all living former presidents of each of the three organizations. A total of seventy-one individuals were identified: twenty-nine from the Academy of Criminal Justice Sciences, twenty seven from the American Society of Criminology, and fifteen from the Law and Society Association. As noted, one person had served as president of two of the associations, reducing our sample to seventy. Drafts of the questionnaire were critiqued by three scholars who have conducted deterrence research. Numbered questionnaires were mailed to our respondents, and follow-ups were sent to non-respondents. In the end, a total of sixty-seven responded (95.7%): twenty-seven from ACJS, twenty-six from the ASC, and fifteen from LSA.

The presidents were clearly asked in both the cover letter and on the questionnaire itself to answer the questions *on the basis of their knowledge of the literature and research in criminology.* We quite purposely did not ask for their personal opinions on the death penalty—information on this might be interesting, but it is irrelevant to the goal of the present study. Eleven questions, all relating to deterrence issues, were included on the questionnaire; the responses to all eleven are reported below.

IV. RESULTS
A. General Questions on Deterrence
The first question explored concerns how the presidents generally view the deterrence question. "Do you feel that the death penalty acts as a deterrent to the commitment of murder—that it lowers the murder rate, or what?" It can be seen that the criminologists are more than twice as likely as the general population to believe that the death penalty does *not* lower the murder rate—41% of the population held this belief in 1991, the last year that Gallup published responses to this question, compared to 83.6% of our experts. Among the sixty four presidents who voiced opinions on this question, fifty-six (87.5%) believe the death penalty does not have deterrent effects.

Further, 86.5% of the criminologists and 46% of the general public say they are "sure" or "think" that "abolishing the death penalty (in a particular state) would not have any significant effects on the murder rate (in that state)." As would be expected, substantially more members of the general public than the criminologists (32.6% vs. 10.4%) say they have no idea whether this statement is true or false.

Similarly, the criminologists are much less likely than members of the general public to agree that "Over the years, states which have had the death penalty have had lower murder rates than neighboring states which did not have a death penalty." Nearly 80% of the criminologists said that they were sure or they thought this was not true, compared to 37% of the general public. Interestingly, more criminologists stated that they had no idea whether this statement was true or false than did members of the general public (14.9% vs. 6.0%).

Approximately 80% of the experts in criminology believe, on the basis of the literature and research in criminology, that the death penalty does not have significant deterrent effects. In addition, no matter how measured, it is clear that the criminologists are much more likely than the general public to dismiss the deterrence argument.

Overall there is widespread agreement between the criminologists and the police chiefs on the deterrent value of the death penalty (or lack thereof), with the criminologists even less likely than the chiefs to see any deterrent value. All of the criminologists, and 85% of the police chiefs, believe it is totally or largely accurate that "politicians support the death penalty as a symbolic way to show they are tough on crime." Almost 87% of the criminologists and 57% of the chiefs find it totally or largely accurate to say that "debates about the death penalty distract Congress and state legislatures from focusing on real solutions to crime problems." None of the criminologists, and only about a quarter of the chiefs, believe there is any accuracy in the statement, "the death penalty significantly reduces the number of homicides." These statements indicate that both academic criminologists and police chiefs view the death penalty as more effective in political rhetoric than as a criminal justice tool.

One of the questions asked of the criminologists focuses on the *unique* deterrent effect of the death penalty above and beyond available alternatives of long imprisonment. Only three of our respondents (4.5%) agreed, and none strongly agreed, with the statement, "overall, over the last twenty years, the threat or use of the death penalty in the United States has been a stronger deterrent to homicide than the threat or use of long (or life) prison sentences." Those disagreeing or strongly disagreeing included 92.6% of the respondents, and 96% of those with an opinion. Responses to the next question indicate that only three respondents felt that the empirical support for the deterrent effects of the death penalty had moderate support; none believed it had strong support. Instead, 94% of the criminologists felt the argument had weak or no support.

B. The Question of Reform

Proponents of the death penalty might concur with the critics of the deterrence argument, but say that the lack of a clear deterrent effect is a result of the fact that only a small proportion of those on death row are executed each year, or that the wait on death row between condemnation and execution is too long. Increasing the frequency and celerity of the death penalty could produce a deterrent effect. The experts responding to our survey, however, disagree with such a position. Almost 80% disagree or strongly disagree with the statement, "if the frequency of executions were to increase significantly, more homicides would be deterred than if the current frequency of executions remained relatively stable." Nearly three-quarters (73.2%) of the experts disagreed or strongly disagreed with the position that decreasing the time on death row would deter more homicides. Much of the research that informs these experts' opinions was done with data from the 1930's, 1940's, and 1950's, when the frequency of executions was higher and the average time spent on death row was shorter than it is today. Hence, criminologists do have some research at their disposal that would enable accurate predictions of what would happen if these proposed death penalty reforms were actually enacted.

C. Support for the Brutalization Hypothesis

In a final question, the experts were asked how they felt about the so-called "brutalization hypothesis." This argument, supported by some research, suggests that the death penalty tends to devalue human life and sends a message that tells citizens that killing people under some circumstances is appropriate. However, this hypothesis does not have widespread support among the experts. Two-thirds (67.1%) of the respondents either disagree or strongly disagree with the statement, "overall, the presence of the death penalty tends to *increase* a state's murder rate rather than to *decrease* it."

The responses to this item help us address some possible reservations about our overall findings: Is there anti-capital punishment bias among the respondents? Were the responses made based on an understanding of the research or are our respondents merely liberal academics who object to the death penalty on moral grounds and would report options that might undermine it, even if the empirical evidence showed otherwise? The responses to the question on brutalization suggest that the answers to these questions are negative. If the respondents simply responded to any question in a way that buttresses the abolitionist position, there should be strong agreement with the notion that the death penalty actually increases the homicide rate, since this is an anti-capital punishment argument. It appears, instead, that the respondents were responding on the grounds we asked—their appraisal of existing research.

V. CONCLUSIONS

The results of this project show that there is a wide consensus among America's top criminologists that scholarly research has demonstrated that the death penalty does, and can do, little to reduce rates of criminal violence. Hence, these leading criminologists do not concur with one of the most important public justifications for the death penalty in modern society.

Do politicians and policy makers pay any attention to expert opinions among members or leaders of scholarly societies? There is some evidence in the recent ASC task force panel reports to the Attorney General that they may on some issues. But that task force, while studying a dozen crime control policy options, did not examine the issue of capital punishment. The advice we would offer, reflecting the opinions of the presidents of the major criminological organizations, is to shift public debates about how to reduce criminal violence in America away from the death penalty.

Capital punishment will continue to generate much public debate in the early decades of the next century and various bodies of opinion will be consulted. One important body of opinion has been revealed by this study. The results show that the question of whether or not the death penalty can reduce criminal violence is—at least for the presidents of the major scholarly societies in criminology—a settled issue. Hopefully this study will provide policy makers with information that might help move political debate beyond "gut" feelings and simplistic demands for the death penalty as a way of "getting tough" on crime.

GUN CONTROL

━━━━►∞◄━━━━

Is Gun Control Likely to Reduce Violent Killings?

FRANK ZIMRING

O ne of the major arguments for the elimination of firearms, and derivatively for gun control laws, is that such measures would reduce the number of criminal homicides. It has been argued, however, that eliminating guns would have no such effect because if somebody wants to kill, he will find a weapon to achieve "his destructive goal"; there is, it is said, more than one way to skin a cat. This paper is an attempt to bring this phase of the gun control debate closer to a resolution, through analysis of data from the Police Department of the City of Chicago on reported criminal homicides and serious, but not fatal, criminal assaults during 1965, 1966, and 1967.

HOMICIDE AND THE INTENTION TO KILL

If all homicides resulted from such a single-minded intention to kill as gangland killings, laws prohibiting firearms would not have a substantial effect on homicide. Even assuming such assassins would be unable to obtain guns—a doubtful supposition—they would resort to other weapons on the order of dynamite to achieve their intention. But not all homicides are so unambiguously motivated. The question is: Do a significant proportion of homicides result from a less deliberate and determined intention? If this question may be answered in the affirmative, and if the probable substitute for firearms in these situations is less likely to lead to death, then the elimination of guns would reduce the number of homicides.

The hypothesis is more easily stated than proved. For obvious reasons, there are no precise data on the intention of an attacker toward his victim—whether he wished to wound or injure, with some apprehension of the risk of death or some desire to kill, or whether he single-mindedly intended to kill at any cost. Either of these mental states would be consistent with a finding of murder if homicide results. But the more ambiguous intention might well lead to the termination of an attack before lethal consequences ensue. The barroom fight ends when one of the two participants has been stabbed, shot, or beaten into submission. At that point the issue has been decided. Similarly, the violent domestic dispute may end decisively without fatal consequences.

A series of statistics for the city of Chicago throws light on the degree to which homicides result from an ambiguous, rather than a single-minded, intention to kill. The first table concerns the relationship between attacker and victim in homicide cases.

> More than two-thirds of all killings involved spouses, lovers, friends, or tavern guests as victim and attacker.

Closely related to data on relationship are statistics about the motive of the attack, as seen in Table 2.

> 82% of the homicides in Chicago in 1967 occurred as a result of altercations— domestic, money, liquor, etc.—precisely the situations where the intention is more apt to be ambiguous rather than single-minded.

Third, a comparison of victims of homicide with victims of serious assaults, with respect to their race and sex, shows:

> Victims of homicides and victims of serious assaults are distributed quite similarly by race and sex among the population and differ substantially in these characteristics from the Chicago population as a whole. (See Table 3.)

Next, it should be noted that only 30% of the victims of fatal gunshot attacks in 1967 were wounded by more than one shot. While data are not available on the number of shots fired, it may be readily assumed that the majority of the 70% of single wound homicides occurred in situations where the attacker did not exhaust the multiple shot capacity of his firearm.

Finally, in 54% of the situations which led to homicide in 1967, the police noted that the offender or the victim or both had been drinking prior to the homicidal attack. This figure probably does not include a number of situations in which the police officer was unable to determine whether intoxicants were involved.

It may be inferred from these data that many homicides are related to variable states of intention and that a significant proportion do not result from an attack committed with the single-minded intention to kill. The next question that must

435

Table 1
Relationship between homicide victim and attacker: Chicago, 1967

Relationship	%
Friends and acquaintances	41
Spouse or lover	20
Other family	7
Neighbors	3
Business	3
no relationship	22
Undetermined	4
Total	100
Number of cases	554

be asked in order to determine whether elimination of firearms would result in a lower homicide rate, is whether firearms as a class are more dangerous in the normal assault situation than the most dangerous probable substitute weapon. If they are not, then their elimination would not reduce the homicide rate, which is a function of the dangerousness of the weapons used multiplied by the number of serious attacks. Before an answer may be sought from the data, it is necessary to define "dangerousness" of a weapon in a manner that permits empirical study.

DEFINING DANGEROUSNESS

To say that weapon A is more dangerous than weapon B might mean either that weapon A can facilitate the implementation of intentions to attack in situations where weapon B cannot, or that consummated attacks with weapon A are more dangerous than consummated attacks with weapon B, or both. Certainly, the capacity of a particular weapon to make a homicidal attack possible—its range—is an element of any definition of weapon dangerousness. But no available experience statistics indicate how many attacks with weapon A would not have been attacks at all if weapon B and not weapon A were available.

We do know (1) that firearms as a class have a greater range for carrying intention into act than any other frequently used assault mechanism, and (2) that most homicides involve individuals who are acquainted with one another and take place in "inside" locations such as homes, taverns, and common passageways. The prior acquaintance of victim and offender and the location of most homicidal attacks suggest that it is correct to assume that weapon

Table 2

Motives of homicide as established by police: Chicago, 1967

Motives	%
Altercations:	
General Domestic	17
Money	9
Liquor	7
Sex	2
Triangle	6
Racial	1
Children	2
Other	38
	82
Teen Gang Disputes:	3
Robbery	
Strong Arm	3
Armed	9
Other Motive:	3
Total	100
Number of cases	551

Table 3

Homicide and serious assault victims and Chicago population by race and sex

	Homicide Victims 1967 %	Serious Assault Victims of Gun and Knife Attacks 5th Period, 1968 %	Chicago Population 1960[a] %
White			
Male	15	15	37
Female	7	4	39
Negro			
Male	59	61	11
Female	12	15	12
Other			
Male	6	5	—[b]
Female	1	1	—[b]
Total	100%	100%	100%
Number	553	480	3,540,100

[a]More recent data on Chicago population by both race and sex are not available. Non-whites are estimated to have comprised 30% of the city's population in April 1968, as compared with 24% in 1960. Hospital Planning Council for Metropolitan Chicago, Chicago Regional Hospital Study: Population Estimates for Municipalities and Counties in the Chicago Consolidated Area, 1967 and 1968, Table 2 (mimeo. July 1968).

[b]less than 0.5%.

range is a critical factor in attack situations in only a comparatively small number of cases. Nonetheless, to the limited extent that range has any bearing on the dangerousness of weapons in attack, guns must be considered more dangerous than alternative weapons in common usage. Where range is important, as in the killing of police, the absence of firearms may have preventive effects beyond the scope of this study.

The Most Dangerous Probable Substitute Weapon

In order to assess the impact of effective gun control on homicide fairly, the dangerousness of firearms in attack situations should be judged against the dangerousness of the most dangerous weapon which probably *would be*—as opposed to *could be*—used in assault situations were firearms not available.

There are a number of dangerous instrumentalities widely available to most of the population. Knives, other cutting instruments, automobiles, and blunt instruments of all kinds are freely available. Hands and feet, potentially lethal instruments in their own right, are a part of man's standard equipment. Some, but not all, poisons are available in various forms. Many flammable and explosive substances are within the average citizen's reach. Thus, weapon availability is a threshold which excludes only a few of the more exotic or technically sophisticated means of destruction. A far more important screening question is whether a particular form of attack instrumentality is available in the perceptual sense—likely to enter the thoughts and physical reach of an individual who is contemplating attack.

A rough estimate of the perceived availability of instrumentalities as murder weapons can be obtained by analyzing the type of weapons actually used in homicides reported to the police:

Homicide by weapon: Chicago, 1968

	%
Firearms	52
Knives	30
Other weapons	8
No weapon	10
Not known	1
Total	100
Total number:	510

It is true, of course, that some attack instruments may be underreported because it is difficult to discover that they have caused a death (e.g., some forms of poison) or because death caused by the instrumentality is not normally suspected as intentionally caused whether or not intention was actually present (e.g. automobiles). Poison is not even listed as a cause of death in Chicago homicide in 1966. An automobile is listed as accounting for one suspected intentional death. The great disproportion between knife and bodily attacks and other instrumentalities does not allow for the serious competition of automobiles and poison.

Thus, unless the people who make homicidal attacks with firearms are radically different from those who make homicidal attacks with other weapons known to the police, the absence of guns would produce a great many more knife attacks and a substantially greater number of attacks using hands or feet as potentially homicidal weapons.

There are two separate kinds of evidence suggesting that guns and knives are used by the same sorts of people:

As Table 4 shows, in general, the same kinds of altercations produce gun and knife killings.

As Table 5 shows, firearms and knives are used by whites and Negroes in about the same proportions.

Although knives result in three times as many homicides as attacks with the hands or feet, it is not necessarily true that knife attacks are more physically dangerous than all kinds of attacks with hands or feet. Some forms of attack involving the hands or feet, such as strangulation, might conceivably result in death in a greater proportion of attacks in earnest than some forms of knife attack. But comparison of the proportions of killings does indicate one of two things: (1) if attacks using the hands or feet are very much more common than the homicide statistics indicate, they are physically very much less dangerous than knife attacks, or (2) if attacks using the hands or feet are physically more dangerous than knife attacks, they ate very much less used and therefore less available in the perceptual sense.

Strangulation is very rare in Chicago. There were six such reported fatalities in 1966: most homicides by hand or foot attack were attributable to beatings. Since beatings are common in attack situations, it is more probable that knives are physically more dangerous. In either case, since we are talking about the predominant probable substitute for gun attacks, the balance would seem to favor the use of knife attacks. The use of beatings would lead to even stronger differences than those noted.

Table 4

Police-nominated motive of homicides by weapon: Chicago, 1966

	% Shot	% STABBED	% Other
Altercations:			
General Domestic	21	25	23
Money	6	7	2
Liquor	2	8	4
Sex	1	3	2
Gambling	2	1	0
Triangle	5	5	3
Theft (alleged)	—	—	2
Children	2	1	1
Other	41	30	28
	80	80	65
Robbery:			
Strong Arm	—	—	10
Armed	9	9	4
Burglary:	—	—	—
Sex:			
Perversion	2	3	5
Assault of woman	—	4	7
Wanton Use of Weapons:	2	—	1
Undetermined:	6	4	4
Gangland Type:			
Organized	1	—	—
Crim. of victim			
Burglar	—	—	—
Undetermined	—	—	1
Other:			
Mercy Killing	—	—	1
Mental Disorder	—	—	2
	100%	100%	100%
Number	265	152	93

Table 5

Homicide weapon used by race and sex of offender: Chicago, 1967

	Male		Female	
	Negro	White	Negro	White
Guns	60	59	40	50
Knives	21	16	54	33
No weapon	12	17	1	0
Other	8	8	4	17
Total	100%	100%	100%	100%
Number of Offenders	330	71	72	12

FATALITY RATES FROM GUN AND KNIFE ATTACKS

Chicago police records include data which permit useful comparison between serious knife and gun attacks and between knife and gun killings. (See Table 6.) For 1967, these data show:

> 2.3 times as many serious knife attacks were reported to the police as gun attacks.
>
> Knives accounted for less than half the number of homicides that guns did.
>
> *The rate of knife deaths per 100 reported knife attacks was less than 1/5 the rate of gun deaths per 100 reported gun attacks.*

These figures support the inference that if knives were substituted for guns, the homicide rate would drop significantly.

The figures, though not the inference, are subject to qualification, however. Not all gun or knife attacks are called to the attention of the police. That attacks reported to the police are not a complete census of weapon attacks in the population would not, by itself, disturb the validity of inferences made from comparisons of police statistics. But if a plausible argument can be made that the police statistics are not a reliable *index* of attack rates in the total population, and if the factors which undermine the use of police statistics as an index could be expected to overstate the proportion of knife relative to gun attacks reported, the validity of inferences from police attack statistics could be questioned.

Table 6
Number of non-fatal attacks and homicides with knives and firearms recorded by police: Chicago, 1965–67

	Non-Fatal Attacks	Homicides
1965		
Knives	5,285	104
Firearms	1,298	195
1966		
Knives	5,230	152
Firearms	1,873	265
1967		
Knives	5,612	135
Firearms	2,412	317
Total		
Knives	16,127	391
Firearms	5,583	777

Two plausible reasons why attacks with one weapon could be more often reported than attacks using a second weapon may be noted. First, the more serious a victim perceives an attack to be, the more likely it is that he will report the attack to the police. Attacks with weapons which are considered more serious will be reported to the police proportionately more often than weapons considered less serious. It must be stated that we do not here deal with the fine distinctions that people may make regarding the lethal potential of various weapons. Thus, if individuals considered both knife and gun attacks to be very serious, the marginal differences in their opinions regarding the two weapons could not be expected to produce significant reporting differentials. Second, to the extent that aggressive patrol, investigation, police pressure on victims to promote disclosure, or a patrolman's decision to report an attack may affect police records, the police perception of weapon dangerousness will influence the proportional relationships found in police statistics. A series of interviews of Chicago police officials at various levels indicates that the unanimous feeling of concerned police officers is that gunshot attacks are more dangerous than knife attacks. To the extent that police and victim perceptions distort police statistics, therefore, they apparently result in underestimation rather than overestimation of the ratio of knife attacks to gun attacks in Chicago.

To rebut the inference that substituting knife attacks for gun attacks would reduce the homicide rate, it can also be argued that because a knife is viewed as a less serious weapon than a gun, a lower proportion of knife attacks represent attacks in earnest. The statistics clarify the form such an argument would have to take. First, it can be noted that the use of attacks reported to the police as a standard to construct attack proportions has already screened out a certain number of attacks which are not considered terribly serious, because it is plausible that attacks perceived of as being more serious are more often reported. Second, in order to equalize the number of deaths per 100 attacks in earnest with each weapon, the "non-earnest knife attack" hypothesis must explain over 75% of the total number of reported knife assaults even if it is assumed that *every* firearm attack reported to the police in 1966 represents an attack in earnest. To the extent that less than all firearm attacks are considered in earnest, an even greater proportion of knife attacks must be discounted. On its face, this seems implausible. The demographic similarity between knife attack victims and homicide victims is an additional indication that the two statistics may be two products of closely similar forms of attack, in essence a continuum rather than two discrete behaviors. Given the magnitude of the difference between reported knife and gun assaults, and the substantial probability that reporting biases underestimate the proportional impact of knife assaults if they have any influence at all, the non-earnest hypothesis seems an incomplete explanation of the different assault/killing ratios noted in Chicago.

THE ATTACK STUDY

To obtain a more accurate impression of the character of knife and firearm attacks reflected in Chicago police records, police assault records for the period November 9–December 6, 1967 were analyzed in detail. The ratio of knife attacks to gun attacks was somewhat lower during this period than in any of the larger periods which have been the basic focus of analysis. Still, the number of knife attacks was substantially greater than the number of firearm attacks. And the ratio of gun killings to knife killings rose even more dramatically in this period than the ratio of gun attacks to knife attacks. There were 34 deaths attributable to firearms during this police period and eight deaths attributable to stabbings. The rate of knife deaths per 100 reported knife assaults was less than one-sixth of the rate of gun deaths per 100 reported gun assaults during this police period. This relationship is consistent with the overall one to five statistic found in the earlier large period comparisons.

One way of estimating the seriousness of an attack is to determine where the attacker sought to wound his victim. It may be assumed that actual wound location is a generally reliable indicator of the intended target, particularly for knives. It is highly unlikely that a great number of individuals intending superficial wounds to a non-vital area of the victim's body would by mistake stab him in the back, chest, neck or abdomen. Indeed, to the extent that "mistakes" produce a patterned difference between intended and actual location of wounds, the bias would probably understate rather than overstate the seriousness of a large group of attacks.

Table 7 sets forth the most serious area of the body where a wound was sustained in a knife or gun attack. It shows:

> 70 knife wounds per 100 knife attacks occurred in areas that are associated with serious attacks—chest, abdomen, head and face, back, and neck—while only 56 gunshot wounds per 100 firearm attacks occurred in these areas.
>
> Knife attacks resulting in wounds to non-vital areas—thighs and extremities—occurred no more frequently per 100 attacks than similar gun wounds. A smaller number of knife wounds to legs and thighs per 100 attacks is balanced against a larger number of knife wounds to arms, hands, and wrists per 100 attacks. Of every 100 reported firearm attacks, 12 resulted in no wound, while there was only one reported knife attack during the period which resulted in no wound.

Table 7
Non-fatal and fatal knife and gun attacks by location of
most serious wound: Chicago, November 9–December 6, 1967

Location of most serious wound	Non-Fatal Attacks		Fatal Attacks		Total	
	Knife %	*Gun* %	*Knife* %	*Gun* %	*Knife* %	*Gun* %
Serious						
Chest	15	13	50	44	15	17
Abdomen	17	12	—	18	17	13
Head	15	11	38	32	16	14
Back	10	3	13	3	10	3
Neck	4	1	—	—	4	1
Shoulders	8	8	—	3	8	7
Total	69	48	100	100	70	56
Non-Serious						
Legs	7	28	—	—	7	24
Arms	24	10	—	—	23	9
Missed	—	14	—	—	—	12
Total	31	52	—	—	30	45
Total	100%	100%	100%	100%	100%	100%
Number	358	213	8	34	366	247

These data appear to support three inferences, each of which will be discussed in turn.

1. *Not all gun attacks can be per se considered attacks in earnest.* About 56% of the reported firearm attacks, including all of the fatal attacks noted during the sample police period, produced wounds in the chest, abdomen, head area, and the back and shoulders. It is, of course, true that many of the gun wounds in locations like the back or chest were not the kinds of wounds which led to fatalities. However,

444

since we are using wound location as an index of the *intended* seriousness of an attack, and wound seriousness is an indication of outcome rather than intention, it is probably safe to assume that a substantial proportion of those gun attacks with dangerous area wounds could qualify as attacks in earnest, since they generated the risk of fatal consequences.

It can be argued, however, that since the relationship between the intended locale of an attack and the actual locale of the wounding is not complete, many of the firearm attacks that have been coded as misses, or attacks culminating in a wound no more serious than an arm, hand, hip, leg, or foot wound, were actually much more seriously intended. A proponent of this position would point out that when a police report indicates that a man firing a gunshot has missed, as it does in a substantial number of cases, there is no information on what area of the body the gunshot wound has missed, and therefore no inference may be drawn about the seriousness of the attack. The normal attack capacity of a firearm, however, is substantially more than one shot. If an individual does not wound a victim as seriously as he intended on the first try, he may try again. Since Table 7 only codes wounds by *location of the most serious wound area of a particular attack*, attacks coded in less serious areas are attacks in which the assailant *did not* try again, or at least had no greater success. If attacks resulting in multiple wounds are presumptively considered serious and added to those resulting in actual wounds to serious areas, the total is less than 58% of all gun attacks. (See Table 8.) Adding shotgun attacks not already included still leaves the total at roughly 60%. It is doubtful, therefore, that *all* gun attacks are accompanied by even ambiguous intentions to kill.

2. *A substantial proportion of the knife attacks reported to police appear to be attacks in earnest.* The data show that a far greater number of knife attacks resulted in wounds to serious than to non-serious locations. If the 29 multiple knife wounds in non-serious locations are added to the knife wounds in serious areas, the total is approximately 77%. (See Table 8.) While it is doubtless true that not all attacks resulting in serious area wounds were in earnest, it may also be presumed that some of the attacks resulting in non-serious wounds to the arms represent attacks in earnest partially thwarted by the victim's defensive use of his arms. In any event, it is difficult to argue that only an insignificant proportion of knife attacks are made in earnest.

3. *There is no evidence that attacks in earnest are much more common with guns than with knives.* Adding multiple wounds in non-serious locations to all serious wound locations makes possible a very rough estimate of the proportion of attacks which are in earnest for guns and knives. As indicated above, these figures are approximately 60% and 77%, respectively. Obviously, these are only rough estimates. Their trend,

Table 8
Knife and gun attacks resulting in multiple
wounds: Chicago, November 9–December 6, 1967

	Knife	*Gun[a]*
Serious Area		
Number of Multiple Wound Attacks	117	19
% of—		
Non-Fatal Attacks	46%	16%
Fatal Attacks	50%	19%
Non-Serious Area		
Number of Multiple Wound Attacks	29	5
% of—		
Non-Fatal Attacks	26%	5%
Fatal Attacks	—	—

[a]Does not include shotgun attacks resulting in multiple, non-serious area wounds.

however, may be usefully compared with police estimates of the gravity of the most serious wound sustained by the victim. Since the gravity of the wound may reflect a number of factors independent of the attacker's intention, the use of these police data should be secondary, to safeguard against any unwarranted inferences from the wound location data.

The police classify knife wounds as "slash" and "puncture" wounds. Slash wounds involve a shallower penetration than puncture wounds. Some gun wounds are classified by the police as "grazing," less serious wounds. The police estimates (see Table 9) indicate:

34% of the serious area knife wounds were slash wounds; 25% involved only one serious area slash wound. If this latter group is excluded, 59% of the knife attacks resulted in puncture wounds to serious areas or multiple knife wounds.

9% of the serious area firearm wounds were grazings. Excluding these leaves 56% of all firearm attacks resulting in serious area or multiple gunshot or shotgun wounds.

Excluding slash and graze wounds from attacks in earnest is not necessarily the best method of arriving at final figures. While slash and graze wounds where there was only one serious area wound may have resulted from less ominous attack intentions than penetrating wounds, the dangerousness of the area where the wound was sustained militates against this interpretation. Nevertheless, the exclusion results in a conservative estimate of the proportions of knife and gun attacks which are in earnest.

Table 9

**Police-noted extent of wound by weapon and area of wound:
non-fatal attacks, Chicago, November 9–December 6, 1967**

	Serious		
Knife[a]		Gun[b]	
Puncture	66	Wound	92
Slash	34	Graze	9
	100%		100%
Number of Cases	247		106
	Non-Serious		
Knife		Gun	
Puncture	70	Wound	99
Slash	30	Graze	1
	100%		100%
Number of Cases	110		81

[a]Does not inlcude one "menaced."
[b]Does not include 29 "missed."

These statistics support two complementary propositions: (1) a roughly equal proportion of knife and gun attacks are of the kind which may not have been attacks in earnest, and (2) a roughly equal proportion of police reported knife and gun attacks are of the kind that suggest the attack was probably seriously intended. If the area of wounding is taken as an index of seriousness, a greater number of knife wounds than gun wounds are presumptively in earnest, and a lesser number of knife wounds than gun wounds are of the kind where the location of the attack creates some doubt about the earnestness of the attack. If the presence or absence of multiple shooting or stabbing is examined, nothing about the data suggests that the average knife attack is any less seriously intended than the average gun attack. Indeed, multiple knife attacks are more common per 100 reported attacks than multiple gun attacks. Finally, if all single knife slash wounds are removed from the class of presumptively serious attacks, this still leaves toughly equal proportions of presumptively serious attacks, with the gun figure slightly higher than the knife figure. If all single and multiple knife slash wounds are removed from the class of presumptively serious attacks, a rather radical use of the data, a gap of less than 10% opens between knife attacks considered presumptively serious and gun attacks considered presumptively serious.

The implications of these data on the basic question posed about weapon dangerousness can best be set into perspective by taking the most negative interpretation of the attack statistics and tracing its implications. If it is assumed that only those wounds inflicted by knives in serious area locations that resulted in police reported punctures can be presumptively considered attacks in earnest, but that every gunshot attack reported is an attack in earnest or worse, the death rate per 100 attacks in earnest by guns would still be two and one-half times that of the death rate per 100 attacks in earnest by knives. Certainly, more reasonable use of these data would involve a substantially smaller number of asymmetrical assumptions. If the comparison is between knife puncture wounds in serious areas and gun wounds in serious areas, guns exhibit a death rate five times greater than knives.

Thus, when the data on the character of assaults are discussed in light of assault rates by weapon in Chicago and death rates by weapon in Chicago, a difference in attack intentions by weapon great enough to explain the differential death rates experienced is highly unlikely.

CONCLUSION

The beginning of the present exercise is found in a crude but suggestive set of ratios: the rate of homicide per 100 police reported attacks is about five times as great for firearms as for knives, the next most dangerous weapon available in Chicago's homicide experience. Since a very substantial part of Chicago's homicide rate appears to be attributable to ambiguously motivated deadly attacks, it seems clear that the deadliness of a particular weapon in an attack situation is a significant determinant of the homicide rate. If this is true, then the killing per 100 attack ratio cited above is a conclusive demonstration that the absence of firearms would depress the otherwise expectable homicide rate, unless the disproportionate number of killings per police reported attack could be explained by a plausible rival hypothesis.

We have sought an explanation which would comport with the reality of homicide in Chicago and still explain the disproportionate killing per attack ratios noted in official statistics. The biases built into the way attacks are reported could only work to understate rather than overstate the disproportionate dangerousness of firearm attacks. The remaining rival hypothesis was then phrased in the form of the prediction that the vast majority of all police reported knife attacks were non-earnest in nature and all of the police reported gun attacks were of the kind that were likely to produce ambiguously motivated homicides or worse. In fact, an investigation of patterns of knife and gun wounding has suggested that a roughly equal proportion of both knife and gun attacks appear to be of a class likely to produce the ambiguously motivated homicide. The negative conclusion available from these data has already been stated: It is highly unlikely that the attack in earnest hypothesis which seeks to differentiate knife and gun attacks could, in the light of our study of wound location, completely explain the difference in kill ratios previously noted. But what of an affirmative conclusion?

It might be thought that the five to one kill ratio relationship between knives and guns, when combined with the apparent similarity of attack in earnest ratios, could lead to a prediction that the absence of firearms in Chicago's population would reduce Chicago's homicide experience by four-fifths of the present gun-attributable total, or by some other finite amount. Unfortunately, this is not the case. First, while a substantial proportion of all homicides can be thought to be ambiguously motivated, we cannot make that assumption about all homicides, and we cannot conclusively isolate the proportion of homicide experience which is attributable to this kind of attack. Since the single-minded attack with intent to kill surely results in death more often per 100 attacks than an ambiguously motivated attack in earnest, we cannot confidently exclude the number of single-minded killings which constitute a part of reported homicides. However, there are some interesting data which might bear on the proportion of single-minded killings. The proportion of multiple woundings is only slightly higher in fatal gun attacks than in non-fatal, serious gun attacks. Further, multiple wound figures in homicides for all of 1967 account for only 30% of the gunshot killing totals. This would tend to limit the number of "kill at any cost" cases which might exaggerate the impression of firearm dangerousness in the attack statistics.

Second, it is not unlikely that the apparent similarity between knife and gun attack figures does conceal some disproportion between the attack in earnest ratios noted in knife versus gun attacks. The only unlikely conclusion is that weapon dangerousness does not affect the gross expectable homicide rate. The precise extent of that effect is a matter for conjecture. On their face, the data suggest that the effect of firearm elimination would itself be quite substantial. But that phrase is a hedge, and the method of this inquiry is non-experimental. The words "quite substantial" are as far as the data will take us.

A final note should be taken of the initial assumption of this enterprise: that a degree of continuity exists between homicide and non-fatal but serious assaults with deadly weapons. The similarities between serious attacks reported by police and homicides are compelling. Both events fall with disproportionate impact on the Negro community, and upon a disproportionately high number of male victims. Since relationship is a confirmed element of a great many such attacks, both phenomena can be attributed to a similarly skewed group of attackers. The attack data do not reveal substantial differences between fatal attacks using particular weapon forms and serious area, non-fatal attacks involving the same weapon. During the sample period:

449

46% of the non-fatal knife attacks resulting in wounds to serious areas, and 50% of the fatal knife attacks, involved multiple wounds.

16% of the non-fatal serious area firearm attacks, and 19% of the fatal shootings, resulted in multiple wounds. (See Table 8.)

Perhaps these data are telling us it would be advisable to shift the focus of concentration from the species of homicide to the genus of deadly attack. The portion of the population subject to this threat is as skewed as the homicide statistics indicate, but the problem is larger. In the final years of this decade, a further study of this culture of violence is an obligation to its survivors.

PREVENTION

Black Homicide:
The Adequacy of Existing Research
for Devising Prevention Strategies

DARNELL F. HAWKINS

ithin the last five years, federal health agencies have taken the unprecedented step of identifying violent death as a major public health concern. This has resulted in efforts to devise treatment and prevention policies that are more systematic and effective than the perennial, but inconsistent, responses of politicians, public officials, and criminal justice personnel for the deterrence of violent crime or other forms of violent life-threatening behavior. Recent government reports and social scientific investigations have shown that homicide currently ranks among the top five causes of death for every age group in the United States from ages 1 through 44. In addition, so significant are the effects of race (and sex) in determining the likelihood that one will be a victim of homicide that the Department of Health and Human Services has specifically targeted young black males between the ages of 15 and 24 for homicide reduction programs. Efforts are now underway to identify aspects of black homicide that may be susceptible to professional intervention aimed at its prevention and incidence reduction.

RACE AND HOMICIDE: PAST AND RECENT FINDINGS

Many of the problems inherent in the application (or anticipated application) of social research are evident in current efforts to use research on black homicide to devise intervention strategies. It would appear that racial difference in homicide offending and victimization is one of the most well-documented and least controversial findings within American criminology. Since 1930, many local, regional, and national studies have been conducted. All such studies have shown consistently higher arrest and victimization rates of homicide among blacks than among whites. Further, recent data show that the black homicide rate is also substantially higher than the of other disadvantaged minority groups such as Hispanics. Most of these studies have found the black homicide arrest rate to be between five and six times greater than that of whites.

Inattention to Etiological Factors

Despite the extensive documentation of a disproportionately high rate of black homicide, researchers have provided surprisingly few explanations for this phenomenon. Brearley offered one of the earliest attempts at explaining this difference. In a chapter on "The Negro and Homicide," he notes that many attempts have been made to find a satisfactory explanation for the high rate of black homicide and that these have ranged from more credible ones to those based on prejudice or hasty generalization. Yet, Brearley himself concludes: "There is some evidence, however, that the Negro is lacking in the power to control himself in accordance with the requirements of others." He goes on to suggest that the higher rates of manslaughter as compared to premeditated murder among blacks is proof of their impulsiveness. On the other hand, he suggests the possibility that the high homicide rate of blacks may be more apparent than real. He speculates that "If interracial slayings were eliminated and a careful study made of comparable groups of whites and Negroes having the same economic, educational, and social status and the same inability to secure justice except by a resort to deeds of violence, there is the possibility that approximately equal homicide rates might be found for the two races."

Meanwhile, cartodemographic researchers such as Lottier were devising another form of explanation, one based on both black-white and southern-nonsouthern differences in the rate of homicide. In summarizing these earlier studies Harries observed that when one considers regional geographies of crime in the United States during the 1930s, 1950s, and 1960s, the most striking finding "is the persistence of high homicide rates in the South." In seeking to explain high rates of black violence, he concludes that "Black violence seems to be but a special case of white southern violence, in the sense that white homicide rates in the South are higher than white rates elsewhere."

Wolfgang devotes surprisingly little attention to explaining the extremely disproportionate rate of black homicide in Philadelphia. However, after cautioning researchers against making hasty judgments about the link between race and crime, he proposed an essentially subcultural explanation for the high rate of black and lower-class white homicide. The ideas of Wolfgang and Ferracuti and the cartodemographic researchers were summarized by Gastil into what has been called a "subculture of violence" explanation for high rates of southern violence and (more or less) for high rates of black violence. This subcultural theory has become the most widely proposed explanation for regional and racial differences in homicide.

Analysts in the subcultural tradition appear to have proceeded on the basis of two rather plausible assumptions. First, they have noted that criminal homicide statistics in contrast to data for other types of crime are less subject to distortion by police and other criminal justice officials (e.g., differing patterns of detection and prosecution). There are also high clearance (arrest) rates for homicide cases in comparison to other crimes. Thus, they conclude that consistently high rates of black homicide represent a real phenomenon. Further, to the extent that whites and other racial groups do not display similar levels of violence, the cause of homicide does not lie within the whole of American culture.

Wolfgang and Ferracuti argued that certain subgroups in America live in a cultural and social milieu that encourages physical aggression, or at least does not actively discourage it. They noted that on the basis of an awareness of social, economic, and political disparities between whites and blacks, any diligent researcher would propose that the black crime rate would be higher than the white rate and that there would be a "large spread to the learning of, resort to, and criminal display of the violence value among minority groups such as Negroes."

I have previously suggested that there are several major limitations of subculture of violence theory, many of which are relevant for the present discussion of the adequacy of past research for devising policies to reduce black homicide. Among the major weaknesses of the theory are the following: (1) There is an extreme emphasis on mentalistic value orientations of individuals—orientations that in the aggregate are said to produce a subculture. (2) The theory lacks empirical grounding and indeed is put in question by some empirical findings. (3) Much of the theory has tended to underemphasize a variety of structural, situational, and institutional variables that affect interpersonal violence. For blacks, these variables range from historical patterns developed during slavery to the immediate racialist social context of an individual homicidal offense to the operation of the criminal justice system, past and present. (4) Subcultural theory underemphasizes the effects of law and law enforcement on patterns of criminal homicide (e.g., deterrence effects). (5) There are other plausible ways apart from the inculcation of proviolence values by which the economic, political, and social disadvantages of American blacks may produce high rates of homicide. It is the lack of a full consideration of economic factors that constitutes a crucial ideological bias of subculture of violence theory. Both the lack of attention to economic correlates of black (and white) homicide and the failure to explore situational factors fully are features of existing theoretical analyses of homicide that raise questions about their adequacy for developing strategies of reduction.

Homicide is primarily a problem of the poor and disadvantaged, though as previously noted the relationship between socioeconomic status and murder has not been thoroughly documented. Consequently it may be argued, as Allen does, that successful prevention must involve not only changes in attitudes and behavior but also "through improving the human condition: better housing, employment, education and health." Indeed, available evidence is sufficient to suggest that black homicide is concentrated in what Glasgow, Wilson, and others have called the "black underclass." This segment of the black population has not benefited from the civil rights gains of the last twenty years and recent studies report that their economic condition is worsening rather than improving. Such worsening of conditions is especially evident among urban black youth. For example, Mare and Winship found that "an important exception to improvements in the relative socioeconomic status of blacks during recent decades is increased levels of joblessness among black youths relative to whites....Although racial convergence on school enrollment and educational attainment has reduced other socioeconomic inequalities between the races, it has widened the employment difference."

Recent crime statistics (to the extent available) show that it is among unemployed and underemployed black youths and young adults that the highest rates of homicide in the black community are found. Thus it is obvious that prevention and intervention strategies must be developed to remedy these larger, macrolevel conditions as well as the more situational and immediate determinants of black homicide. Although it appears to be a generally accepted social fact among social scientists that economic factors influence homicide rates, they have conducted relatively little research that explores the dynamics of that influence. Still left unresolved are such questions as absolute versus relative deprivation, and economic condition versus cultural context. For example, Henry and Short and numerous other researchers have suggested that unemployment and worsening economic conditions lead to increases in the rate of violent crime, but a recent study by Cook and Zarkin finds that homicide rates in general are largely unaffected by the business cycle. They do not provide race-specific analyses and are not able to test Henry and Short's proposition that blacks are more affected by such economic trends than are whites. Researchers must also seek to explain why homicide rates decline during severe downturns in the economy and why many of the poorest among rural blacks have comparatively low rates of homicide.

Inattention to the Situational Correlates of Homicide

Although the macrosocietal level etiological factors discussed above are of importance for social scientists and must be considered when devising sound homicide reduction strategies, the inattention of past researchers to the more immediate, situational determinants of homicide may be more problematic. It is at least arguable that homicide, like other problems of the poor, can be remedied successfully only through major political and socioeconomic changes. On the other hand, the kind of social reform sentiments that underlie current homicide reduction efforts are not necessarily compatible with the advocacy of such major changes. At best, major changes in the socioeconomic status of the black poor will be cited as a long-term goal and prevention efforts will be targeted at perceived short-term solutions. It is also true that acts of homicide are relatively rare even among the poorest segments of the population. These two factors—the unlikelihood of major changes in the socioeconomic status of poor blacks and the relative rareness of homicide—have caused many prevention advocates to focus on situational determinants of homicide rather than on larger societal causative factors.

With these kinds of considerations as an organizing perspective, Wolfgang and Ferracuti, Allen, Hawkins, and a few other researchers have proceeded to identify several forms of potential intervention. In general, these may be said to be targeted at either the individual criminal or at the larger community from which homicide offenders are likely to come. Each of these efforts usually considers both victims and offenders. Among the various areas of prevention and intervention discussed are the following:

1. The identification of high risk groups (both offenders and victims).
2. More effective and rapid police and medical personnel response to prehomicide behavior, e.g., assaults, verbal threats, and murder attempts.
3. Gun control.
4. Educational programs, especially those targeted at the young.
5. Community organization and education, including the physical rehabilitation of blighted neighborhoods.
6. Mental health centers for counseling and other forms of intervention for offenders, victims, and their families.
7. Social scientific studies to help identify the social interactional clues to homicide, e.g., verbal and nonverbal behaviors, threats, and social histories of hostilities.

8. More effective control and rehabilitation of potential and actual offenders by the various agencies of the criminal justice system.

Most researchers and other analysts of homicide agree that very few of these intervention efforts have been implemented. They also agree that there are very few social scientific investigations of the effectiveness (or potential effectiveness) of these various strategies. There is also the expression of doubt concerning the potential effectiveness of some intervention strategies. For example, Allen, cites the earlier work of Bromberg who emphasized that it is questionable whether the homicidal acts of specific individuals can be regularly predicted even if all of the personality variables correlated with homicide were known. This reinforces Wolfgang and Ferracuti's suggestion that predicting rare events such as homicide is extremely difficult. The difficulty of such a task has led many to deemphasize the more individual, especially psychological-psychiatric approaches to homicide intervention, and to advocate either more group or law enforcement-oriented prevention including such strategies as gun control and preventive detention of aggressive criminals.

Yet, whatever the approach taken, such efforts must be informed by careful studies of the situational and individually-based determinants of homicide. For example, before counseling, educational prerehabilitation, preventive detention, or similar programs can be applied effectively, we must be able to identify high-risk groups. Current research and statistics identify young, black males as having an extremely high risk of homicide. But such a broad categorization of risk identifies too large a population to be useful for implementing any but the most general preventive programs. In fact, even more detailed sociodemographic groupings of that population (through the use of such measures as income, employment status, urban-rural residence, and education) may not prove useful for precise risk calculation efforts and resulting intervention. As earlier noted, previous research and data sources do not allow policy makers to go beyond these general categorizations to identify various levels of risk within the young, black male population. For example, while it has been shown that black males in 1978 had a homicide risk rate around six times that of white males, certain segments of that population may be shown to have rates exceeding that rate. In addition some segments of the young black male population may have rates lower than the overall rate for white males. How can these groups be identified? Can they be identified with the kind of aggregate-level, sociodemographic analyses generally used by researchers?

At the purely descriptive level, some previous investigations have analyzed various situational and individual level correlates of homicide. For example, Wolfgang considered such factors as the time of day, week, month, and year of the homicide act; site of the act (within or outside of the home); victim-offender relationship; level of violence used in committing the act; alcohol use, and so forth. What is needed, however, are studies that go beyond mere description to discuss the various way in which these and other factors "cause" a given homicide act. Studies such as that of Athens that use a symbolic interactionist approach may be more useful for analyzing the dynamics of the interpersonal encounters that are likely to lead to homicide. Such studies consider not only personal traits but also the processes that lead to acts of aggression. Concern for the situational correlates of homicide and their impact on the effectiveness of prevention efforts has led Jason et al. to argue that primary (family, acquaintance) homicides may be more preventable than secondary homicide (those involving strangers). On the other hand, some researchers have argued that secondary homicide offenders may be more responsive to efforts at legal deterrence such as swift prosecution and conviction.

SUMMARY AND CONCLUSIONS

In this article I have suggested that efforts at black homicide prevention will be impeded by the inadequacy of basic research on the phenomenon of homicide itself, including a paucity of studies on black homicide. In reviewing existing research on homicide, it is evident that there are several major shortcomings. First, most of the research does not go beyond a mere calculation of rates for various racial groups, usually at the state or national level. Even if multivariate techniques are used, the focus is on the magnitude of rate differences rather than other aspects of the patterning of homicide that are correlated with rate differences. Second, few studies have specifically analyzed the variation and patterning of homicide within the black community. Third, studies that do attempt to examine the patterning of homicide (black or white) most often use a limited range of variables. Certain of the more situational correlates of homicide are never fully analyzed. This may be largely a consequence of the limited data on homicide collected by law enforcement or health agencies and the difficulty researchers encounter when collecting these data themselves. For example, socioeconomic status data for offenders and victims are seldom available. But there also appears to be a kind of selective inattention by researchers to the non-aggregate-level correlates of homicide. That is, existing empirical research has been cast within a theoretical framework that limits the range of variables considered.

In many ways the work of criminologists and social scientists who have studied homicide has not lived up to Marvin Wolfgang's pioneering expectations:

If the criminologist is to acquire general principles that are essential to effective control, prevention and treatment, he must seek patterns, similarities and repetitions that can become the basis for classification and generalization....Analysis of a particular type of crime, the individuals who commit it, and those who are victims of it, is relatively rare. Such analysis, provided it is as detailed and specific as the best available data permit, may produce insights into etiology, prediction and control as yet unknown and unexplored.

Without insight into the phenomenon of homicide such as that described here, goals of reduction will be largely unrealized. For example, agreed upon preliminary steps toward intervention—identification of high risks groups apart from race, identification of the social interactional clues, and so on—depend upon the availability of sound empirical and theoretical work on homicide. Many observers have questioned the extent to which the devising of social policy is dependent upon the availability of research data. Policy decisions, sometimes sound ones, are made even in the absence of reliable data. On the other hand, even sound research findings are not always easily translated into specific policies. Despite these observations, sound empirical and nonempirical social science research is an asset for the policymaker.

The following kinds of studies are needed to begin to provide a basis for the kind of intervention efforts currently proposed by the federal government:

1. More detailed analyses of the sociodemographic characteristics of homicide victims and offenders. These should include such previously underanalyzed characteristics as socioeconomic status (absolute and comparative), residence (within and across regions), and intercorrelation among various sociodemographic variables.

2. Improved studies of the individual-level and situational correlates of homicide. These studies should be geared toward not only identifying high risk individuals or circumstances but also toward identifying those conditions and persons for whom intervention might be possible and effective.

3. Beyond basic research, there is a need to conduct studies that evaluate intervention efforts. Only through such application and evaluation of existing knowledge will researchers be able to identify successful forms of intervention.

Finally, researchers must seek to define what is meant by intervention and prevention more carefully. They must also determine which kinds of interventions work most effectively with which types of homicide. There is also a need to evaluate the impact of intervention efforts on those persons involved and on the larger society. Homicide prevention may be accomplished by direct intervention with high risk individuals or groups. Such direct intervention may be more effective than the post facto, exemplary deterrence assumptions currently underlying criminal law and law enforcement. It is possible that these kinds of strategies may be more effective but they also pose the greatest risk of violating the rights and dignity of those targeted for intervention. Crime prevention efforts, perhaps more so than other forms of applied social science, have the potential for abuse. In the words of Wolfgang and Ferracuti, we must ask, "To what extent are we willing to change the traditional democratic constraints that normally function to restrict society's manipulative control over behavior, even the conduct of criminals, in order to reduce crimes of violence?" A major task of social researchers will be to devise prevention strategies for homicide that do not contribute further to the victimization of the American underclass.

Responding to Missing and Murdered Children in America

ERIC HICKEY

The purpose of this chapter is to examine the extent of missing and murdered children in the United States and our response to these crimes. Parents, school officials, and social service agencies must be aware of avenues for educating children about the inherent dangers of becoming involved with some strangers. Libraries and police departments can prove to be valuable resources in educating children about strangers. Parents of murdered children experience tremendous grief and anguish, which often turns into anger toward the offender and a criminal justice system that has been slow to respond to these atrocities. During the past several years, victim coalition groups have emerged to take up the plight of the victim and those who are the survivors. To date, victim rights/advocacy groups and groups catering especially to those involved with missing or murdered children have formed a grass-roots movement.

LURING CHILDREN

We all hear the horror stories about abducted children. Many who have never experienced such a crime or have never been a family member or friend of a victim may want to discount tales of abduction as distortions of reality. Unfortunately, child abductors can be particularly creative in their methods of finding suitable victims. One 16-year-old offender being evaluated for a sex-offender program in a western U.S. psychiatric facility noted how simple it was for him to find child victims to molest. His favorite hunting grounds were shopping malls because he always found parents who were willing to leave their children, sometimes even young children, alone for a few minutes around the toy counters. The children whom he approached, escorted to the washroom, and molested inevitably seemed to trust him. Some of his victims were so young he was sure they would not understand what had occurred once he allowed them to leave. On a "good" night he claimed he could lure three or four children to the washroom.

In 1977, Operation Police Lure was organized in Oakland County, Michigan, by a law enforcement task force in response to a series of seven unsolved child homicides. Some believed at the time that a serial killer was responsible for several of the abductions. A survey was administered to 54 elementary and junior high school students in grades four through nine in efforts to gather more data on child molestation and abduction. The children reported 782 incidents of attempted or actual cases of molestation that had never been reported to authorities. They also found that children ages 10–12 were the most likely targets and that males and females were victimized at about the same rates. Although victims were approached at varying times of the day, 3:00–6:00 p.m. was the period most frequently reported. Children profiled the offenders as White males, usually in their 20s or 30s, who often attempted to lure them by asking for help, such as looking for a lost puppy. When vehicles were used the abductors and molesters also seemed to prefer two-door models and cars that were blue in color.

Child abductors, of course, do not come in only one mold and generally do not fit the stereotype of the peculiar-looking "dirty old man." Some individuals of very benign appearance are arrested for child abduction molestations. Creating a new stereotype of such offenders becomes problematic, as it excludes many variations of that stereotype. There are, however, some important concepts that should be noted about the nature of child abductions. While coercion, bribery, and other methods of luring victims are frequently employed, the ploy of asking for help from a child is not only effective—from an offender's perspective—but also creates difficulty for parents in protecting their children. The thought of helping find a lost puppy or kitten can easily preclude attention by the child to the person seeking the assistance. Similarly, an offender may use a badge or a blue vehicle to appear as an authority figure to intended victims. Most children are taught or have learned by experience a degree of respect for authority figures and will automatically respond to their commands.

Wooden outlines a variety of child lures used by offenders, including an appeal to a child's ego, by telling the child he or she is to be in a beauty contest or television commercial. Some offenders tell the child an emergency has occurred and they

461

have come to escort the child home immediately. Wayne Williams, involved in the Atlanta child murders, was known to have posted employment advertisements for young men throughout the area in which he resided. In the case of Ted Bundy and others like him, similar themes are used but in a more sophisticated manner. For offenders, wearing a cast to evoke sympathy or displaying fictitious business cards can initially alleviate a child's fears of dealing with a stranger. Offenders who have become adept at manipulation can exert complete control over others, especially children.

There are many ways in which child abductions can be avoided if parents, school officials, and community leaders are prepared to carry out intervention strategies. Parents or guardians must ensure the safety of their children. The most important tool ever used in preventing abductions is that of educating children. The following list of strategies has been compiled and adapted from recommendations made by the National Center for Missing and Exploited Children, the Indiana Missing Children Clearinghouse in Indianapolis, and the National Finger Print Center for Child Identification in Kirksville, Missouri:

1. Never leave children unattended while in a public place. This includes being left alone in a car, store, or shopping cart. Telling children, especially younger children, not to unlock the car door until mom or dad returns places the child at a distinct disadvantage in attempting to make quick decisions when being confronted by an adult stranger. Some parents find using expanding cords to tether their small children to them useful in keeping toddlers from wandering off. Tethering lines are available that can be attached to the wrist of the parent and the clothing of the child. More elaborate and expensive beeper devices can be purchased by parents who wish to allow their children more movement. With these, a beeper alarm automatically is triggered when the child crosses over a preset radius.

2. If children do become separated for any reason from their parents, they should know to go to the nearest store employee, checkout counter, or police or security officer and ask for assistance. Children must understand that wandering around often makes it more difficult for parents to locate them. Having children go to a prearranged location if they are separated from their parents is a good idea.

3. Children should be taught that strangers are all persons they do not know, or persons they do not know very well. Consequently, children must learn to avoid going anywhere with strangers—such as entering cars—without the prior verbal approval of the parents.

4. Children must know they are not to get close to strangers who may be following them or calling them to their cars.

5. Children must understand that adults who need assistance should be asking other adults for help, not children. Many children easily succumb to the lure of helping a stranger "look for the lost puppy."

6. Children should be taught that if they feel they are being followed or if they become afraid of an adult, the best course of action is to yell out for assistance rather than to hide.

7. Parents should inform their children which homes in the area are designated as "block watchers" or that otherwise participate in community programs designed to assist and protect children.

8. Children should be taught that if they are being forced to go somewhere, they need to protest loudly, screaming and yelling that this person is not their parent or guardian.

9. Children should be taught how to reach the telephone operator in an emergency.

10. Children should learn as young as possible their own names, full addresses, telephone numbers—including area codes—and full names of both parents.

11. Children should avoid going places alone.

12. When children are alone at home, they should never open the door to strangers. They should also be taught to tell unfamiliar phone callers that neither parent can come to the phone at that moment (rather than saying the parents are out) but will return the call later.

13. Children should always ask permission of parents when leaving their homes or play areas, or when entering other people's homes.

14. Children should never hitchhike, and should accept rides only with those who have been approved by the parents.

15. When in public, children should not wear clothing emblazoned with their names, because they are more likely to respond if strangers call them by name.

16. Children should be taught that if strangers want to photograph them, they should immediately inform their parents and/or school officials.

17. Children must be taught that others do not have the right to touch them inappropriately and that any occurrence of such touching should be reported immediately to parents or teachers.

18. Divorced parents should understand their legal rights if they fear noncustodial parental abduction. School officials should be aware of children's custody status.

(19.) Babysitters, daycare centers, and schools should release children only to those specifically designated by the parents.

20. Children should be fingerprinted by properly trained personnel.

If a child does disappear, the parents should contact authorities immediately and be prepared to give a complete description of what the child was last seen wearing, unique physical characteristics (such as braces or glasses) and the child's height, weight, hair color, eye color, and date of birth. A recent close-up color photograph of the child should be provided to the police. Recent dental charts and medical records of the child should be obtained from the family doctor and dentist.

EDUCATIONAL RESOURCES

As parents, school administrators, and law enforcement officials have become more cognizant of the potential dangers children may encounter, we have begun to see more resources available for educating our children. Parents should consult their local libraries for books addressing the protection of children. Some books are designed and written especially for children and can be augmented through discussion of the meanings of these stories with parents or teachers. For example, Vogel and Coldner, in their book *The Danger of Strangers*, deal with advances made by strangers toward children. Illustrated and written especially for children, the text is endorsed by the American School and Community Safety Association and is designed to help children understand why they must be wary of strangers. Parents should consult their public libraries for this and other books written for children.

Parents should be cautious, however, in their efforts to educate children about strangers. Children should be taught only to follow the recommended safety guidelines. Estrella and Forst note that scaring children into compliance can be dangerous in itself. Making children suspicious and fearful of strangers can make them fearful of all adults, even as they mature. Indeed, a measured response by parents toward their children when educating them about potential dangers involving strangers is usually the best course of action. Most strangers have no designs to harm anyone, and they often prove to be valuable resources in times of need. Children, like parents, must know what to do when approached by strangers. Simple strategies of knowing how to use a pay phone, locking doors, and practicing street safety can prove invaluable to children.

Police departments are usually prepared to send representatives to schools or community action groups to discuss ways in which to protect children. Police will stress the importance of children's carrying some form of identification and maintaining regular check-in times with parents, and parents' knowing where their children are supposed to be at all times. Older children usually express an interest in why some strangers are dangerous, while younger children are not prepared to understand such motivations. Therefore, parents must be sensitive to how much information they should try to convey to their children. Children's questions should be answered if they are raised, and they should be allowed to raise them. Police representatives usually are prepared to answer such questions during their visits to schools and often will provide students and parents with literature discussing the inherent dangers of some strangers.

Parents can organize themselves and operate block parent programs in which volunteers who are at home during the day open their homes to children who may encounter problems. Such homes are usually designated by a sign in a window. Dixon points out that it is important for parents to introduce children to block parents before an emergency or crisis occurs. Block parents often are parents or grandparents themselves, and they usually are registered with and investigated by police when they first volunteer for a block parent program. Usually such programs can be implemented with the assistance of local law enforcement agencies.

PROTECTION AND PREVENTION: GETTING PARENTS INVOLVED

Many people today feel a sense of impending doom, believing that they will inevitably fall prey to criminal victimization. A great deal of this fear is created by constant news media reports focusing on the most heinous crimes that individuals in our society can produce. However, we must never forget there are many factors that play a role in the dynamics of victimization. Age, race, sex, socioeconomic status, place of residence, employment, education, and lifestyle—all of which can affect the types of crimes occurring in particular areas—must be considered when one is weighing risk factors. Even so, crimes do occur that appear to have little or no correlation to most risk factors. It becomes disconcerting for people to feel they may be at risk and yet powerless to respond effectively to such concerns. Regardless of their utility, most strategies embraced by adults to protect themselves—such as enrolling in self-defense courses, carrying weapons, or increasing home security—are not viable for children. More important, we may delude ourselves into believing that law enforcement can provide sufficient protection for our children and that school officials can always provide adequate supervision.

The increasing perceived randomness of child victimization outside the home has initiated awareness and action on the part of concerned parents and community activists. The impact of victimization often serves as a catalyst for involvement in victim rights and victim advocacy groups. Some organizations function primarily as support groups, while others focus on introducing legislation aimed at addressing the rights of victims, including the handling of criminals in our judicial system. The impact of a murdered child extends far beyond the loss of life, as is evidenced by parents of child victims. While some may seek vengeance on offenders, others become involved with groups that work to prevent future victimizations, assist other victims who are being processed through the criminal justice system, and provide counseling. We may quickly forget a child murder after the headlines subside, but the agony is only beginning for many of those related to the victim.

Acknowledgements

Bowers, W. and G. Pierce, 1975. "The Illusion of Deterrence in Isaac
Ehrlich's Research on Capital Punishment." Reprinted by permission of The
Yale Law Journal Company and Fred B. Rothman & Company from The Yale Law Journal,
Vol. 85, pages 187-208.

Busch, K. et al, 1990 "Adolescents Who Kill." Journal of Clinical
Psychology, 46, 4. Reprinted by permission.

Canter, Missen, and Hodge. "A Case for Special Agents." Policing Today,
1997, pp. 9-12. Reprinted by permission.

Chesnais. "The History of Violence: Homicide and Suicide Through the Ages."
International Social Science Journal, 1992, 44/2(132): 217-234. Reprinted
by permission of Blackwell Publishers.

Daly, M. and M. Wilson, 1988. "Evolutionary Social Psychology and Family
Homicide" Reprinted with permission from Science, 242, 1988. Copyright
1988 American Association for the Advancement of Science.

De Hart, D. and J. Mahoney, 1994. "The Serial Murderer's Motivations: An Interdisciplinary
Review." Omega: Journal of Death and Dying, 29.1.
Reprinted by permission.

Dietz, P., 1986. "Mass, Serial and Sensational Homicides." Bulletin of the
New York Academy of Medicine, 62, 5. Reprinted by permission of The New
York Academy of Medicine.

Erlanger, H. 1974. "The Empirical Status of the Subculture of Violence
Thesis." Social Problems, 22. c 1974 by The Society for the Study of Social Problems.
Reprinted by permission.

Gastil, R., 1971. "Homicide and a Regional Culture of Violence." American
Sociological Review, 37. Reprinted by permission of the American
Sociological Association.

Geberth and Turco. "Antisocial Personality Disorder, Sexual Sadism,
Malignant Narcissism, and Serial Murder." Reprinted with permission from
the Journal of Forensic Sciences, 1997, 42/1:49-60. Copyright American
Society for Testing and Materials, 100 Barr Harbor Drive, West
Conshohocken, PA 19428.

Given, J., 1977. "The Frequency of Homicide." Reprinted from Society and
Homicide in 13th Century England by James Buchanan Given with the
permission of the publishers, Stanford University Press. c 1977 by the
Board of Trustees of the Leland Stanford Junior University.

Goetting, A., 1989. "Patterns of Marital Homicide: A Comparison of Husbands and Wives." Journal of Comparative Family Studies, 8. Reprinted by permission.

Grubin, D. 1994. "Sexual Murder: British Journal of Psychiatry, 165.5, pp. 624-629. Reprinted by permission of The Royal College of Psychiatrists.

Haglund, W., D. Reay, and C. Snow. 1987. 'Identification of Serial Homicide Victims in the 'Green River Murder' Investigation." Reprinted with permission from the Journal of Forensic Sciences, November. Copyright American Society for Testing and Materials, 100 Barr Harbor Drive, West Conshohocken, PA 19428.

Hawkins, D. 1985. "Black Homicide: The Adequacy of Existing Research for Devising Prevention Strategies." Journal of Research in Crime and Delinquency, 31. Copyright c 1985 by Sage Publications. Reprinted by permission of Sage Publications.

Hickey, E., 1990. "Responding to Missing and Murdered Children in America." In Roberts (ed.) Helping Crime Victims. Copyright c 19890 by Sage Publications. Reprinted by permission of Sage Publications.

Hotaling, G. and D. Finkelhor. 1990. "Estimating the Number of Stranger-Abduction Homicides of Children: A Review of Available Evidence." Journal of Criminal Justice, 18.5. Reprinted by permission of Elsevier Science.

Keppel, R. and J. Weis. 1994. "Time and Distance as Solvability Factors in Murder Cases." Reprinted with permission from the Journal of Forensic Sciences, June 1994. Copyright American Society for Testing and Materials, 100 Barr Harbor Drive, West Conshohocken, PA 19428.

Keppel, R., 1995. "Signature Murders: A Report of Several Related Cases." Reprinted with permission from the Journal of Forensic Sciences, July. Copyright American Society for Testing and Materials, 100 Barr Harbor Drive, West Conshohocken, PA 19428.

Keppel, R. and J. Weis. 1993. "Improving the Investigation of Violent Crime; The Homicide Investigation and Tracking System." Research in Brief (August). Washington, D.C.: U.S. Department of Justice.

Luckenbill, D. 197. "Criminal Homicide as a Situated Transaction." Social Problems, 25. c 1977 by The Society for the Study of Social Problems. Reprinted by permission.

Maxson, C. et al. 1985. "Differences Between Gang and Nongang Homicides." Criminology, 23. Reprinted by permission.